Painting the Secrets of the Forest with Watercolors

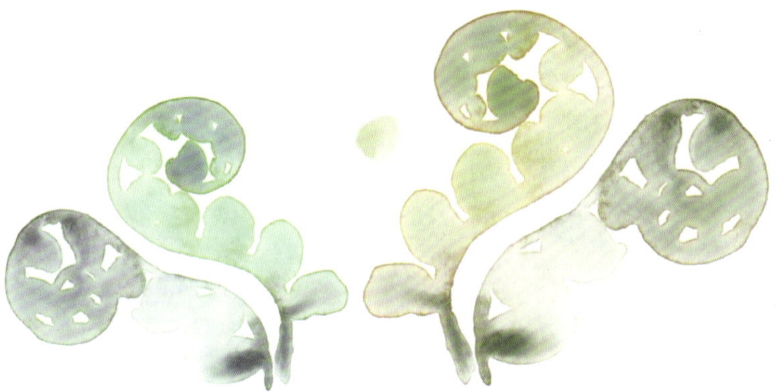

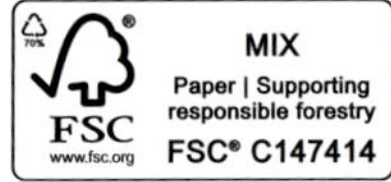
MIX
Paper | Supporting
responsible forestry
FSC
www.fsc.org
FSC® C147414

Painting the Secrets of the Forest *with Watercolors*

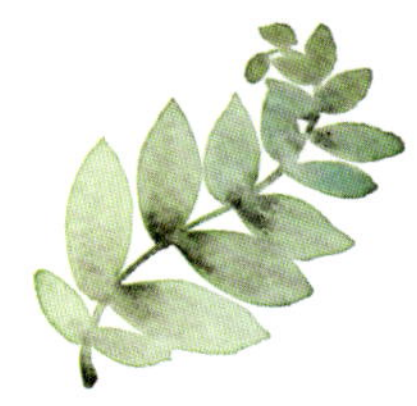

Jennifer Lefèvre

DESIGN ORIGINALS

an Imprint of Fox Chapel Publishing

www.d-originals.com

Contents

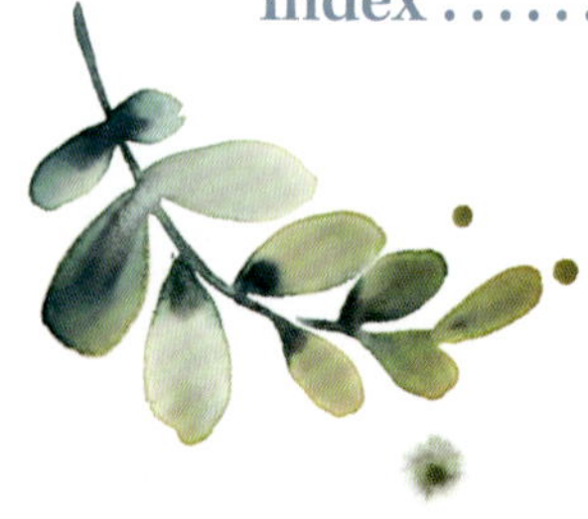

Introduction

I have always been fascinated by the forest and the many secrets that surround its ecosystem. When I was a child, the woods were always a source of escape for me. In my imagination, I liked to give it an appearance that was sometimes magical, sometimes disturbing. During family walks, I spent long hours observing all the strange little things that inhabit the forest, such as insects, mushrooms on tree stumps, or mosses that are so soft when you touch them with your fingertips. It is therefore natural that I gradually combined my vision of the forest with my artistic universe as a watercolorist.

In this book, you'll discover how to explore the shapes and colors of the forest to inspire your work. You'll learn how to choose the right materials; master watercolor techniques; and create floral arrangements, small forest scenes, or abstract plant motifs with fluidity and intuition, whatever your skill level.

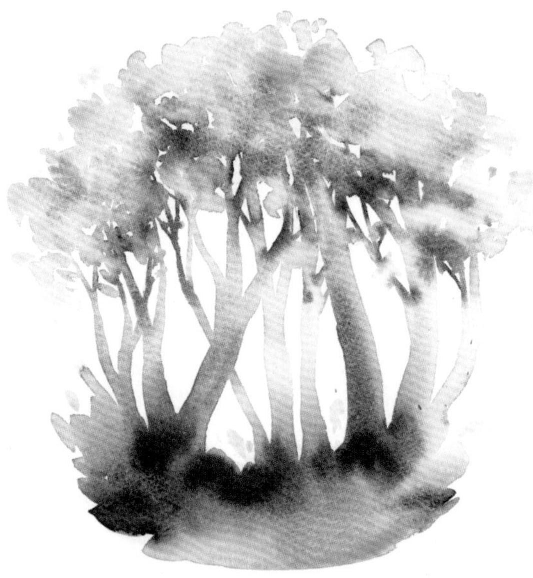

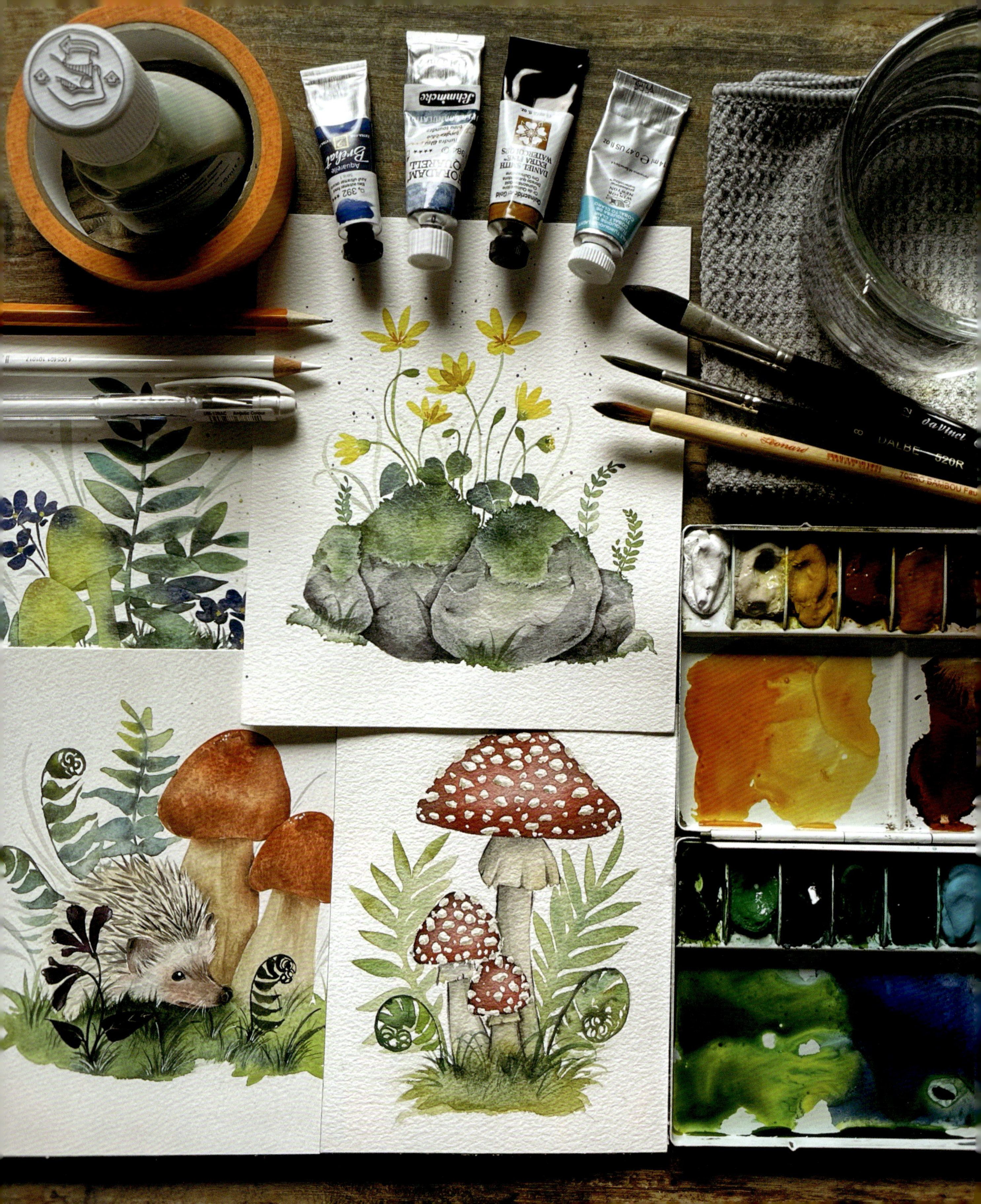

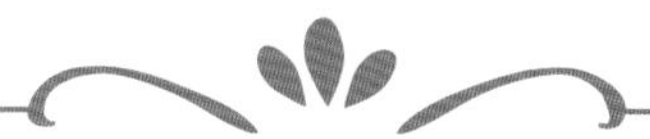

Tools & Materials

In this chapter, I detail all the equipment I use on a daily basis to carry out my artistic studies and imagine beautiful forest scenes. Keep in mind, however, that this is a matter of personal preference. Each artist bases their choices on what works best for them.

Choosing Your Supplies

There are a wide variety of tools on the market, with prices that vary greatly depending on your skill level. Keep in mind that the better quality of your materials, the better results you will achieve. Whether it's the paper, paints, or brush fibers, each plays a role in the creation of your works. The ideal paper, 100% cotton, will allow the pigments to adhere well and blend well with each other. It will also have good water absorption for more uniform drying. As for the quality of the pigments, the nicer options will give your works better durability and greater color intensity. Finally, higher quality brushes will have greater water retention, and they will retain their shape better after being placed on the paper.

There are, however, some very good, affordable alternatives for complete beginners. Since you don't have to use the exact same tools as I did to achieve the same results shown in this book, I'll offer these options as alternatives to mine.

Also note that in the following chapters, I will no longer mention the brands I use but rather broad terms to designate them; for example: "use a fine, firm brush" or "use a soft, thick brush." Regarding the mixtures, I will describe the colors I used without mentioning the brands. As for the paper, it will always be cotton paper. Feel free to come back here when you need help choosing your tools.

Papers & Brushes

THE DIFFERENCES IN WATERCOLOR PAPER

Composition

As I mentioned, cotton paper offers better results than other watercolor papers because it allows you to work longer in wet conditions and achieve uniform color blends. However, there is a less expensive option: cellulose paper.

Designed to withstand large quantities of water, cellulose is recommended for beginners in watercolor painting. However, the pigments adhere less to its surface due to its smooth and soft texture. The mixtures will be less fine and will dry more quickly than on cotton paper. For me, this is an important factor because I work my watercolors for a long time in the wet. I like to be able to move and readjust the pigments that I place on the paper.

The paint blends made on cotton paper (bottom) are finer and more subtle than those on cellulose paper (top).

Weight

When painting with watercolors, it is recommended to use a specific paper designed for this medium. Its weight and highly resistant design will allows watercolor paper to withstand numerous layers of water without damaging it.

The standard thickness is around 140 lbs. (300g/m^2), but this can vary. Some manufacturers offer very thick weights, over 300 lbs. (640g/m^2). The higher the weight, the less the paper will curl. However, when this happens, it is more difficult to control the way the water moves and to give the desired shape to your watercolor. It is possible to paint on mixed-media paper with a low weight (70 lbs. [150g/m^2]); however, the paper will deteriorate more quickly and will not support a large amount of water. I sometimes use it to practice before painting my final watercolor.

Texture

Watercolor paper has three texture levels: satin (very smooth), fine grain (lightly textured), and torchon (very textured). These vary slightly depending on the manufacturer.

I like satin paper when I want to draw and paint with transparency. It holds pigments well; however, water dries rather quickly on its surface. Blending is a little more difficult to achieve than on other textures.

The fine grain is more textured, and I particularly appreciate it for its versatility. The slower drying time allows for more work in the wet and for obtaining uniform mixtures.

Finally, the torchon grain is the one of that allows you to work the longest in wet conditions, which makes it very popular with landscape (plein air) painters.

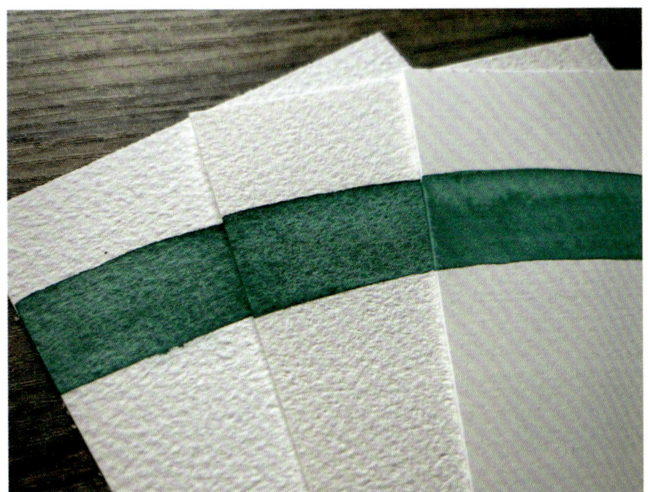

From left to right: torchon, fine grain, and satin papers.

NOTEBOOKS

There aren't many 100% cotton watercolor notebooks on the market, but there are a few manufacturers I particularly appreciate for the quality of their products. I also recommend painting on fairly large formats because, this way, you'll have more freedom and space to let your imagination run wild.

Hahnemühle notebook, 100% cotton, A4 or A5 portrait format, 120 lbs. (250g/m²)

- *Alternative 1*: Etchr notebook, 100% cotton, fine grain, B5 portrait format, 105 lbs. (230g/m²)
- *Alternative 2*: Hahnemühle notebook, cellulose, A5 portrait format, 120 lbs. (250g/m²)

BLOCKS

Blocks are loose sheets of paper. They allow me to tackle larger and more complex projects—something I'm less likely to do in my watercolor notebooks, as they serve more as a place to explore and have fun.

With watercolor blocks, I also like being able to easily change the texture of my paper depending on the project I want to tackle. This gives the subject a completely different look. The papers below are my favorites, but the list is long, so everyone should experiment and choose what they like best.

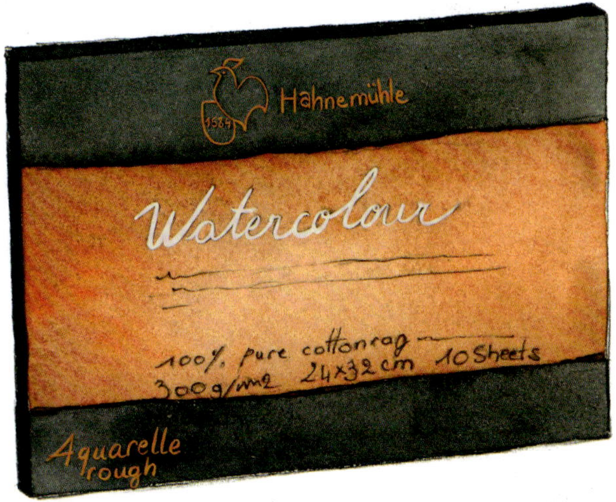

Hahnemühle Watercolor The Collection, 100% cotton, fine grain, 140 lbs. (300g/m²)

- *Alternative 1*: Dalbe, 100% cotton, fine grain or satin, 140 lbs. (300g/m²)
- *Alternative 2*: Moulin du Coq "Le Rouge," 100% cellulose, fine grain, 160 lbs. (325g/m²)

BRUSHES

Having a variety of brushes will help you feel more comfortable painting patterns of varying sizes and achieving specific textures by varying their angle or shape. You will paint different subjects depending on the softness of the fibers. A firm brush will give you greater precision, while a soft brush will cover larger areas more easily due to its ability to hold water better.

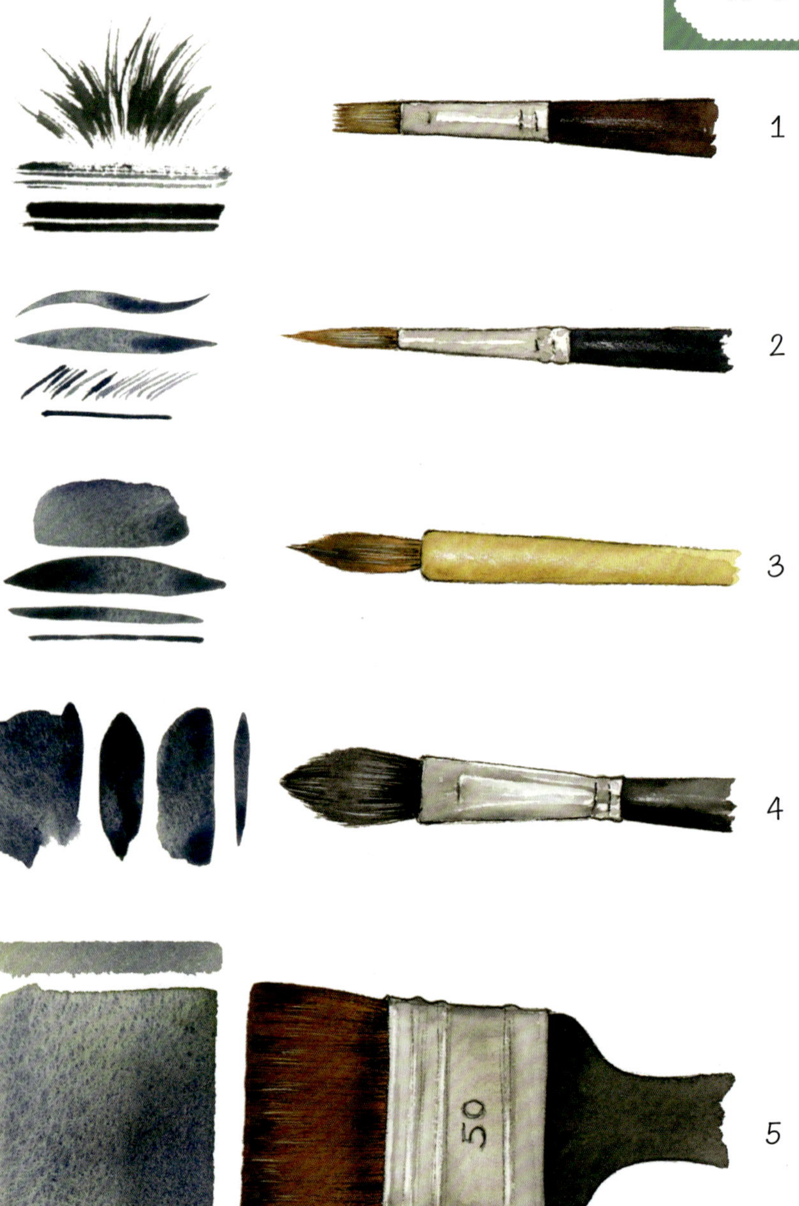

1

2

3

4

5

1. **Flat brush:** Da Vinci VARIO TIP, series 1381, size 6

2. **Round brush (firm):** Dalbe, series 520R, sizes 6 and 8

3. **Round brush (soft):** Léonard Fawn Bamboo, series 700RO, size 2

4. **Oval wash/cat's tongue brush:** Da Vinci CASANEO, series 898, size 12

5. **Mottler/spalter brush:** Dalbe, series 555, size 50

Miscellaneous Supplies

I often use the following tools to preserve the white of the paper or to add white after painting.

1. **White gel ink pen:** uniball™ SIGNO™

2. **White colored pencil:** Faber-Castell Polychromos

3. **Painter's tape:** Nippon Gold Tape

4. **White gouache:** Winsor & Newton Designers Gouache

5. **Masking fluid:** Winsor & Newton

To create white, I prefer white pens because they allow me to give small light effects. Painter's tape, on the other hand, is mainly used to limit or border an area that you do not want to paint on; for example, to create a clean frame for your watercolor.

Once you have chosen and gathered your different tools, equip yourself with a **bowl of water** and a **cloth**.

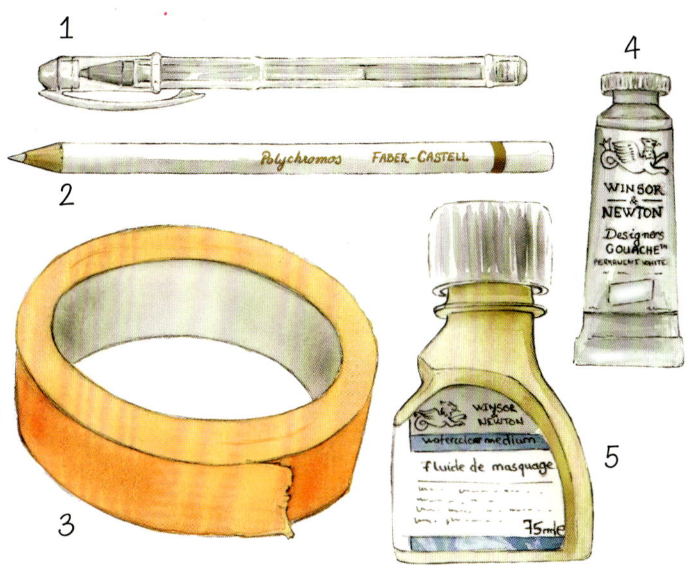

Watercolors

When purchased, watercolors come in two forms: liquid and solid. The former is packaged in tubes, the latter in small containers, called pans.

For my daily use, I prefer tubes because, this way, I can independently refill the ones that empty more quickly. Compared to pans, tubes are also more economical. Another important point: The **palette** I use is specifically designed for liquid paints. I really like its wide wells that allow me to mix many colors.

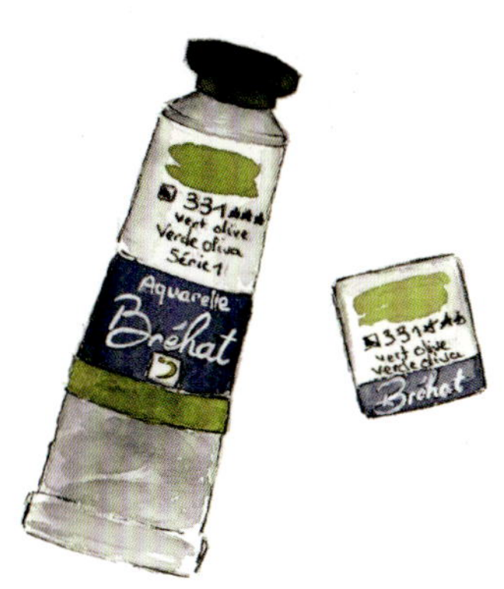

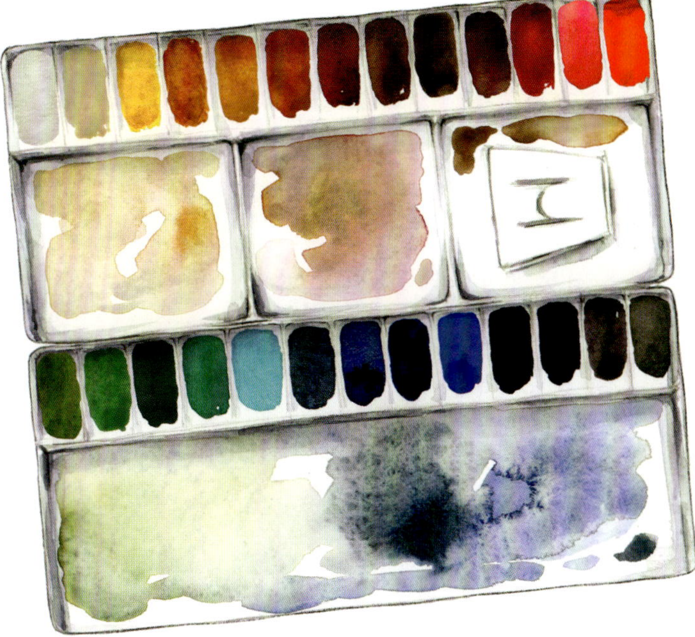

A good palette has large wells for you to mix colors together.

Here's a look at the colors I selected to fill my watercolor palette.

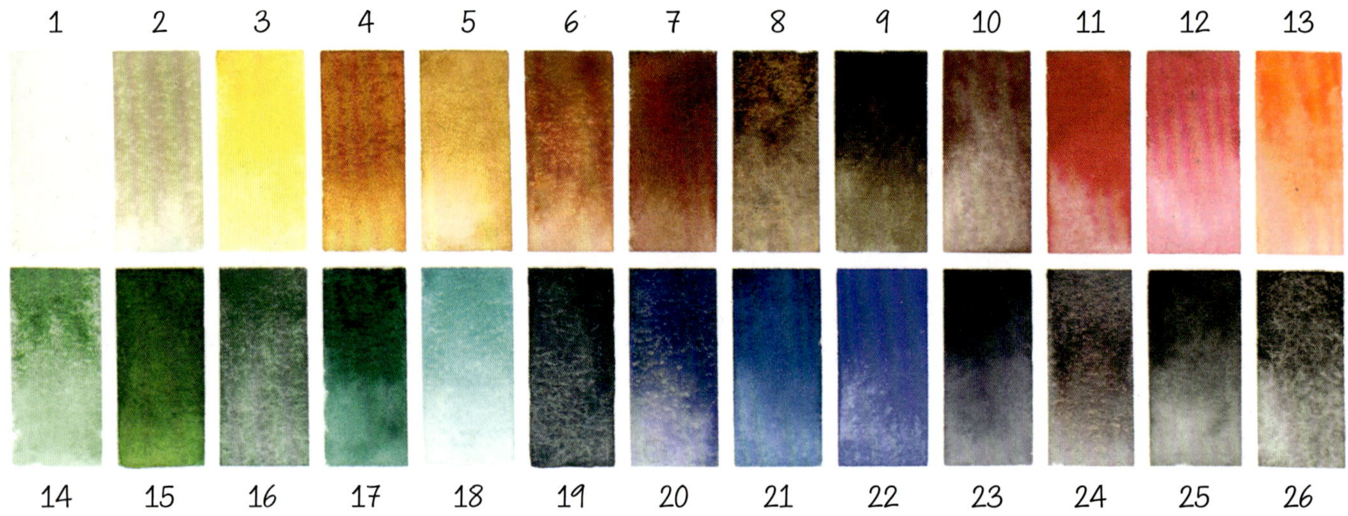

1. Permanent White gouache (Winsor & Newton)
2. Buff Titanium (Daniel Smith)
3. Indian Yellow (Daniel Smith)
4. Quinacridone Gold (Daniel Smith)
5. Yellow Ochre (Winsor & Newton)
6. Burgundy Red Ochre (Daniel Smith)
7. Permanent Brown (Daniel Smith)
8. Enviro-Friendly Brown Iron Oxide (Daniel Smith)
9. Sepia (Daniel Smith)
10. Caput Mortuum (Winsor & Newton)
11. Alizarin Crimson (Daniel Smith)
12. Permanent Rose (Winsor & Newton)
13. Pyrrole Orange (Daniel Smith)
14. Cobalt Green (Daniel Smith)
15. Sap Green (Daniel Smith)
16. Cobalt Green Dark (Schmincke)
17. Phthalo Green (Blue Shade) (Daniel Smith)
18. Cobalt Turquoise Light (Winsor & Newton)
19. Lunar Blue (Daniel Smith)
20. Tundra Blue (Schmincke)
21. Prussian Blue (Dalbe)
22. Dark Ultramarine Blue (Dalbe)
23. Payne's Gray (Dalbe)
24. Shadow Violet (Daniel Smith)
25. Lamp Black (Daniel Smith)
26. Mars Black (Winsor & Newton)

Generally speaking, you'll find more or less the same colors in palettes already prefilled by watercolor manufacturers. They're also a great alternative for beginners or those on a budget. Some of them have specific features, particularly in terms of granulation, which cannot be reproduced by mixing with traditional colors.

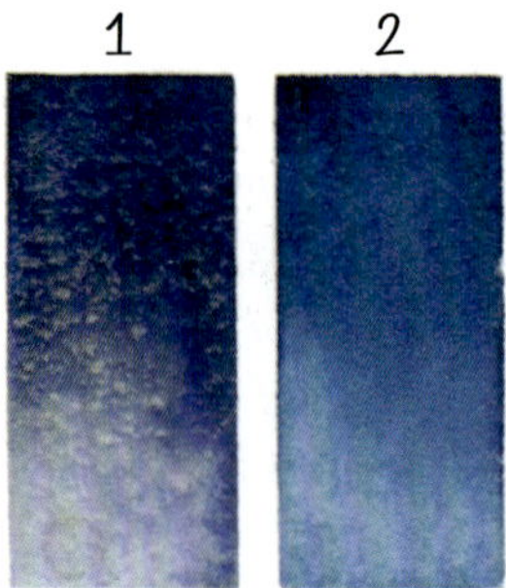

1. Tundra blue with granulation.
2. Prussian blue without granulation.

Pigment granulation occurs when certain pigments disperse unevenly in water, creating unique textures. If the pigments dry on a rough surface, such as torchon watercolor paper, it will be even more pronounced. Granulation is particularly useful if you want to represent natural materials like rock, wood, or even earth. I invite you to create these types of textures using the processes starting on page 30.

Some pigments granulate more than others, so it's important to know their properties to create specific effects. For example, because of its coarser particles, black iron oxide granulates more than ultramarine blue. You'll find the latter in prefilled palettes because its versatility makes it very popular with artists.

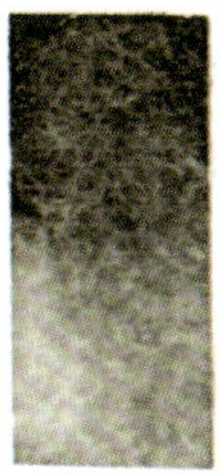 

A black iron oxide (left) granulates more than ultramarine blue (right).

The Color Index

All color pigments have a unique code, established by the Color Index, which provides, among other things, the characteristics of a color, such as its chemical or mineral nature. This list is useful to artists because it allows them to better understand colors and anticipate how they will react on paper.

A color's code will also help identify it with a manufacturer, especially if they have chosen a different name for the same configuration, and will help you determine its composition. For example, at Daniel Smith, the color Lunar Black is composed of the pigment PBk 11, a black iron oxide that is found under the name Mars Black at Winsor & Newton.

For my mixing experiments, I chose to integrate into my palette some colors that granulate, allowing me to create the effect of rock and other natural textures. For example, browns, reds, and oranges will be ideal for representing different soils or barks; a black will naturally give relief to the rock; while greens and blues will bring depth to mosses and the various plants of the forest.

Here are some pigments that I like and that generally fill my palette.

1. Cobalt Green Dark (PG 26)—high granulation
2. Cobalt Green (PG 50)—high granulation
3. Black Iron Oxide (PBk 11)—very high granulation
4. Enviro-Friendly Brown Iron Oxide (PBr 6)—high granulation
5. Caput Mortuum (PR 101), a very dark red iron oxide—high granulation
6. Burgundy Red Ochre (PR 102), a dull orange-brown pigment—medium granulation
7. Tundra Blue (PB 29 + PBr 7), a blue with green variations—intense granulation

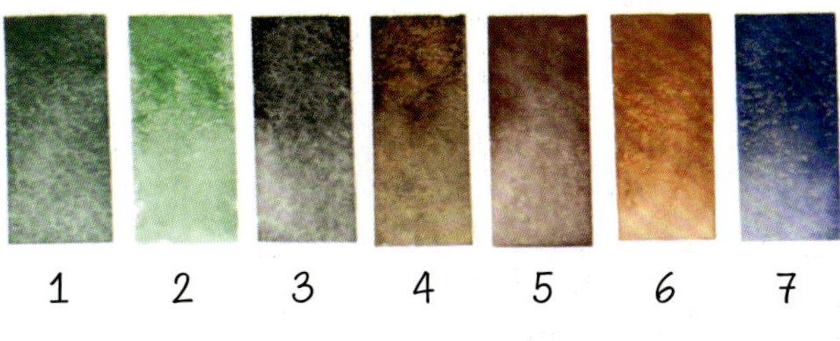

Note

These colors will be very present in this book, which is why I recommend you buy them.

When you're a little more experienced and want to mix your own colors in your watercolor palette, I recommend purchasing color charts sold by manufacturers. These allow you to see and try all the colors in their catalog before deciding.

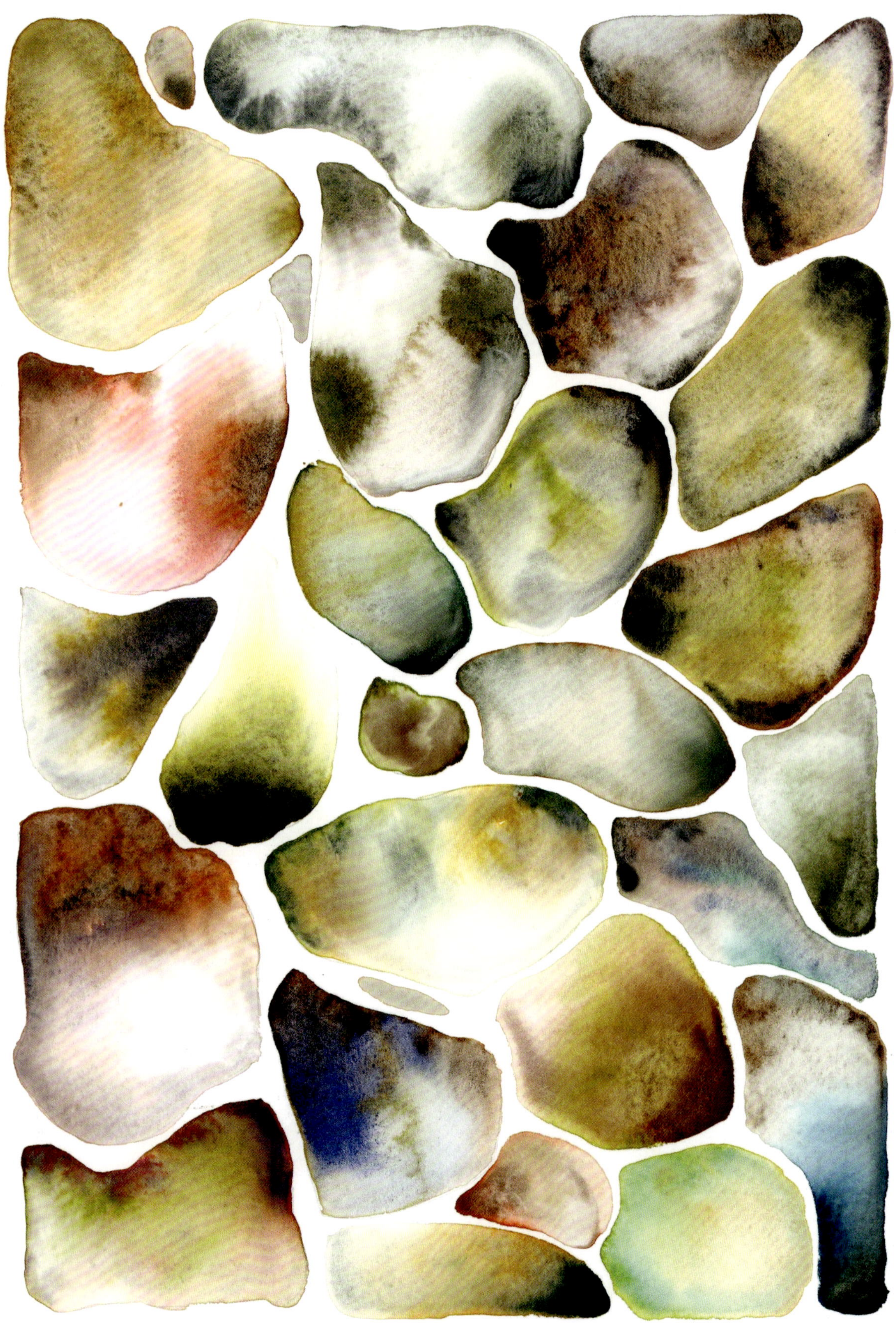

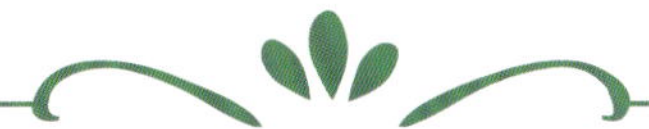

Techniques

After exploring the different tools for watercolor painting, discover in this chapter
all the techniques that will be useful to you in creating beautiful works.

Taming Watercolors

Mastering different watercolor techniques is important because it's how you can bring your creative ideas to fruition. When I paint forest scenes, I play with blurring, transparency, depth, and so on. And all of this contributes to developing my artistic style.

KNOWING YOUR COLORS

Start by developing your palette's color chart. This will allow you to quickly visualize all your colors and be more efficient when you plan to make new mixtures.

Set up your workspace with a medium-sized round brush, a bowl of water, and a cloth. On a piece of watercolor paper, place a little paint on your sheet and spread it slightly with a rinsed brush to visualize it clear and intense.

Note

If you're not satisfied with the results of your work, don't be discouraged. Learning a technique takes time and patience. I advise you to apply each new skill on paper as quickly as possible. You will learn it much more effectively that way.

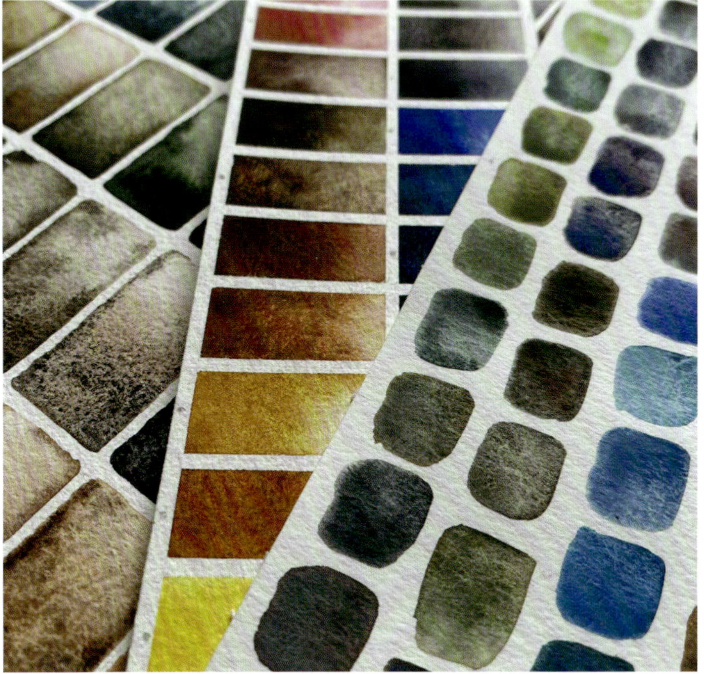

I personally have several color charts for each of the palettes I own.

DILUTING A COLOR

Knowing how to create a beautiful gradient is essential for creating many blending effects. To practice, draw a 2" x 2" (5.1 x 5.1cm) square and apply the most concentrated color to the top of the square. Rinse your brush completely with clean water and then blend the color. Repeat this process, gradually moving down to the base of the square while trying to achieve a lighter and lighter color.

The larger the area, the larger your brush should be, because the difficulty with this exercise lies in how quickly you can blend the color using the right amount of water. The longer you wait between steps, the longer your paper will have time to dry, and you'll have difficulty moving the pigments evenly. If your brush is too small for your colored area, lines will have time to appear.

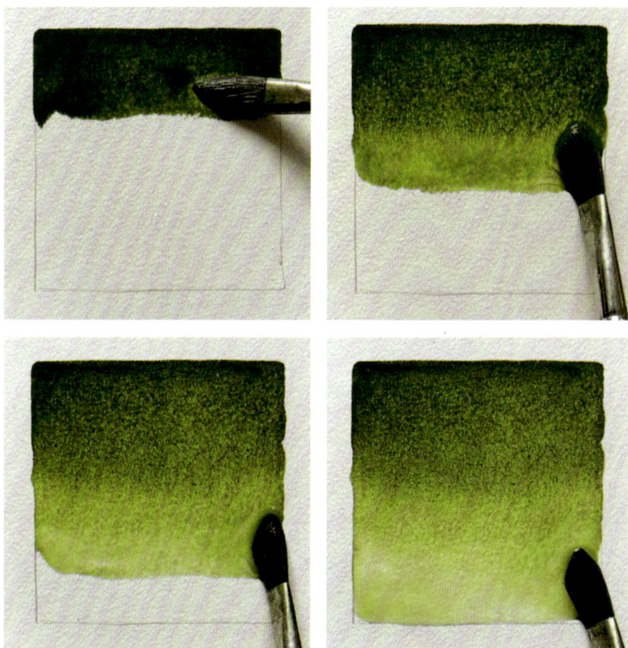

Create a color chart that shows pigment blending by starting with a concentration of color and slowly diluting it as you move down.

OBTAINING NEW COLORS

By mixing the 26 colors in my palette together, I can create a huge number of new colors. If you're new to watercolor, I highly recommend creating a color wheel to familiarize yourself with the theory of color mixing. This involves taking the three primary colors (yellow, blue, and red) and mixing them to create the three secondary colors (orange, green, and purple).

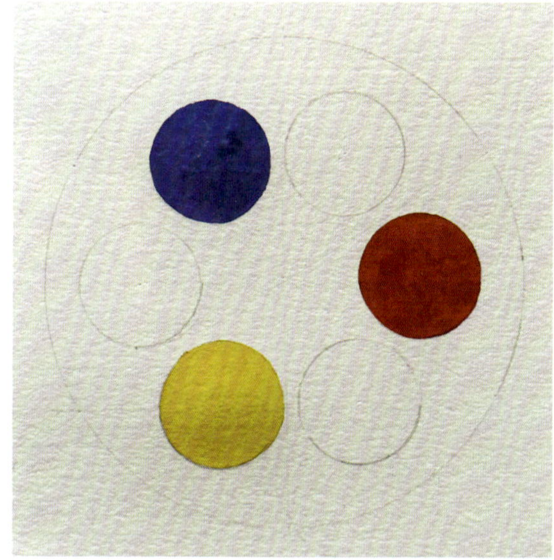

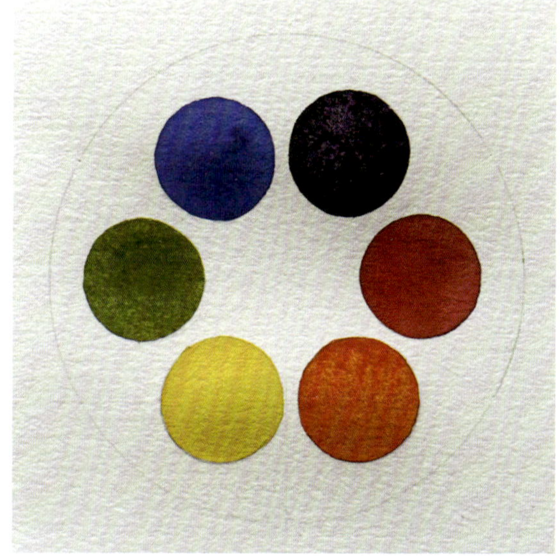

Primary colors (top) are mixed to create secondary colors.

Here's my improved color wheel with a thumbtack that allows me to turn each disc to better visualize color associations. This is useful in most of my work, but when I paint the forest, I'm more into matching my colors based on observation of the environment.

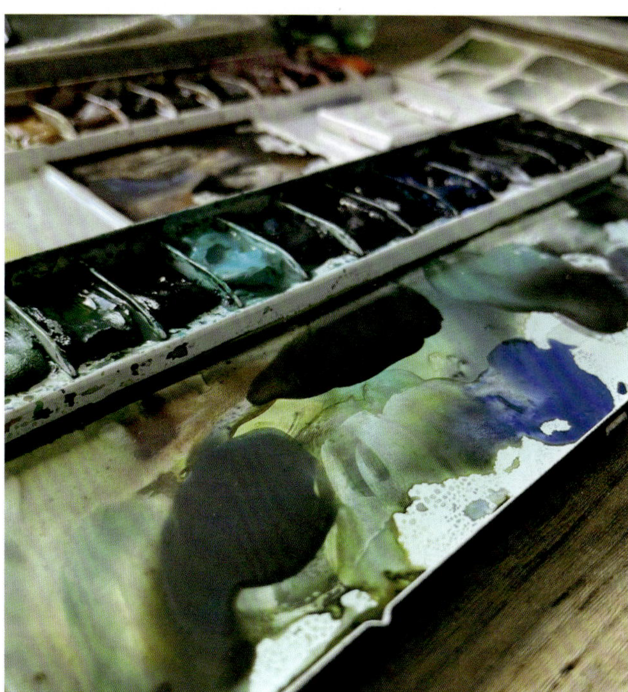

Each level shows how colors are mixed or how vibrant they are.

MAINTAINING YOUR COLORS

Water reactivates watercolor endlessly, so you can definitely keep your favorite blends at the bottom of your wells and continue to use them in your next watercolors. This is something I do regularly with my greens, which saves a lot of money on my pigments.

Let your paints dry in the palette. They can be activated with water and reused.

Painting Wet-on-Wet, Creating Blends

Knowing how to create beautiful color blends with your pigments is an essential technique for mastering different effects. This technique requires a larger amount of water in order to work with the watercolors for longer. This also allows you to create blurry effects and to lay down the first colors that form the base.

Playing with color blends can be very satisfying. For example, I often place small puddles of water with my brush, then put two colors at opposite points to observe the mixture that is created when they merge in the middle.

Create Mixtures in a Square

Add water, then take the time to distribute warm, cool, light, or dark colors to produce a rich visual effect.

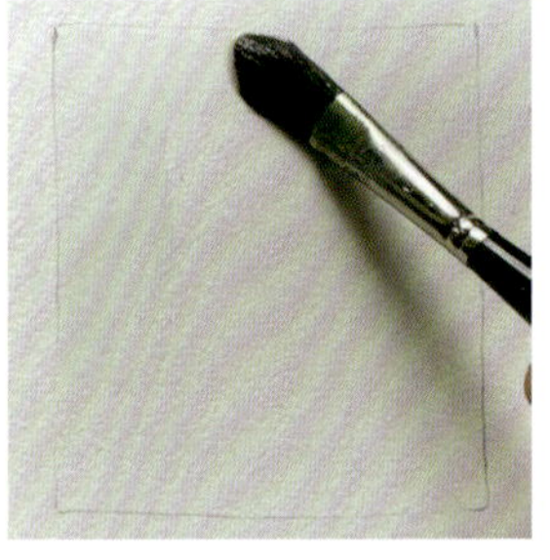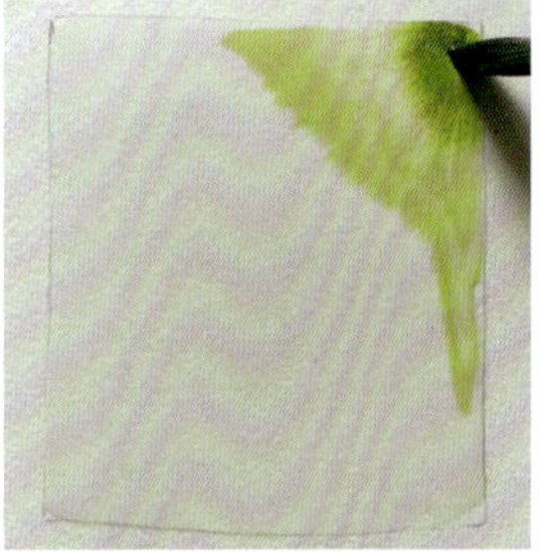

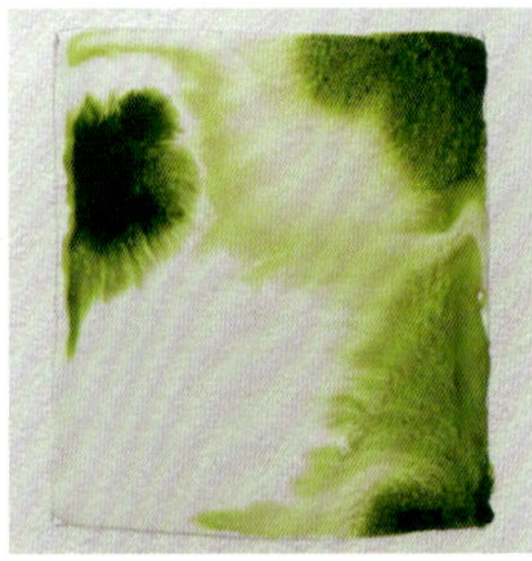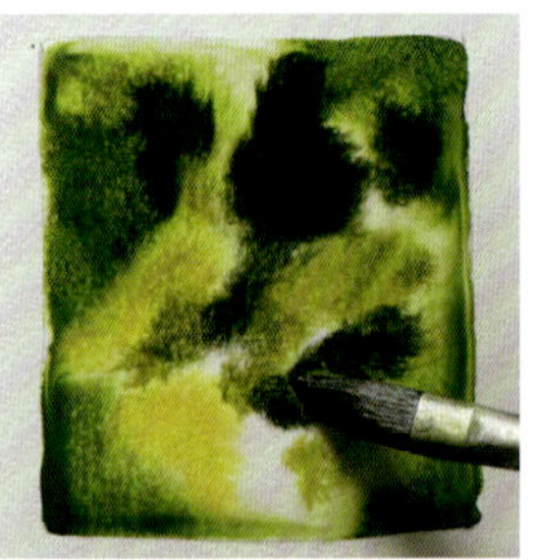

Be careful to distribute the water evenly across the surface of the paper. If you notice any puddles that are too high, don't hesitate to remove the excess with a lightly wrung-out brush.

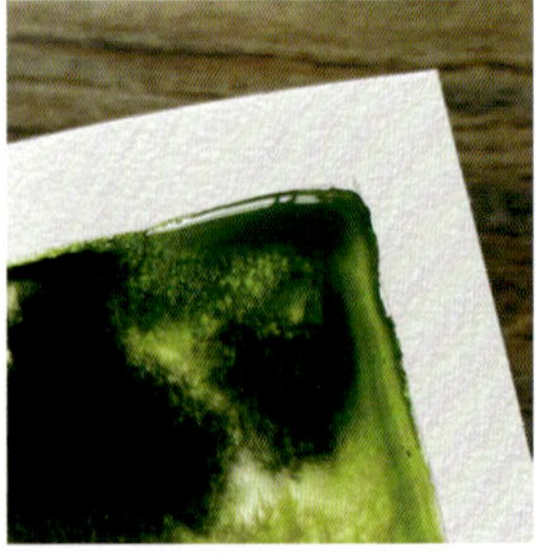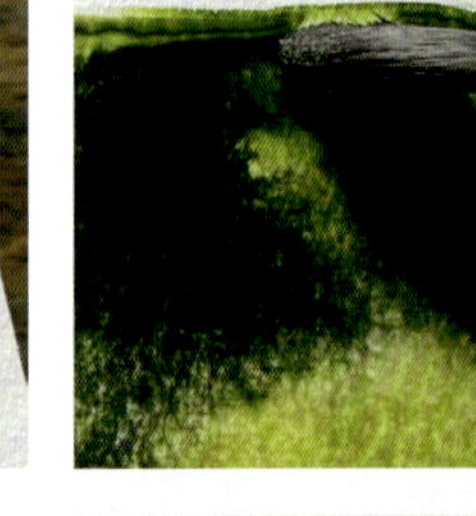

Continue to play with the still-wet watercolor until you are happy with the effect.

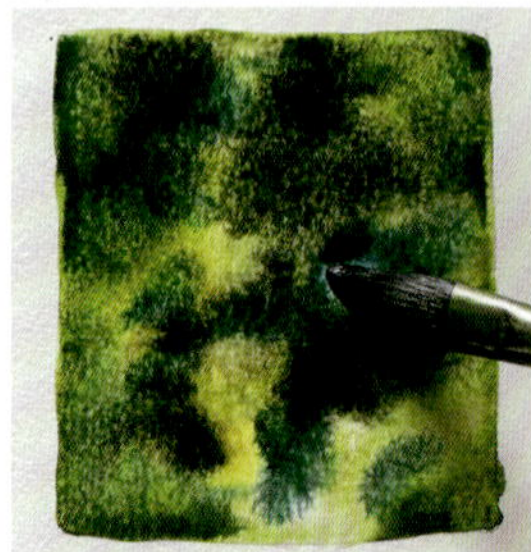

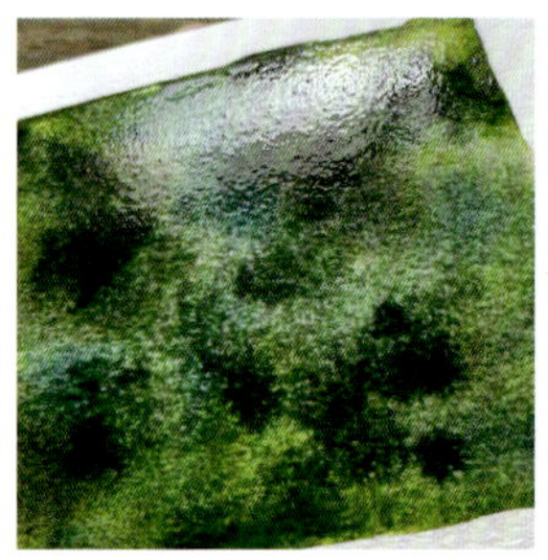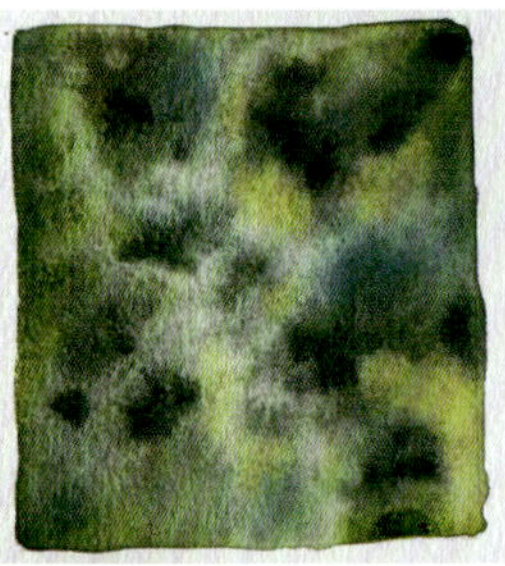

Check that the water is evenly distributed to avoid streaks and let it dry.

AVOIDING LINES

Lines, often unsightly, occur when watercolor doesn't dry evenly on the paper. To give you a concrete example, among these four rectangles, you can see a streak on the two left rectangles and a nice blur on the two right rectangles. In the top right, the moisture is very homogeneous. When I added blue, it blended perfectly into the green, as shown on the bottom right.

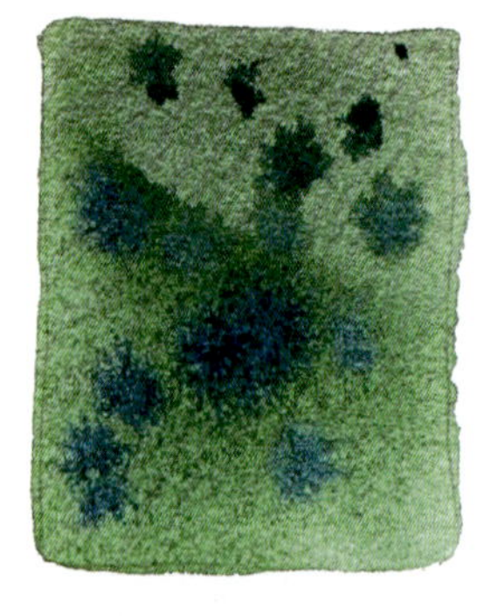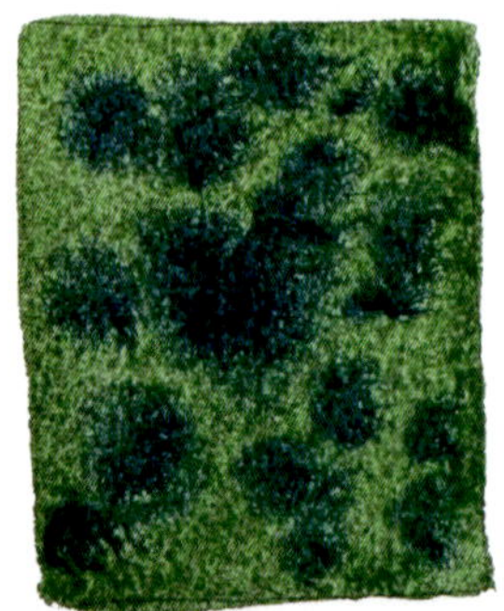

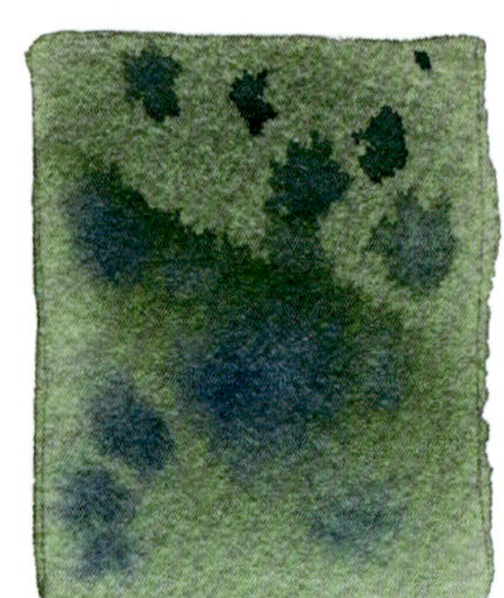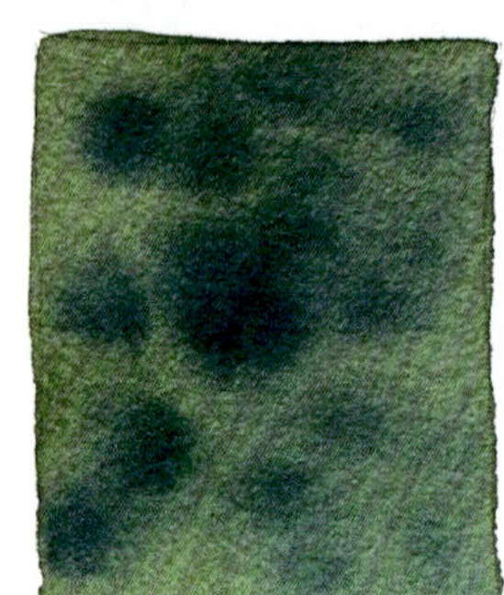

On the left, the green didn't dry evenly, creating a dividing line between the top and bottom. When I added blue to the top part of the top-left rectangle, the pigments got stuck in the green without blending in.

In the bottom-right rectangle, the moisture was still satisfactory, which allowed the pigments to disperse well and provide a nice blur.

CONTROLLING PIGMENTS IN WATER

Learning how to control paints when they touch a wet spot will be very useful. Indeed, if you want to deposit pigments in a specific spot of your illustration without them escaping and spreading everywhere, you will have to control the amount of water and paint on your brush. This will have a direct impact on how you play with the colors of your illustration during its wet phase.

To the right are two concrete examples. I spread water in identical circles and placed sap green only at the base.

On the left, I deliberately put too much water in my brush. As you can see, the pigments escape into the water on the paper because the water on my brush is added to the water already there.

On the right, my brush contains less water and a little more pure pigment. This has the effect of managing the way the pigments will be transported by the water already present on the paper.

GAINING SPEED

Painting quickly is essential for creating beautiful blends and working wet for as long as possible. To do this, before you begin:

- Prepare your colors and materials.
- Make a small sketch of your watercolor and color it lightly to visualize the final version.
- Practice on a scrap sheet of paper.

This way, you will be able to anticipate each step of your watercolor and make quick decisions that will allow you to gain precious minutes to paint for as long as possible in the still-wet watercolor.

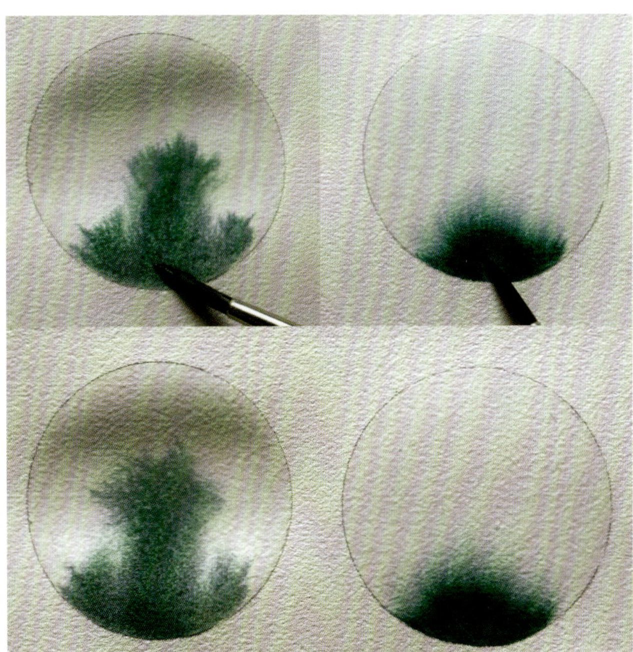

More water (left) means the paint will spread in ways you cannot predict. Less water (right) allows you to control the effect more.

Painting Wet-on-Dry, Creating Transparency

One of the techniques I use most in my watercolors is transparency. This allows me to make dense vegetation without weighing it down, since watercolor is a naturally transparent medium. I can therefore add several layers of paint and achieve a soft and light result. I also suggest creating transparent ferns in the step-by-step project on page 121.

To practice creating transparency, choose a light color, arrange a few shapes inside a square, and then wait for the watercolor to dry completely. Then using a light blend, add new shapes on top of the first ones to reveal the elements on top of each other.

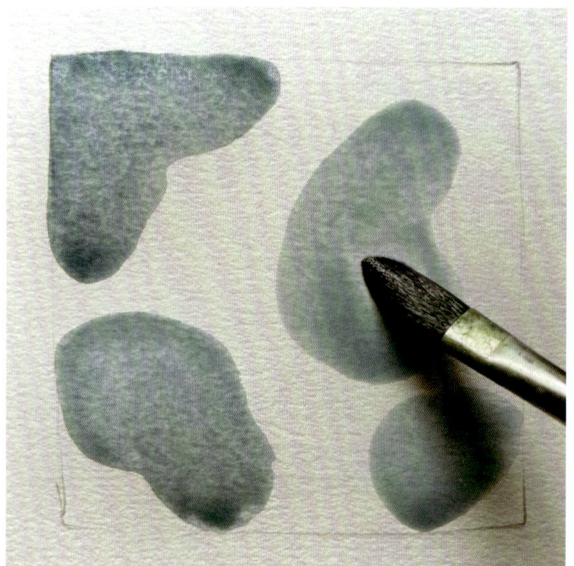
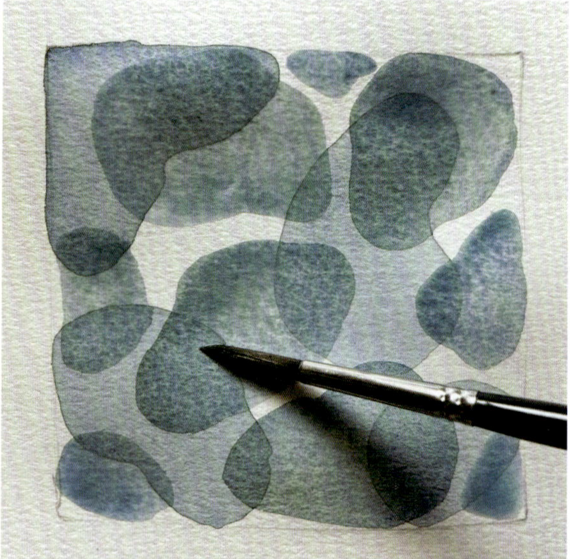

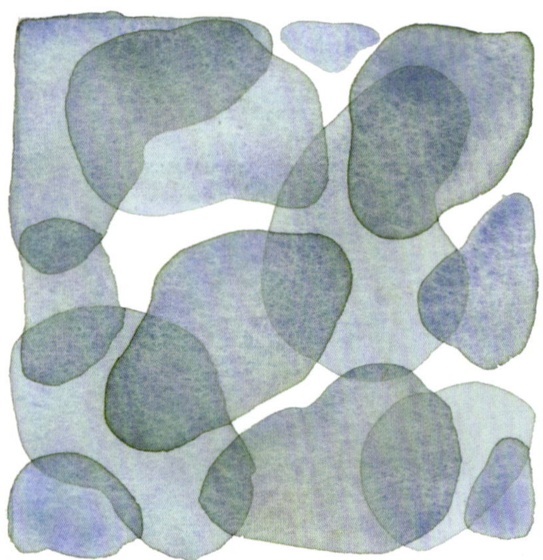

Making Light Areas Appear

The main difficulty with watercolor is managing the white areas. Indeed, it is a medium that requires preparation and anticipation, because once you have applied a dark or dark color, you will not be able to go back to lighten a large area—unlike gouache, for example. You will therefore have to anticipate the areas you want to leave white or light, then paint from lightest to darkest. Find concrete examples starting on page 30, though this is explored more in "Painting Forest Landscapes" on page 131.

However, there are a few techniques to lighten some dark areas of your watercolor.

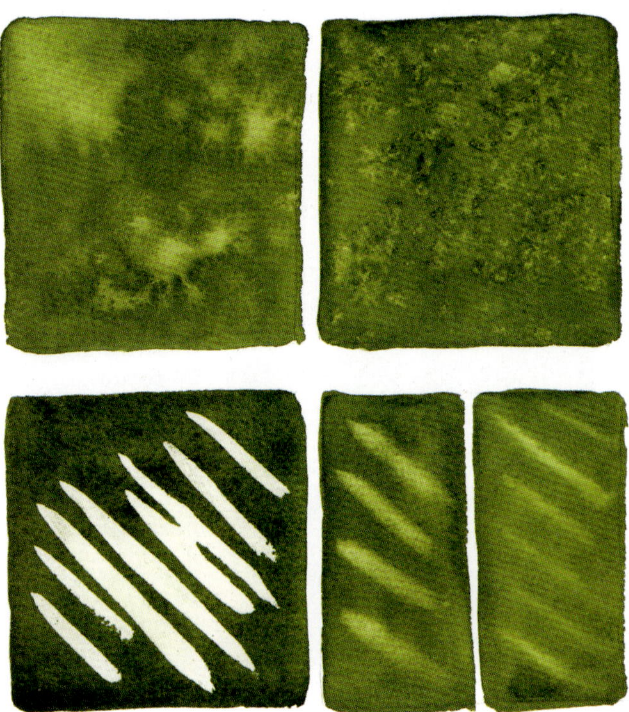

These examples show different techniques for repelling pigments or preserving the white of the paper.

PUSHING BACK PIGMENTS

With Water

If the watercolor is still wet, you can move the pigments from an area you want to leave light. Try filling a square with a dark color and, using a clean brush containing only water, scatter a few drops of water. You can also experiment at different stages of drying the watercolor to see that the drier the watercolor, the less mobile the pigments will be.

With Salt

To create a speckled effect in your watercolors, you can also use salt, which will absorb both water and pigments. The larger the salt grains, the greater the absorption. This is a popular effect in snowy landscapes, for example.

Test by placing a dark color in a 2" x 2" (5.1 x 5.1cm) square and scattering a few grains of salt over the still-wet watercolor. Wait until it is completely dry before removing the salt with a cloth, then observe the result.

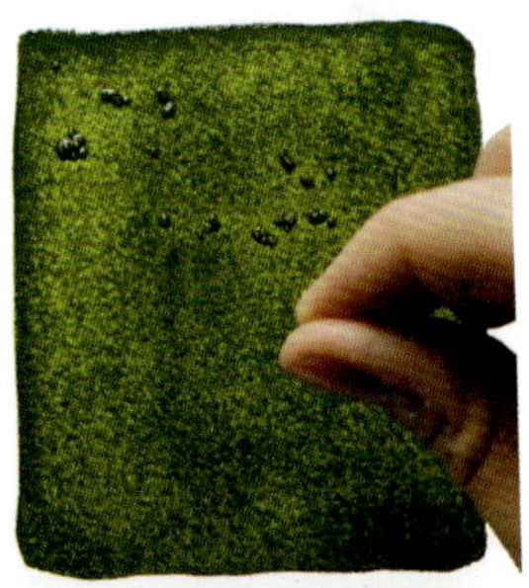

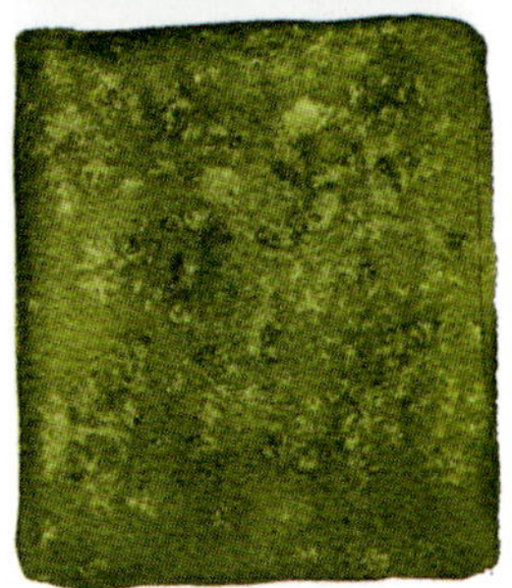

With a Wrung-Out Brush

When you want to precisely remove pigments from wet watercolors, you can use a clean, wrung-out brush. Simply place your brush on the desired area; you will notice that the pigments and water will be absorbed by the brush fibers, revealing a lighter area.

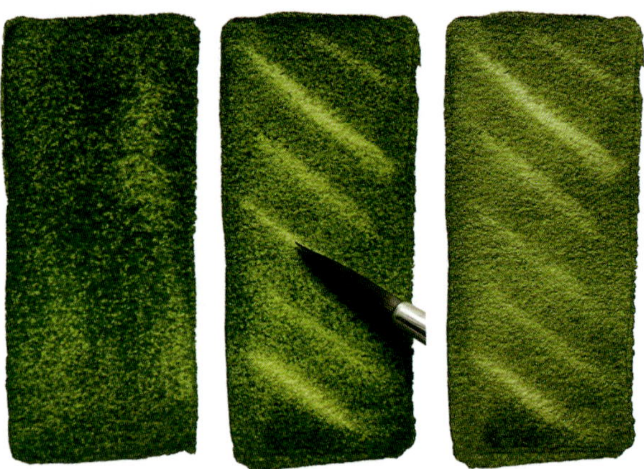

If the watercolor is dry, a little more effort will be required, as you will need to reactivate the pigments by lightly rubbing your paper with a brush.

Make sure the brush is not too dry, or the pigments won't be reactivated enough and you'll damage your brush. When the pigments are mobile again, pat the previously moistened area with a tissue. The pigments are removed from the paper.

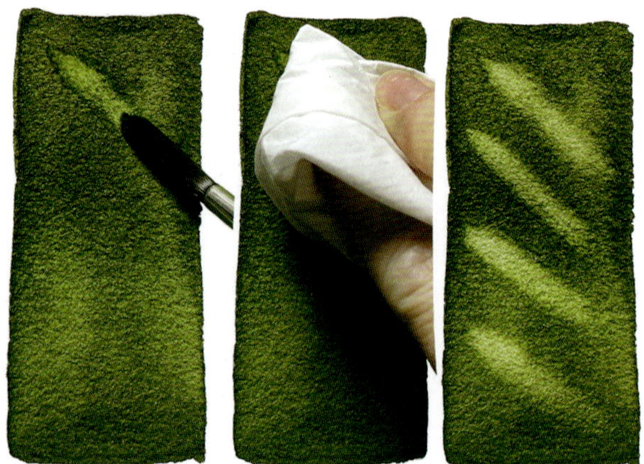

MASKING FLUID

I recommend using masking fluid if you want to perfectly maintain the white of the paper. For example, you might want this to paint a pattern lighter than your background. When it dries, this liquid latex prevents the pigments from touching the sheet.

To apply the liquid, moisten the brush slightly before application and rinse it thoroughly with clean water after use. I recommend using a cheap brush because the fluid can damage the fibers. When the fluid is completely dry on your sheet, you can paint over it without worrying about the watercolor touching this area. Once the paint is dry, you can gently remove the fluid, which has become elastic, by rubbing it with your finger or a small cloth.

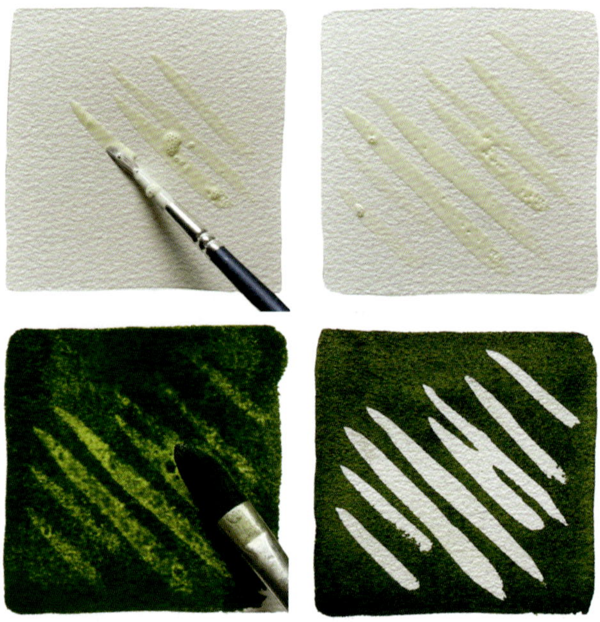

Creating Contrasts with Color

Color contrasts convey visual emotion and demonstrate artistic identity. The more numerous and striking they are, the more your work will engage the viewer.

PLAYING WITH TEMPERATURE

On the color wheel, we quickly perceive the colors that warm us (red, orange, and yellow) and those that cool us (green, blue, and purple). I like to vary the temperature of my colors to bring dynamism to my watercolors.

Green is a color used a lot in this book. It comes from mixing yellow, which is a warm color, and blue, which is a cool color. Therefore, depending on the amount of yellow or blue you add, your green will appear warmer or cooler. Take this into account to create a contrast of warm and cool colors, even within the same color family, to give a strong visual impact on your composition.

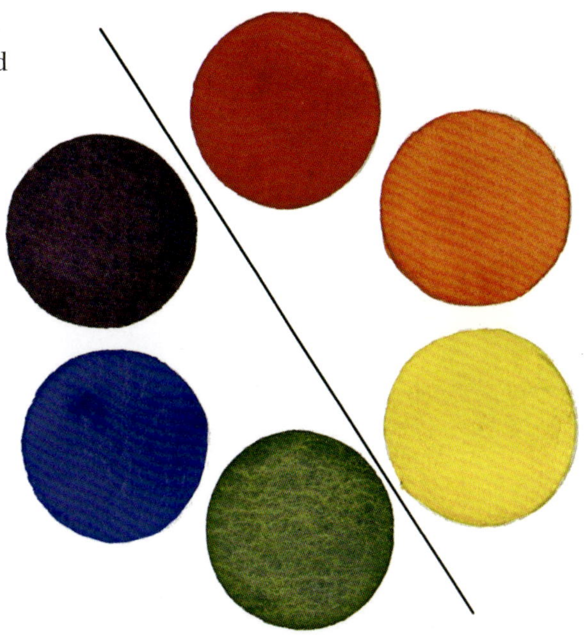

The line separates this color wheel into cool colors (left) and warm colors (right).

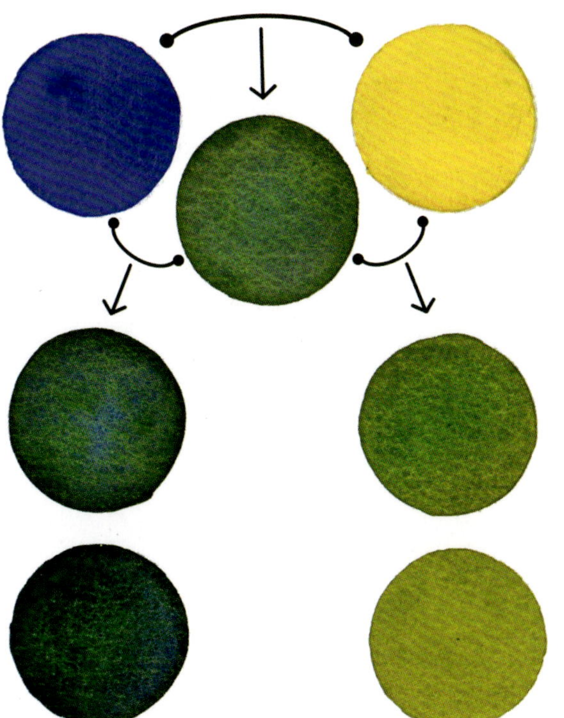

Combine blue and yellow to get green. Adding more yellow or blue creates a variety of greens that look very different from one another.

PLAYING WITH VALUE

Value is defined as a color's level of brightness. Using different color values can create contrasts. For example, using lighter colors for lit areas and darker colors for shaded areas creates a sense of texture, shadow, or depth.

Try lightening one of your colors by gradually adding water to your mixture (also called blending).

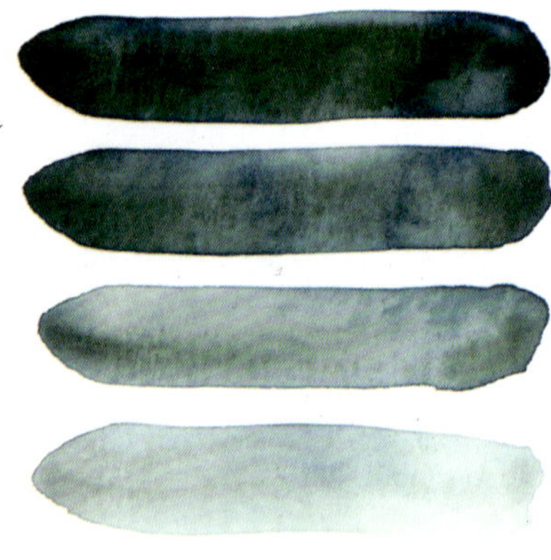

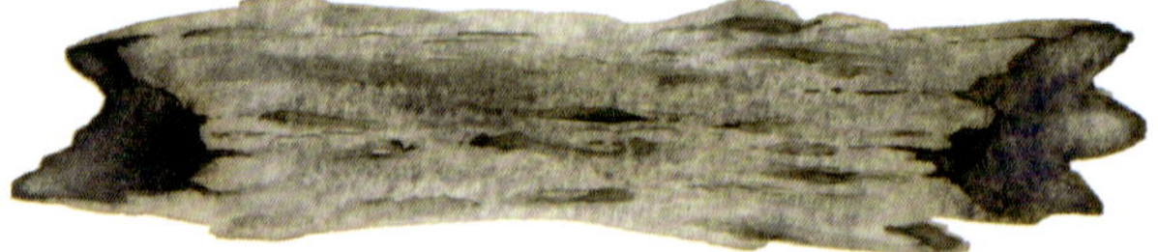

Here, values are essential to give volume to this branch.

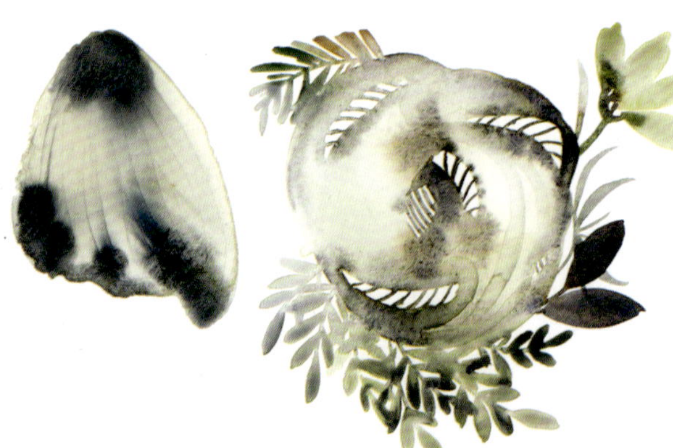

PLAYING WITH SATURATION

Saturation is defined by the purity of a color. For example, saturated colors are more intense and vivid, while desaturated colors are duller and grayish. With this type of contrast, artists can create more expressive works, richer in detail and depth.

To desaturate a color, mix with its complementary color, Payne's gray, or brown. Combining complementary colors usually results in a brown. If you use black, you will get a muted tone.

Here, I'm desaturating one of my greens with Payne's gray. At the top, you can see that the color is pure and intense, but it dulls as I add more gray. Try experimenting on your palette by mixing green with black, white, grays, and earth tones.

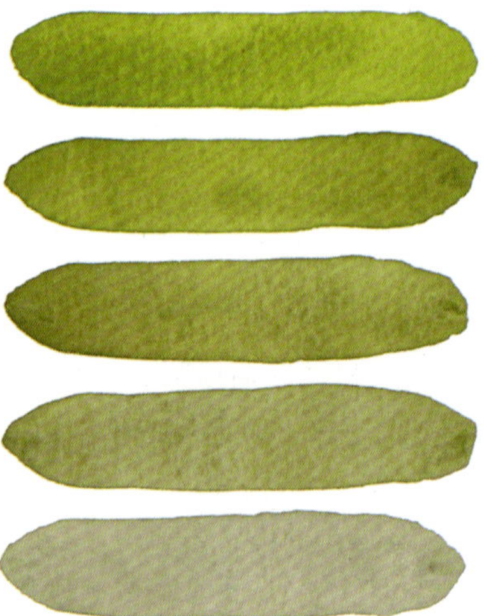

As the greens gradually desaturate, they provide more options for colors found in nature.

Painting with Intuition

For me, watercolor is a meditative medium because the way the water guides the pigments onto the paper is something very satisfying to observe. Playing with shapes, colors, and the unexpected can help you relax your movements before you begin painting. I often practice "letting go exercises," such as pages 33–35, drawing inspiration from plants to guide my movements, while using as many contrasts as possible to work on my technique. This also sharpens the imagination and helps you find new creative ideas.

FREEING YOURSELF FROM DRAWING

Throughout my artistic explorations, I noticed that when I drew a beautiful sketch before painting, I tended to spontaneously move toward something realistic. Even though I appreciate this style, I prefer to let myself be guided by interpretation and letting go, because it brings me more serenity and creativity.

Starting without drawing first is a method that requires a little practice but which very quickly becomes instinctive. Little by little, the brain places its demands and expectations differently. Your priority will be to highlight the unique attributes of the subject rather than making the details as perfect as possible. If you force yourself to no longer draw before painting, you will, for example, pay more attention to the association of colors or the shape of your patterns. As you explore, you will notice that your artistic style develops.

Painting without drawing is a process I've learned over time, and it's extremely liberating for me. Before I got there, I tried to understand how nature was made around me by making small sketches with minimalist coloring.

The technique I use is to visualize the overall shape of my subject without paying attention to details. I look at the volumes as well as where the light and shaded areas are located. I then focus on the number of colors, and before painting, mix them in the wells of my palette. This allows me to save time on drying my paint, because this technique requires knowing how to paint wet, and therefore quickly.

MASTERING BRUSH PRESSURE

Learning to control your brush is essential for creating many different shapes. I highly recommend practicing using it in different positions on a piece of cellulose paper.

When I started, my favorite exercise was creating simple leaves. This allows you to work on the pressure applied to the brush: the fine line made by using the tip and the thick shapes made by flattening it completely onto the leaf.

For fine lines, I recommend first using a small amount of water on your brush to get a nice tip, then picking up

Note

I am not talking here about light sketches that serve as reference points to better anticipate light and dark areas or that mark particular shapes like the step-by-step "Snowdrop" (page 53), "Mushroom Sphere" (page 118), or even "Insect Branch" (page 123).

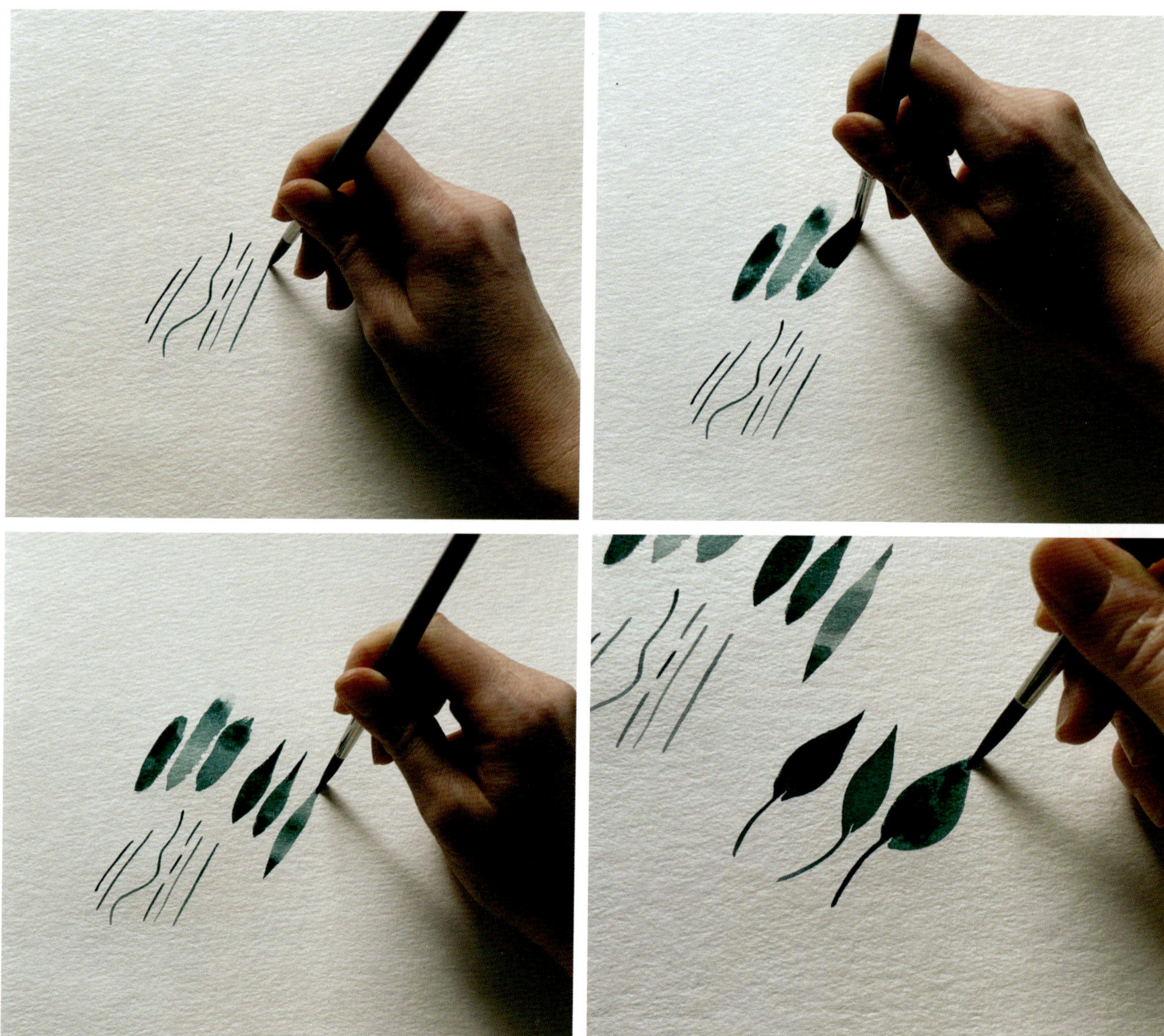

a little pigment. Hold your brush almost vertically and practice drawing small lines (top-left photo).

For thick shapes, take a larger quantity of water so that you only make one pass, then press the brush generously (top-right photo on the next page).

Repeat the exercise, gradually releasing the pressure so as to create a point at the end of your thick line (bottom-left photo).

Now that you have mastered the pressure of the brush, put all these elements together to build a simple leaf (bottom-right photo).

Don't be discouraged if it's not perfect! I personally had to repeat these movements many, many times before feeling completely comfortable with this exercise.

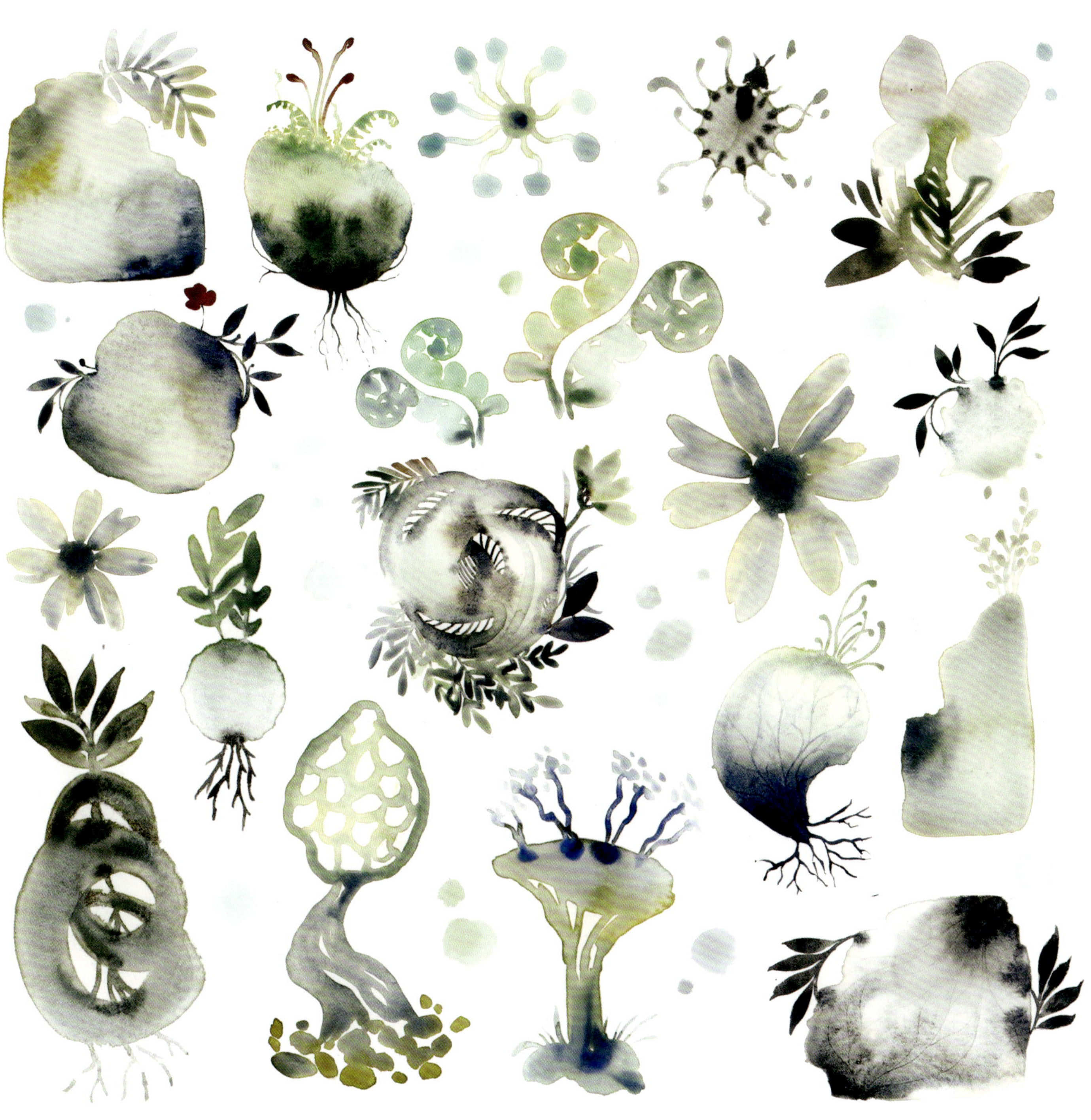

Practice

WORKING WITH NATURAL TEXTURES

In these step-by-step tutorials, I invite you to practice texture effects using various natural materials as a reference. You'll master several techniques, such as using transparency to create highlights, blending colors, or using wet-on-dry and wet-on-wet watercolors. Finally, using granular pigments, you'll learn how to give your surfaces a realistic look.

Wood

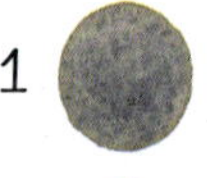

1 • **Mixture 1** - Tundra blue + brown iron oxide (very diluted)

2 • **Mixture 2** - Tundra blue + brown iron oxide (highly concentrated)

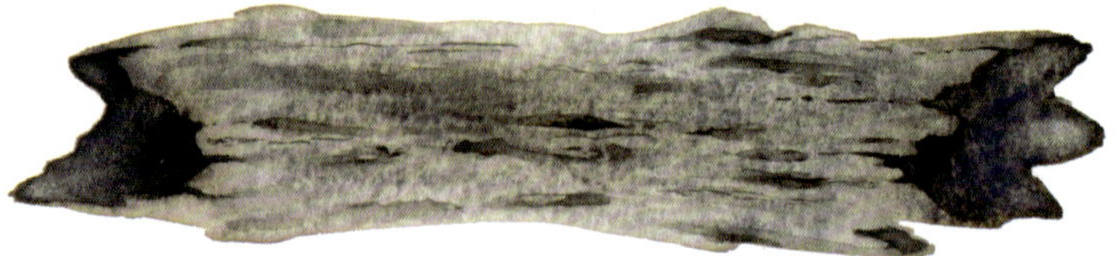

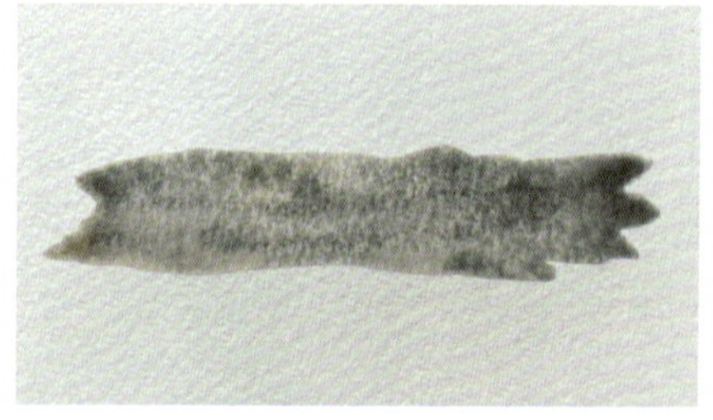

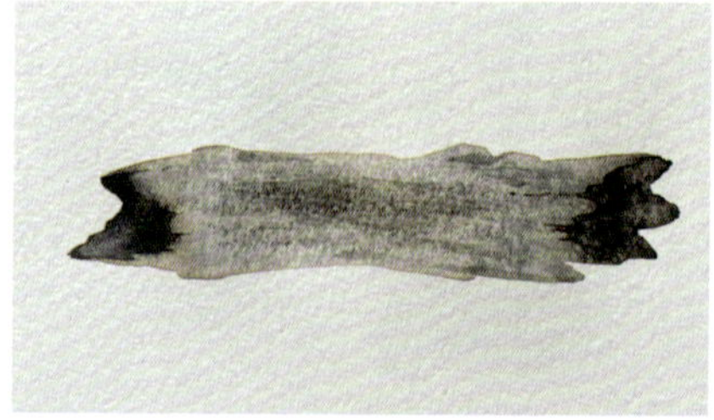

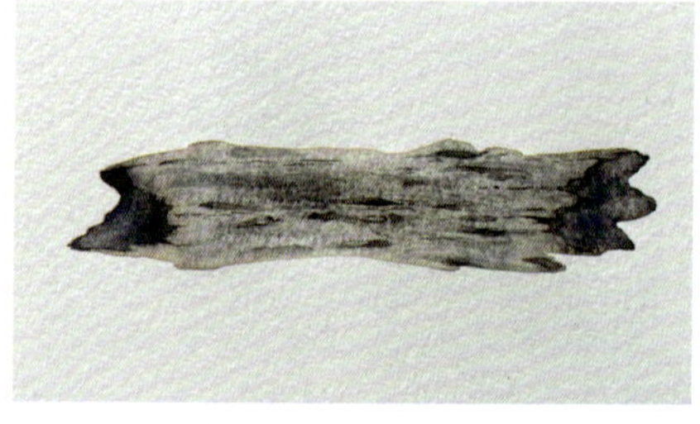

1. Using a firm brush and Mixture 1, paint the shape of the log. The granular pigments will naturally give your painting the appearance of bark. Let it dry.

2. Using the same brush, apply Mixture 2 to the edges of the log, so as to give the impression of a hollow.

3. Add small thin lines on the light part for the grain.

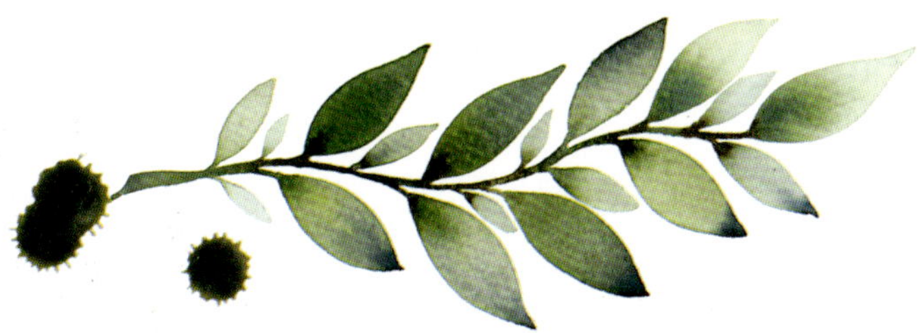

Rock

1

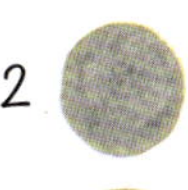
2

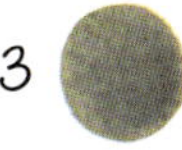
3

- **Mixture 1** - Yellow ochre + tundra blue + black iron oxide (diluted)
- **Mixture 2** - Yellow ochre + tundra blue + black iron oxide (slightly diluted)
- **Mixture 3** - Yellow ochre + tundra blue + black iron oxide

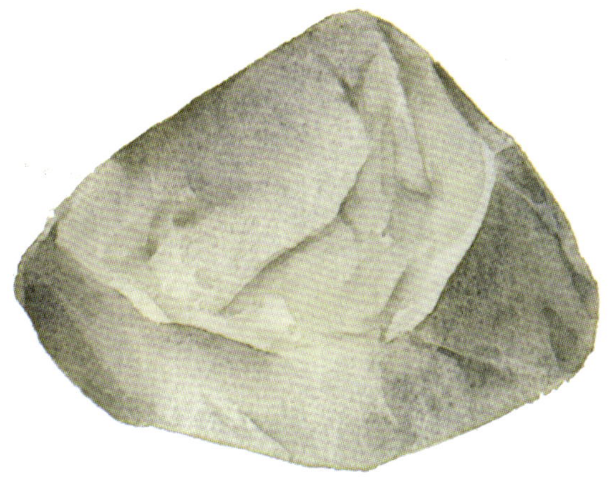

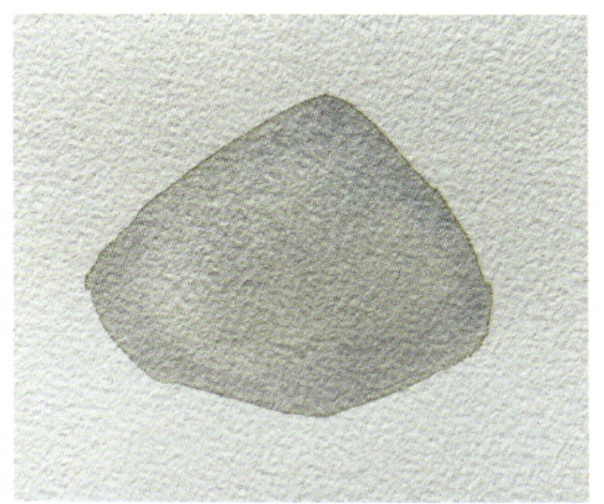

1. Take a soft brush and apply Mixture 1, shaping your rock. Wait for the watercolor to dry completely.

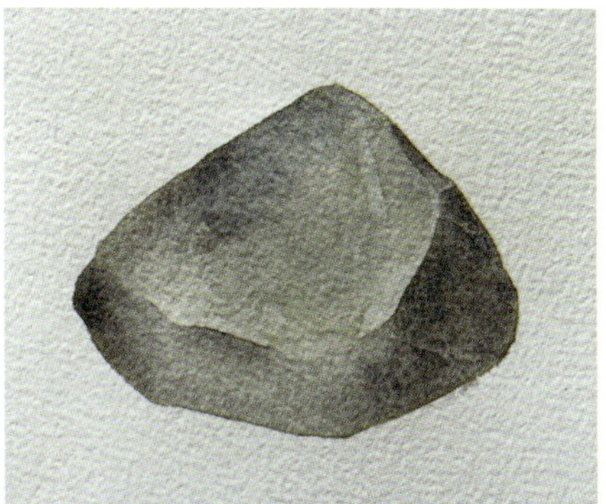

2. Using the same brush and Mixture 2, mark the edges of the rock to reveal the relief effect. Wait for the watercolor to dry, then add new marks.

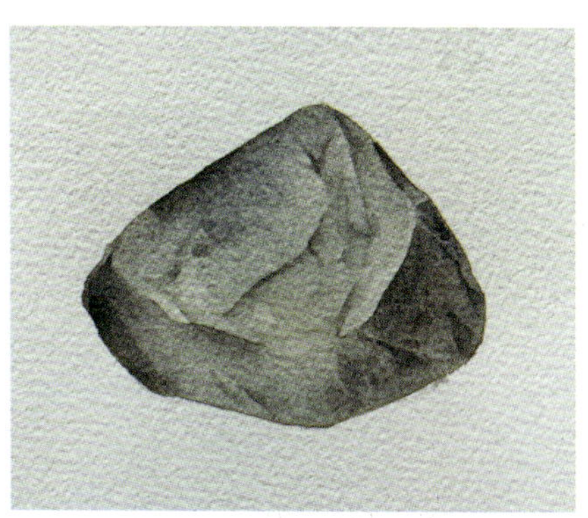

3. With Mixture 3, dig deeper into the rock, creating more intense cracks and marks in the shadows.

Ground

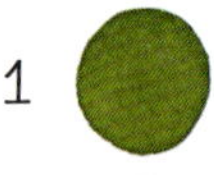

1

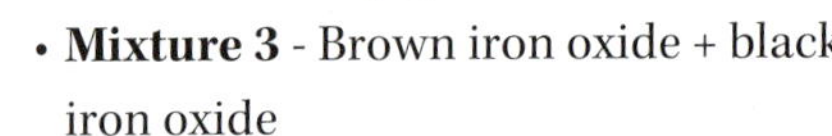

- **Mixture 1** - Sap green + Indian yellow
- **Mixture 2** - Sap green + ultramarine blue
- **Mixture 3** - Brown iron oxide + black iron oxide

2

3

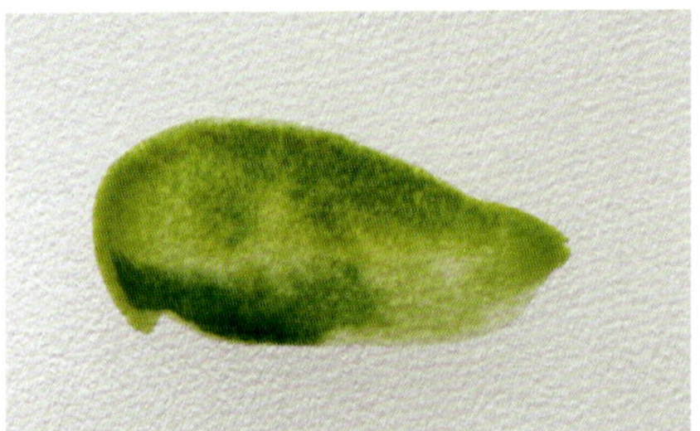

1. Using a soft brush and Mixture 1, create a small oval patch of grass.

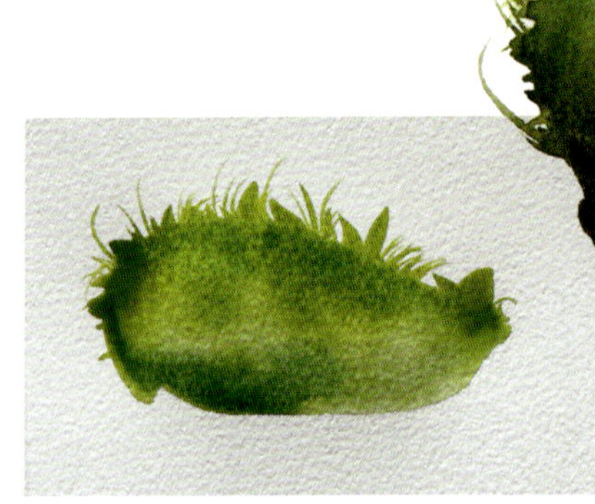

2. With the tip of your brush and the same mixture, draw small blades of grass on top. In the still-wet watercolor, place Mixture 2 to give color variations to the grass.

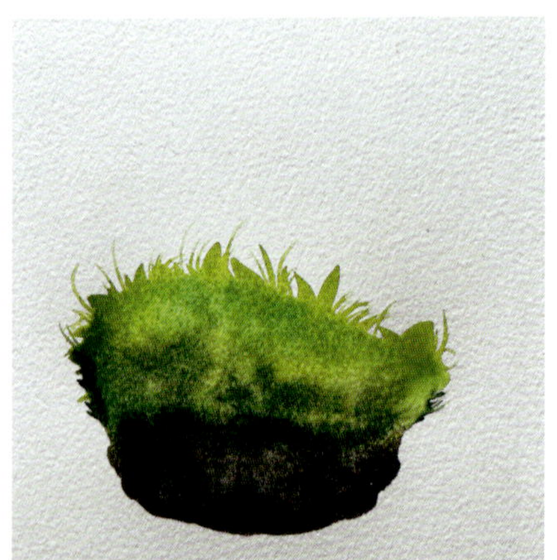

3. In the still-wet watercolor, form the soil under the grass with Mixture 3.

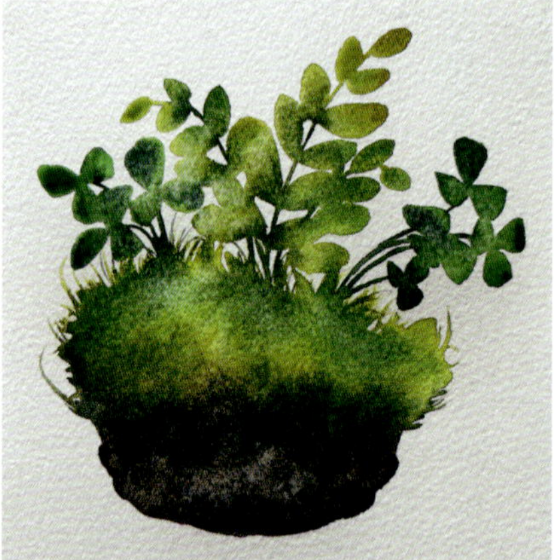

4. In the still-wet watercolor, add vegetation above the grass using Mixtures 1 and 2, then wait for the watercolor to dry completely.

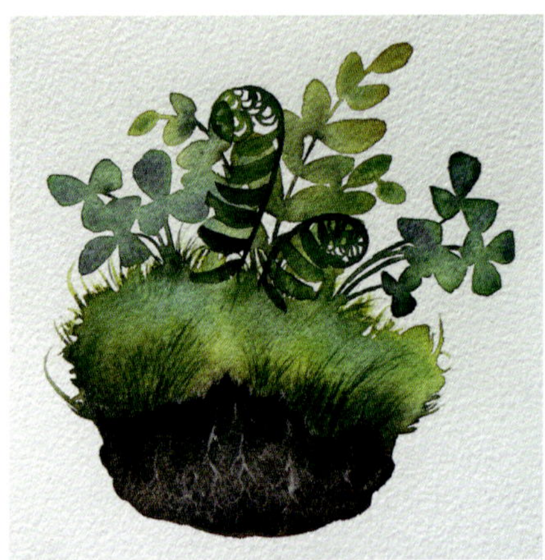

5. Use Mixture 2 to make the ferns. Use Mixture 3 to add depth to the soil, creating a more shadows under the grass. Also, have fun creating small roots using a white colored pencil.

HAVE FUN WITH LETTING GO

In these exercises, I suggest you don't necessarily follow the colors I use but rather explore the possibilities of your palette. These aren't necessarily realistic but work as practice with organic shapes. Have fun alternating between light and dark, warm and cool colors, and adding more or less water to your mixtures.

Little Drop

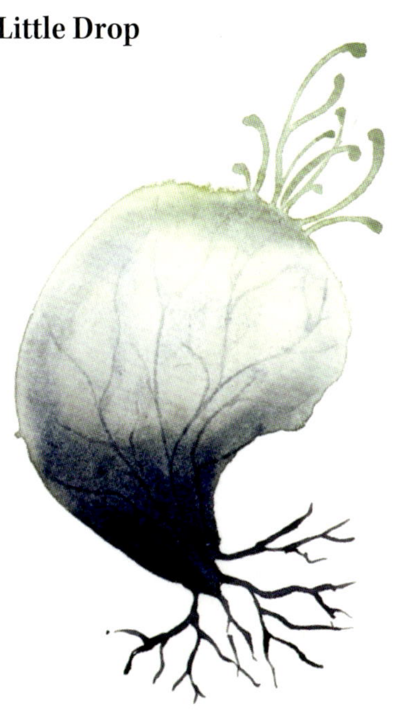

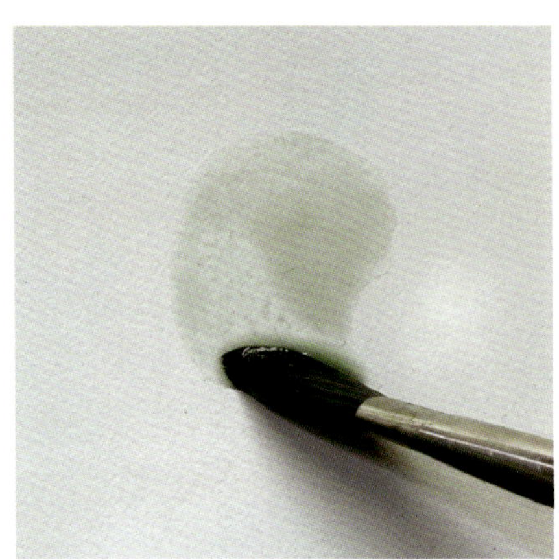

1. Using a wide, soft brush, draw a shape resembling a water droplet. I used a very diluted buff titanium color.

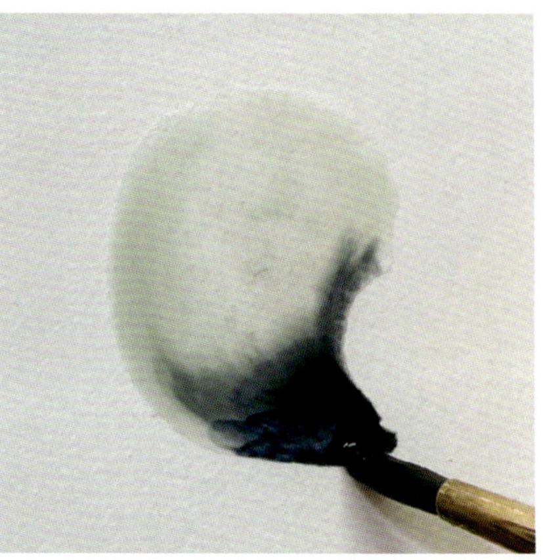

2. Using a smaller brush, apply a touch of tundra blue to the bottom of the drop.

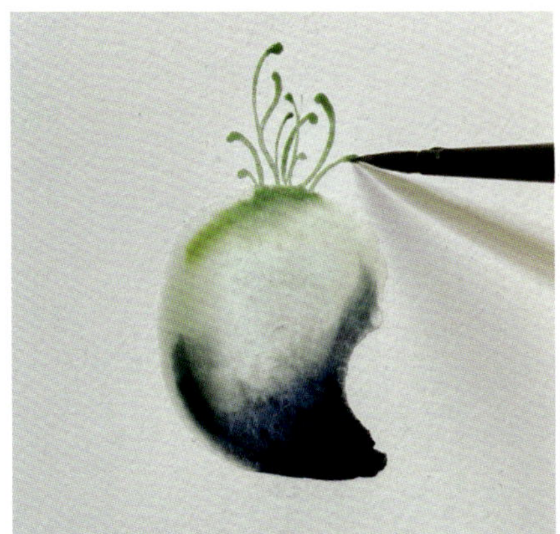

3. Using a liner brush and light green, draw tentacle shapes on top.

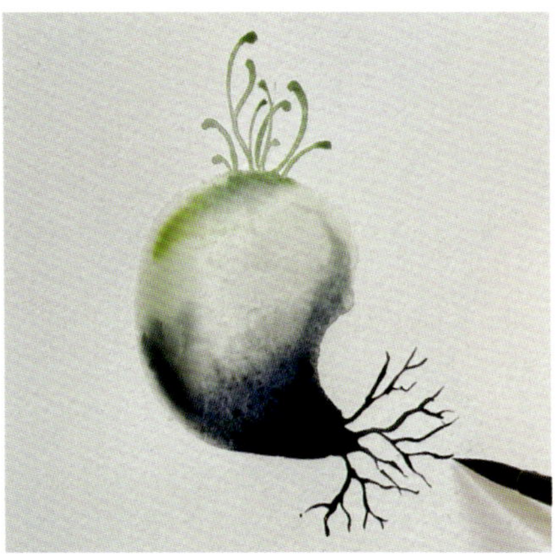

4. Do the same with tundra blue for some roots.

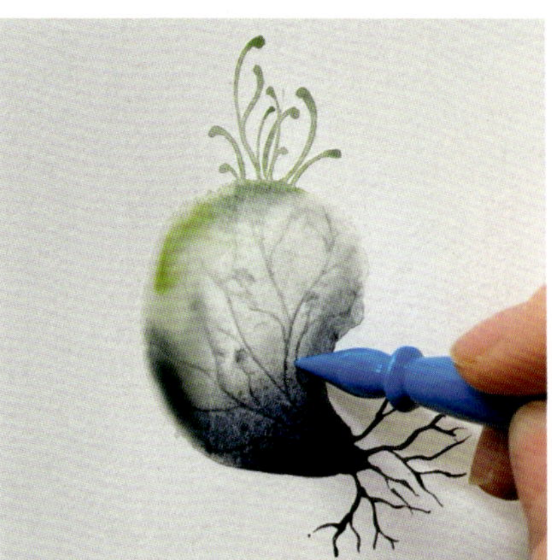

5. Draw veins with a pointed object to imitate the wings of a butterfly.

Honeycomb Morel

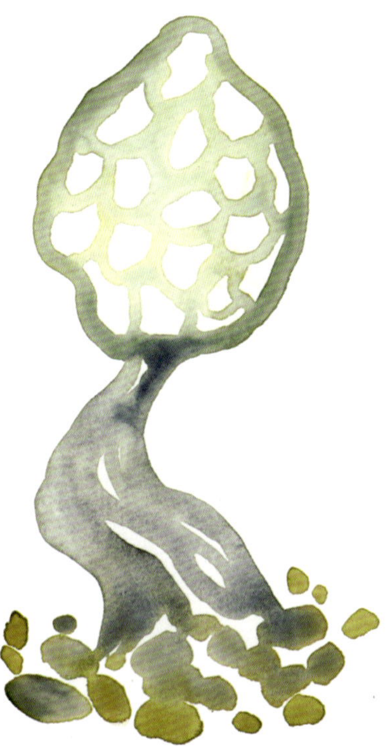

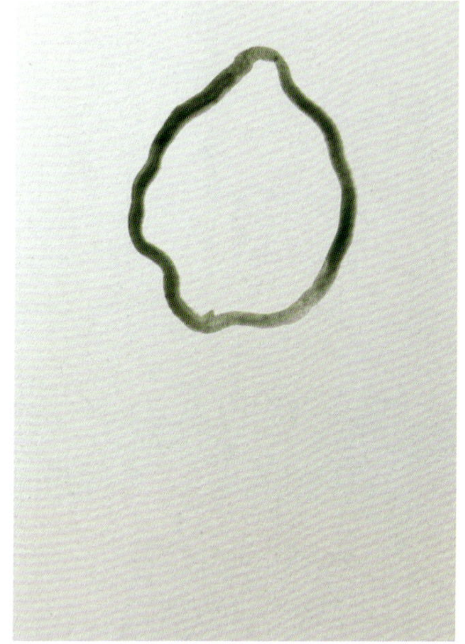

1. Using a very diluted mixture of Mars black and tundra blue, trace the shape of the morel cap.

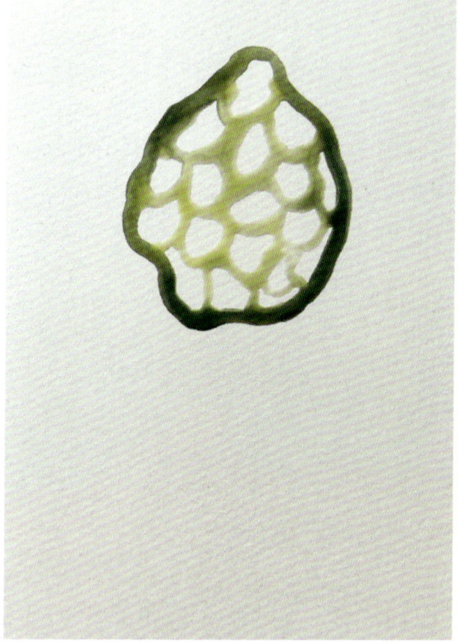

2. Using the buff titanium color, draw small honeycomb shapes in the mushroom cap.

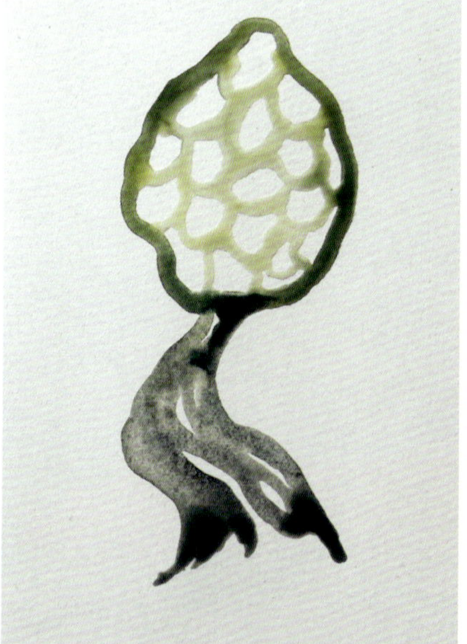

3. Reuse the first mixture to paint the base, forming roots.

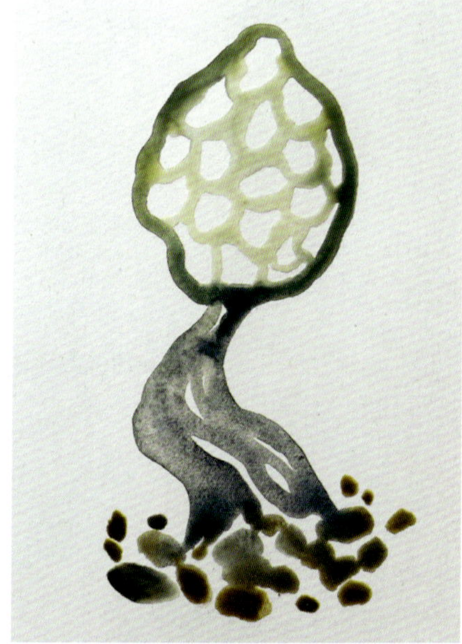

4. Place small pebbles at the base of the mushroom, mixing the quinacridone gold and the tundra blue.

Water Mushroom

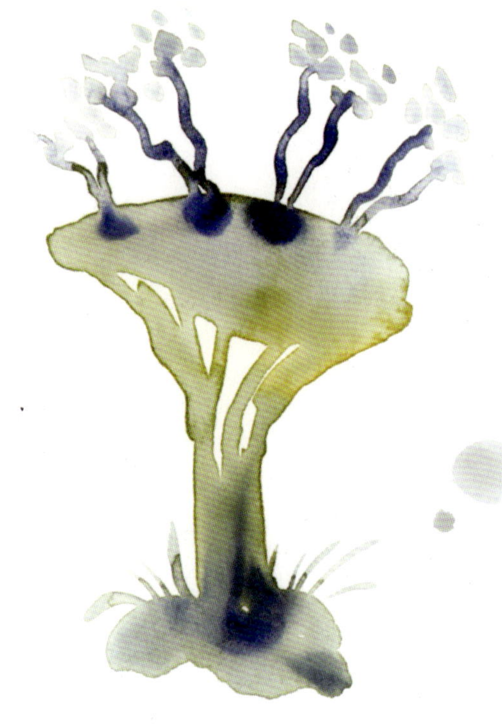

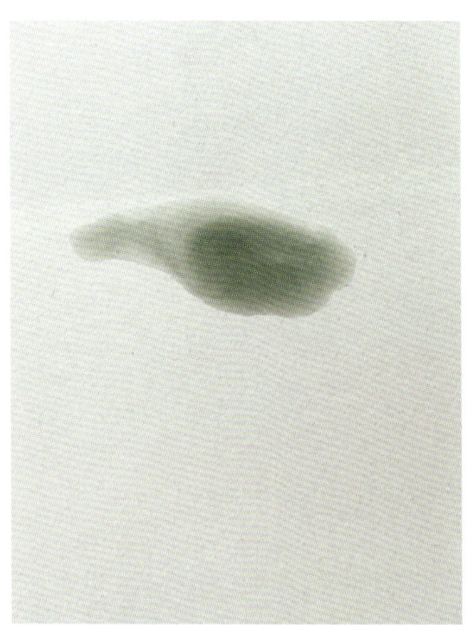

1. Paint the mushroom cap with a very light mixture of yellow ochre and tundra blue.

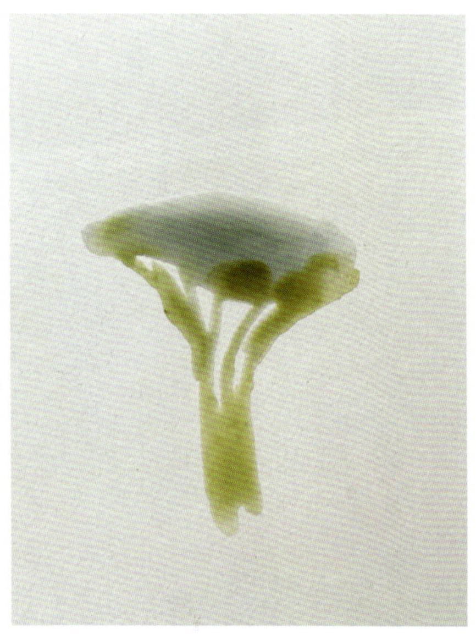

2. Using yellow ochre, paint the base of the mushroom in the still-wet watercolor, having fun creating strange shapes.

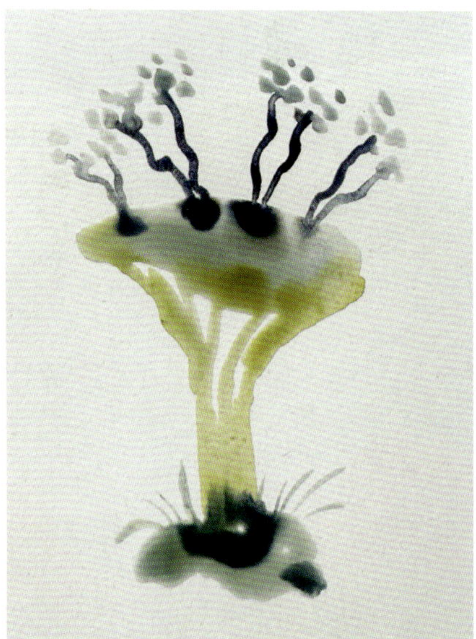

3. In the still-wet watercolor, draw some seaweed-like shapes on the mushroom cap and below the stem.

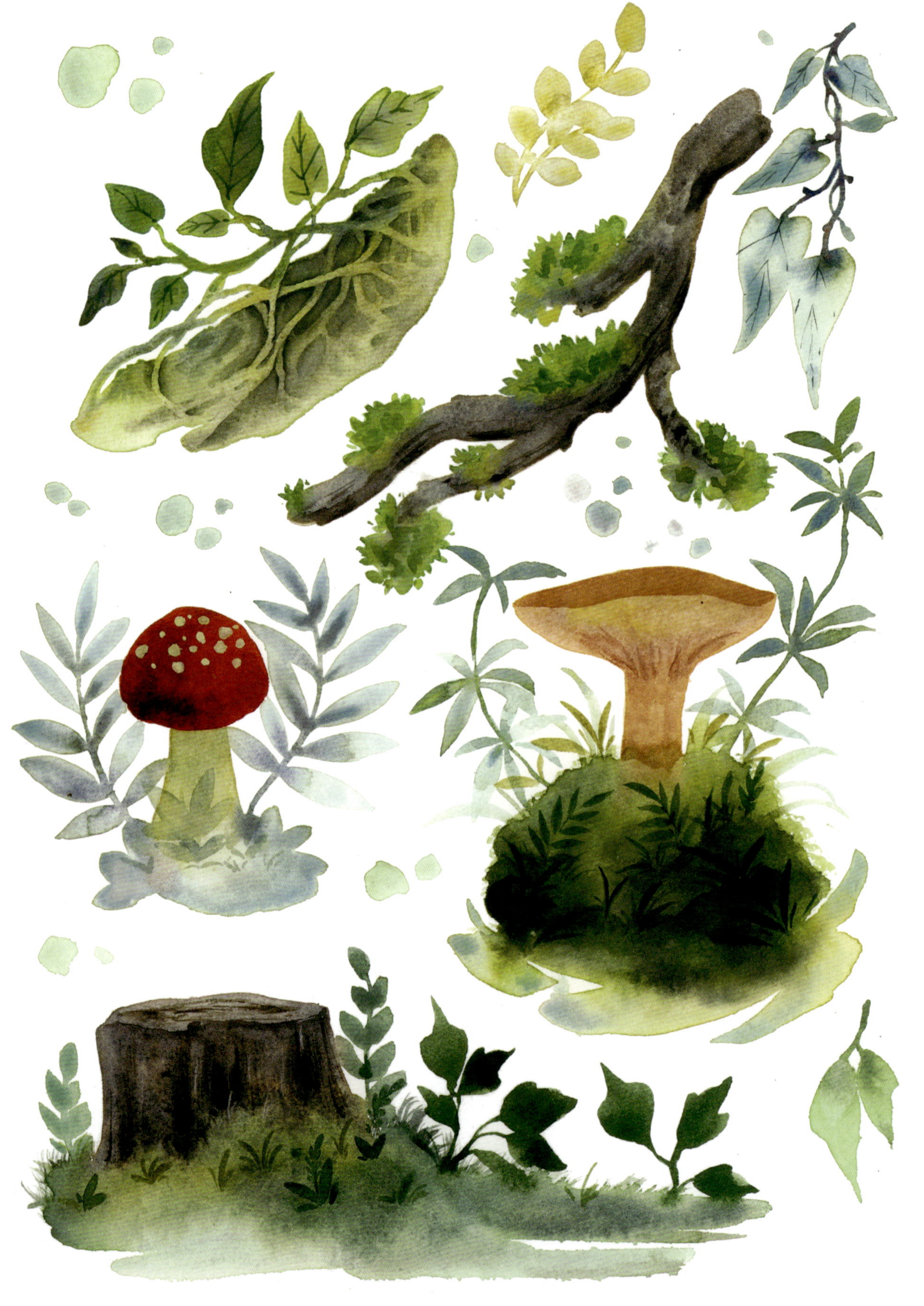

Observing Nature

Taking the time to observe and study plants and minerals is essential to better understanding the colors, shapes, and textures of nature. This will allow you to paint them more accurately later. Sometimes, certain details become a source of inspiration and lead to new creative explorations.

Finding Inspiration

Often right in front of our eyes, it's sometimes difficult to perceive inspiration or imagine it in our art. Years can sometimes go by without being able to conceptualize creative ideas. That's why doing research will help you achieve your goal. The more you practice, the faster you'll reach it.

Here are some ideas I suggest for exploring nature:

- Collect or photograph natural elements and observe them in daylight. Analyze the different shades of color, variations in textures, and the shapes that characterize them.

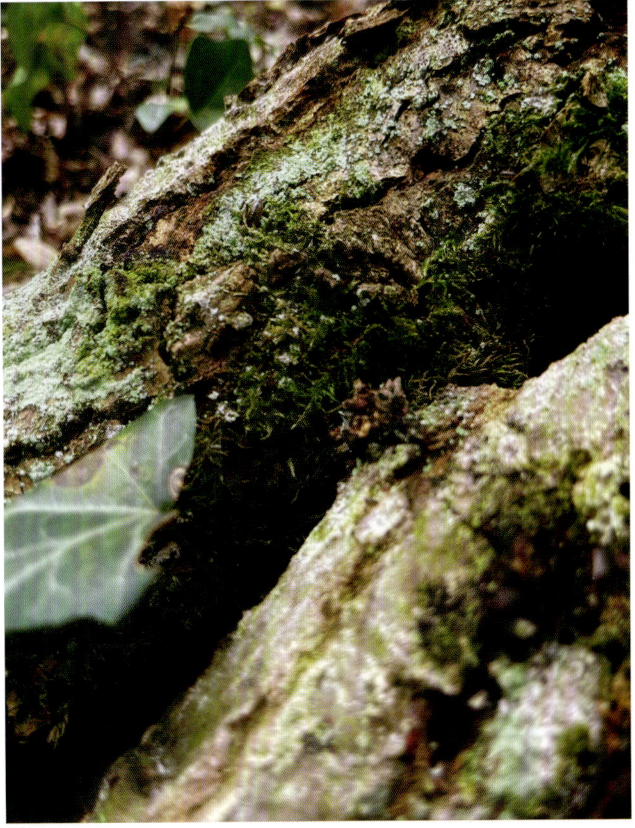

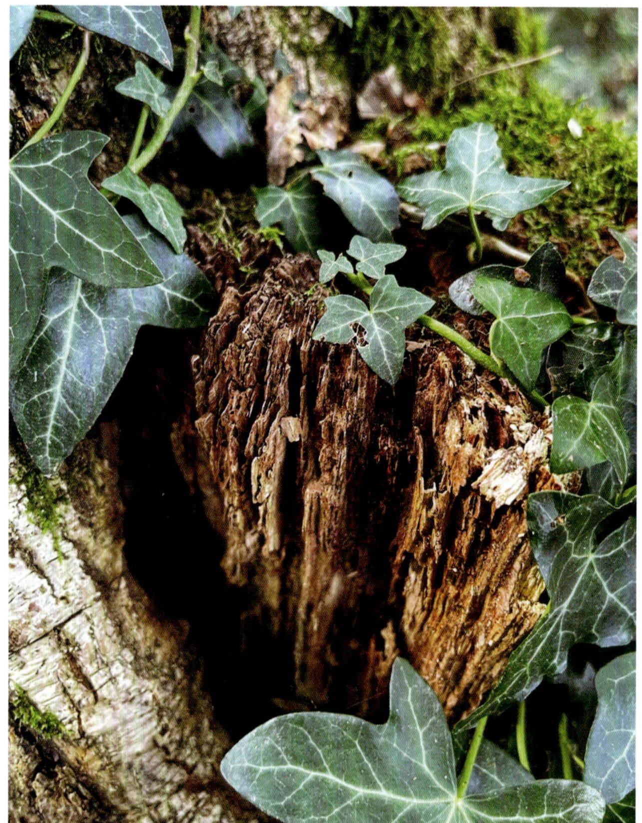

- If possible and safe, try to touch the texture of tree bark or a small rock to better understand the depth and relief.

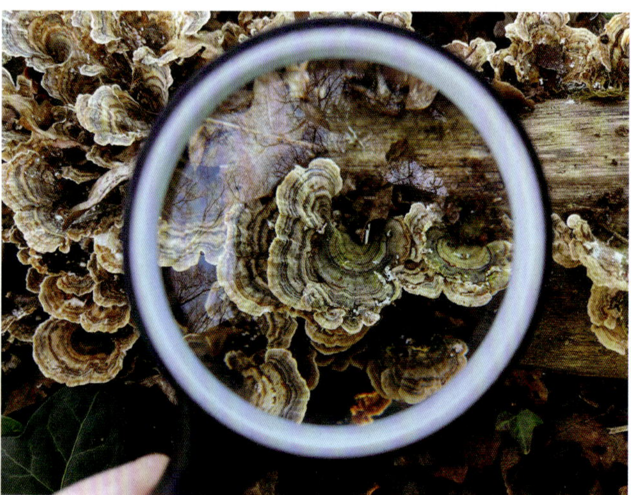

- Use a magnifying glass to better study the details that form on the surface of plants.

Being a very visual person, I need to supplement my resources with the internet. The many inspiring and quality images found there allow me to gather my ideas. Nature has always been at the heart of my research—the forest in particular—and I noticed that the illustrations or photos I spent the most time on mainly represented the small things that we only perceive when we get very close. Textures, shapes, and colors fascinate me, so I very quickly turned my explorations toward these types of subjects. This is good, because the nature is full of inspiring ideas!

I also consult the following books, which offer valuable advice for better understanding the forest ecosystem and its environment.

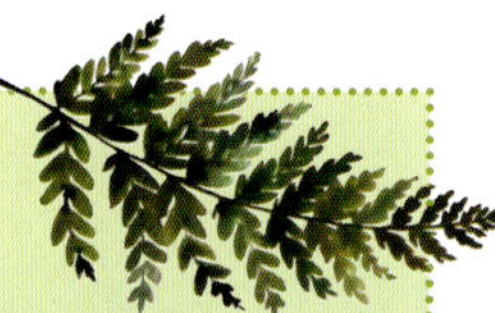

My Favorite Books About Nature

Most of these books are only in French. However, they are mostly comprised of photos and illustrations, which could be useful for anyone, even if you do not know the language.

- Vignes, Pierre and Délia Vignes. *L'herbier des plantes sauvages*. Larousse, 2011.
- Olsen, Lars-Henrik, Jakob Sunesen, and Bente Vita Pedersen. *Small Woodland Creatures*. Oxford University Press, 2001.
- Guillot, Gerard. *Guide des fleurs des forêts*. Belin, 2014.
- Milochau, Fabrice and Eve Gandossi. *Forêts enchantées de France*. GEO, 2022.
- Massé, Franck. *Les mousses, les lichens et les fougères, ces méconnus essentiels à la forêt*. CNPF, 2020.
- Pichard, Gilles. *Le champignon, allié de l'arbre et de la forêt*. CNPF, 2015.

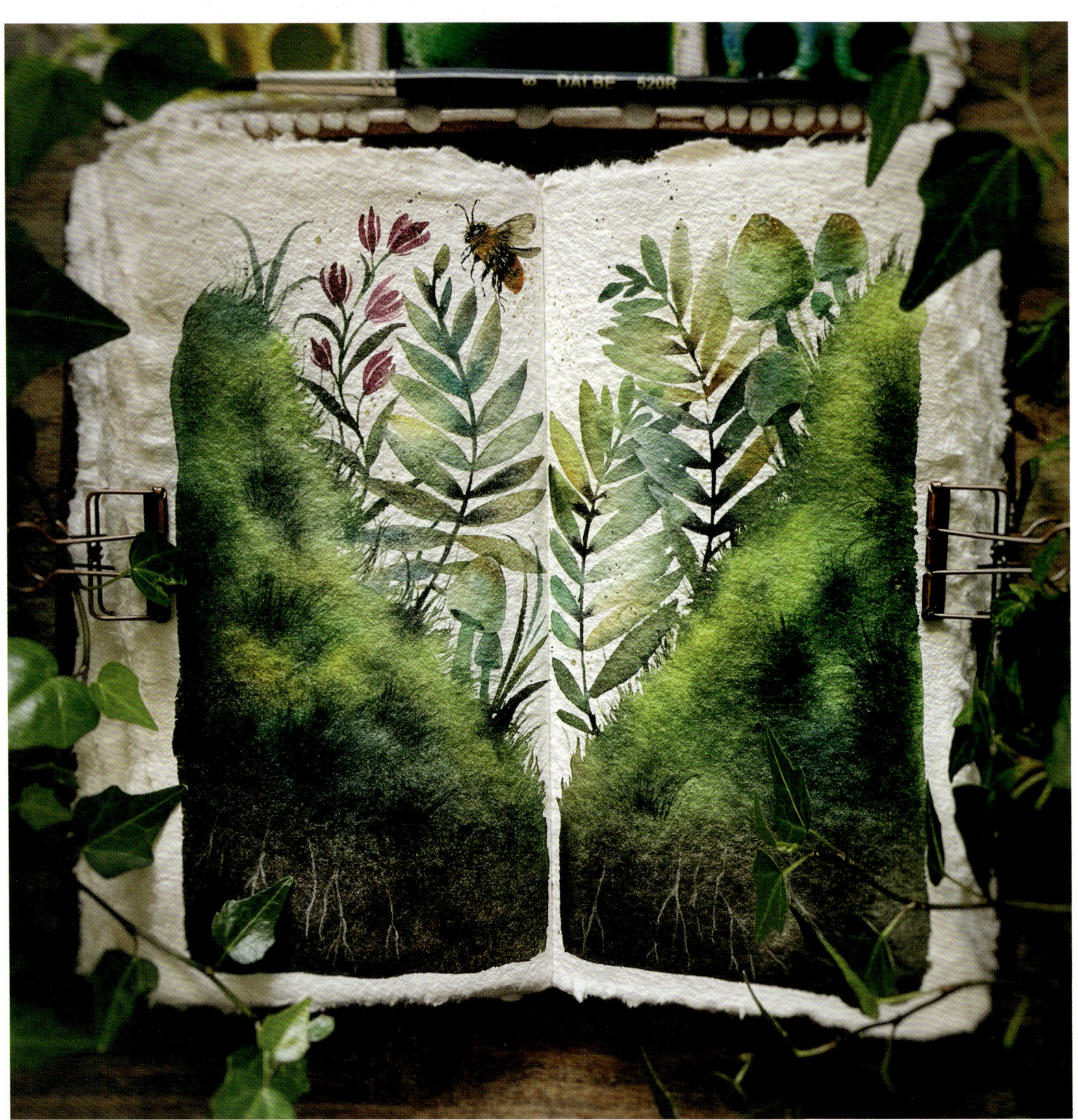

Your observations about nature can be gathered into a book of your own!

Creating Herbariums

I like to draw inspiration from my research to create herbariums inside my watercolor notebooks. This allows me to practice, then to better visualize the plants before integrating them into my creations. Introducing insects or wildflowers into my paintings gives them a poetic note. Imagining a story around these little animals makes the scene softer and more pleasant to view.

On these pages are some examples of flowers I photograph with my phone while out walking. They're also good models if you'd like to practice drawing them. See the exercises that start on page 49 for the method I use to paint woodland flowers.

You'll probably notice that certain plants recur frequently from one page to the next. I've listed several plants (below) of varying size, shape, and color that often find a place in any of my creations. I carefully chose my subjects based on their ease of reproduction and the visual effect they bring to my watercolors. I highly recommend creating pages with references to your favorite plants.

Here is my personal list: ferns, mosses, lichens, mushrooms, forest fruits, wild berries, ivy, cranberries, bindweed leaves . . . You will be able to paint most of these elements as you follow the step-by-step instructions I suggest in this book.

For my part, my favorites generally find their place inside my watercolor notebooks because I like to immerse myself in my explorations like a personal diary. They also have the advantage of preserving the evolution of your research over time.

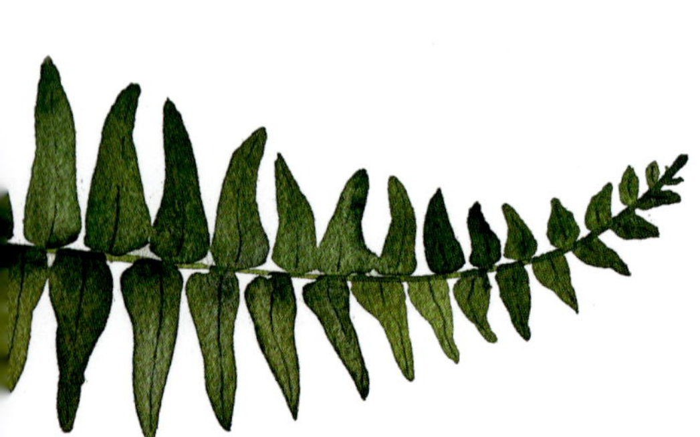

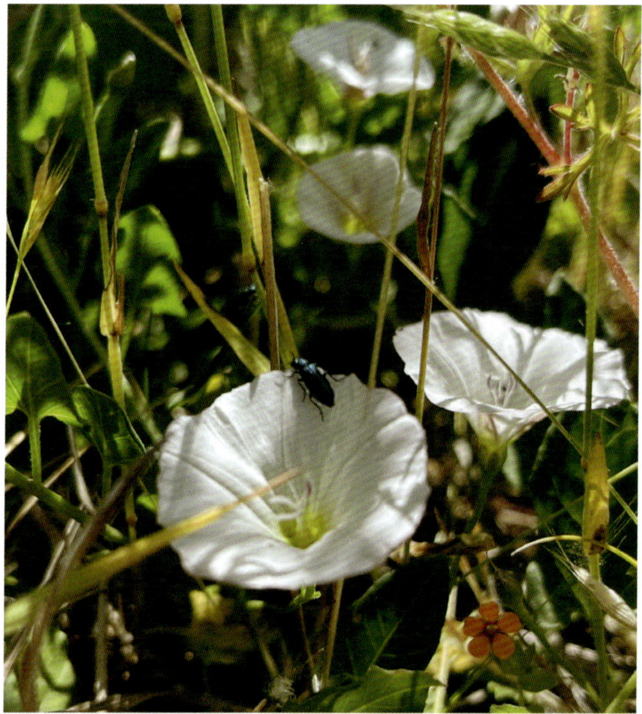

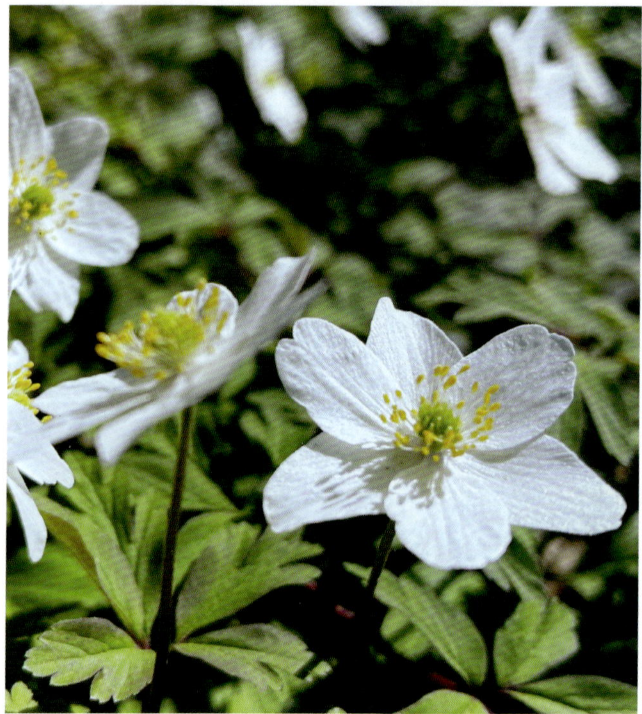

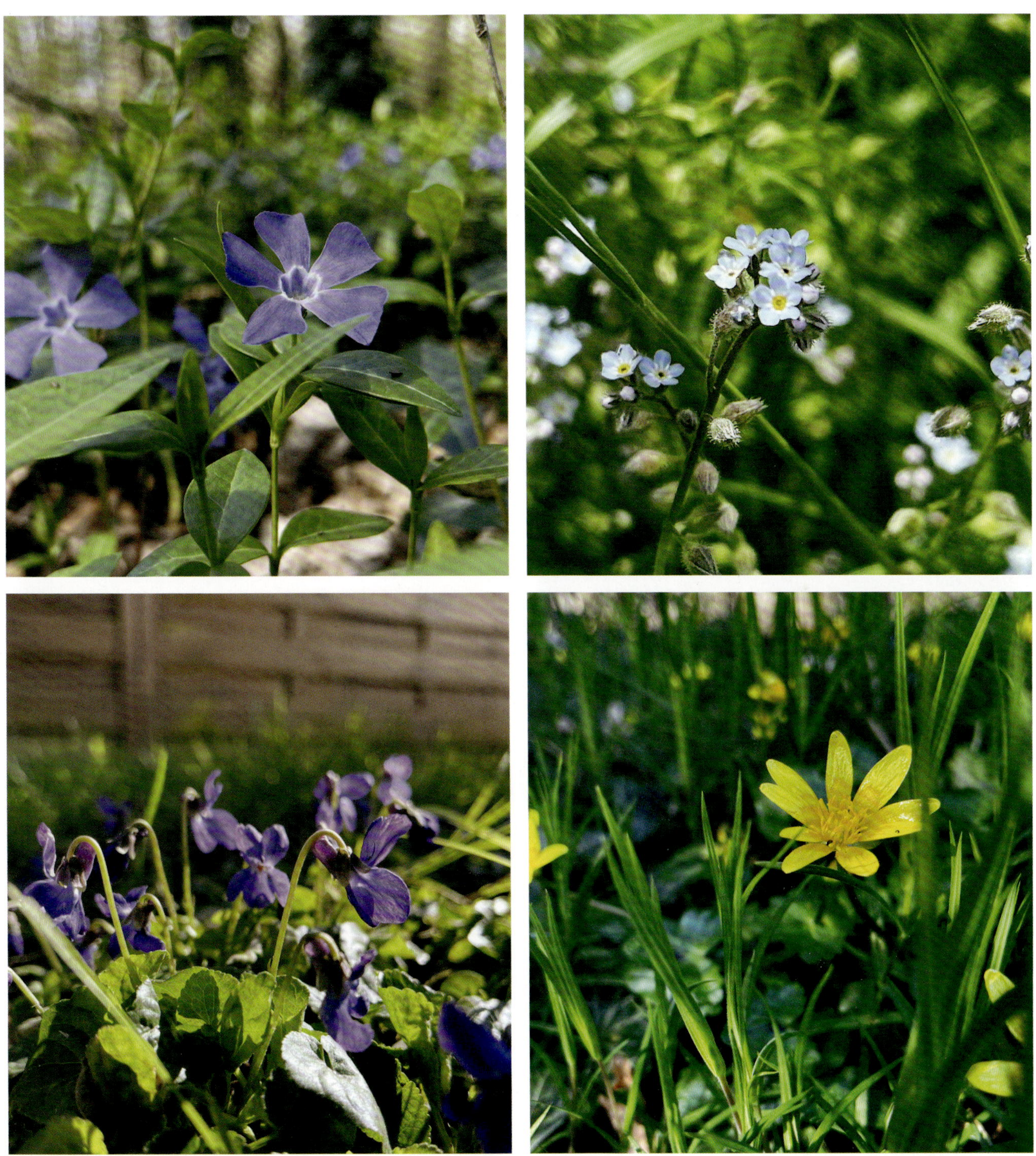

Using Notebooks

Keep a small sketchbook with you to stay connected to your creativity at all times. This will inspire you to continue observing the beauty of nature wherever you are. You'll more easily find the impulse to find a brief moment in your day to draw, and this moment will quickly turn into a creative routine. By getting into the habit, you'll learn faster and more efficiently. Once you get home, you can add some colors to your notebook using your color charts or the photos you've taken.

Drawing or painting from real subjects is also a very good exercise to better understand the role of light and shadow, because you will be able to observe all angles of your model.

Once you've gained some skill in sketching from nature, you can improve your drawings by putting small scenes you've imagined on paper. Before painting, you'll be able to combine multiple images to create a unique, personal creation.

Here is an example: I took a photo of a tree stump in the forest that I used as reference for painting a watercolor.

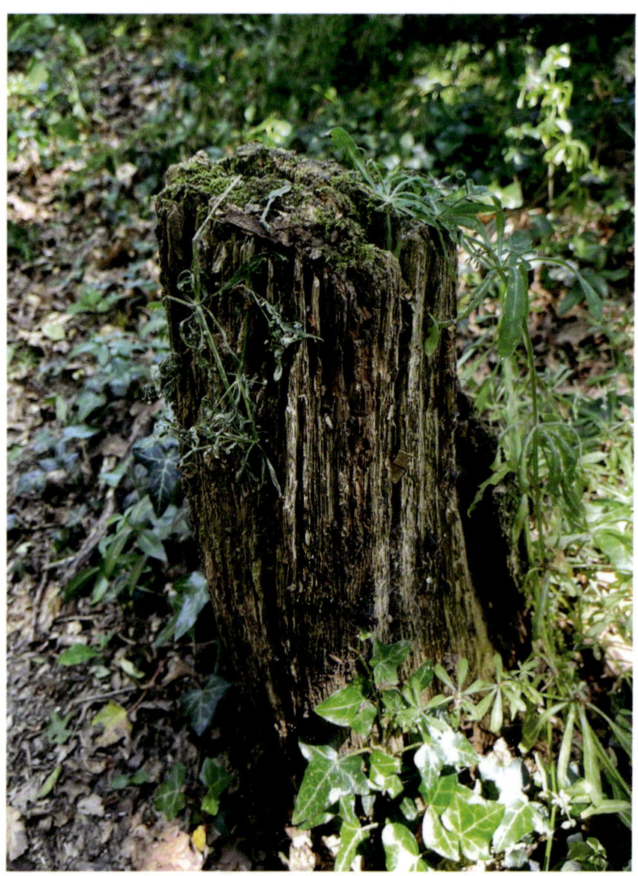

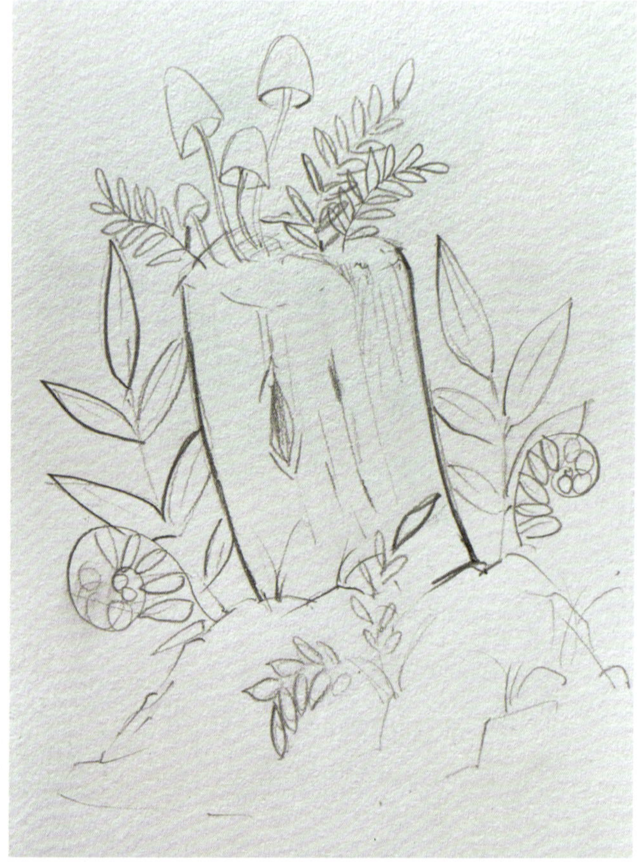

1. Before I jump to painting directly what I see, I make a quick sketch. Here, I analyze how to simplify the stump while taking care to preserve the essential parts.

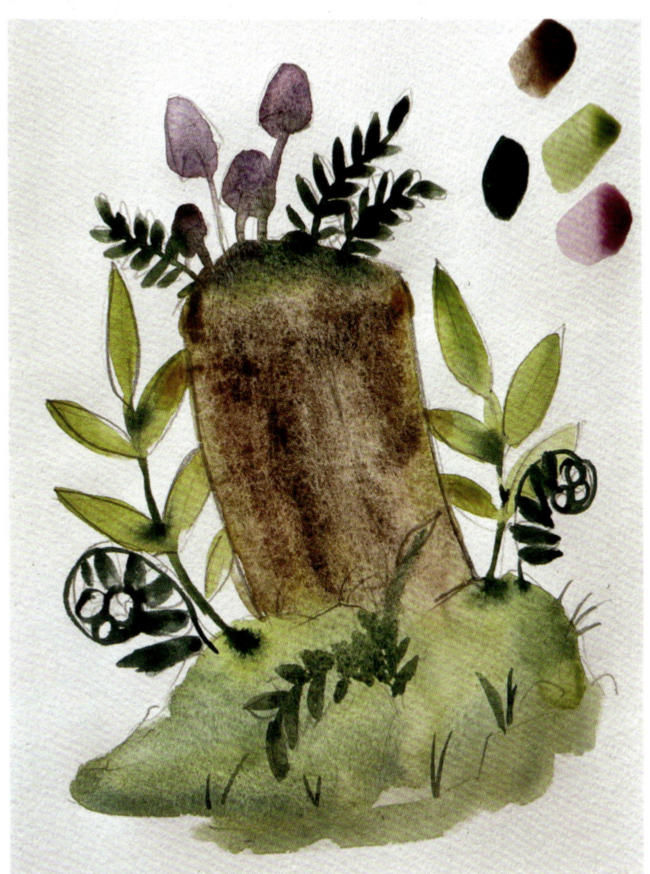

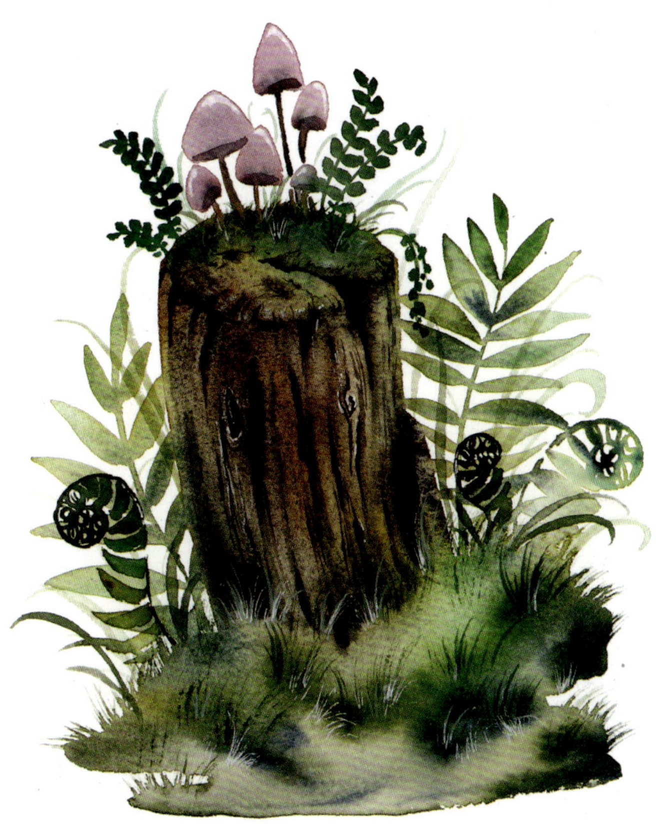

2. I apply some colors to help me visualize the appearance of my stump. You may notice that I added some vegetation that wasn't in my reference photo. I incorporated elements from other photos and illustrations into my painting.

3. Studying my subject on a rough draft allowed me to feel completely at ease when I started on my cotton paper. It's a technique I often use when I want to deviate slightly from the original photo to move toward something more personal.

Perhaps you've noticed, but I like to give a certain coherence to the subjects I paint in my notebooks, which is often the result of long reflections. The main block that artists encounter in their notebooks is the fear of failing and wasting the pages. To overcome this fear, I prefer to paint several small subjects that disorient my need for perfection, rather than tackling vast projects that block me. Thus, my notebooks are more explorations in which I allow myself to make mistakes. I also find it pleasant and fun to think about the organization and arrangement of the elements on the pages of the notebook and then observe the final result.

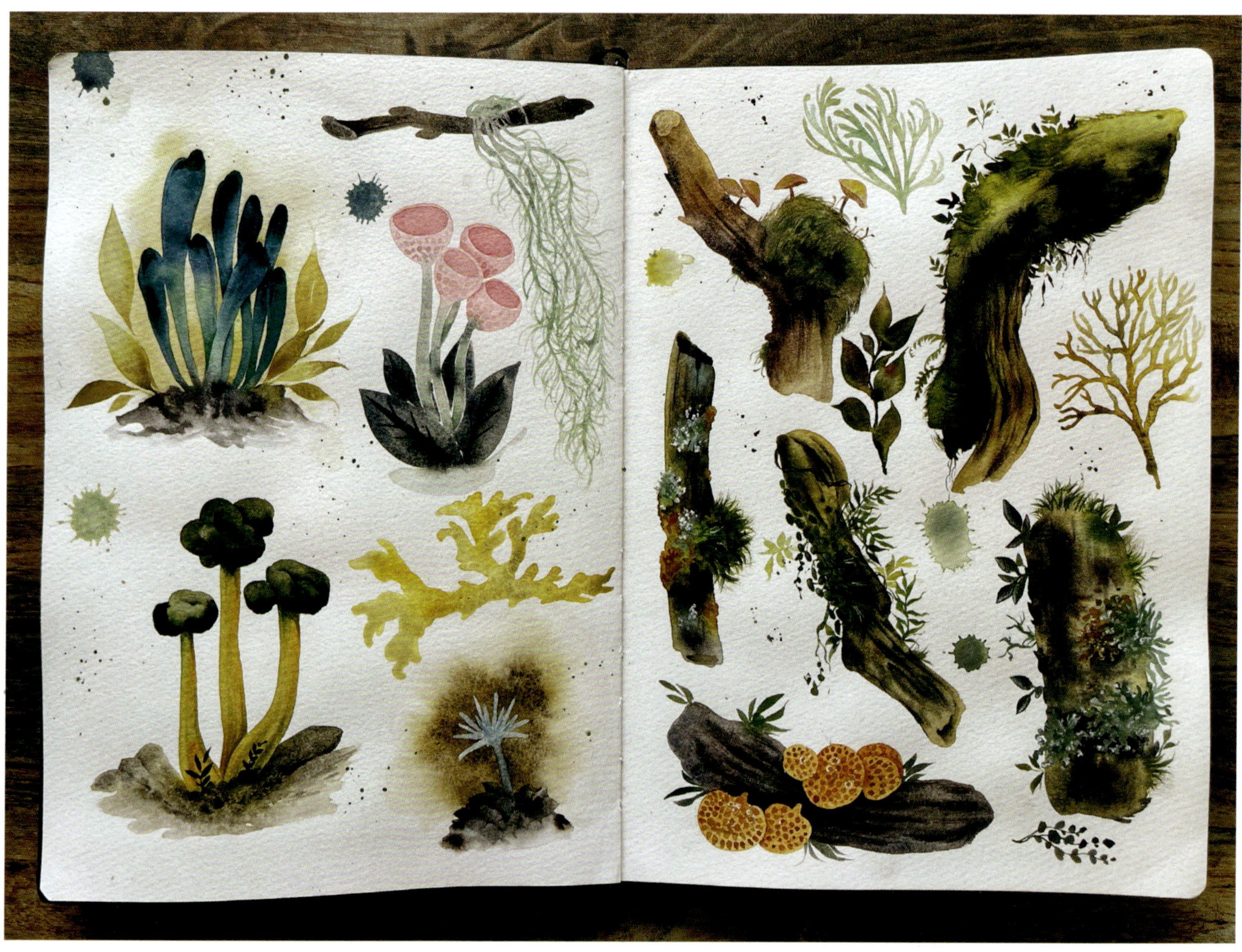

The left page focuses more on mushrooms while the right is an exploration of wood with mosses, lichens, and mushrooms growing on it. They are separate themes, yet they make sense paired together on a spread.

Here are some tips for filling the pages of your notebooks.

First, think of a broad enough theme that will guide your paintings. Then, on a page or spread, have fun painting subjects that come from the main theme. For example, I chose the forest flora, a theme that is both broad but narrow. To guide me, I visualize something in particular that I would like to explore: wood, mushrooms, undergrowth, terrariums, forest flowers, etc. But I could also orient my work more toward colors, atmospheres, or techniques to master, such as transparency or mixtures.

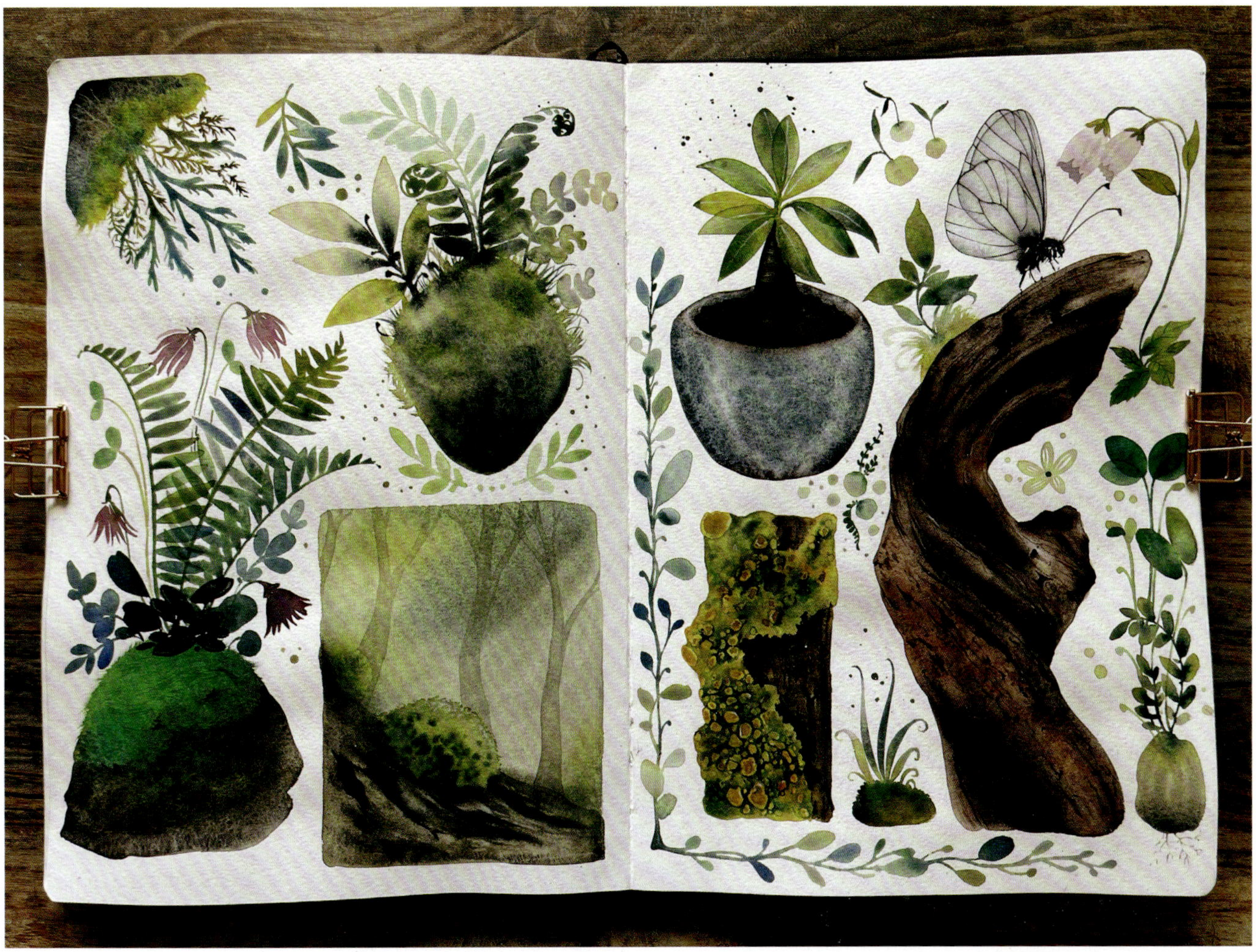

This spread has a more general plant theme, but I let no white space go to waste by experimenting with different shapes and sizes.

The topic remains specific enough that others can be added to the same page without creating inconsistencies. The key is to harmonize them well.

To create unity between my subjects, I try to vary their size and shape, and to manage the room on my page as best as possible without leaving too much empty space. I sometimes paint very small elements to avoid white space as much as possible.

Furthermore, I chose to paint in an A4-sized notebook, which allows me to work on several subjects per page and add many details to them without difficulty. When I am looking for more complexity in a larger piece, I use my notebooks as a guide and opt for loose sheets to make this reference easy.

Practice

REPRODUCING THE COLORS OF NATURE

Nature is full of different colors. In the previous chapter, I explained how to create new ones through mixing, using the color wheel, and your color charts. This will allow you to practice getting as close as possible to the colors you see in nature.

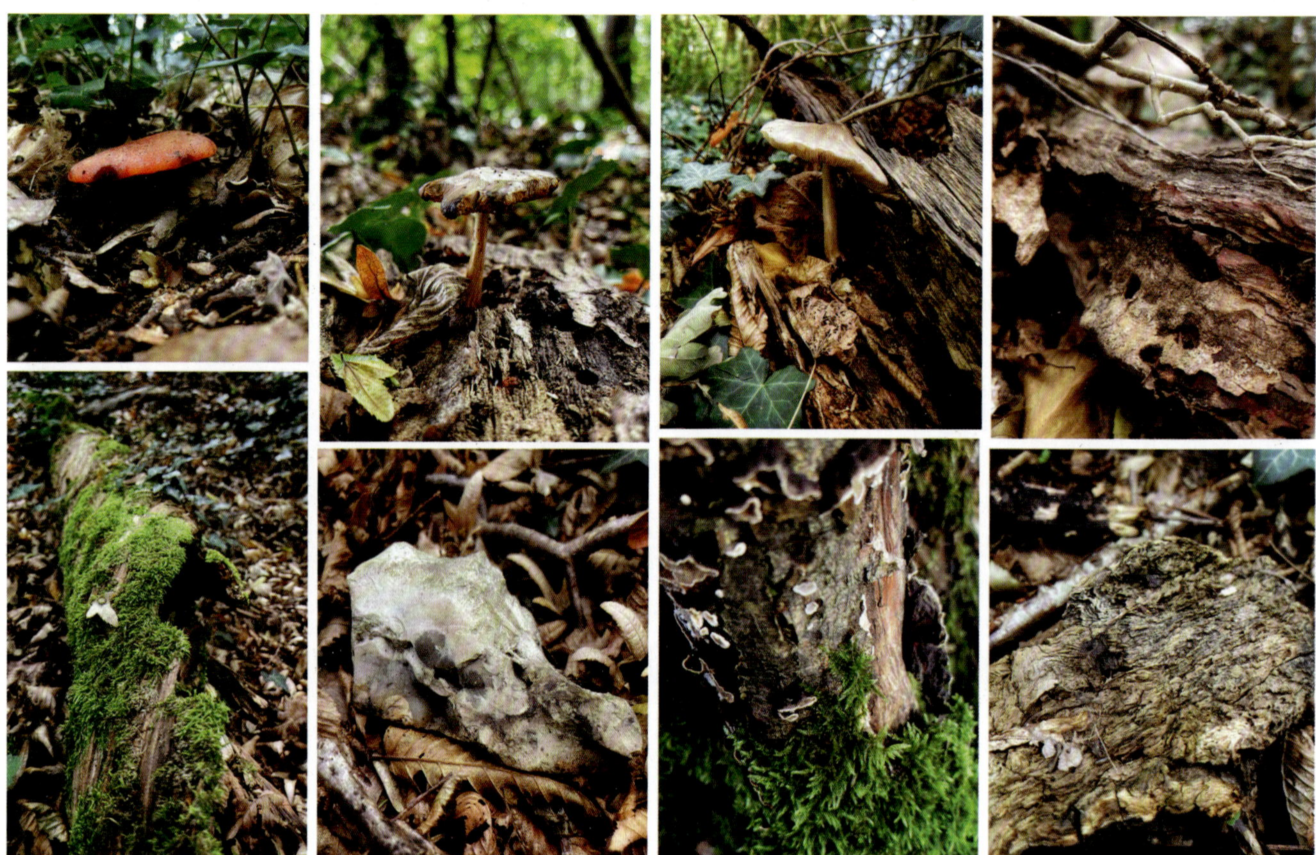

These are just some examples of photos I've taken for inspiration.

1. Gather a small collection of images and elements from nature; for example: bark, a stone, an acorn, leaves, flowers. If you cannot collect them, photograph them. Observe the textures, shapes, and colors.

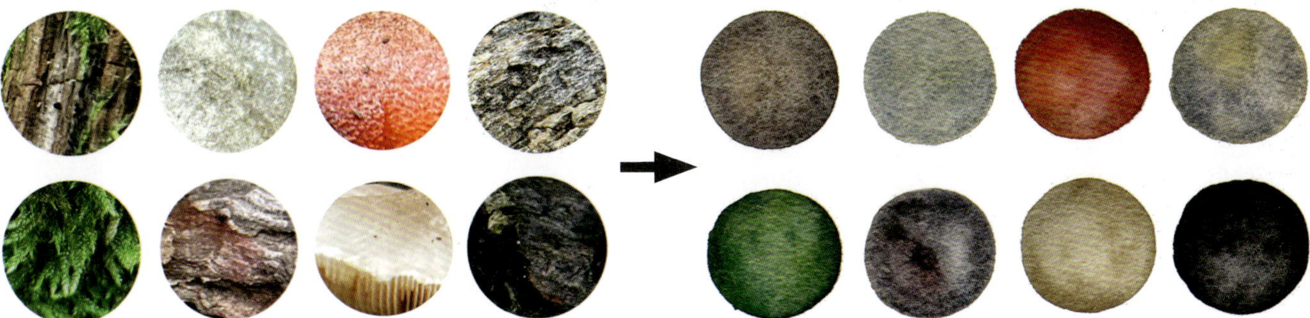

2. Once you've collected enough specimens, practice reproducing their colors or those present in your images. To do this, target each hue and connect each of them with the colors in your palette. For example, for the photos selected on the opposite page, here are the eight colors I wanted to reproduce for practice (left), along with the final mix (right).

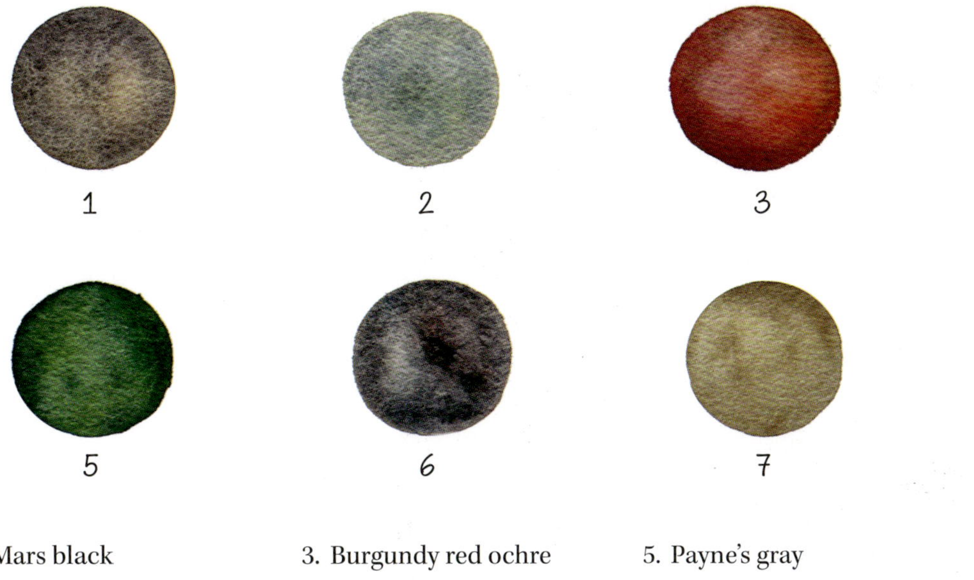

1   2   3   4

5   6   7   8

1. Mars black
   Brown iron oxide
   Yellow ochre
2. Tundra blue
   Sap green
   Mars black

3. Burgundy red ochre
   Alizarin crimson +
   Payne's gray
   Pyrrole orange
4. Mars black
   Tundra blue
   Yellow ochre

5. Payne's gray
   Phthalo green
   Prussian blue
   Indian yellow
6. Mars black
   Tundra blue
   Caput mortuum

7. Sepia
   Yellow ochre
   Buff titanium
8. Mars black
   Brown iron oxide
   Payne's gray

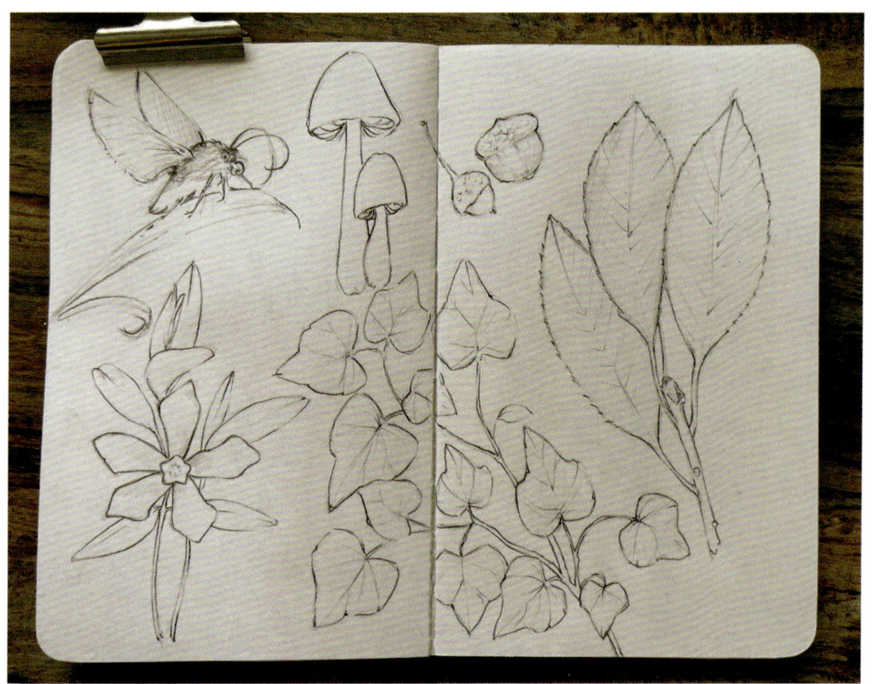

3. Make sketches to perfect your observation of texture and volume. Carefully analyze the proportions, curves, and movements. With a pencil, begin sketching. Then, with a darker pencil, reinforce your lines so that they are clearly visible. With a kneaded eraser, blend the initial lines to retain only the most important ones.

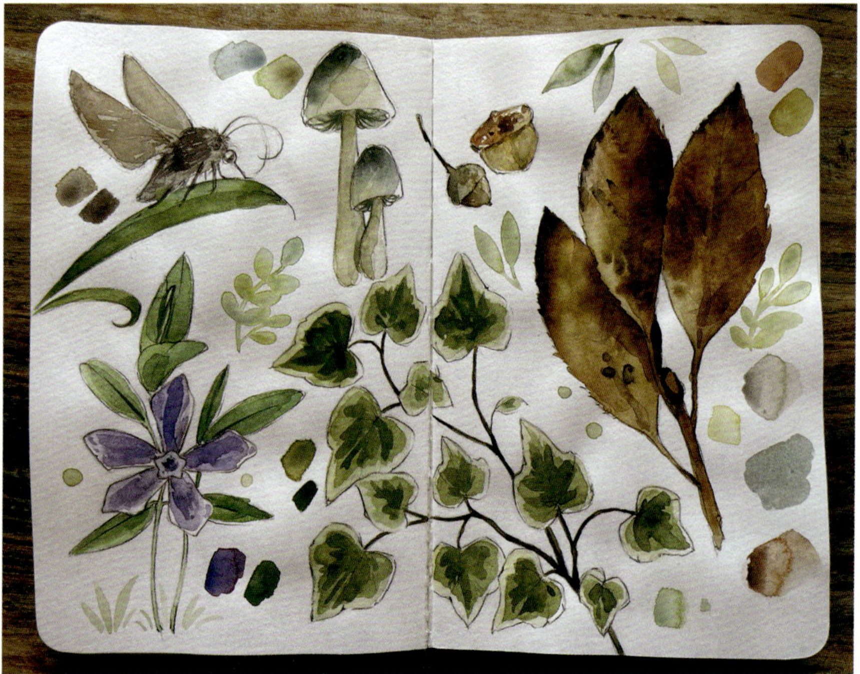

4. Paint lightly, focusing on the main colors that characterize your subjects. When necessary, wait for the watercolor to dry and gradually return to the different elements to add a few additional shades. You can reuse your colors to add small drawings in the empty spaces on your page.

Note

This drawing was done in a Stillman & Birn Alpha Series notebook.

WOODLAND FLOWERS

In this chapter, I invite you to learn how to create wildflowers in the style of modern watercolor painting—intuitively, without drawing. Using your photos or internet research, you can build a reference base to fuel your artistic projects. In the following exercises, practice painting a few flower species to better understand the process.

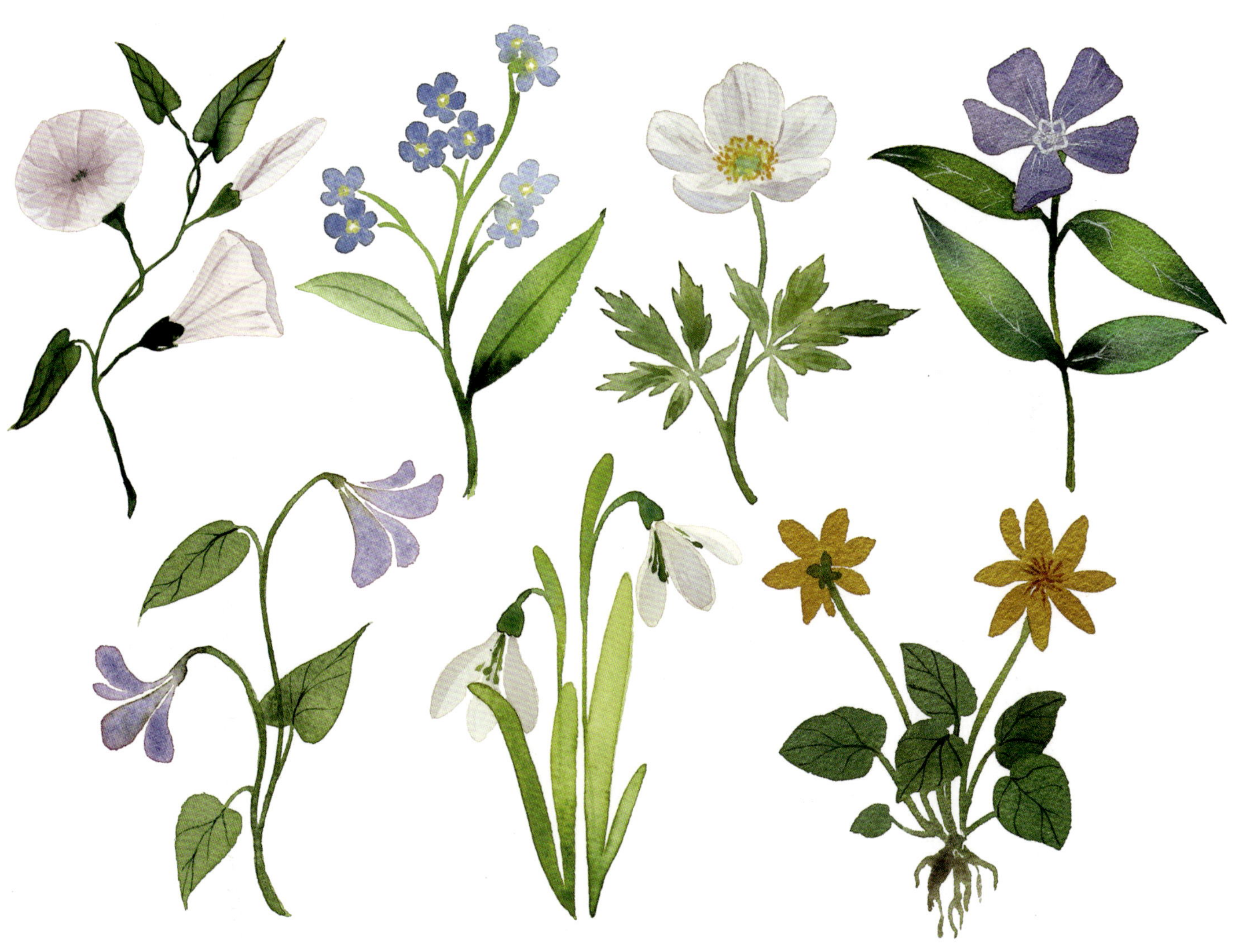

Forget-Me-Not

1
- **Mixture 1** - Ultramarine blue + white gouache

2
- **Mixture 2** - Sap green
- **Mixture 3** - Sap green + ultramarine blue + Payne's gray

3

- **Mixture 4** - Indian yellow + white gouache

4

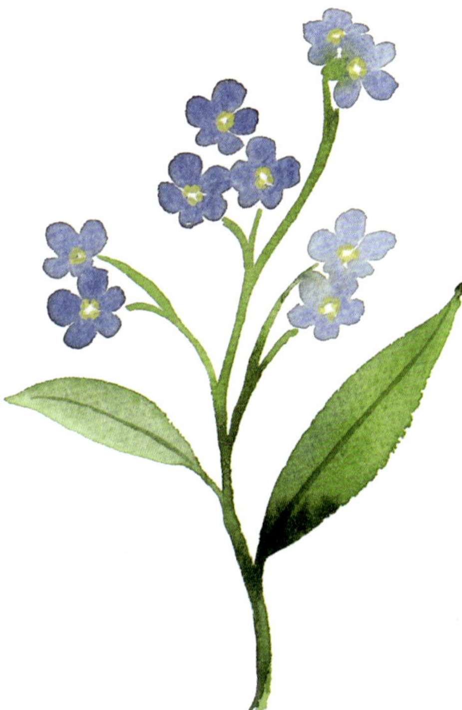

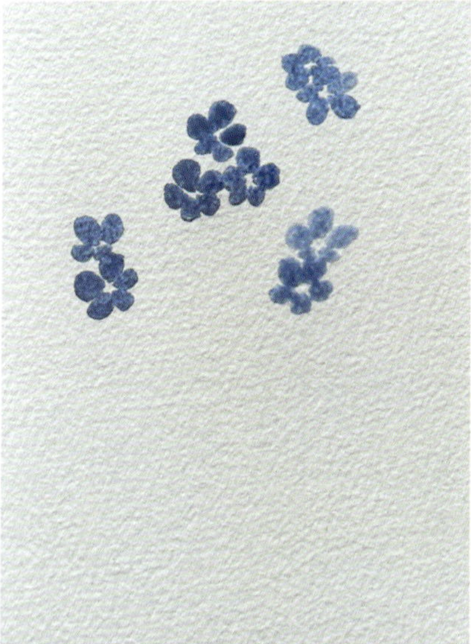

1. Using a small, fine brush and Mixture 1, create a few blue flowers in clusters of two or three.

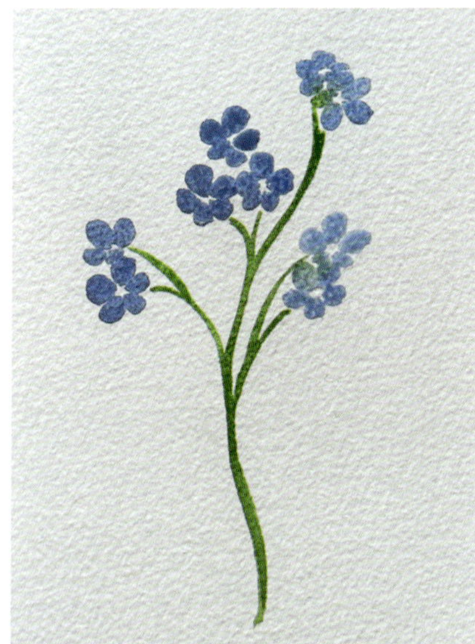

2. Using a small brush and Mixture 2, draw the stem of the flowers.

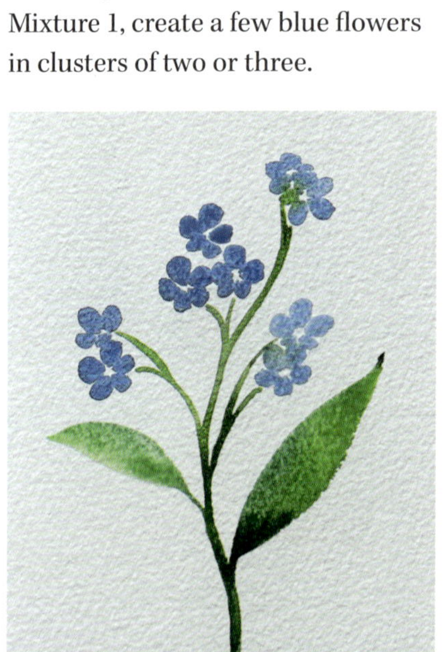

3. Using a soft brush and Mixture 2, create the leaves. Place a few drops of Mixture 3 pigment between the stem and the leaf to add contrast. Wait for the watercolor to dry completely.

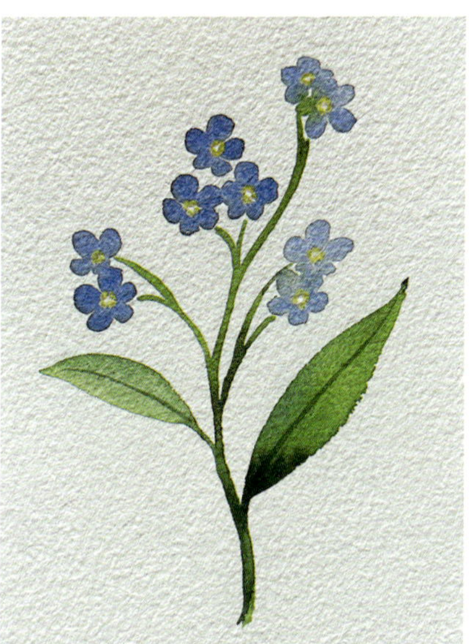

4. Make the center of the forget-me-nots using Mixture 4. With Mixture 3, draw a thin line down the center of the leaves.

Periwinkle

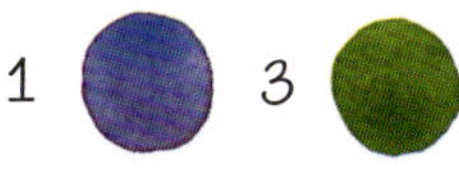

1 · 3 · 2 · 4

- **Mixture 1** - Ultramarine blue + permanent rose
- **Mixture 2** - Sap green + phthalo green + Indian yellow (diluted)
- **Mixture 3** - Sap green + quinacridone gold
- **Mixture 4** - Sap green + ultramarine blue + Payne's gray

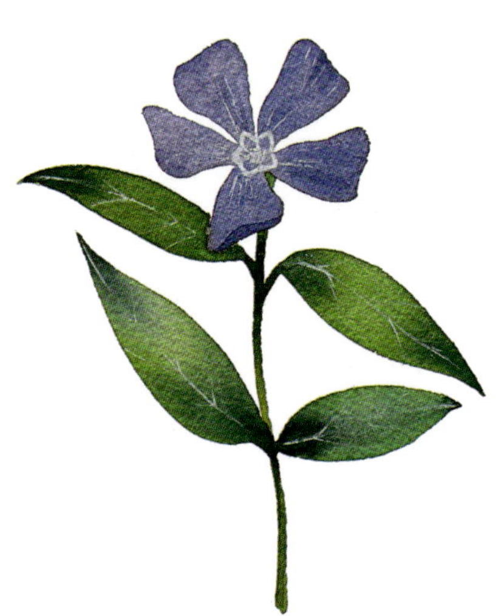

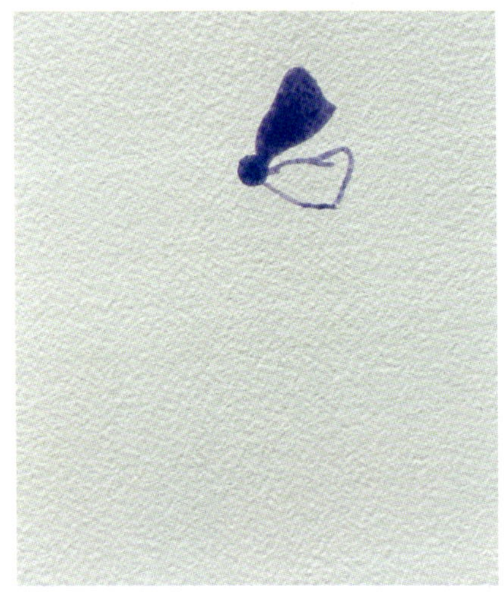

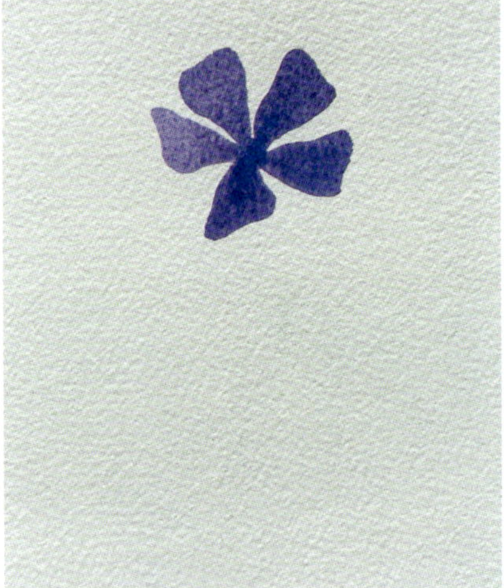

1. Using a fine brush and Mixture 1, create a small circle for the center of the flower. Add a couple of petals around it.

2. With a rinsed, clean brush, remove a little pigment from the center. Continue until you have five petals. Let them dry.

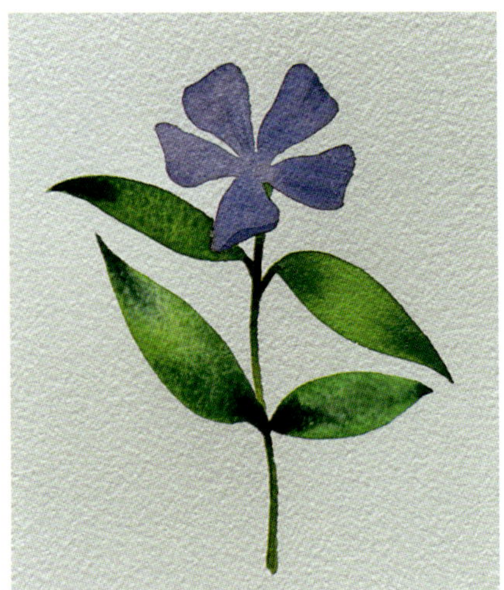

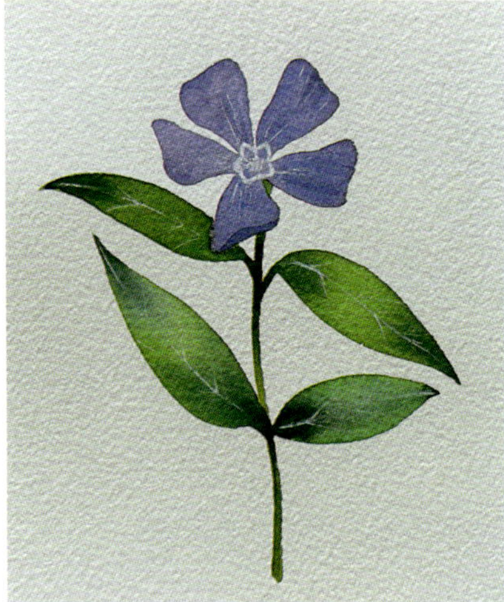

3. Using a small brush and Mixture 1, create curls on the petals and shade them lightly.

4. Using the same brush, draw the stem of the flower and add four leaves. Vary the green pigments by playing with Mixtures 2 and 3, then adding Mixture 4 in spots on the still-wet stem.

5. With a white gel ink pen, draw the center of the flower, add touches of light on the petals, and draw veins on the leaves.

Wild Violet

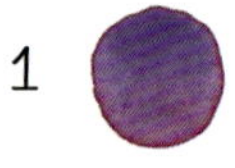

1 • **Mixture 1** - Ultramarine blue + permanent rose
2 • **Mixture 2** - Sap green + ultramarine blue
3 • **Mixture 3** - Sap green + ultramarine blue + Payne's gray

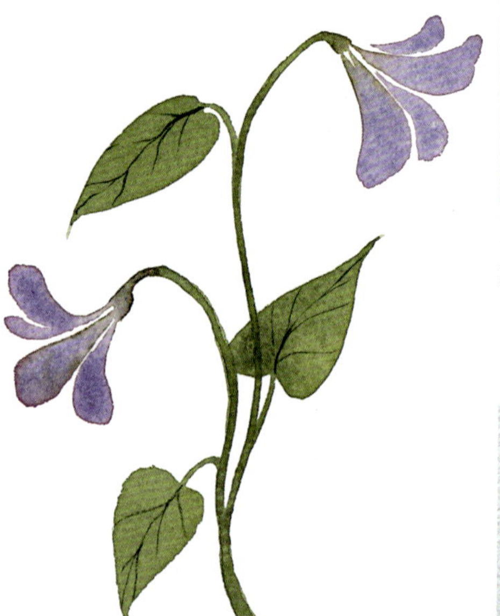

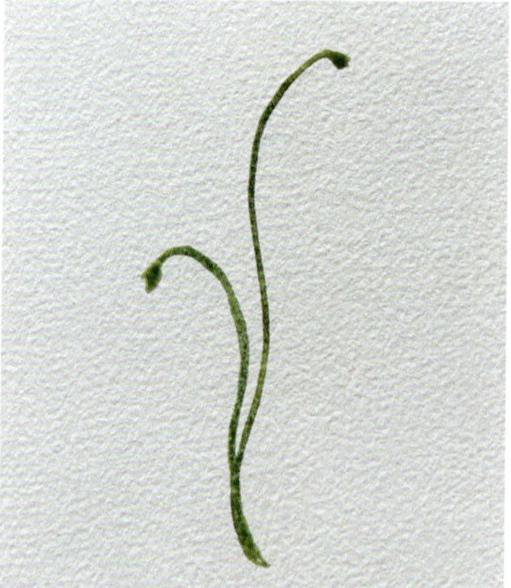

1. Using a small brush and Mixture 2, draw the stem of the flower.

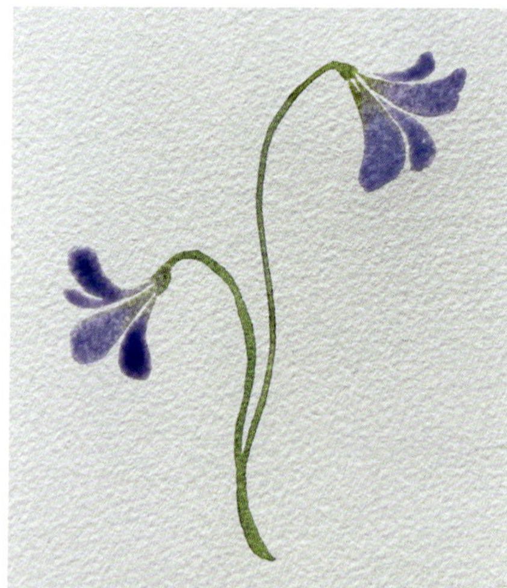

2. Using the same brush and Mixture 1, add the petals to the ends of the stems.

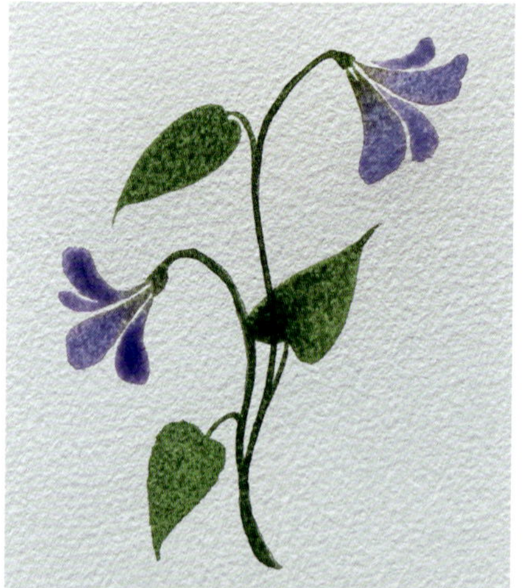

3. Add heart-shaped leaves to different places on the stems with Mixture 2. I made it darker where one leaf overlapped the stem. Let it dry.

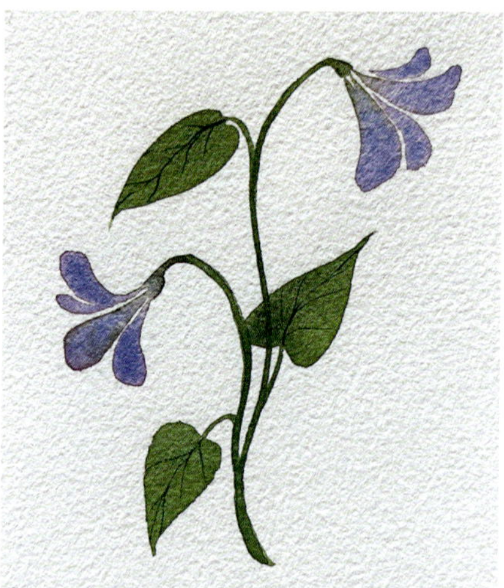

4. Using a very fine brush and Mixture 3, draw the veins of the leaves.

Snowdrop

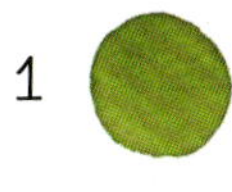

1

2

- **Mixture 1** - Sap green + Indian yellow
- **Mixture 2** - Indian yellow + Payne's gray (diluted)

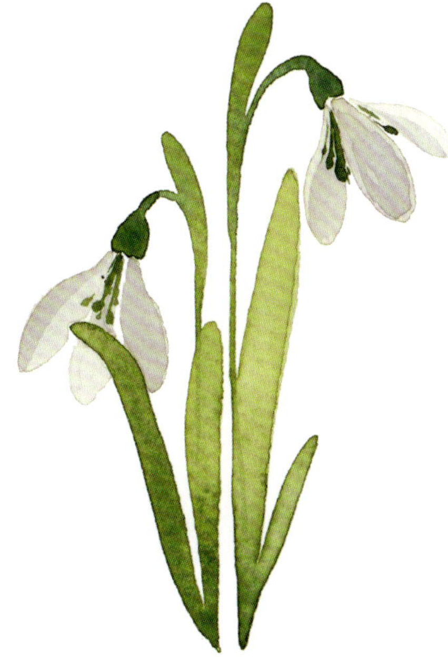

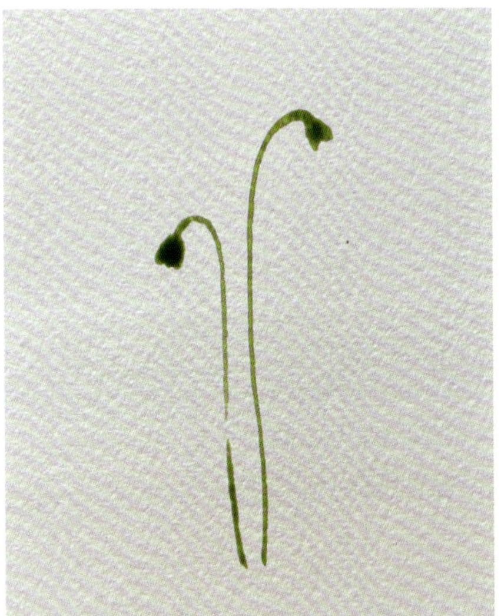

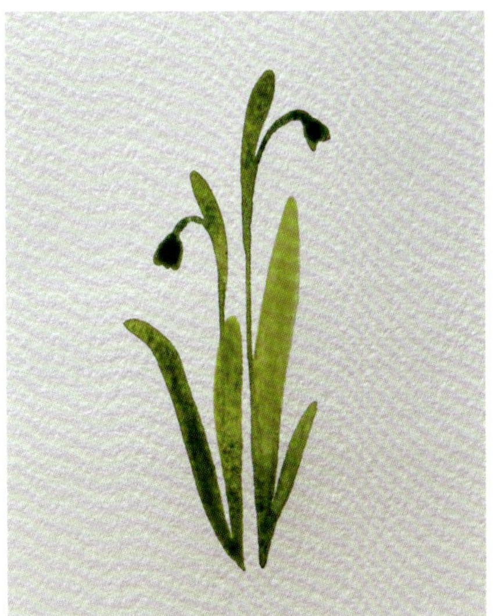

1. Using a small brush and Mixture 1, draw the stems of the snowdrops.

2. Without changing brushes or mixtures, create the elongated, rounded leaves. Let it dry.

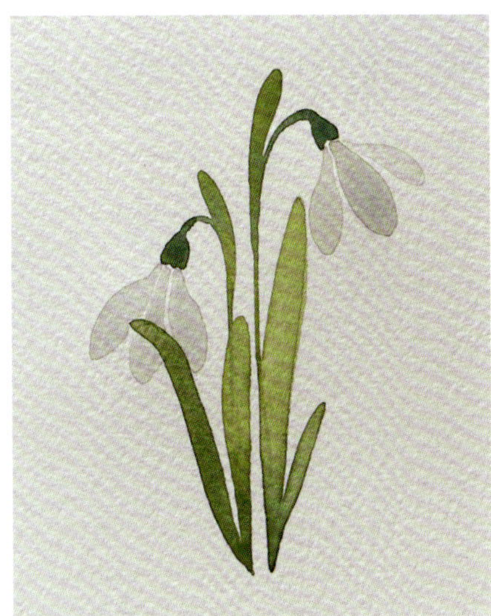

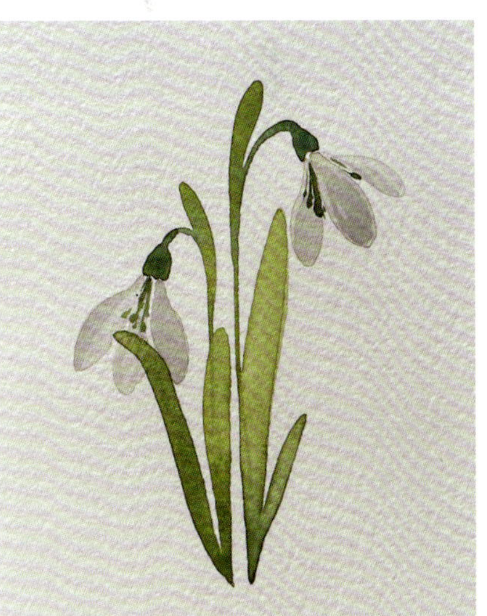

3. With Mixture 2, add the petals, leaving a small space between each. Wait for the watercolor to dry.

4. Add depth to the petals by applying a light layer of paint in certain areas with Mixture 2, then detail the interior with Mixture 1.

Lesser Celandine

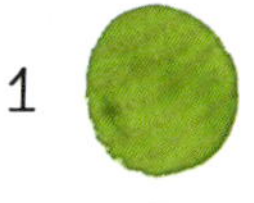

1 • **Mixture 1** - Sap green + Indian yellow

2 • **Mixture 2** - Sap green + ultramarine blue

3 • **Mixture 3** - Brown iron oxide + Indian yellow

4 • **Mixture 4** - Indian yellow + quinacridone gold

5 • **Mixture 5** - Quinacridone gold

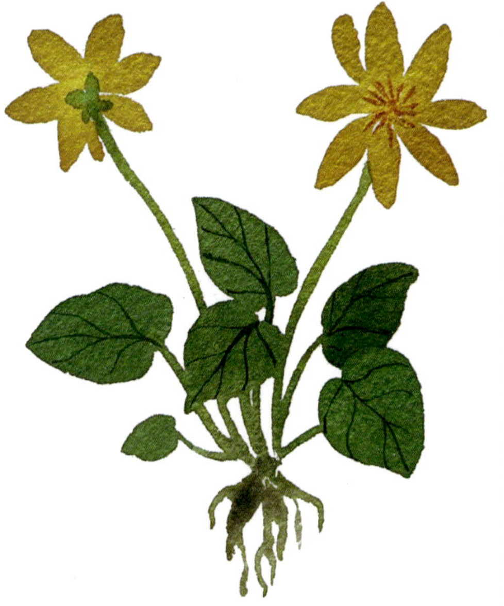

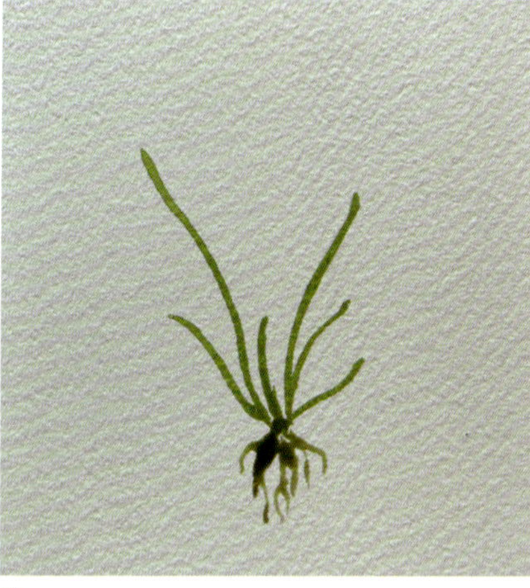

1. Using a fine brush and Mixture 1, trace the stems of the lesser celandine. Add some roots with Mixture 3.

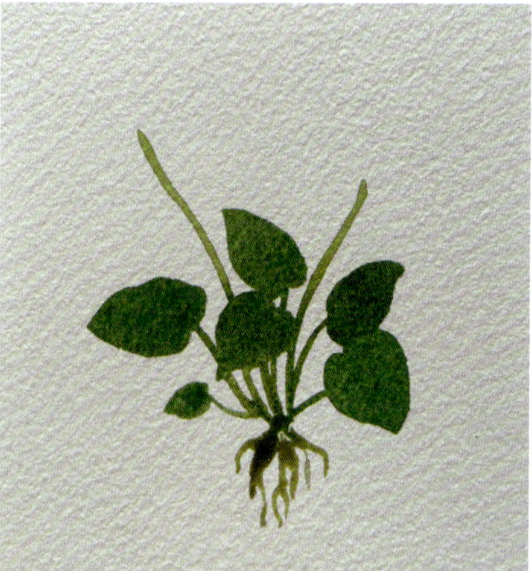

2. In the still-wet watercolor and using Mixture 2, place the slightly rounded, heart-shaped leaves at the ends of the stems. Let them dry.

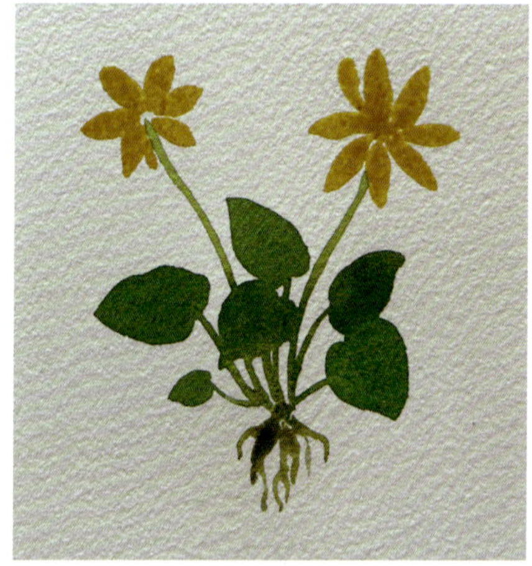

3. Using a small brush and Mixture 4, place small, elongated petals at the ends of the stems to form a flower. Wait for the watercolor to dry.

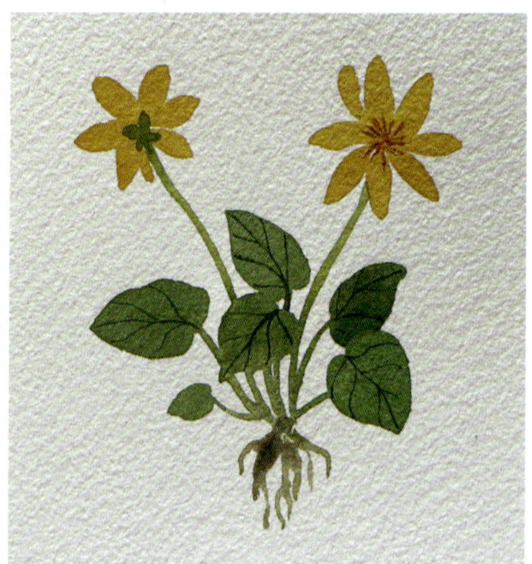

4. Using Mixture 5, detail the inside of the right flower to indicate that it is facing you. Add small leaves to the left flower to show it's facing away. Add veins with Mixture 3.

Wood Anemone

 1
 2
3
4

- **Mixture 1** - Ultramarine blue + permanent rose + Payne's gray (diluted)
- **Mixture 2** - Sap green + ultramarine blue
- **Mixture 3** - Cobalt green + white gouache
- **Mixture 4** - Quinacridone gold + white gouache

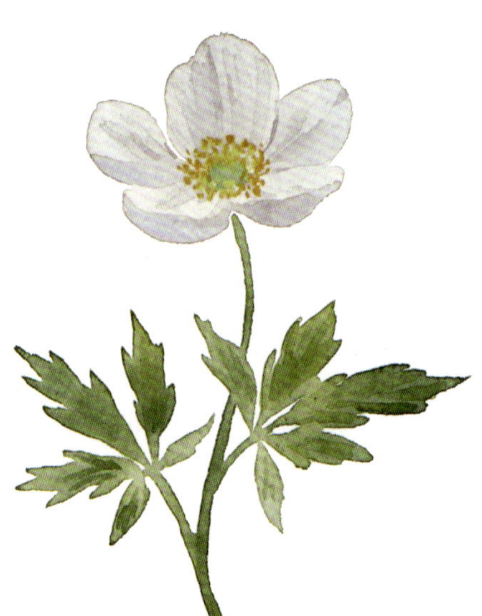

1. Create the petals using a small, soft brush and Mixture 1.

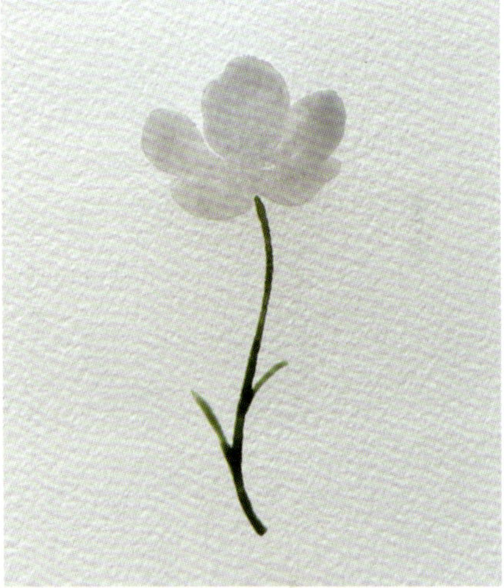

2. Using a fine brush and Mixture 2, draw the stem of the flower.

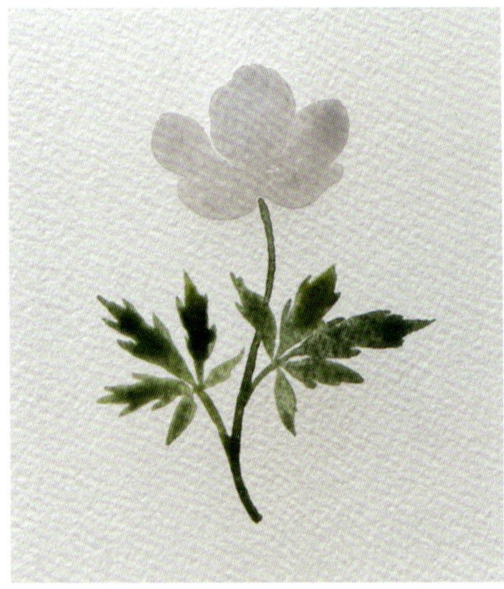

3. Without changing the mixture, create the serrated leaves. Wait for the watercolor to dry.

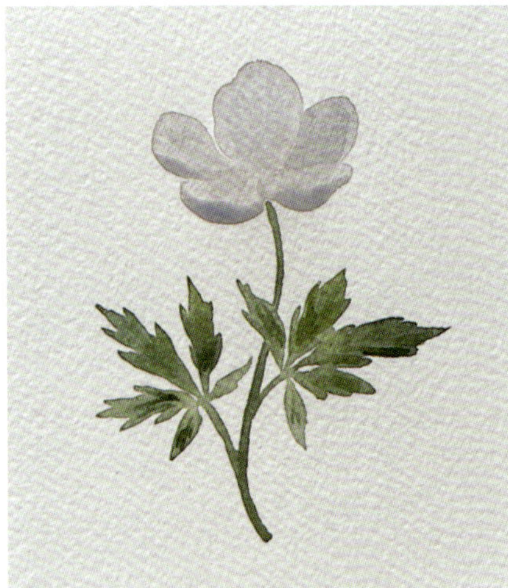

4. Add depth to the petals and leaves by applying a light layer of paint in certain areas with Mixtures 1 and 2 respectively.

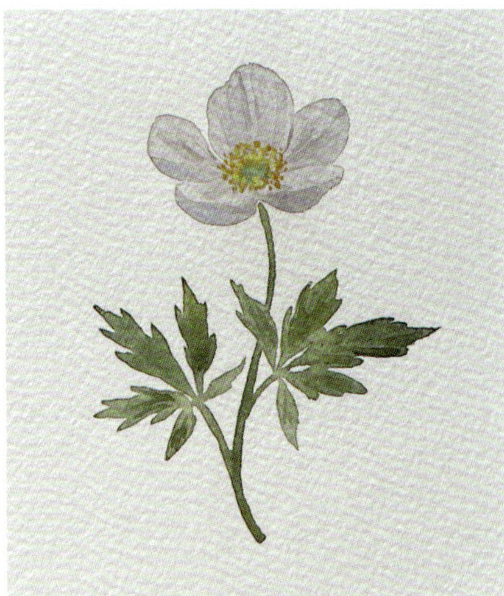

5. Detail the center of the flower. Form a small circle in its center with Mixture 3 and make pistils with Mixture 4.

Bindweed

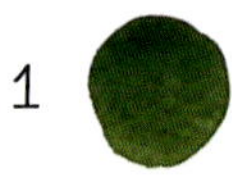

- 1 **Mixture 1** - Sap green + ultramarine blue
- 2 **Mixture 2** - Sap green + ultramarine blue + Payne's gray
- 3 **Mixture 3** - Ultramarine blue + permanent rose (diluted)
- 4 **Mixture 4** - Ultramarine blue + permanent rose + Payne's gray (diluted)

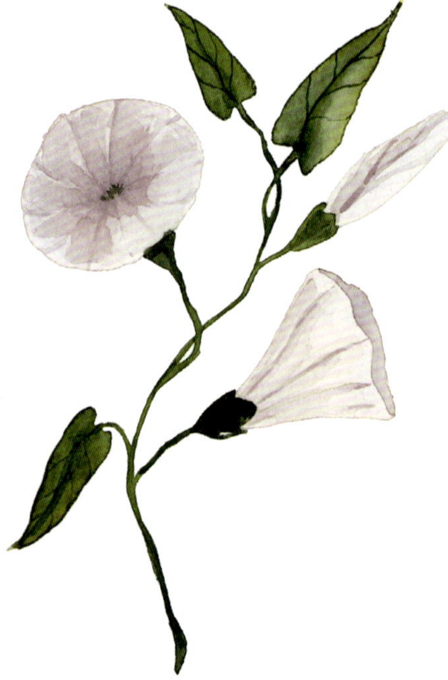

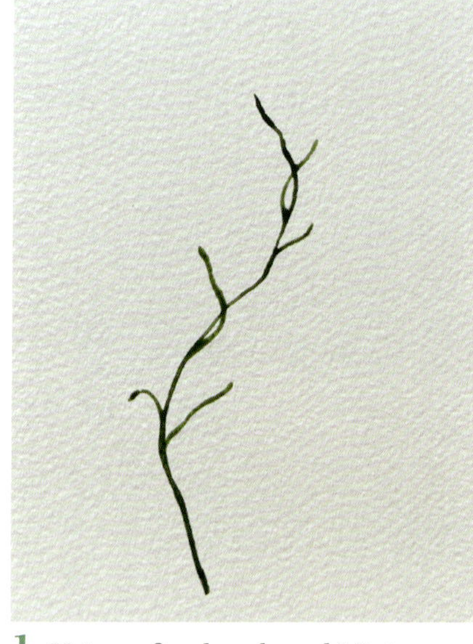

1. Using a fine brush and Mixture 1, draw an irregular stem. From this central stem, create several small ones going off in random directions.

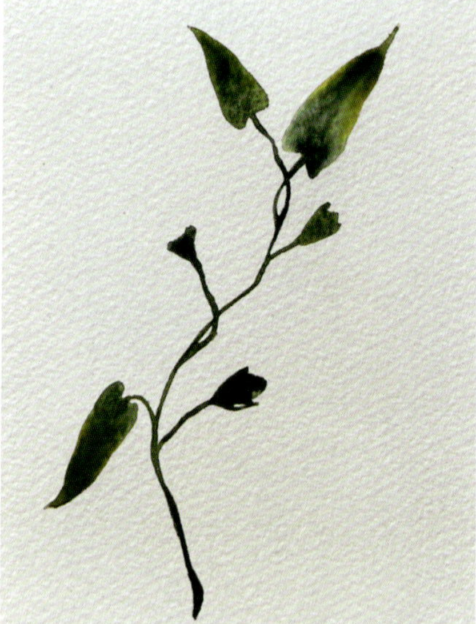

2. On some of these small stems, paint leaves and flower bases with Mixtures 1 and 2. Let it dry.

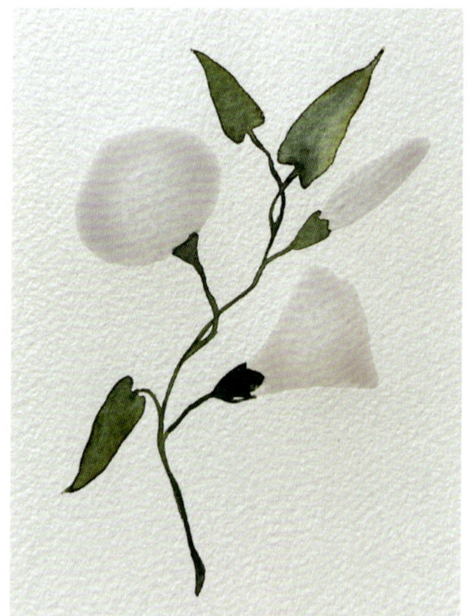

3. Add bindweed flowers to the bases using Mixture 3. Vary their opening to give dynamism to the watercolor. Let it dry.

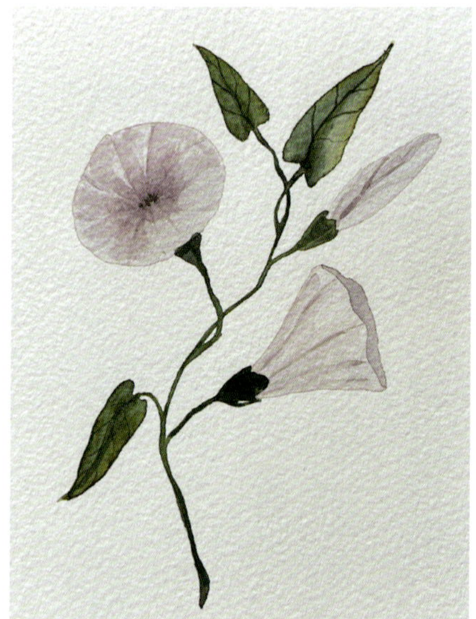

4. Add depth to the petals and detail them by applying Mixture 4 in certain areas. Make the leaf veins with Mixture 2.

FOREST PLANTS

There are many species of forest plants you can create to enrich your watercolors. As with the woodland flowers, I suggest you create mushrooms, ferns, leaves, and lichens from your own research and from these directions. Use brushes and pigments in a variety of ways to understand the unique characteristics of these plants.

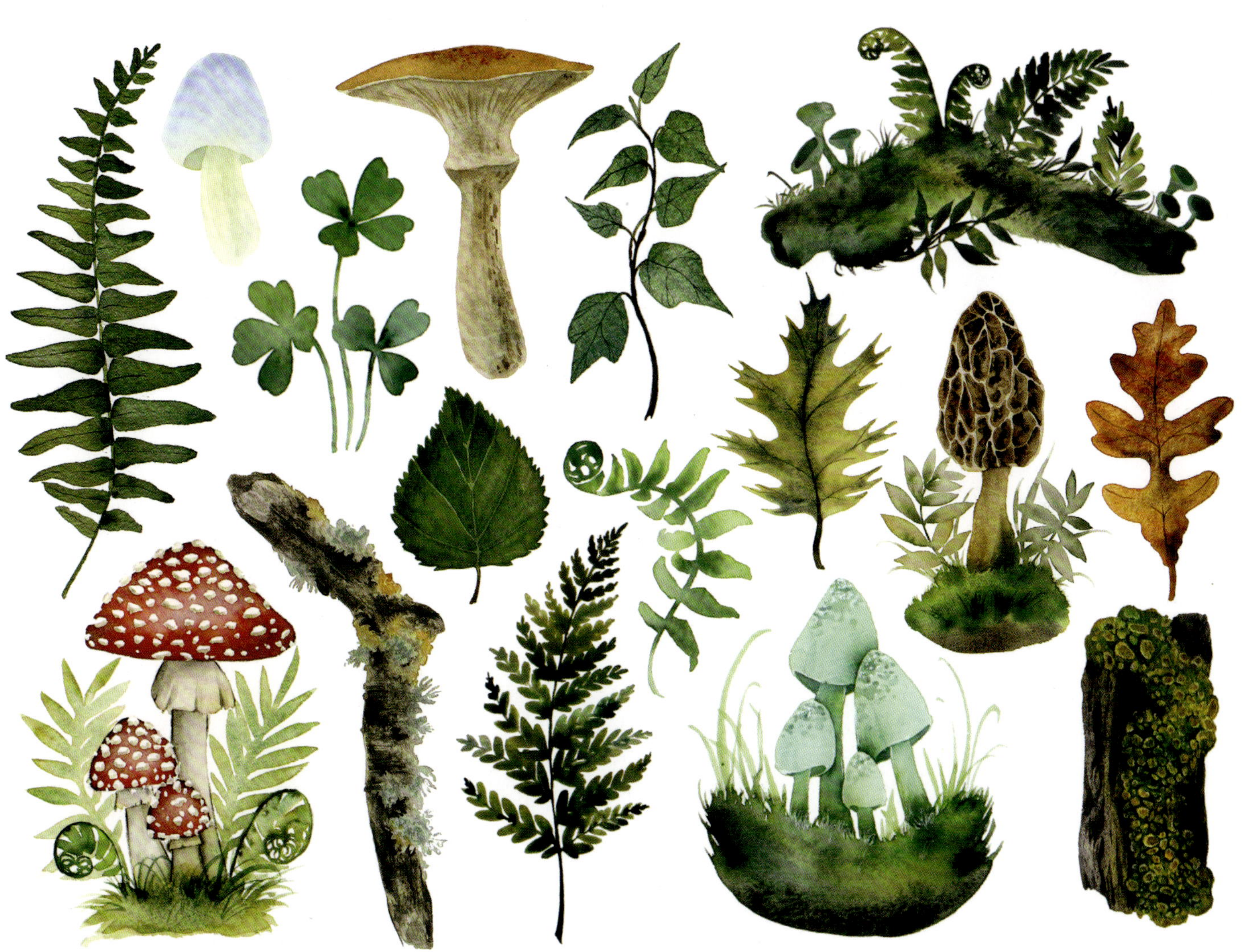

Lichen

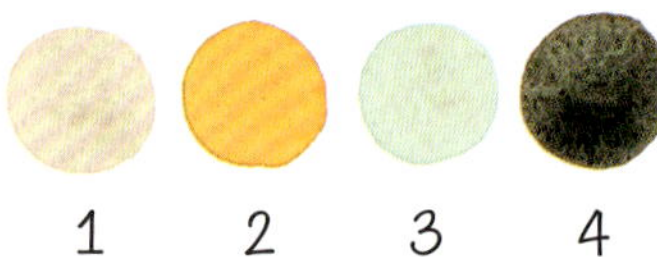

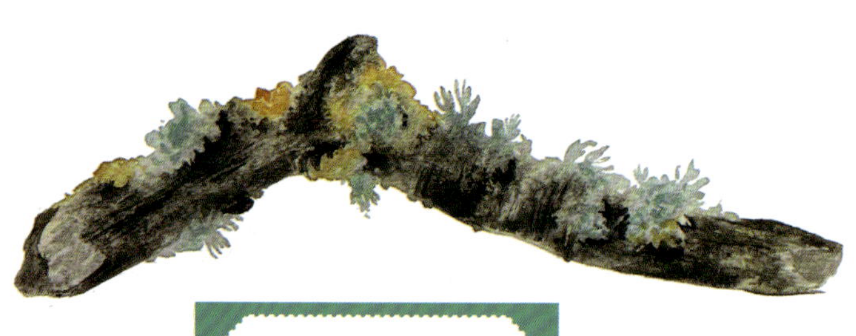

- **Mixture 1** - Buff titanium + brown iron oxide (diluted)
- **Mixture 2** - Quinacridone gold
- **Mixture 3** - Buff titanium + phthalo green (diluted)
- **Mixture 4** - Mars black + brown iron oxide + cobalt green (diluted)

Note

Steps 1–5 are all worked in the wet.

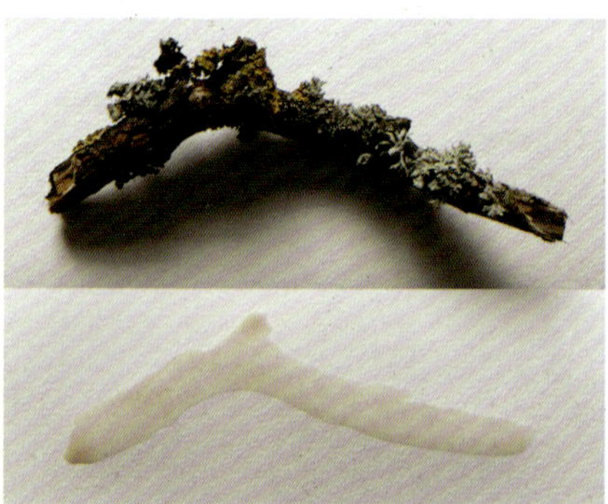

1. Observe the branch and its lightest color. Using a soft brush and Mixture 1, paint the shape of the branch. For this first step, add more water to retain moisture as long as possible.

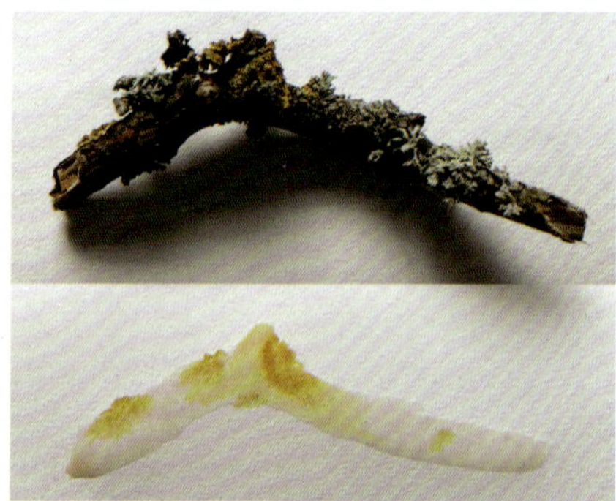

2. Apply Mixture 2 using a firm, precise, round brush. Mark small lichen shapes slightly above the branch.

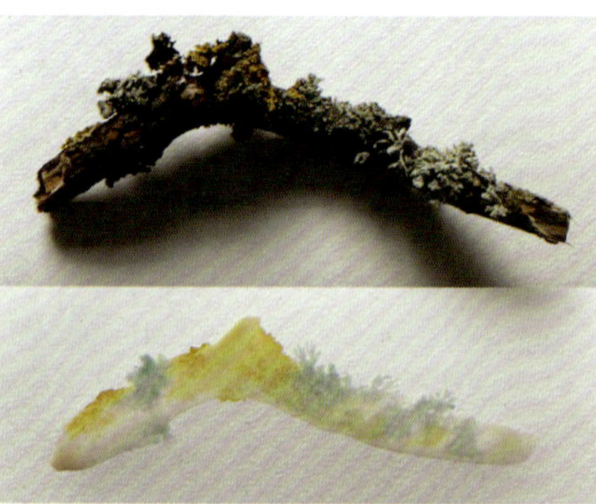

3. Using the same brush, apply Mixture 3 to paint the pale green lichen. As before, give it the shape of little hands clinging to the branch.

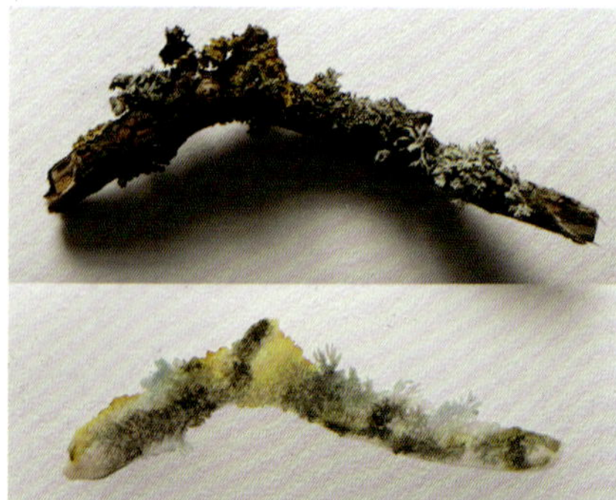

4. Reproduce the color of the wood with Mixture 4. Without changing brushes, apply the color so as to outline the position of the lichen and the wood on the branch.

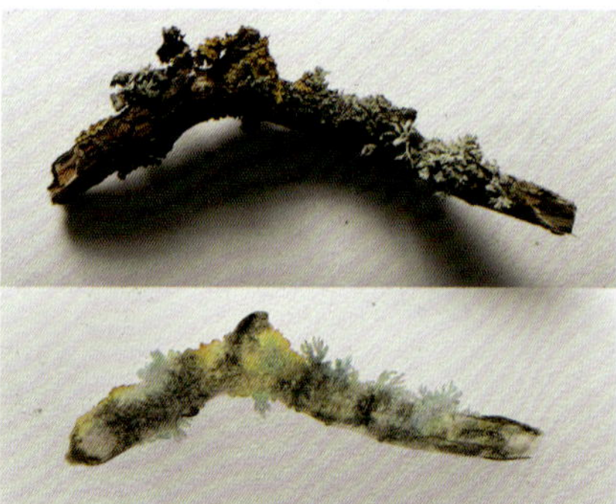

5. Using Mixture 4 and a fine, firm brush, draw small grooves to place the future bases of the cracked wood. Wait until the watercolor is completely dry.

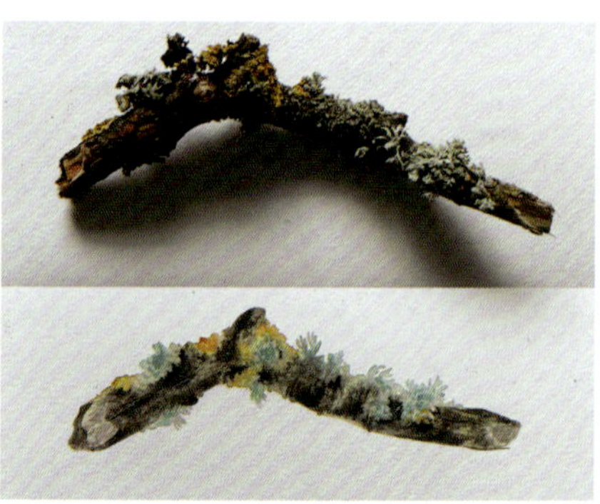

6. Accentuate the structure of the branch to give more precise shapes to the lichens and texture to the wood. Intensify the depth of the lichen by applying Mixtures 2 and 3 on top.

Mossy Branch

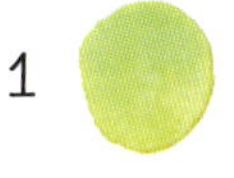

1

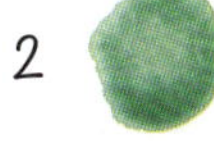

2

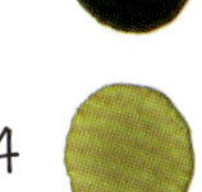

3

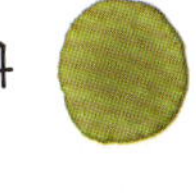

4

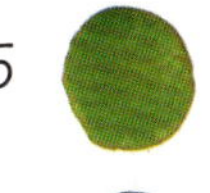

5

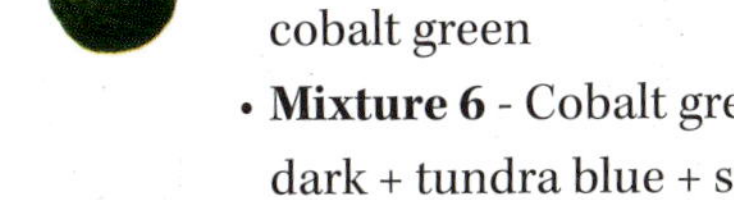

6

- **Mixture 1** - Indian yellow + cobalt turquoise light + cobalt green (diluted)
- **Mixture 2** - Cobalt turquoise light + cobalt green dark + cobalt green (diluted)
- **Mixture 3** - Cobalt green dark + brown iron oxide
- **Mixture 4** - Sap green + yellow ochre + brown iron oxide
- **Mixture 5** - Quinacridone gold + cobalt green
- **Mixture 6** - Cobalt green dark + tundra blue + sap green + Mars black

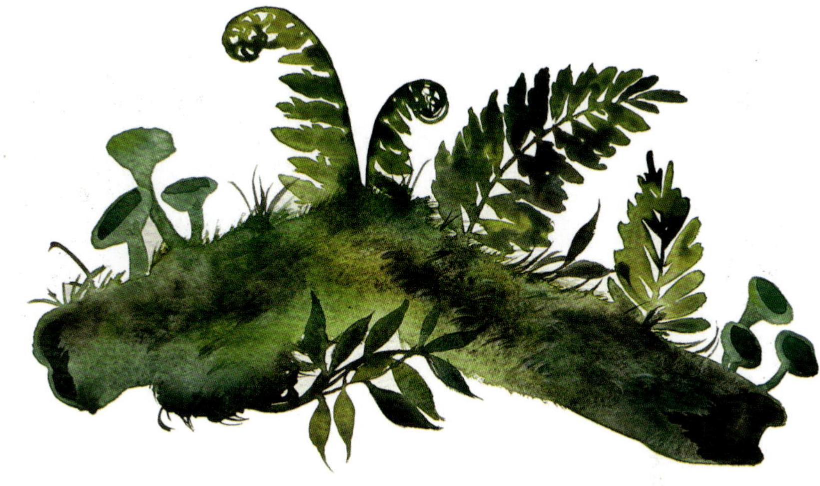

> ## *Note*
>
> *What's interesting about this exercise is being able to work with the many shades of green to create the moss and vegetation. Remember to vary the intensity of the pigments you use to give your watercolor painting beautiful contrasts.*

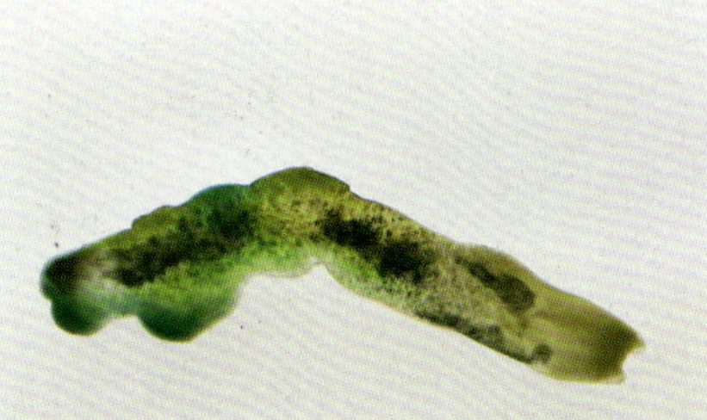

1. Using a wide, soft brush, create the shape of the branch using small strokes to represent the structure of the moss. Play with different shades of green using Mixtures 1, 2, 3, and 4.

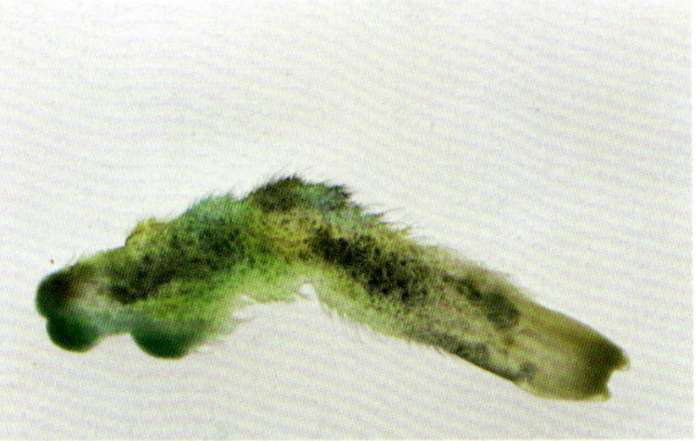

2. Using a tapered or very small brush, create the small blades of grass on the surface of the branch. Wait for your watercolor to dry.

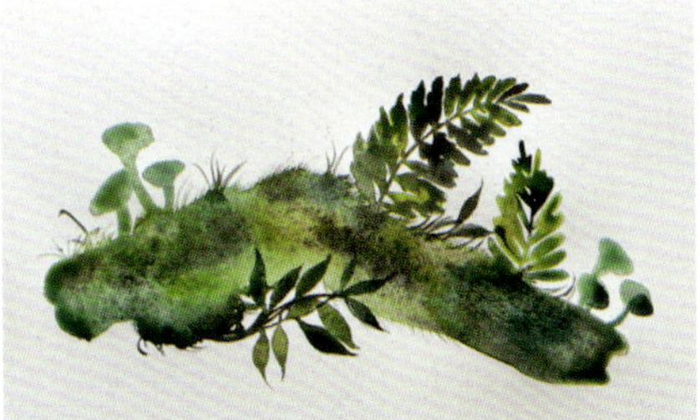

3. Add various plants above and below the branch with Mixtures 2, 5, and 6.

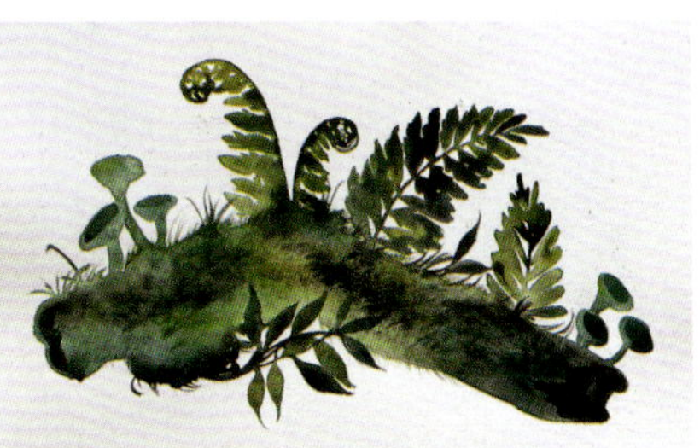

4. Reinforce the shapes of the moss and branch by outlining different areas of your watercolor with darker pigments. With a white pencil, you can add a little light to the top of the moss to represent grass.

Lichen on Bark

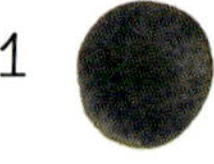

1 • **Mixture 1** - Tundra blue + brown iron oxide + Mars black

2 • **Mixture 2** - Indian yellow + cobalt green (diluted)

3 • **Mixture 3** - Cobalt green dark + sap green

4 • **Mixture 4** - Quinacridone gold

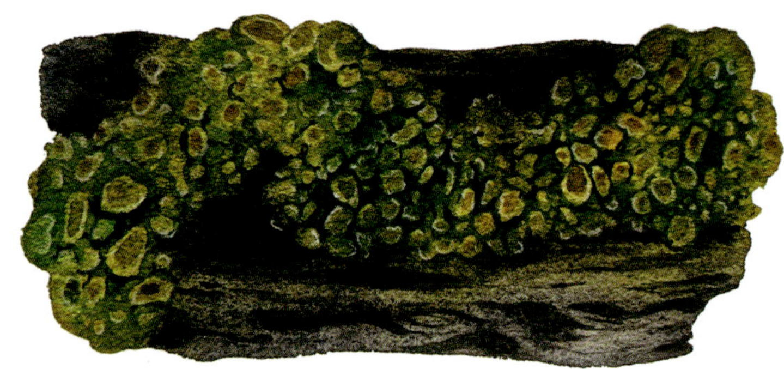

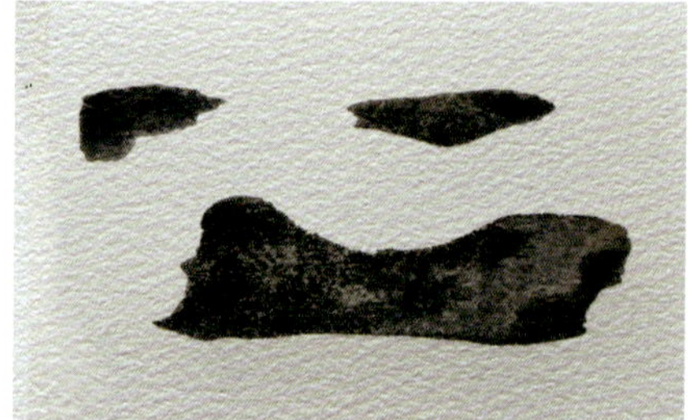

1. Start the bark shape using a soft, round brush and Mixture 1. Leave gaps to add the lichen.

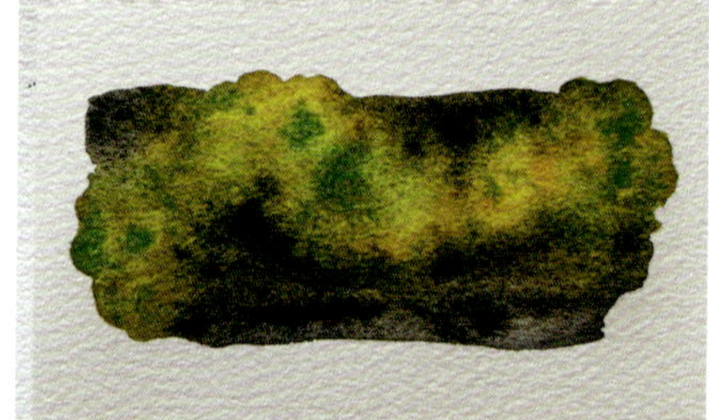

2. In the still-wet watercolor, place Mixture 2 inside the bark. Gradually, redefine the curves of the lichen more precisely by accentuating further with Mixture 1. Let it dry.

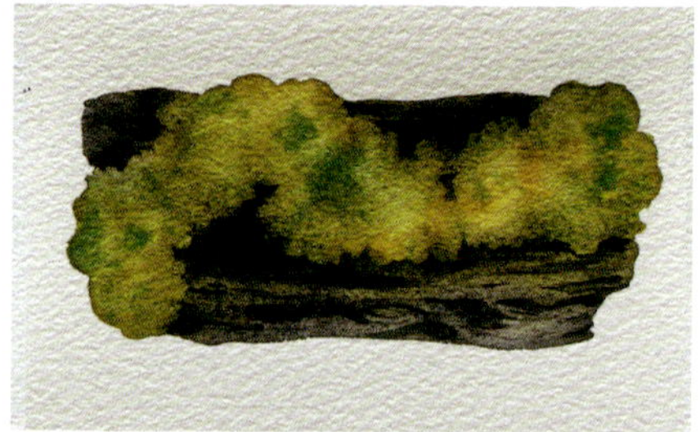

3. Using a fine brush and Mixture 1, sculpt the lichen shape again with more precision and form the wood grain on the bark.

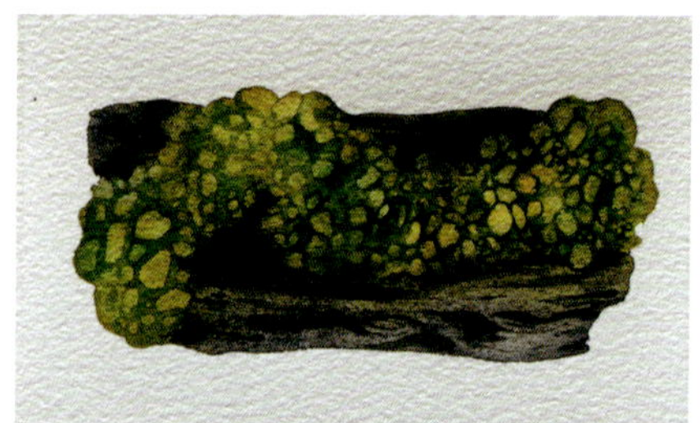

4. Using a small brush and Mixture 3, draw several oval shapes inside the lichen to reproduce its honeycomb texture. Then accentuate the depth of the green part by applying increasingly darker pigments.

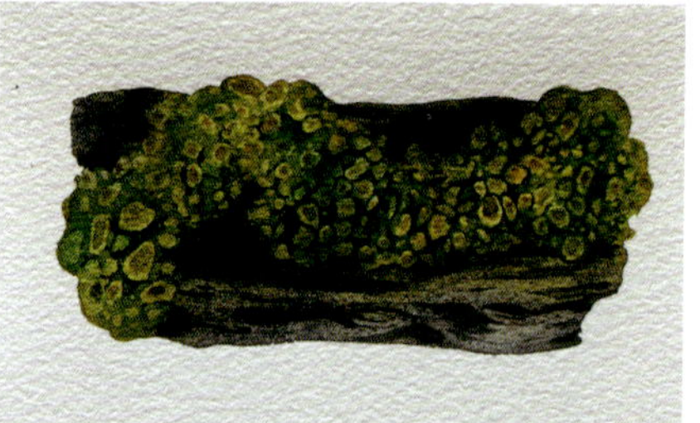

5. Use Mixture 4 to do the same with the yellow lichen.

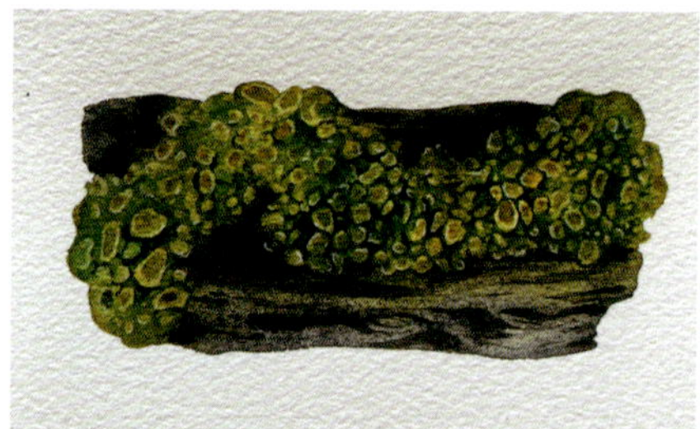

6. Using a white colored pencil, add highlights to the edges of the lichen cells to accentuate the depth and relief.

Imaginary Blue Mushroom

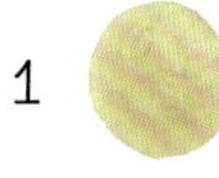

1 • **Mixture 1** - Buff titanium (diluted)
• **Mixture 2** - Buff titanium + phthalo green (diluted)

2 • **Mixture 3** - Ultramarine blue + cobalt turquoise light (diluted)

3

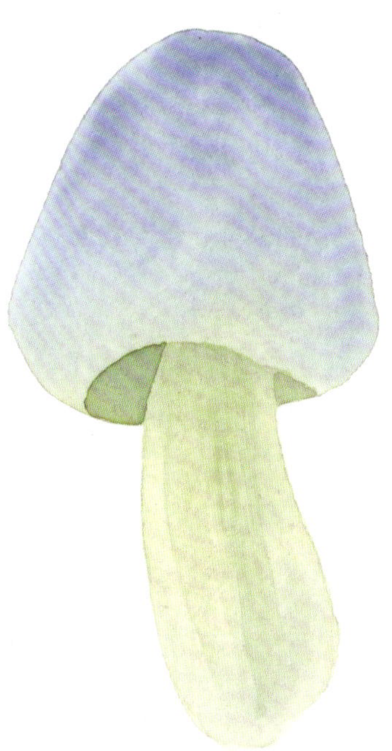

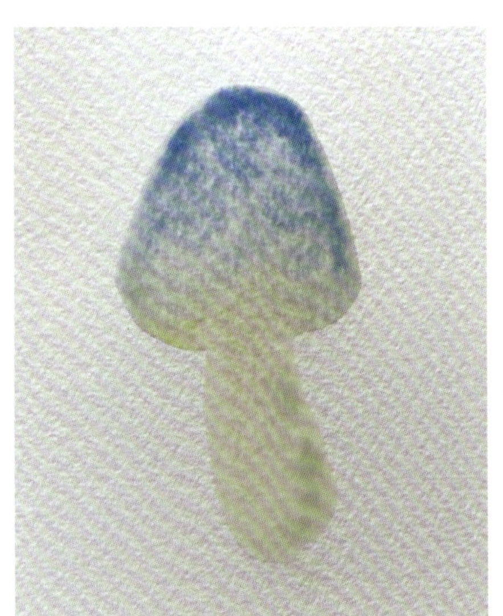

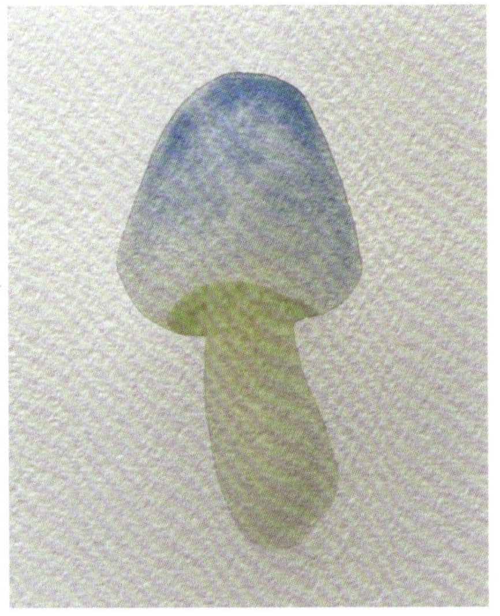

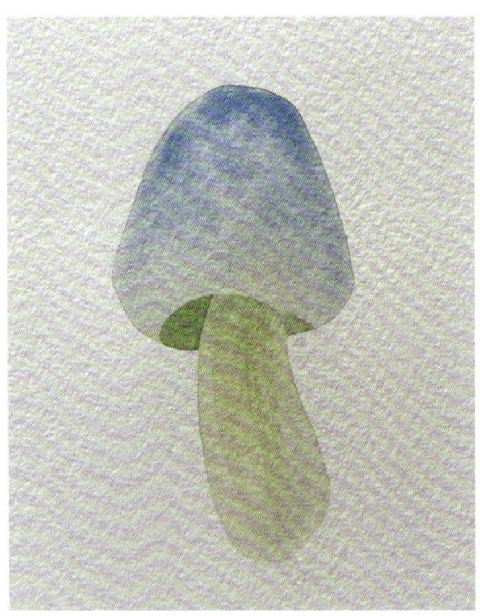

1. Paint the shape of the mushroom using a soft, round brush and Mixture 1. With the tip of the brush, place a little pigment from Mixture 3 on the top of the cap. Let it dry.

2. Using Mixture 2, create depth under the mushroom cap by making an oval shape that extends down to the base of the mushroom to avoid any lines. Let it dry.

3. Intensify the hollow under the hat a little more, this time without painting on the base to clearly distinguish the two elements.

Mushroom Family

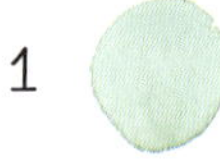

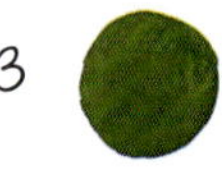

1
2
3
4

- **Mixture 1** - Phthalo green + Indian yellow (diluted)
- **Mixture 2** - Sap green + ultramarine blue + lamp black
- **Mixture 3** - Sap green
- **Mixture 4** - Phthalo green + cobalt green dark + Payne's gray

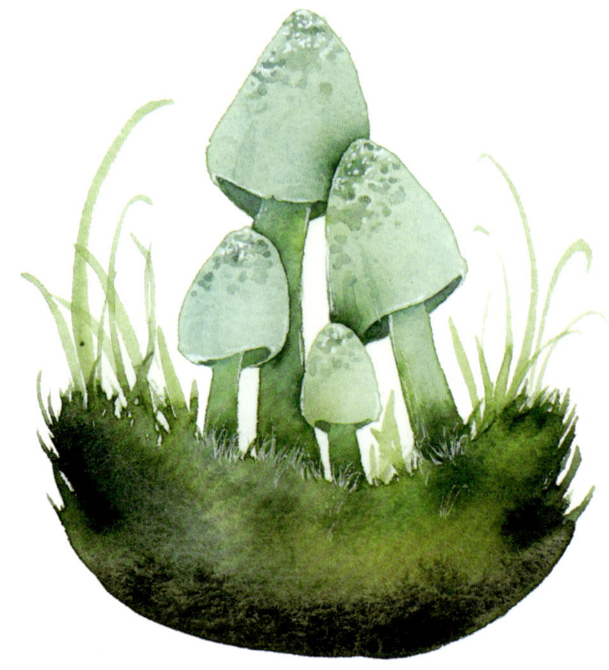

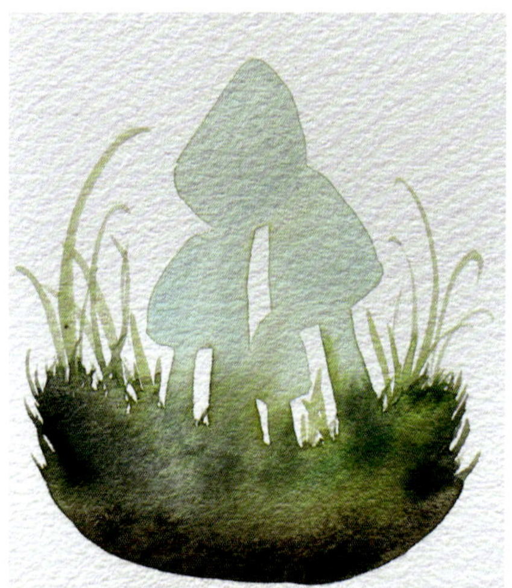

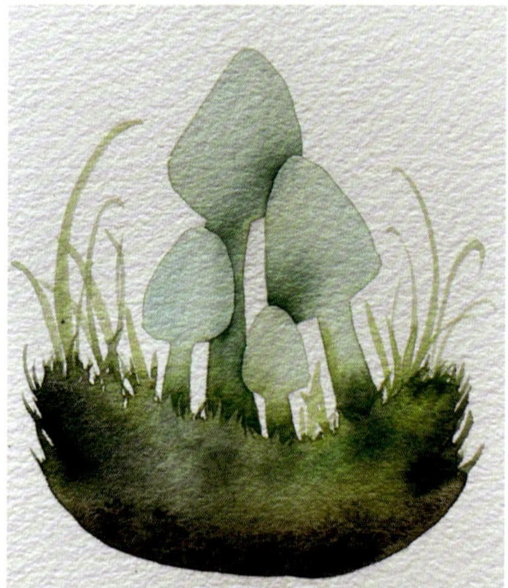

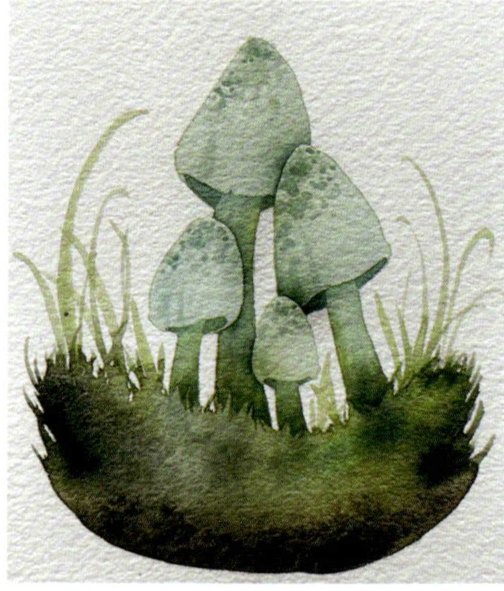

1. Paint the shapes of all the mushrooms using a soft, round brush and Mixture 1. Make sure they overlap. While the watercolor is still wet, add the grass to the mushroom stems using Mixtures 2 and 3.

2. Using Mixture 4, add shadows to the mushrooms to indicate they are in a foreground or background position. This creates depth.

3. Without changing the mixture, create volume by intensifying the pigments under the caps. Also, have fun adding texture to the top of the mushrooms.

Slippery Jack Mushroom

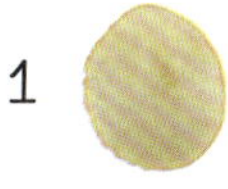
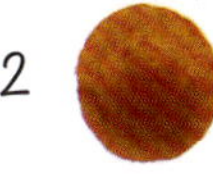
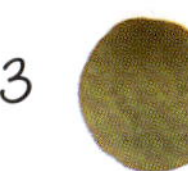

- **Mixture 1** - Yellow ochre + shadow violet
- **Mixture 2** - Quinacridone gold + burgundy red ochre
- **Mixture 3** - Yellow ochre + shadow violet

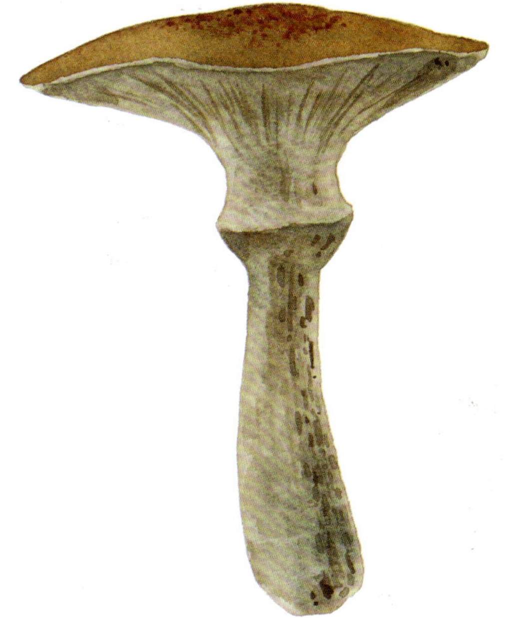

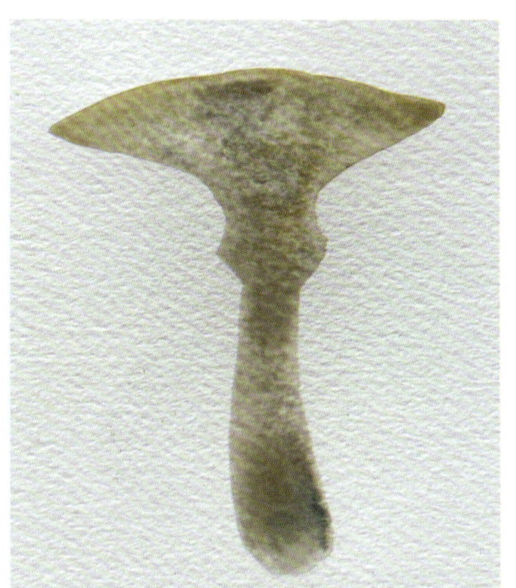

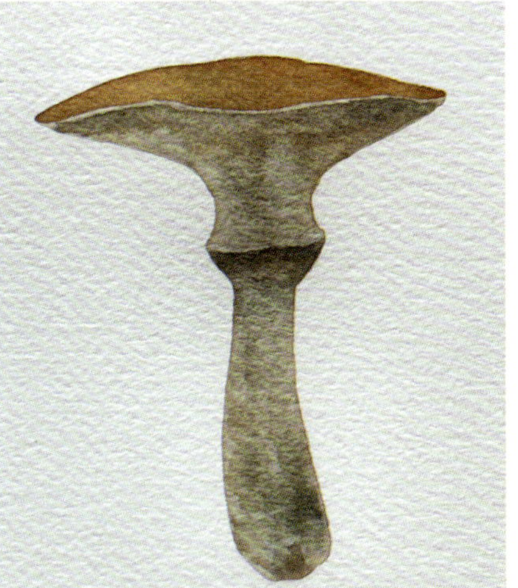

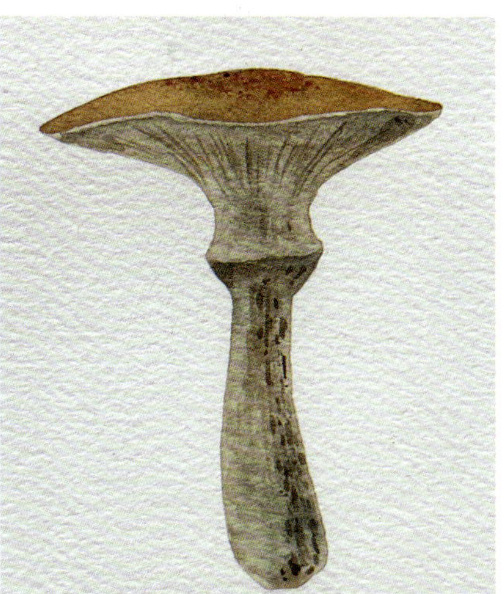

1. Using a soft brush, paint the mushroom shape using Mixture 1. Let it dry.

2. Using Mixture 2, outline the top of the cap by drawing a fairly wide strip. Leave a thin gap, and using Mixture 3, paint a shadow to distinguish between the top and bottom of the cap. Add a shadow to the stem that accentuates the relief. Let it dry.

3. Continuing with Mixture 3, add textures all over the mushroom.

Morel

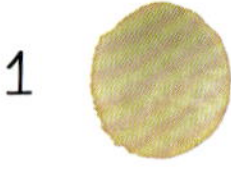

1   • **Mixture 1** - Shadow violet + yellow ochre (diluted)

2   • **Mixture 2** - Sap green + quinacridone gold

3   • **Mixture 3** - Sap green + ultramarine blue + Payne's gray

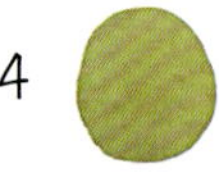

4   • **Mixture 4** - Sap green + yellow ochre (diluted)

5   • **Mixture 5** - Shadow violet + brown iron oxide + yellow ochre

6   • **Mixture 6** - Sepia + lamp black

Note

This mushroom seems more complex to make because of its many pits, but don't worry. Painting them becomes intuitive.

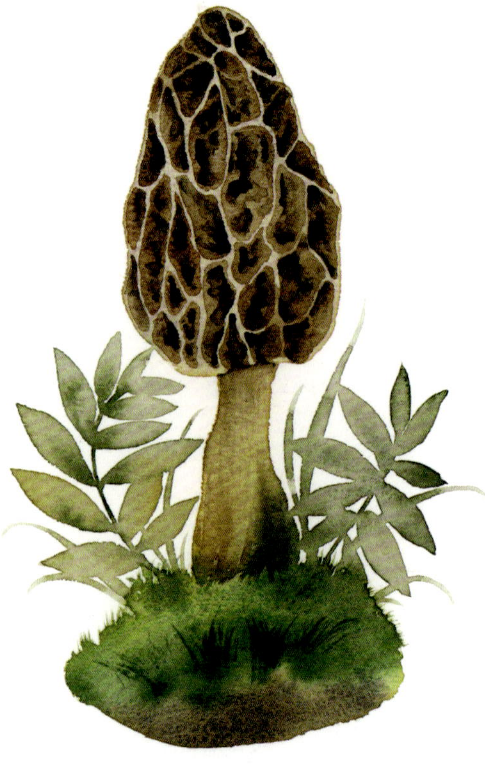

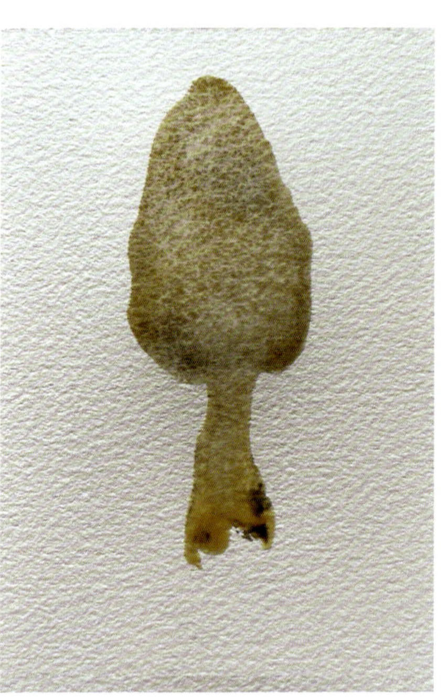

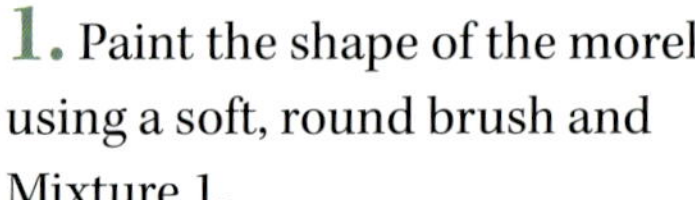

1. Paint the shape of the morel using a soft, round brush and Mixture 1.

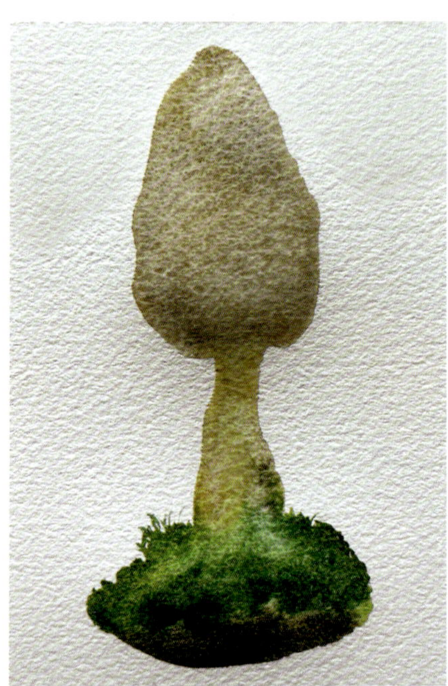

2. In the still-wet watercolor, add moss to the base of the mushroom using Mixtures 2 and 3.

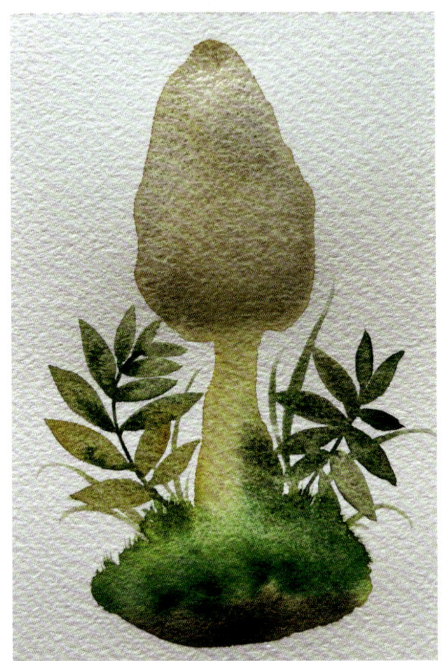 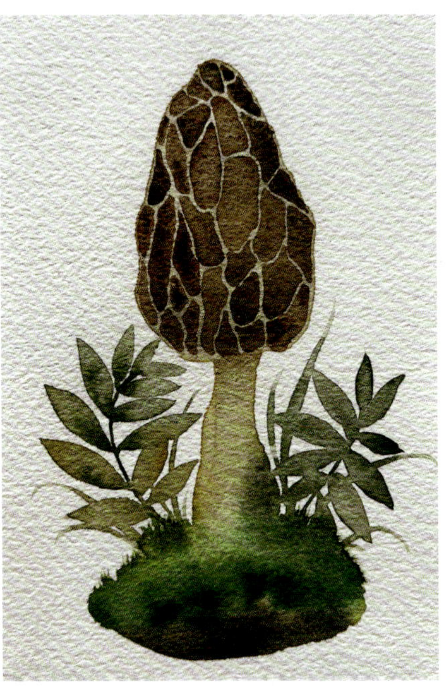 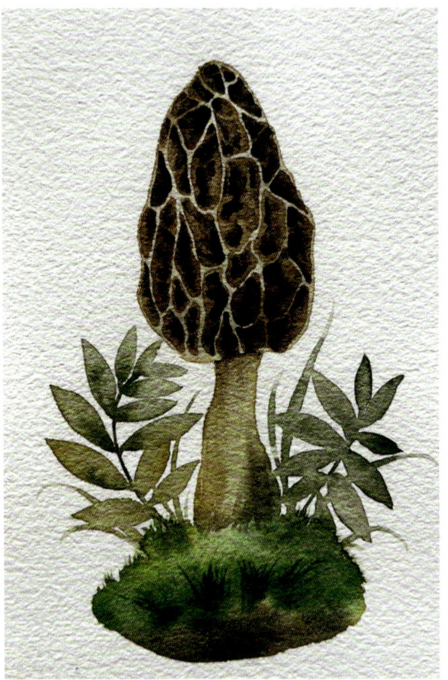

3. In the still-wet watercolor, add plants to the right and left of the stem using Mixtures 3 and 4. Let it dry.

4. Using a small brush and Mixture 5, shape the indents on the morel cap, starting at the top. Play with the shapes of each one, making sure they don't touch. Wait for the watercolor to dry completely.

5. Add depth to the pits with Mixture 6, forming small irregular spots in each of them.

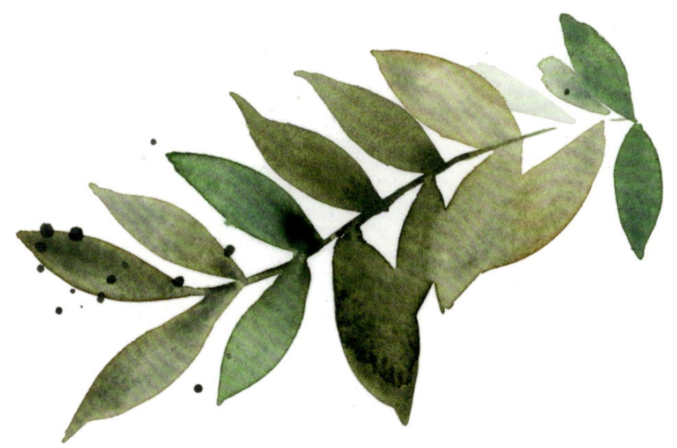

Fly Agaric

1 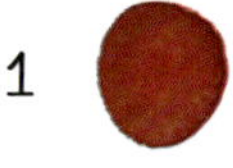

2 

3 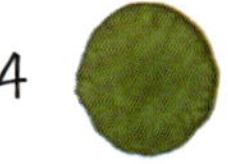

- **Mixture 1** - Alizarin crimson + quinacridone gold + permanent brown
- **Mixture 2** - Alizarin crimson + permanent brown + Payne's gray
- **Mixture 3** - Buff titanium + yellow ochre (diluted)

4 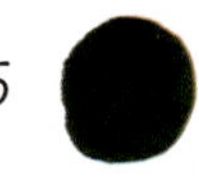

5 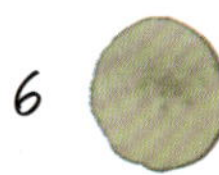

6 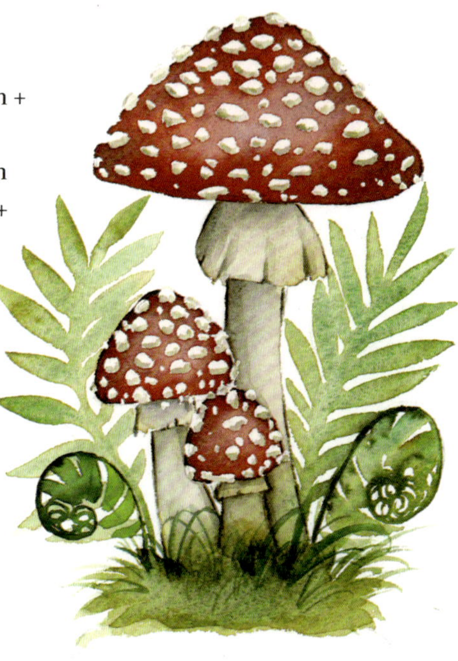

- **Mixture 4** - Sap green + quinacridone gold
- **Mixture 5** - Sap green + quinacridone gold + Payne's gray
- **Mixture 6** - Buff titanium + Payne's gray (diluted)

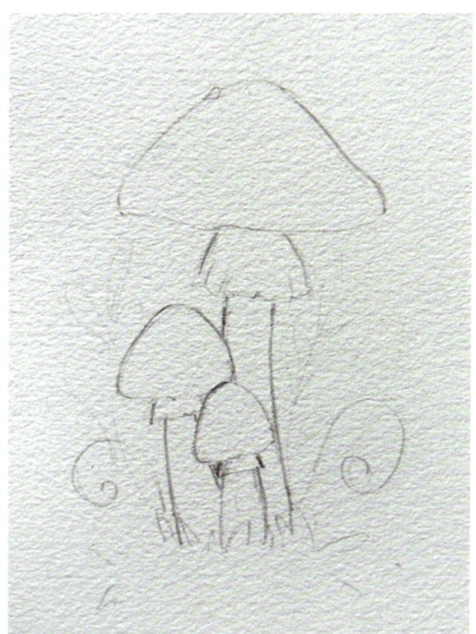

1. Using a pencil, sketch the three mushrooms.

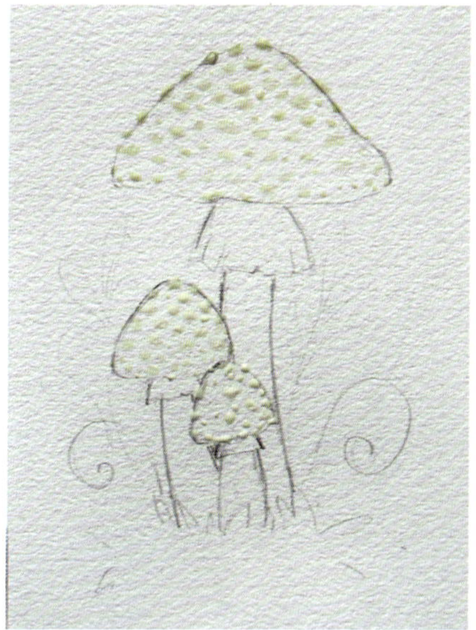

2. Form small, irregular oval shapes on the mushroom caps using masking fluid. Wait until it dries completely.

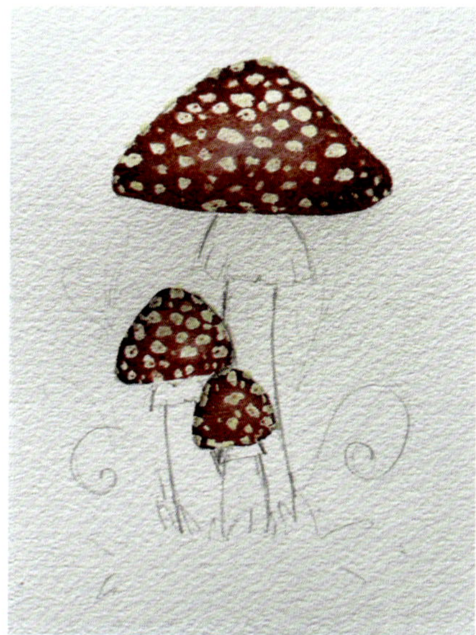

3. Using a soft brush, apply Mixture 1 to the mushroom caps. Then use Mixture 2 to darken the edges. Let it dry.

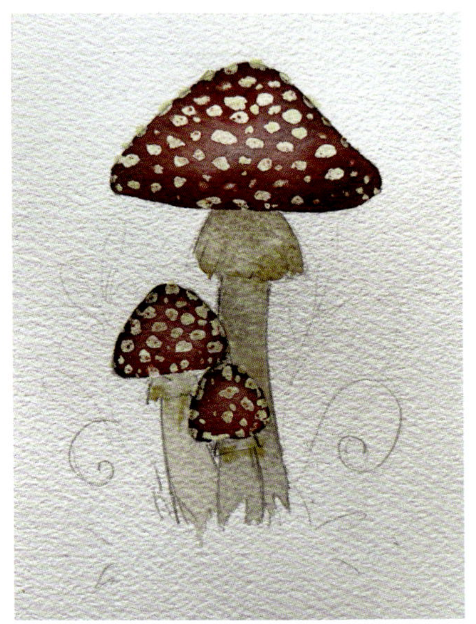

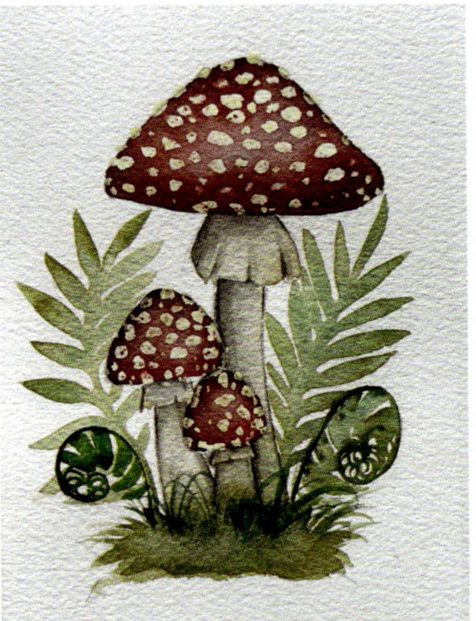

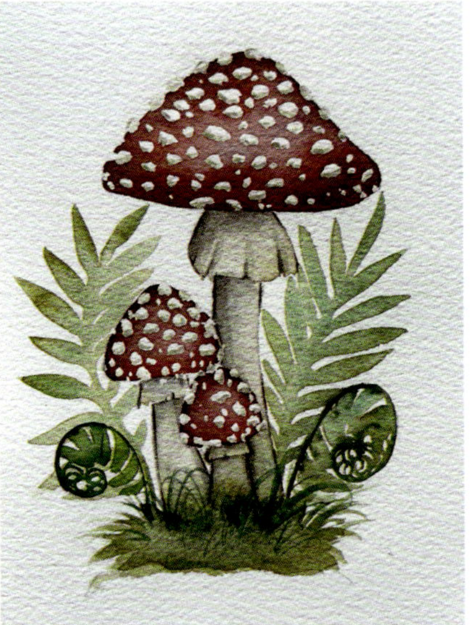

4. Using the same brush and Mixture 3, create the mushroom stems.

5. In the still-wet watercolor, add the moss and vegetation at the base of the mushrooms using Mixtures 4 and 5. Once the watercolor is dry, create the shadows under the caps and on the stems with Mixture 6. Let it dry.

6. Using a cloth or your finger, gently remove the masking fluid to reveal the white of the paper. Finally, use Mixture 6 to create small shadows at the bottom of the white marks for depth.

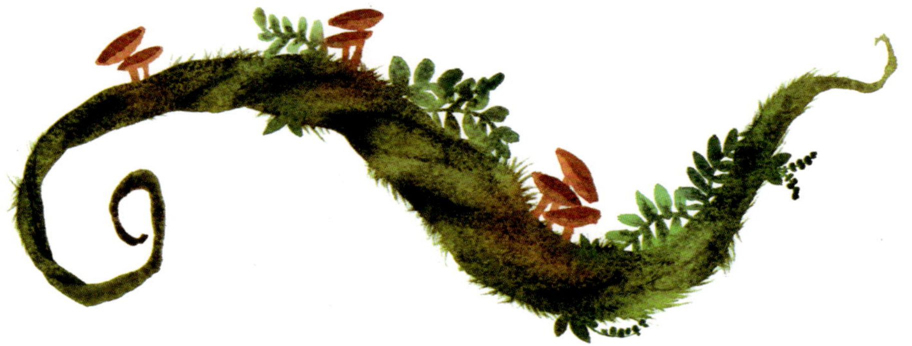

Ivy

1 • **Mixture 1** - Brown iron oxide + lamp black

2 • **Mixture 2** - Sap green + phthalo green

3 • **Mixture 3** - Phthalo green + lamp black

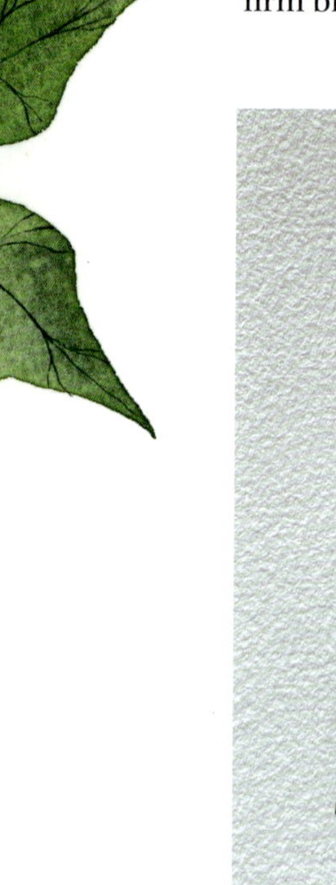

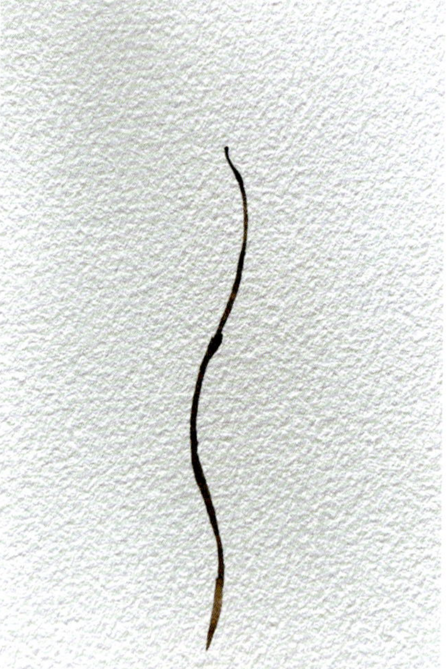

1. Draw the ivy stem using a fine, firm brush and Mixture 1.

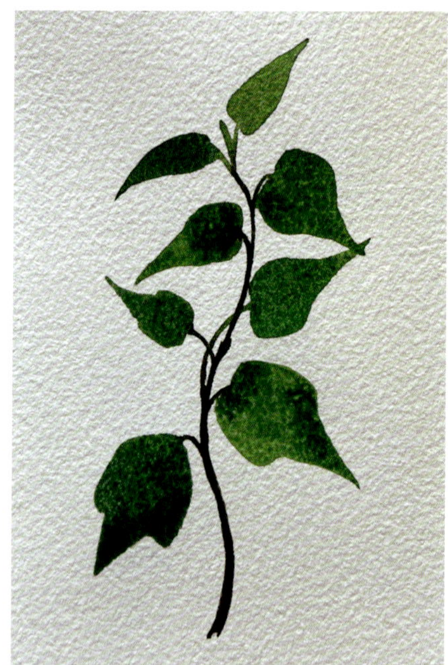

2. Using Mixture 2 and a small brush, add pairs of heart-shaped leaves along the stem. Wait for the watercolor to dry.

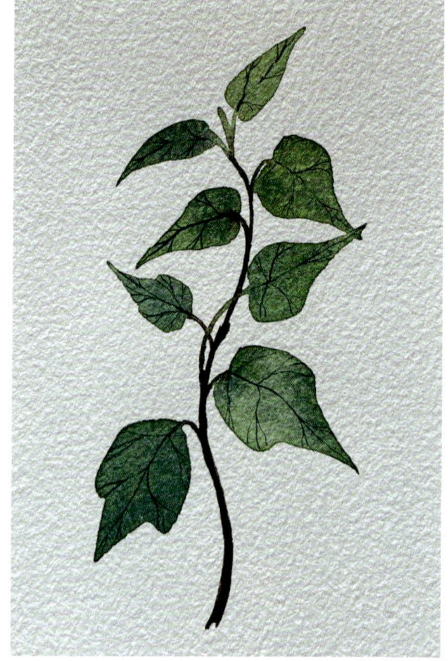

3. Add the veins of the leaves using a very fine brush and Mixture 3.

Eagle Fern

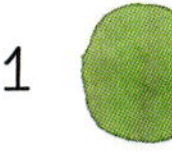 1
- **Mixture 1** - Phthalo green + sap green (diluted)

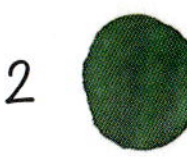 2
- **Mixture 2** - Sap green (diluted)

3
- **Mixture 3** - Phthalo green + cobalt green dark

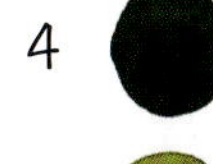 4
- **Mixture 4** - Sap green + phthalo green + lamp black

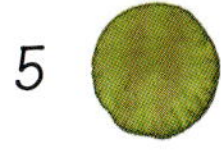 5
- **Mixture 5** - Sap green + quinacridone gold

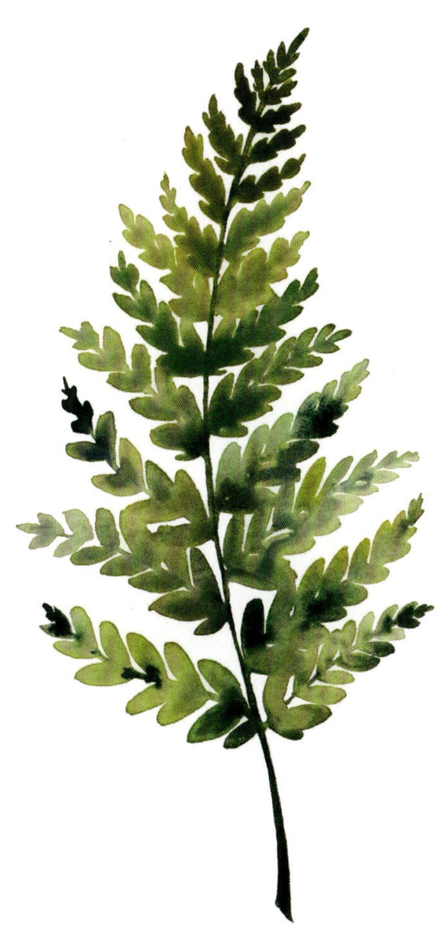

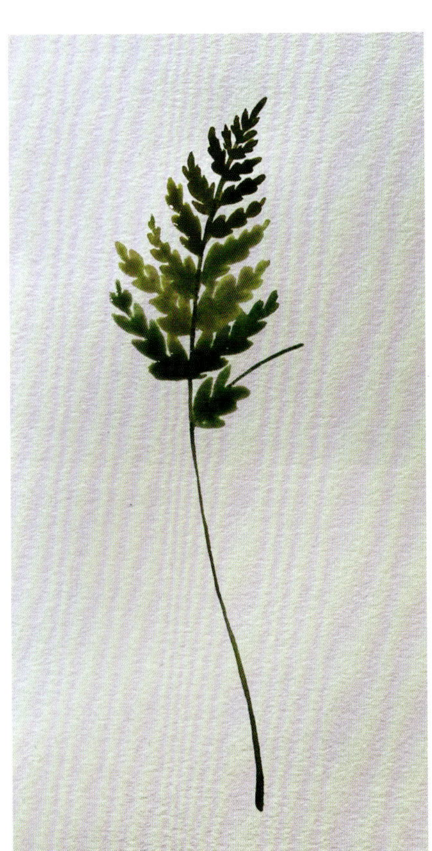

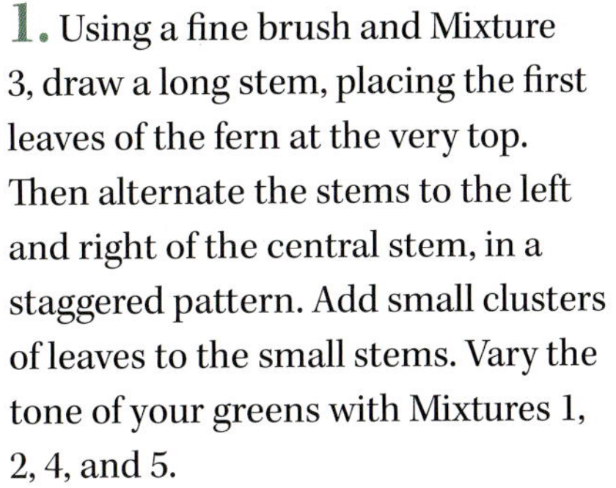

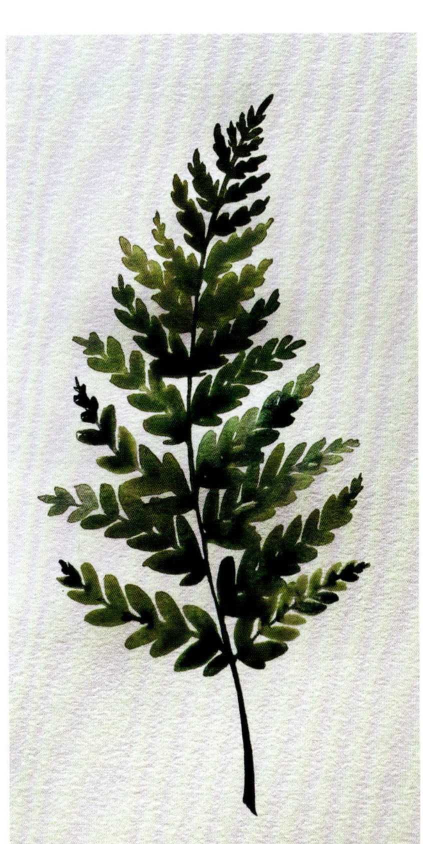

1. Using a fine brush and Mixture 3, draw a long stem, placing the first leaves of the fern at the very top. Then alternate the stems to the left and right of the central stem, in a staggered pattern. Add small clusters of leaves to the small stems. Vary the tone of your greens with Mixtures 1, 2, 4, and 5.

2. Gradually move down the central stem, taking care to increase the length of the stems and size of the leaves as you go down.

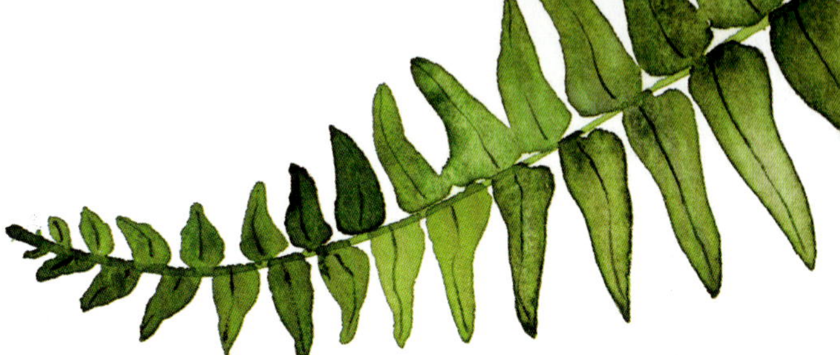

Boston Fern

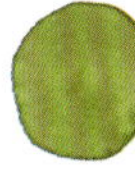

1

- **Mixture 1** - Sap green + quinacridone gold

2

- **Mixture 2** - Cobalt green dark + sap green + ultramarine blue

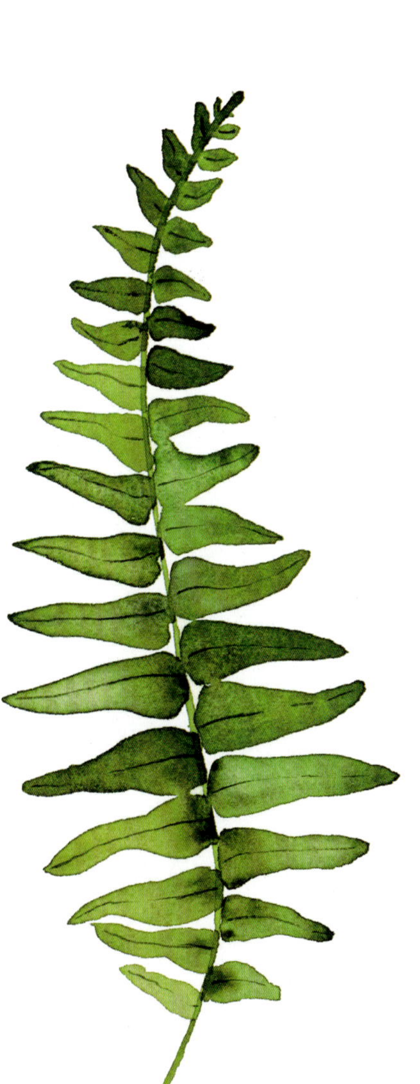

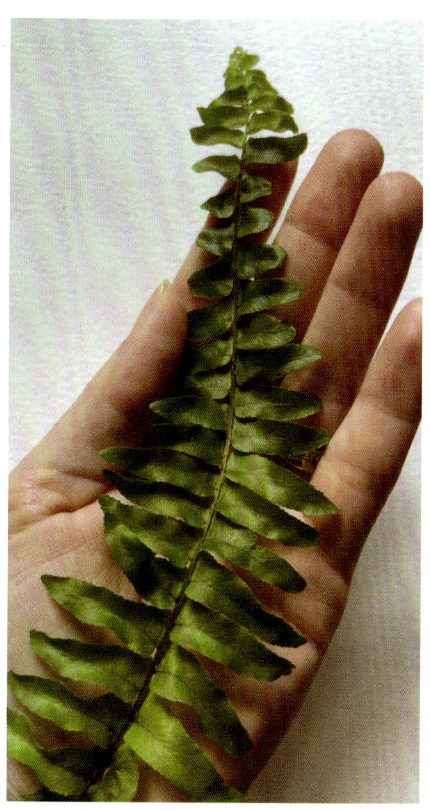

1. Observe the fern carefully: its shape, its movement, its color, its textures.

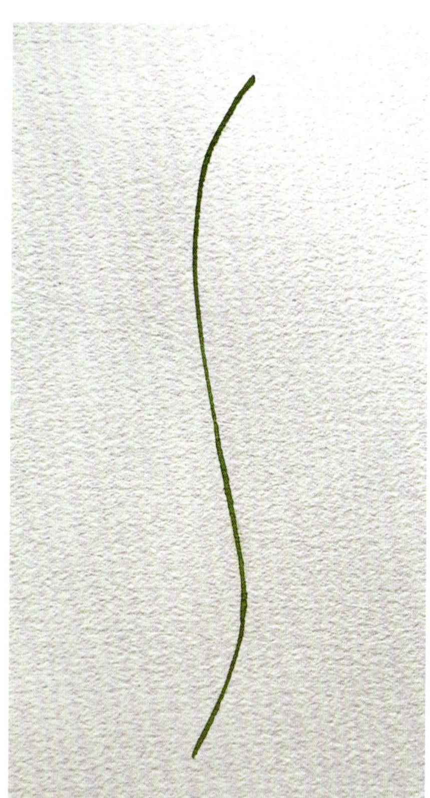

2. Using Mixture 1 and a fine brush, draw a slightly wavy stem.

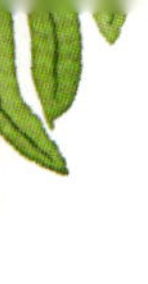

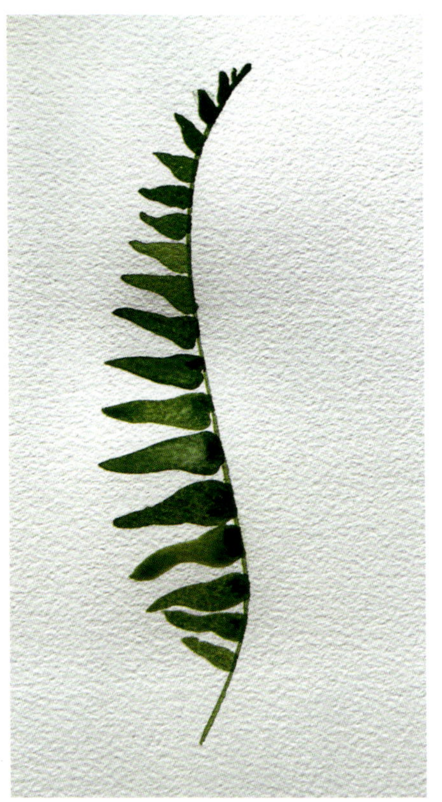

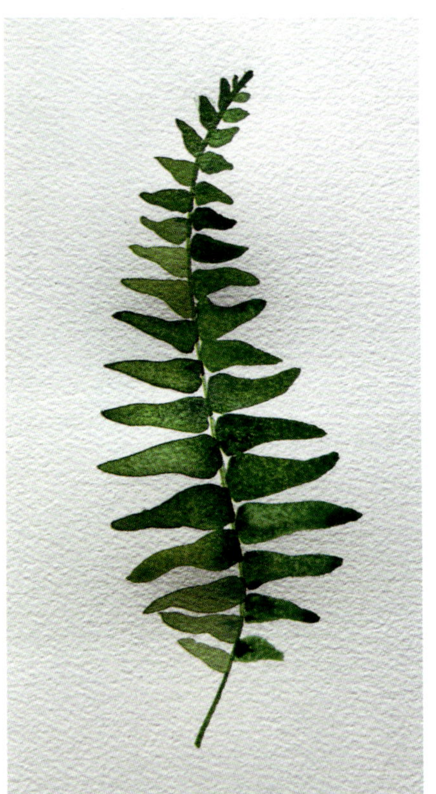

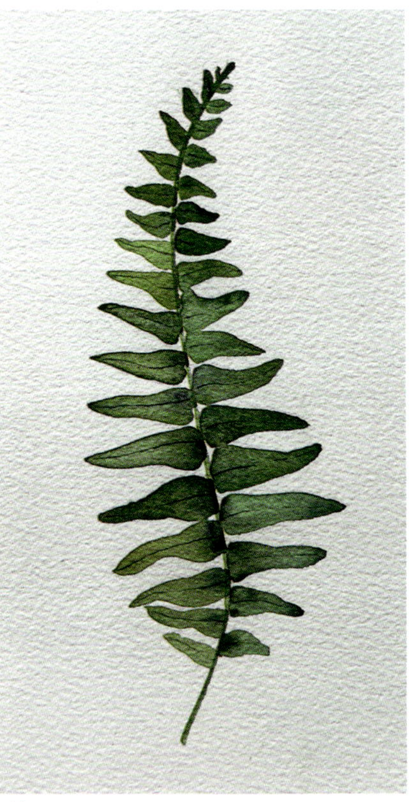

3. Paint all the leaves on the same side, from top to bottom, to maintain the same movement with your wrist. Make sure your leaves are thicker on the stem side and thinner on the outside, like a triangle. Vary Mixtures 1 and 2 to create light and shadow effects.

4. Paint the other side. Make sure to position the leaves in a staggered pattern, not a mirror image. Wait for the watercolor to dry.

5. Using a fine brush, draw a thin vein along the middle of each leaf with Mixture 2.

Advice

The leaves are each an elongated triangle. To easily create them in one stroke, use the tip of your brush as a starting point, then lengthen and widen the leaf shape by increasing the pressure to thicken your line.

Young Fern

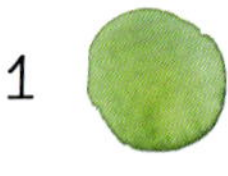

1 **Mixture 1** - Phthalo green + sap green (diluted)

2 **Mixture 2** - Phthalo green + sap green + cobalt green dark

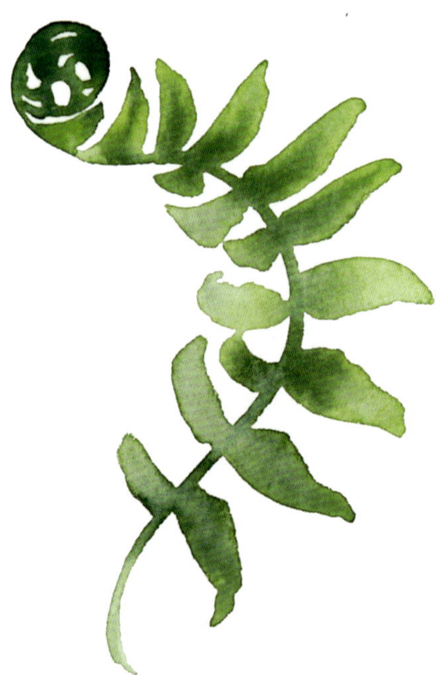

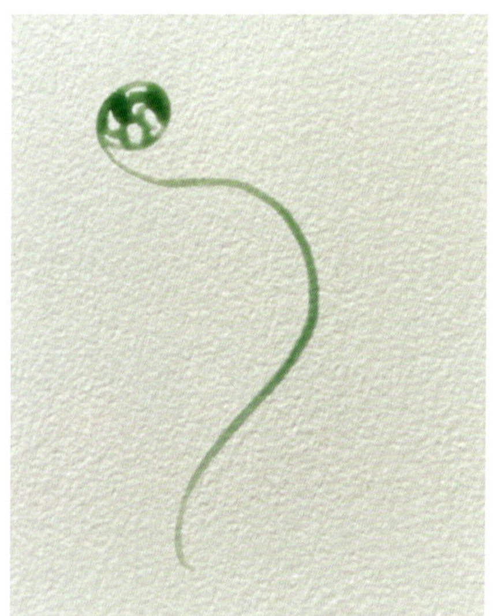

1. Using a fine brush and Mixture 1, draw the stem of the fern. End with a small swirl in which you will form several small ones.

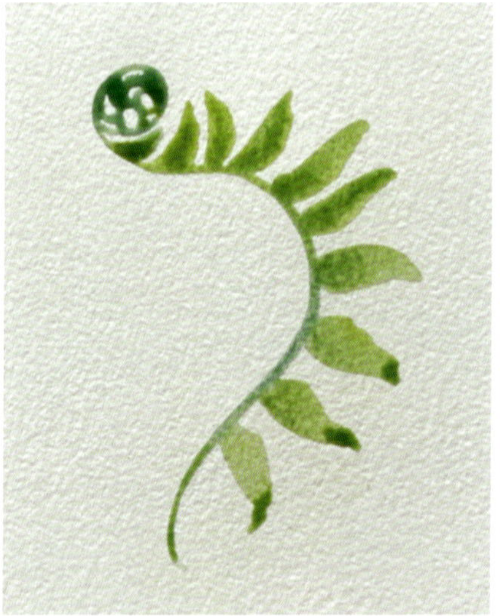

2. Below the swirl, place small leaves on the right side of the stem with Mixture 1.

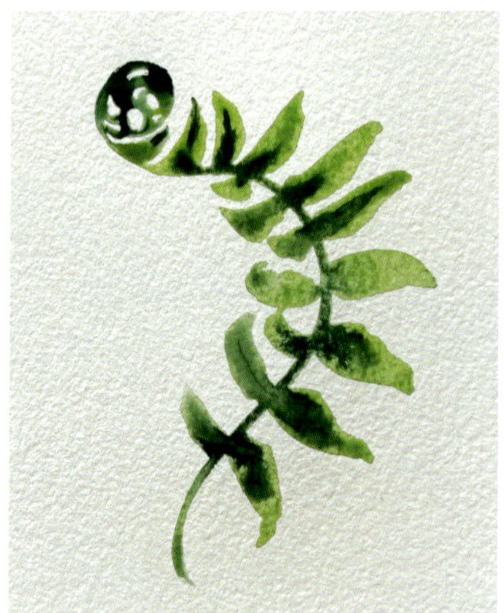

3. Add new leaves on the left side, making sure to give them a dynamic upward movement. Place Mixture 2 on the stem, centered between the leaves, to create contrast.

Clover

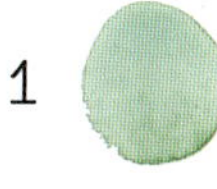

1

Mixture 1 - Cobalt turquoise light + phthalo green (diluted)

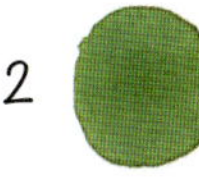

2

Mixture 2 - Sap green + cobalt turquoise light

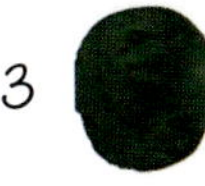

3

Mixture 3 - Phthalo green + lamp black

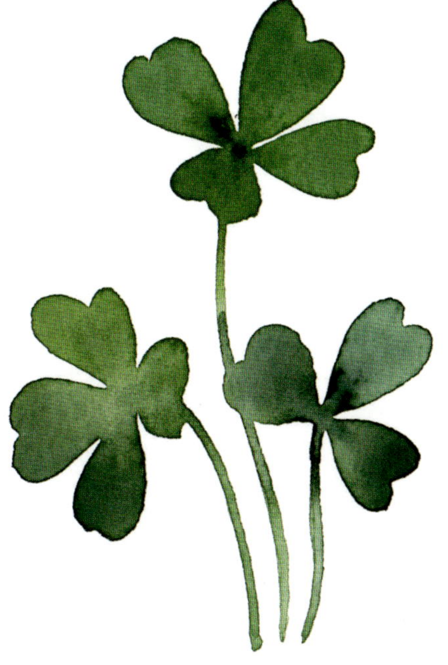

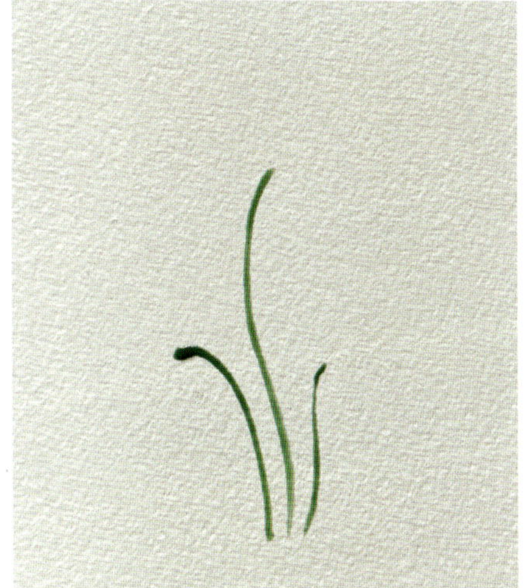

1. Using a fine brush and Mixture 1, draw three small stems.

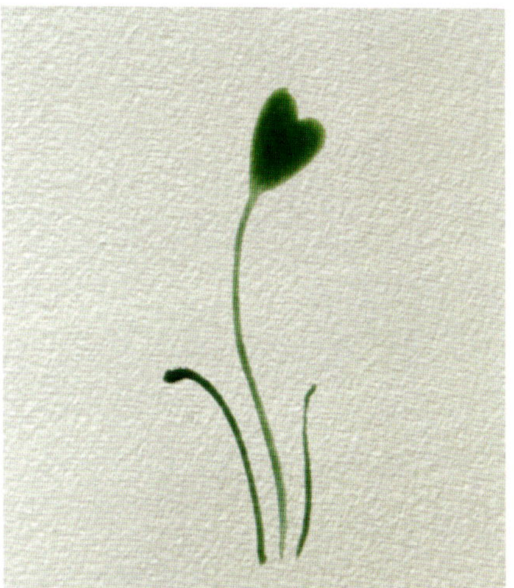

2. Place your brush at the end of the central stem and gently press the thick part of the brush onto the leaf, creating a small flat area. Repeat to create a heart shape for your leaf.

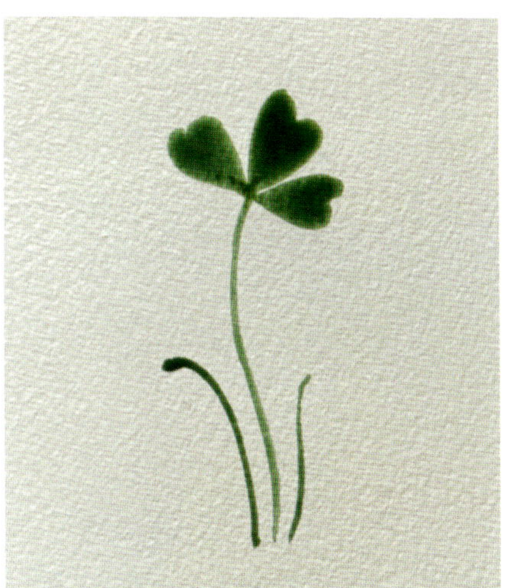

3. Do the same for the other two leaves.

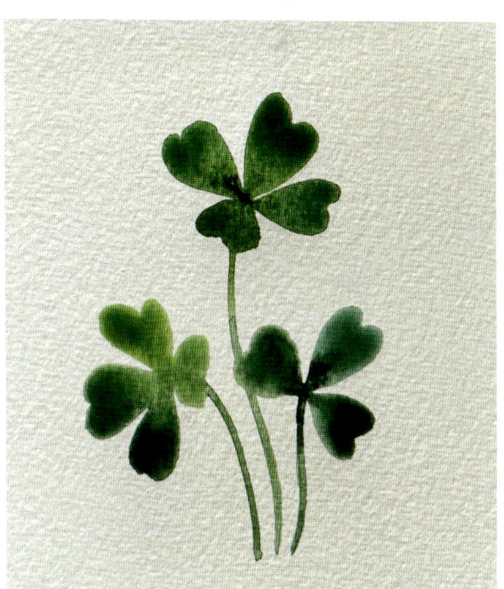

4. The process is similar for the three clovers but vary the number of leaves on each stem. Take care to vary the shades of green to obtain a contrasting result.

Poplar Leaf

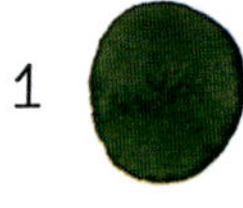

1

- **Mixture 1** - Sap green + phthalo green

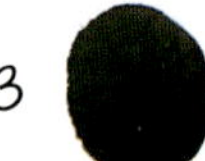

2

- **Mixture 2** - Sap green + cobalt green dark

3

- **Mixture 3** - Sap green + lamp black

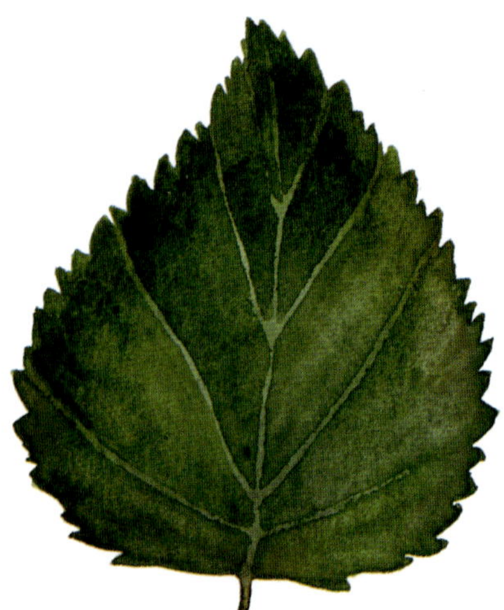

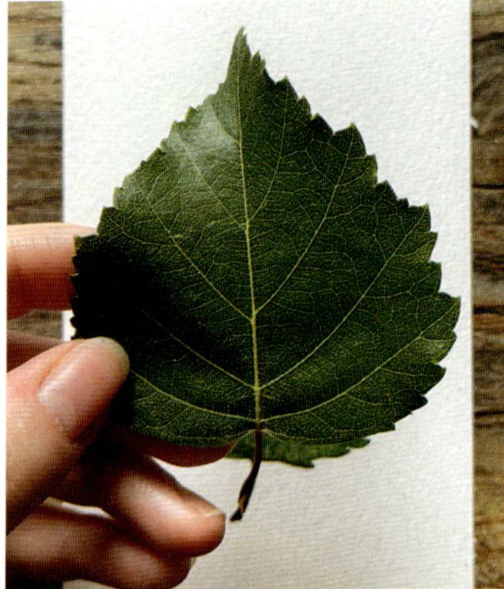

1. Observe the characteristics of the leaf: its colors, its veins, its contours.

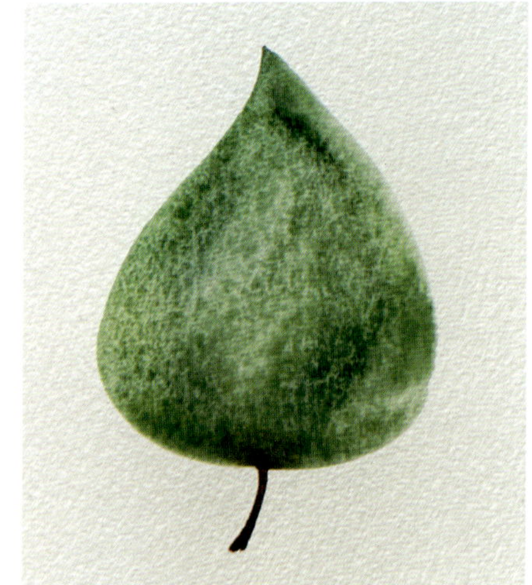

2. Paint the overall shape of the leaf, using a soft, round brush and playing with Mixtures 1 and 2.

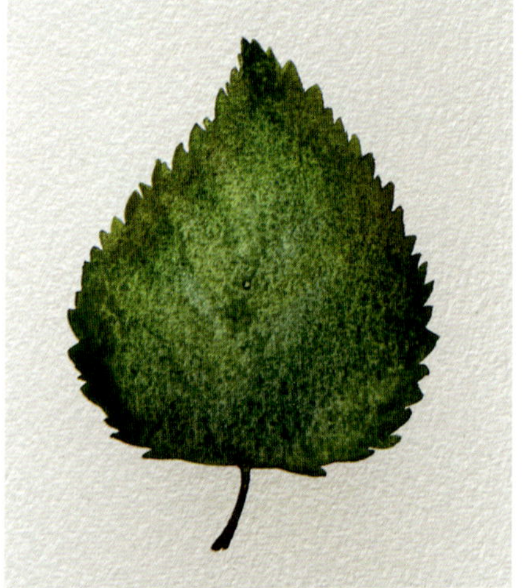

3. While the watercolor is still wet, create the teeth of the leaf by simply placing the tip of the brush along the edge. In this example, use Mixture 3 on the bottom. Let it dry.

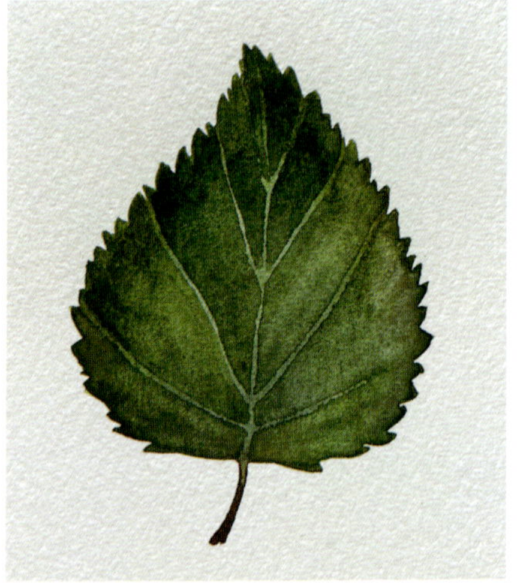

4. Add veins by painting thin lines with Mixture 1.

Red Oak Leaf

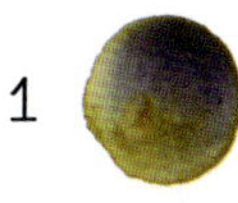

1

- **Mixture 1** - Quinacridone gold + tundra blue

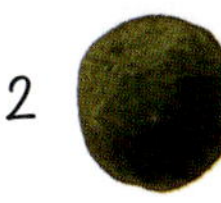

2

- **Mixture 2** - Brown iron oxide + cobalt green dark

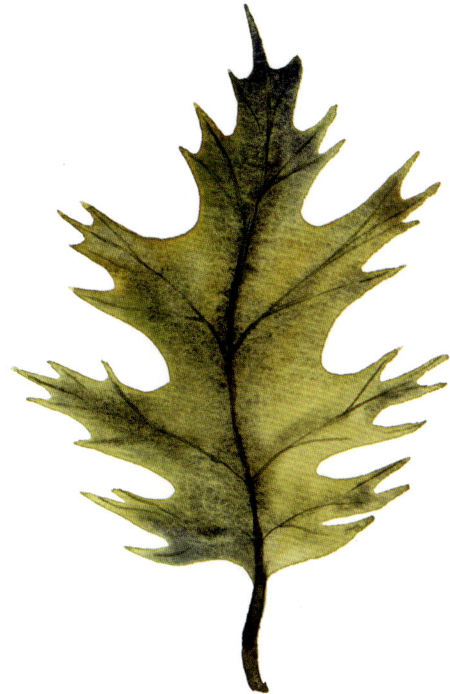

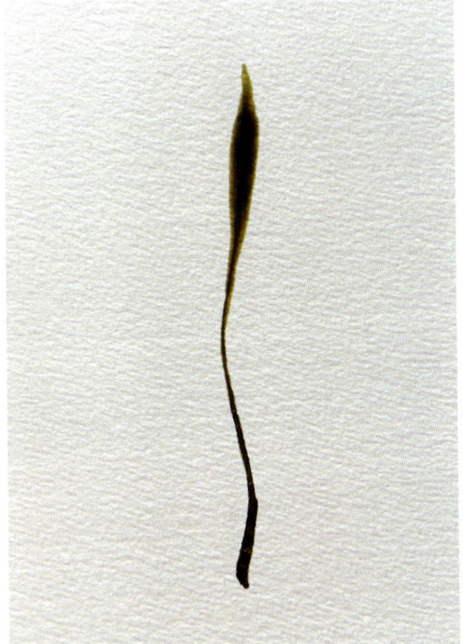

1. Using a small brush, draw the center of the leaf. End with a point. Use Mixture 1 with different pigment intensities.

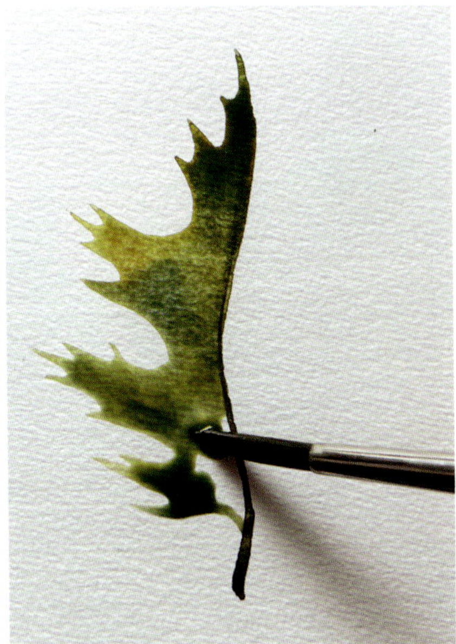

2. Without changing brushes, outline the shapes of the leaf, making sure each curve ends in a point. Only work on one side. Using Mixture 1, fill in the inside of the outlines.

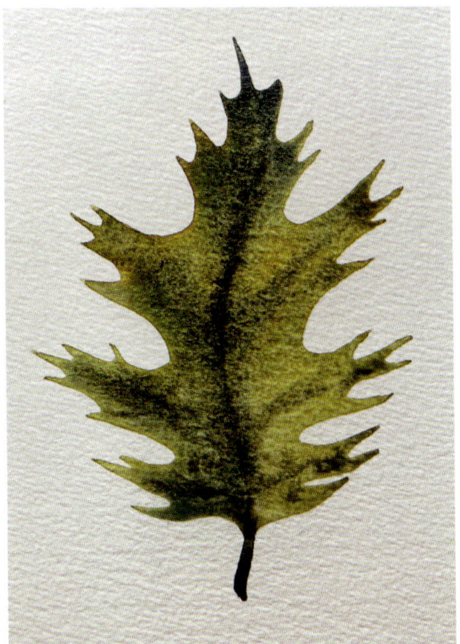

3. Repeat on the other side, playing with the different pigments. Wait for the watercolor to dry.

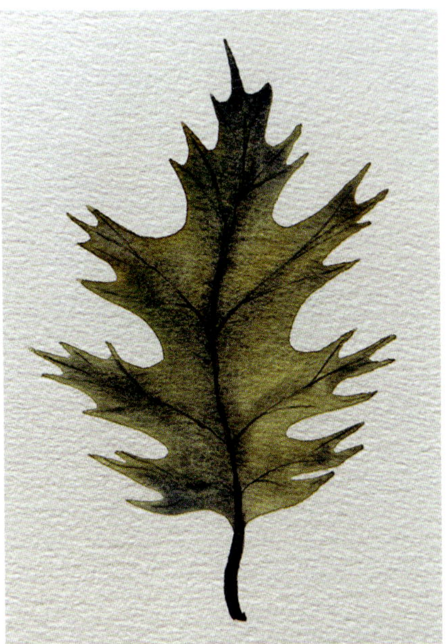

4. Using a very fine brush and Mixture 2, draw the veins of the leaf.

English Oak Leaf

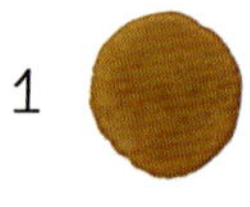
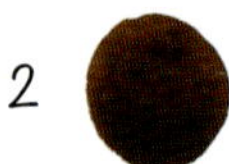

1
2

- **Mixture 1** - Burgundy red ochre + quinacridone gold
- **Mixture 2** - Brown iron oxide + burgundy red ochre

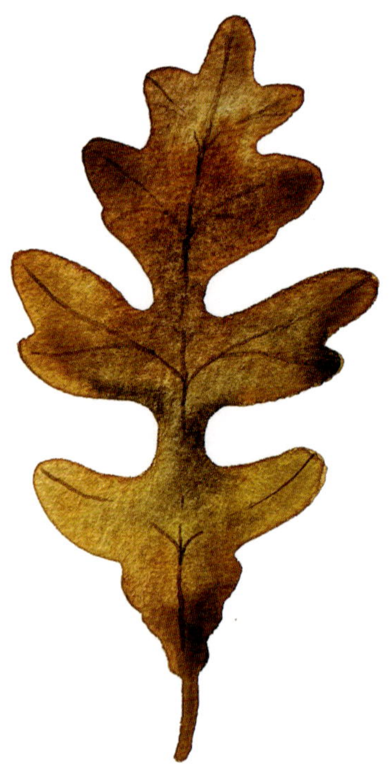

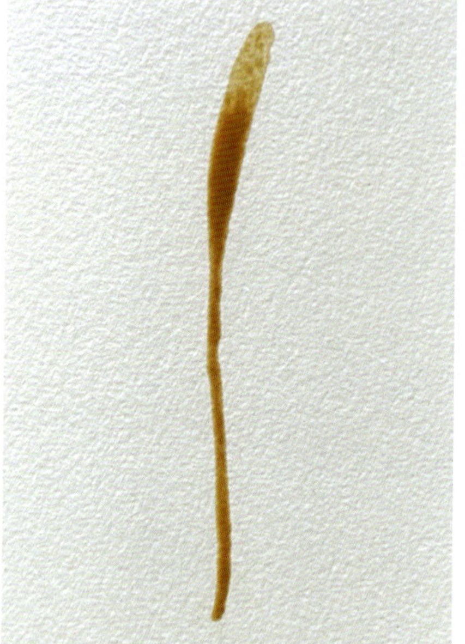

1. Using a firm brush and Mixture 1, draw the center of the leaf, ending with a slightly rounded shape.

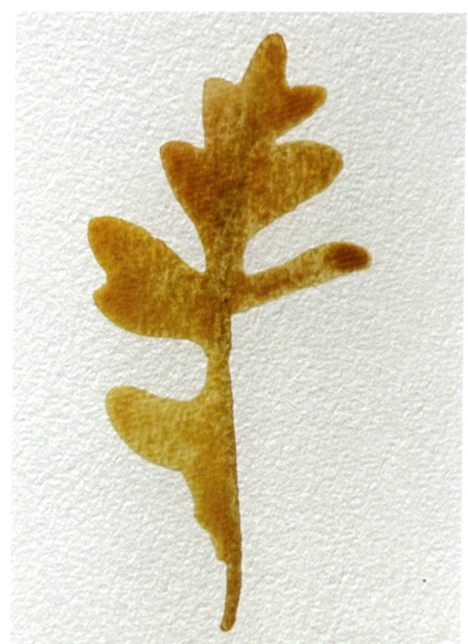

2. Form small waves with your brush on the left side, then on the right, trying to be more or less symmetrical.

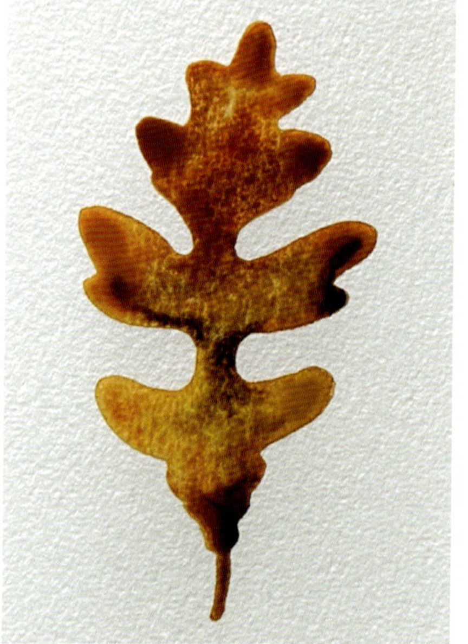

3. In the still-wet watercolor, place Mixture 2 so as to have variations of orange and brown colors on the paper. Let it dry.

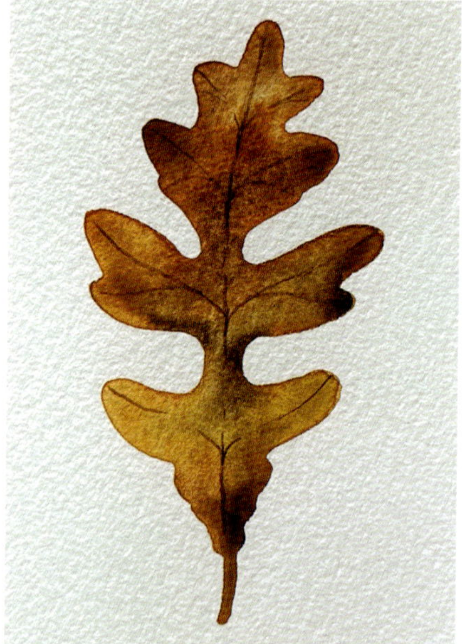

4. Using a very precise brush and Mixture 2, draw the veins of the leaf.

LITTLE CREATURES

In the following exercises, I approach the painting of the little forest critters from different artistic perspectives. As mentioned earlier, it's not always necessary to sketch before painting, which I suggest you experiment with here. However, I understand that this can be intimidating, which is why the frog and snail step-by-step tutorials begin with a drawing. See which technique you're most comfortable with.

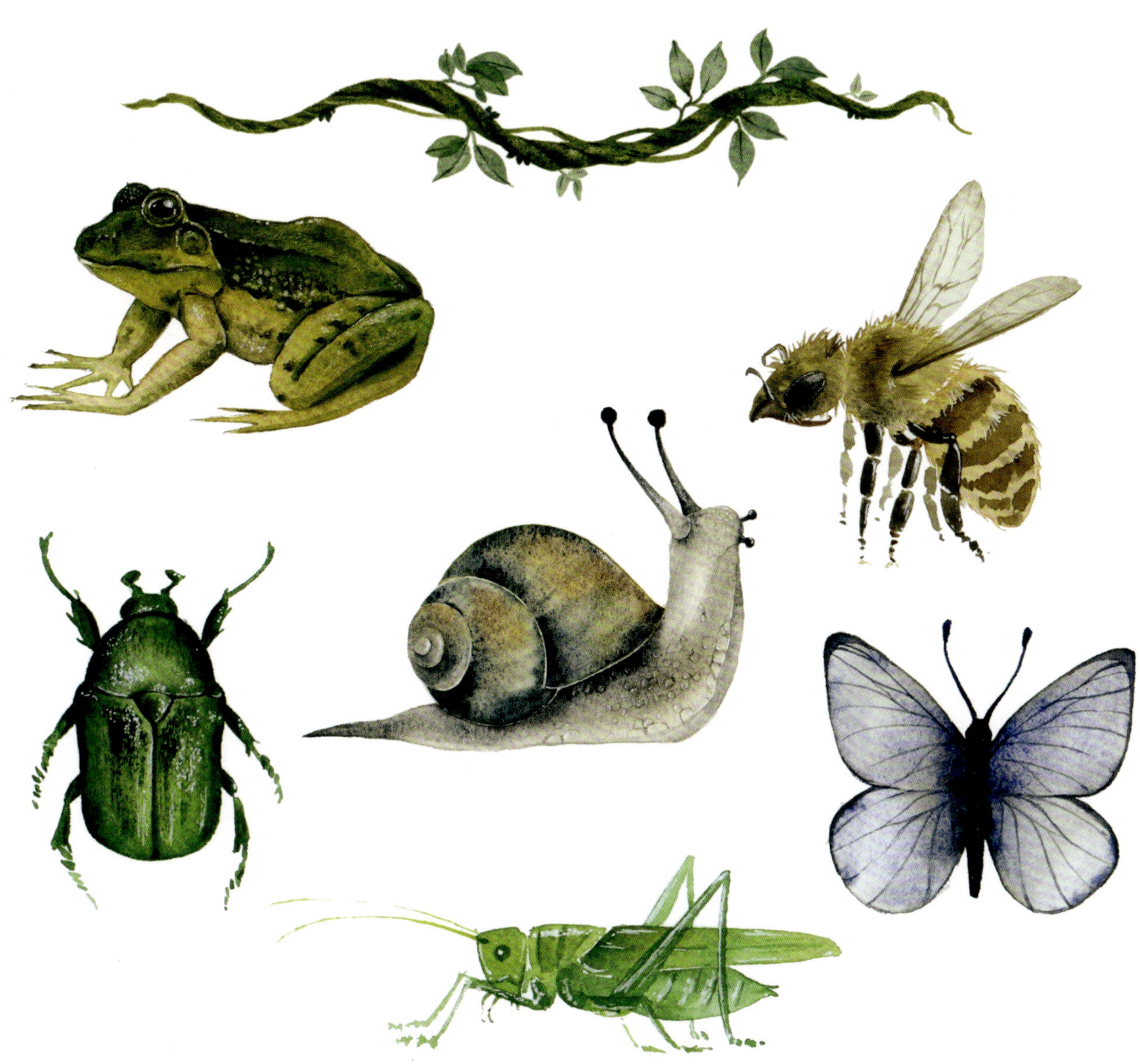

Bee

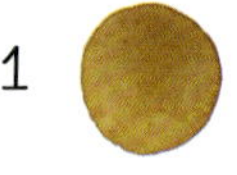

1

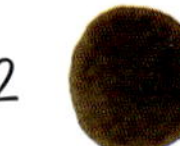

2

- **Mixture 1** - Ocher yellow + quinacridone gold
- **Mixture 2** - Sepia + Mars black

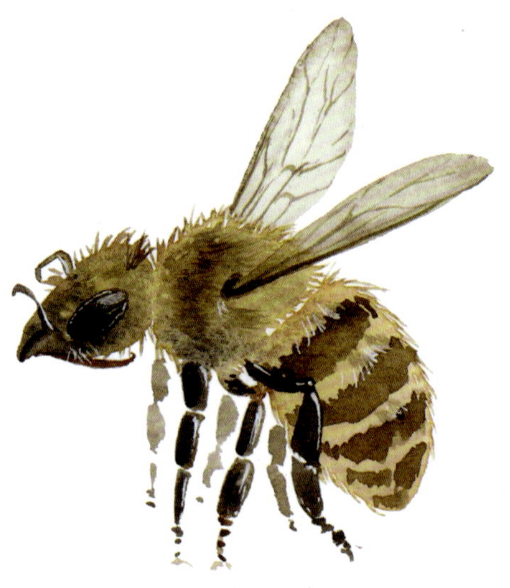

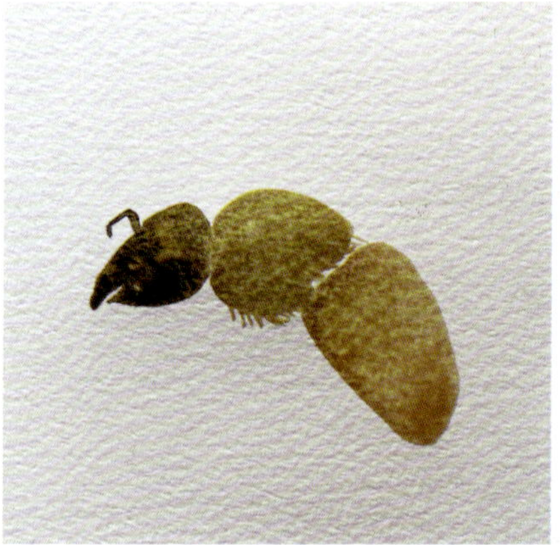

1. Using a small brush and Mixtures 1 and 2, create the bee's head. With Mixture 1, add the two oval-shaped body parts.

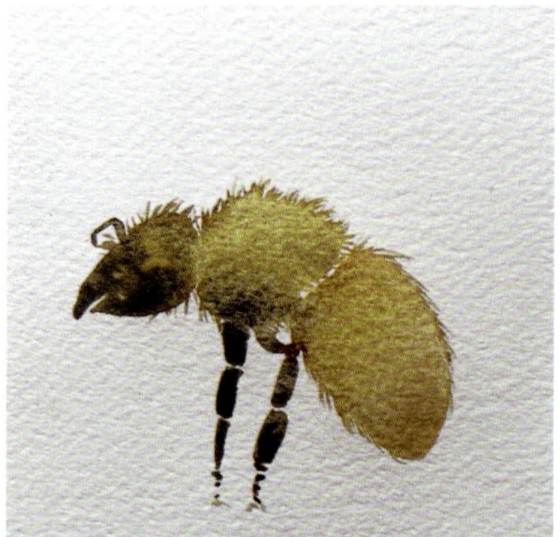

2. Using a fine brush and Mixture 2, apply the first two legs. Draw small hairs on the head and body with Mixture 1. Let it dry.

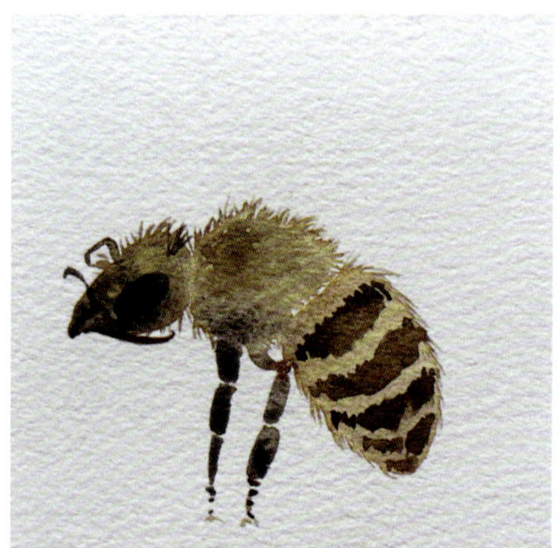

3. Using Mixture 2, paint the bee's eye and the stripes on its abdomen.

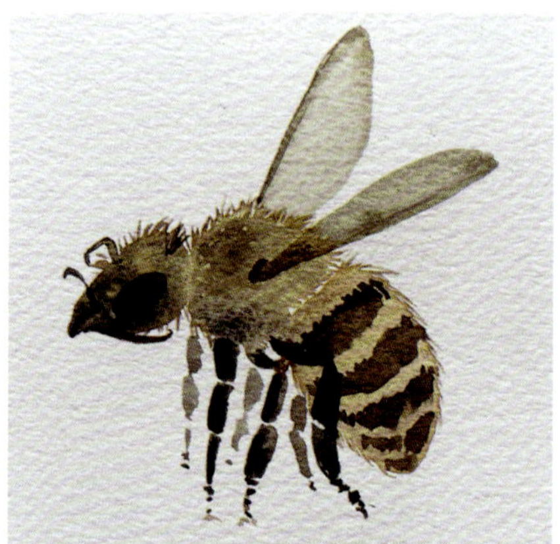

4. With Mixtures 1 and 2 very diluted, then add the wings. Indicate shadows by intensifying the pigments on the wings. Wait for the watercolor to dry.

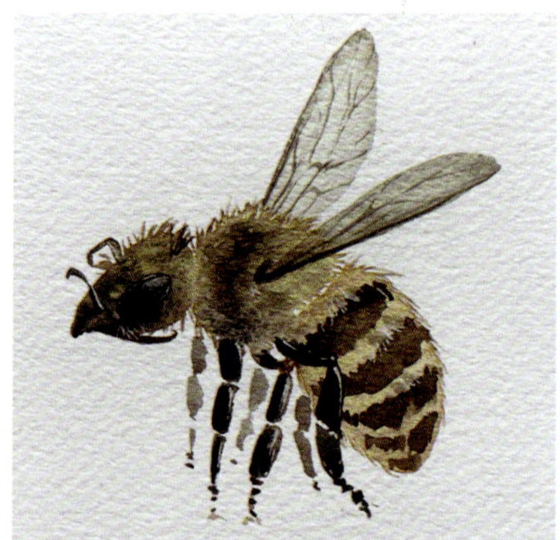

5. With Mixture 2, detail the inside of the wings and add touches of light with a white gel ink pen.

Butterfly

• **Mixture 1** - Payne's gray + tundra blue

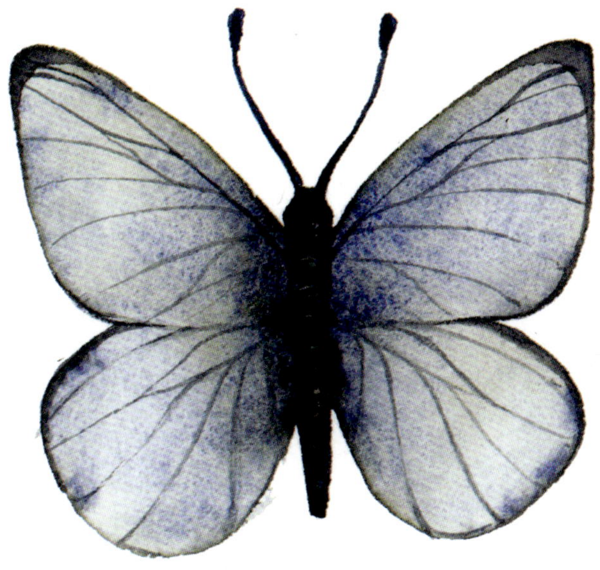

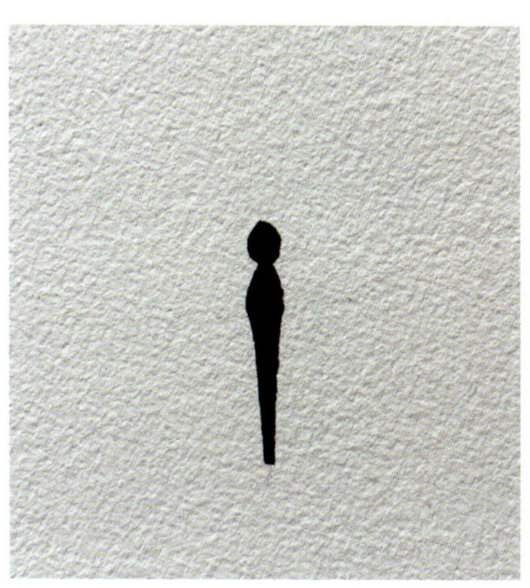

1. Using a small brush, draw the body of the butterfly.

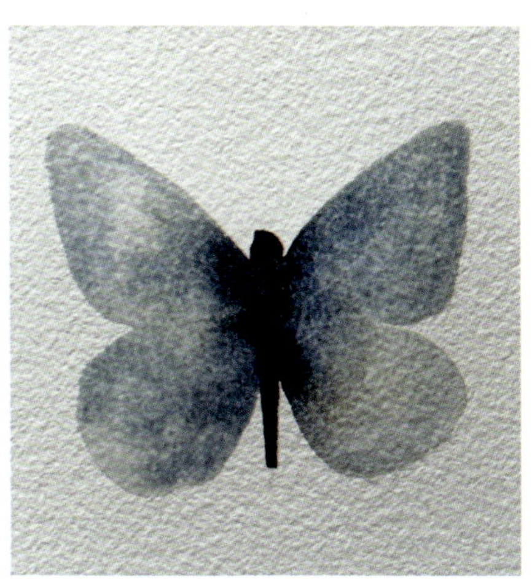

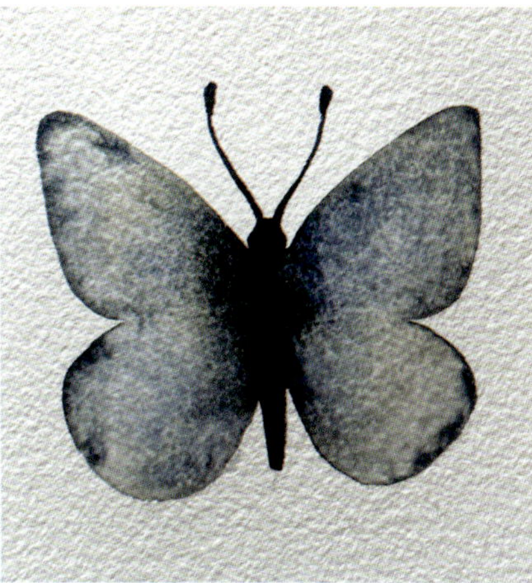

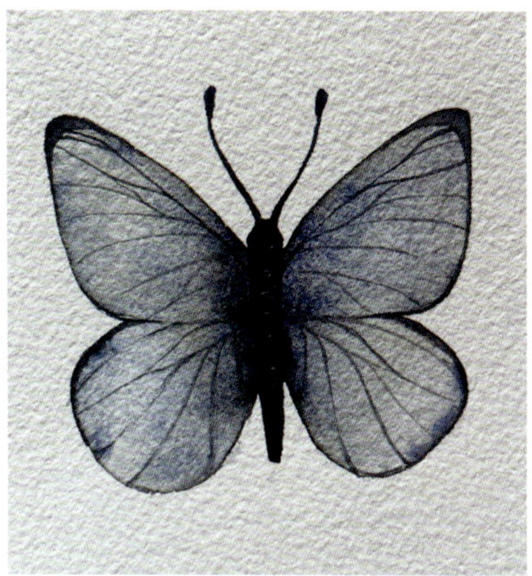

2. Using the same brush, only soaked in water this time, stretch the still-wet pigments to form the wings. If necessary, add more pigments to the body.

3. In the still-wet watercolor, add a few touches of pigment to the ends of the wings, then draw the antennae. Let it dry.

4. Use a very fine brush to detail the inside of the butterfly's wings. With a white colored pencil, add a few touches of light to the body.

Grasshopper

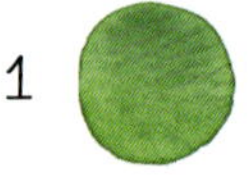

- **Mixture 1** - Phthalo green + sap green
- **Mixture 2** - Phthalo green + quinacridone gold

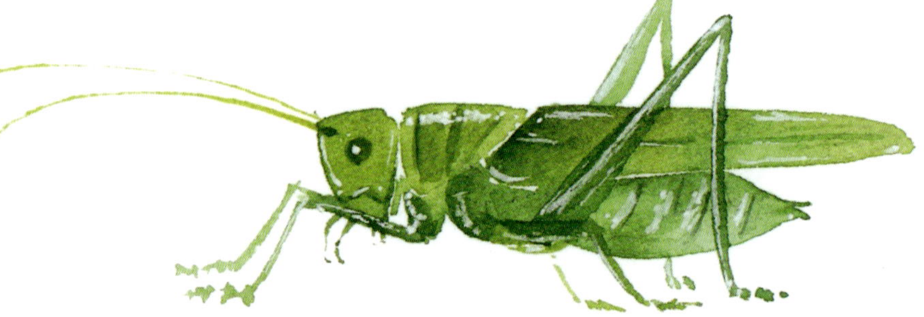

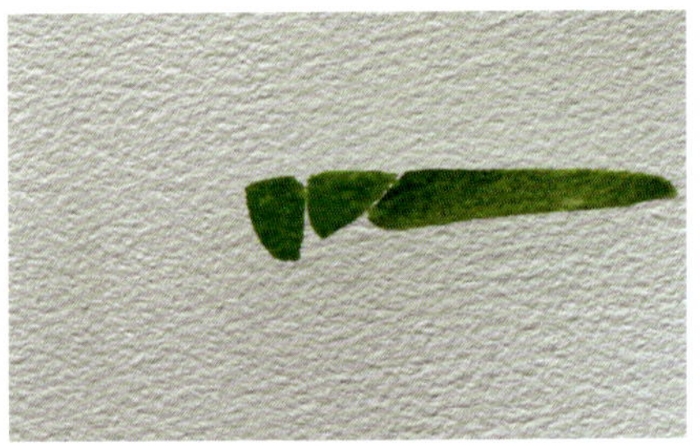

1. Using Mixture 2, start by painting the three upper parts of the grasshopper's body. Use a precise brush to help you shape the different sections.

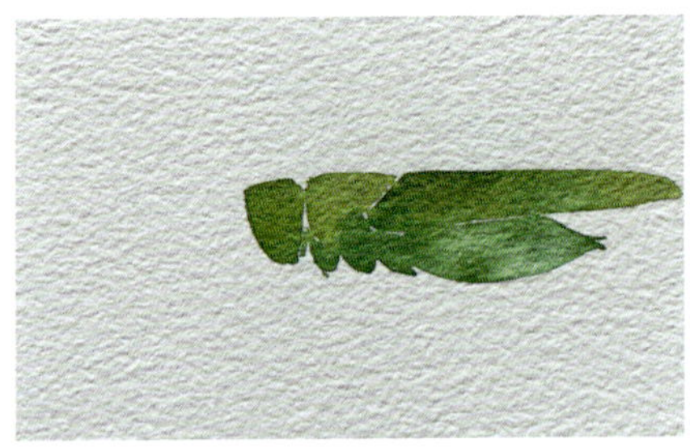

2. Using the same brush and Mixture 1, paint the grasshopper's abdomen and thorax. Let it dry.

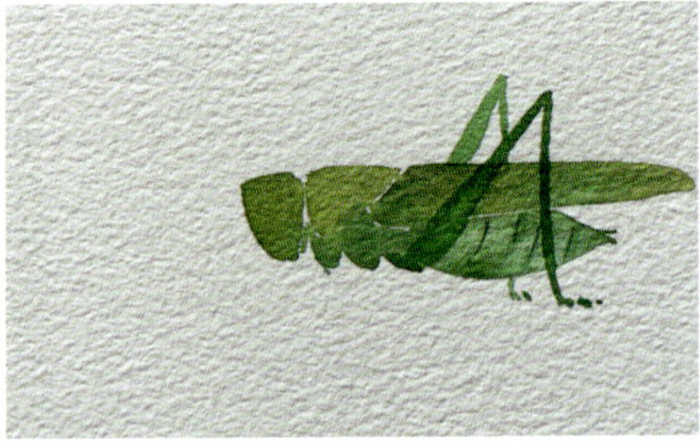

3. Using Mixture 1, add the insect's hind legs, drawing them over its body with transparency. Then wait for the watercolor to dry.

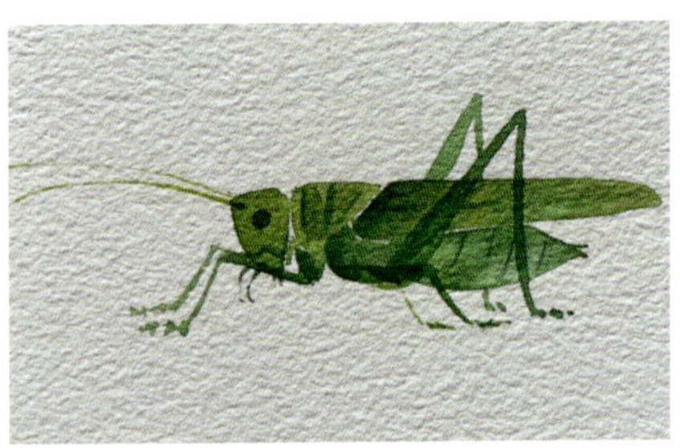

4. Using Mixture 1, paint the front legs, middle legs, and eye of the grasshopper. Using Mixture 2, draw the antennae.

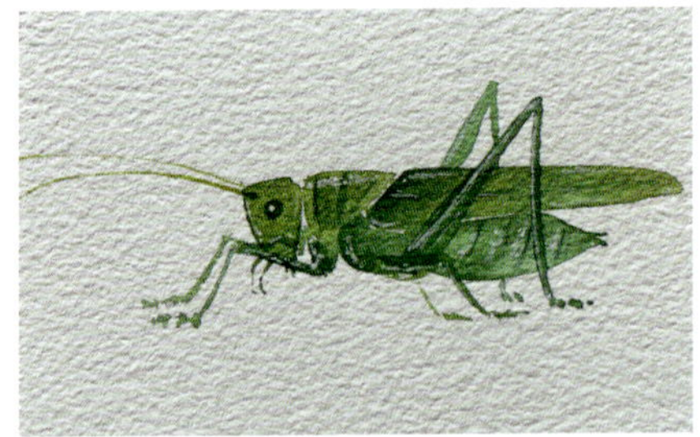

5. Add touches of light using a white gel ink pen and areas of shadow with the pigments remaining in the wells of your palette.

Beetle

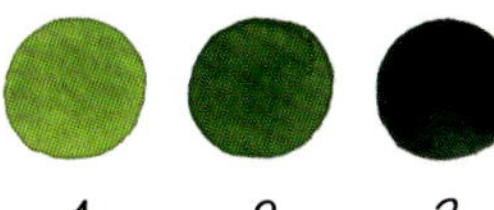

- **Mixture 1** - Indian yellow + phthalo green
- **Mixture 2** - Phthalo green + sap green
- **Mixture 3** - Sap green + Payne's gray + Prussian blue

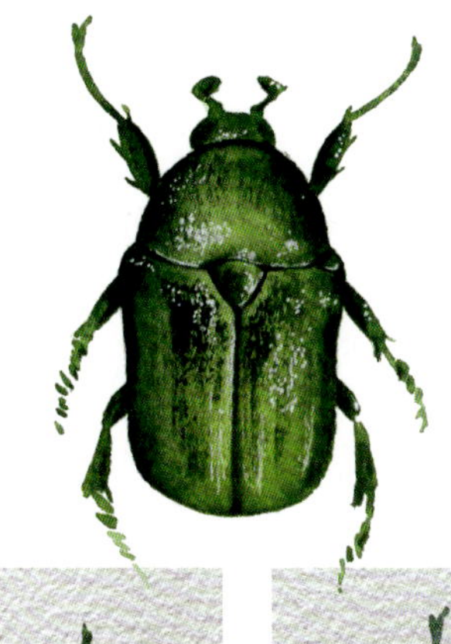

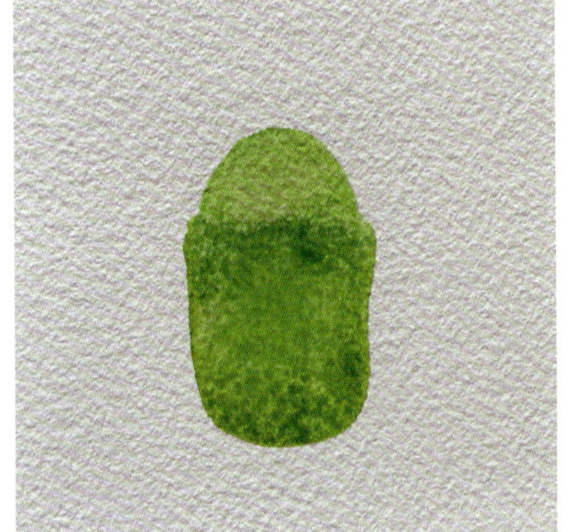

1. Using a small brush and Mixture 1, create the body of the beetle in two stages: the bottom then the top.

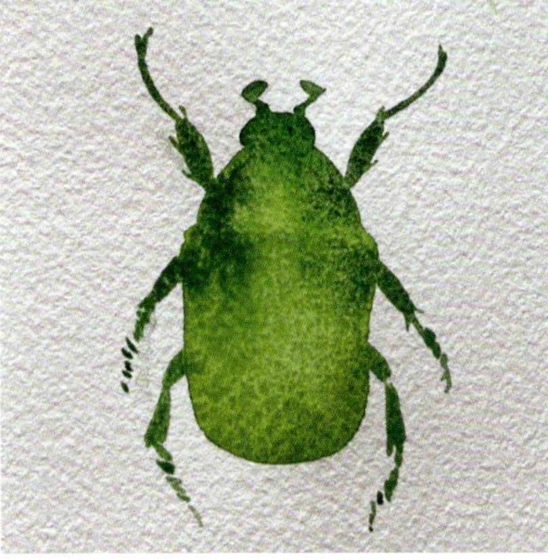

2. In the still-wet watercolor, paint the head then the legs using Mixtures 1 and 2. Place a little Mixture 2 on the edges of the shell to create volume. Don't be worried if the symmetries are not perfect.

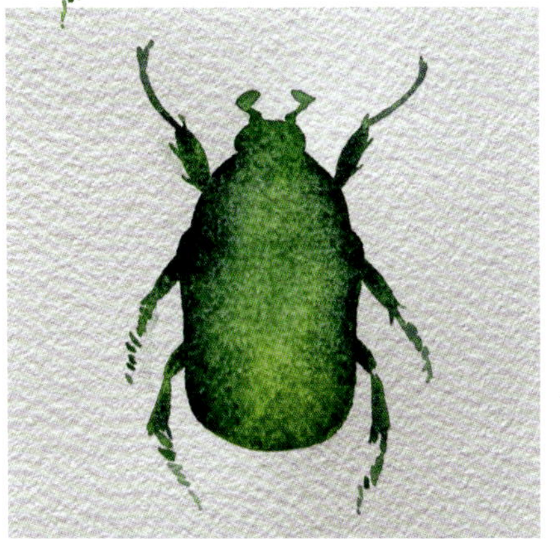

3. Add Mixture 3 to the edges of the shell to further accentuate its rounded shape. Be sure to leave Mixture 1 visible in the center. Wait for the watercolor to dry completely.

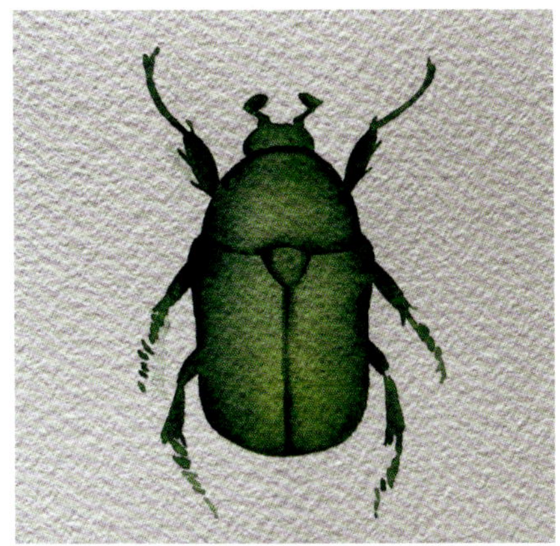

4. Using a fine brush and Mixture 3, draw the lines of the shell. You can add light shadows to make them slightly deeper.

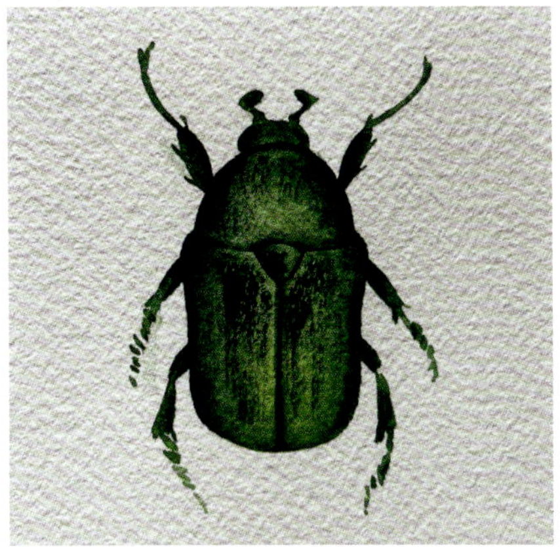

5. Using the same brush, pick up dark pigments from Mixture 3, removing as much water as possible. Gently rub the brush fibers over the rounded areas to give the beetle an uneven shine.

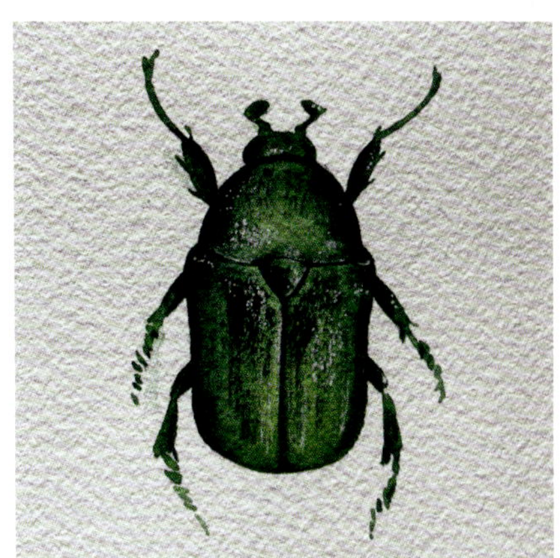

6. With a white gel ink pen, accentuate the shine of the shell by placing a few small dots and lines between the dark traces of the previous step.

Frog

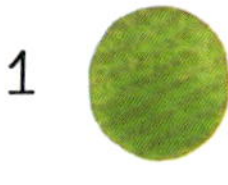

1 • **Mixture 1** - Indian yellow + cobalt green

2 • **Mixture 2** - Quinacridone gold + cobalt green + brown iron oxide

3 • **Mixture 3** - Buff titanium

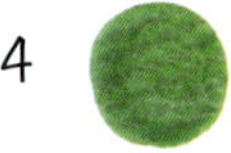

4 • **Mixture 4** - Cobalt green

5 • **Mixture 5** - Payne's gray + brown iron oxide

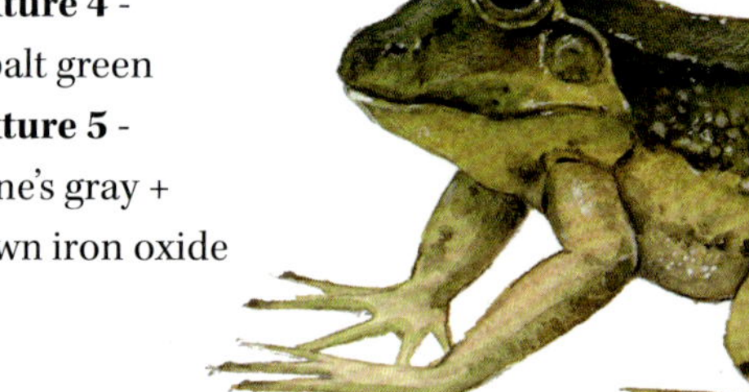

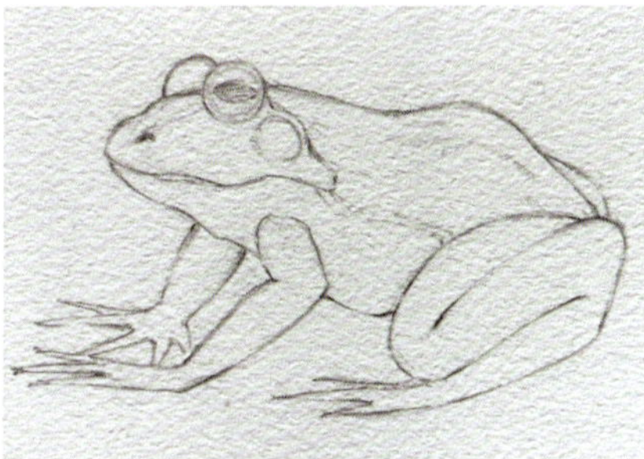

1. Using a pencil, sketch the shape of the frog.

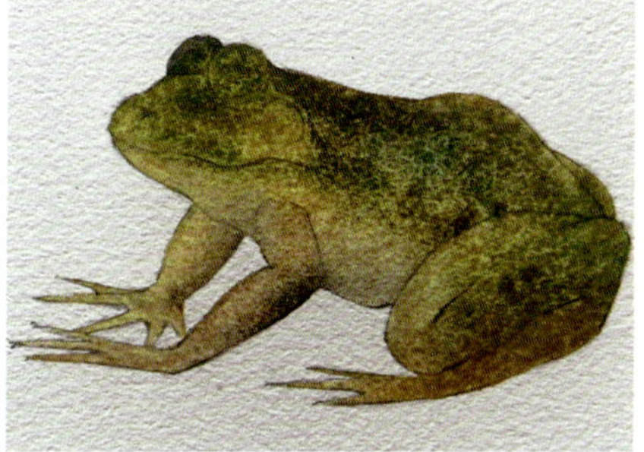

2. Using a soft brush, paint the frog's snout with Mixture 1, its back and lower hind legs with Mixture 2, and its belly with Mixture 3. Apply a few touches of Color 4 to the back, then let it dry.

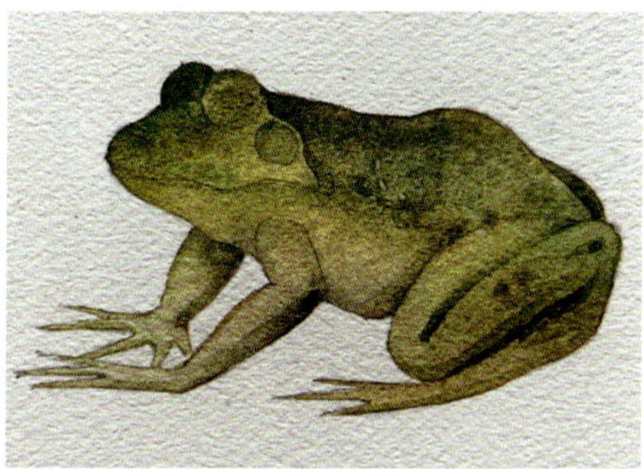

3. Using a small brush and Mixture 2, add some shadows to the farther parts of the body, and where there are bends and creases.

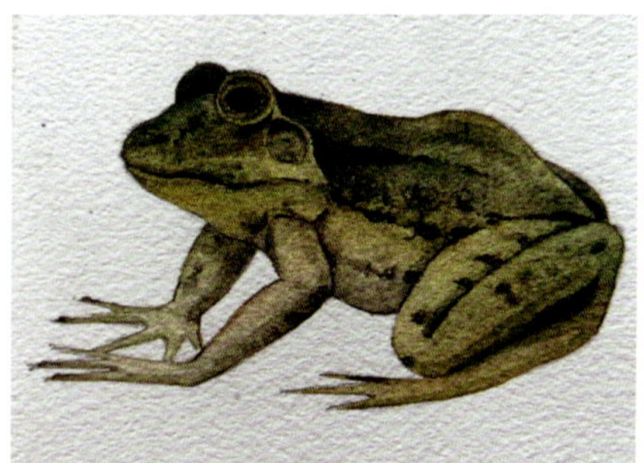

4. Using the same brush and Mixture 5, make small dark marks on the body, then darken the center of the eye.

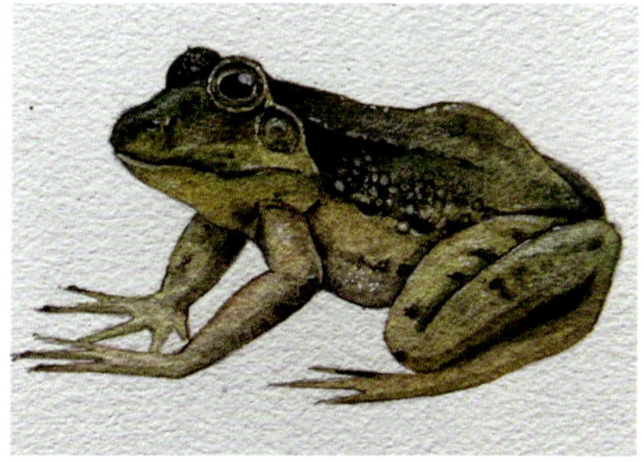

5. Add touches of light: use a white gel pen for very bright areas, and use a white colored pencil for softly lit areas.

> ## *Tip*
>
> *If the colors are duller than expected, know that you can definitely come back to your watercolor with a brighter color, because the colors will continue to show through thanks to the transparency of the paint. This frog is an example.*

Snail

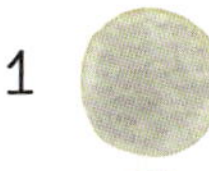 • **Mixture 1** - Indian yellow + lunar blue (diluted)

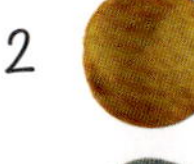 • **Mixture 2** - Indian yellow + caput mortuum

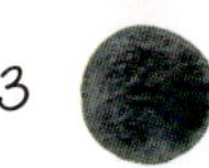 • **Mixture 3** - Lunar blue + caput mortuum (diluted)

 • **Mixture 4** - Buff titanium + shadow violet (diluted)

 • **Mixture 5** - Payne's gray + shadow violet

 • **Mixture 6** - Shadow violet + quinacridone gold (diluted)

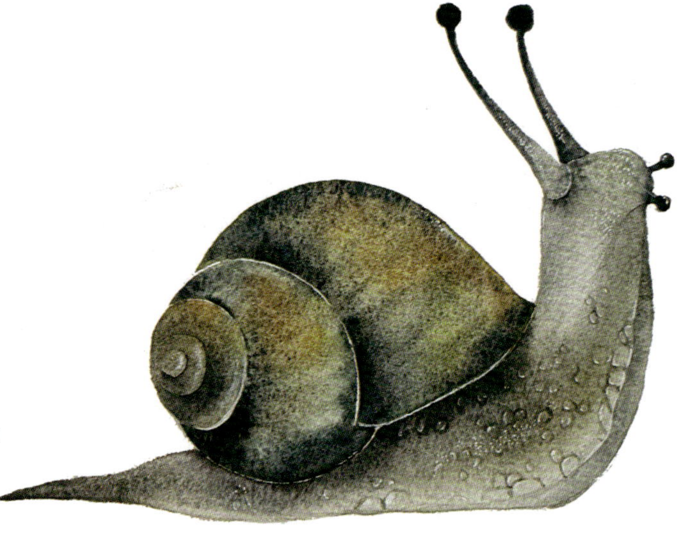

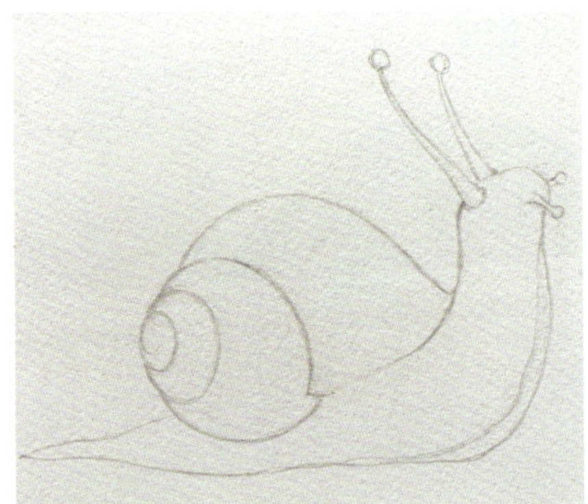

1. Using a pencil, sketch the shapes of the snail, starting with its shell. There is no need to make the lines too bold.

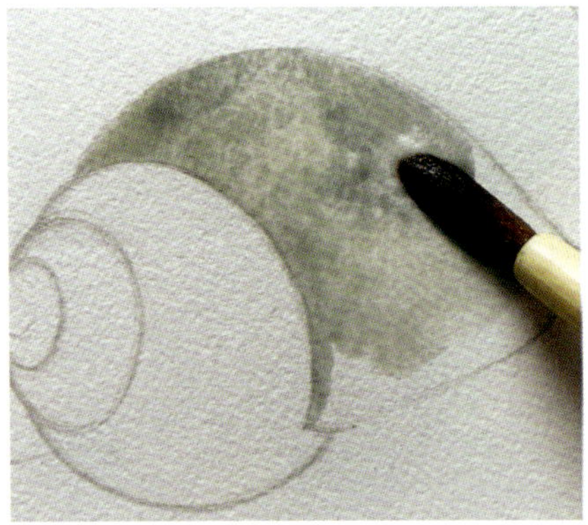

2. Using a soft brush and Mixture 1, paint the upper part of the shell.

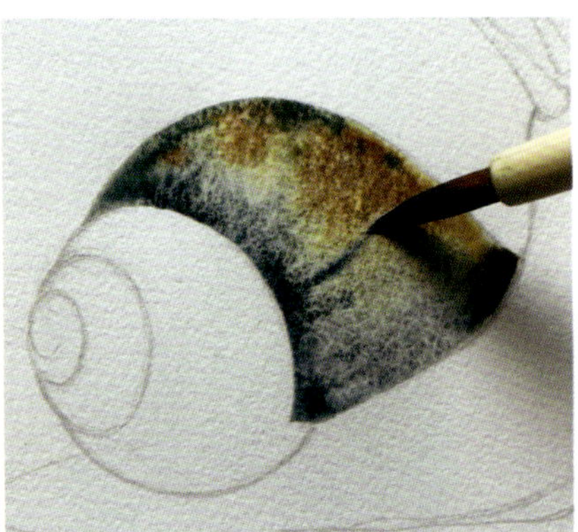

3. In the still-wet watercolor, add Mixture 2. Place Mixture 3 toward the edges of the painted area, then move the pigments using light strokes to form grooves and accentuate the rounded shape.

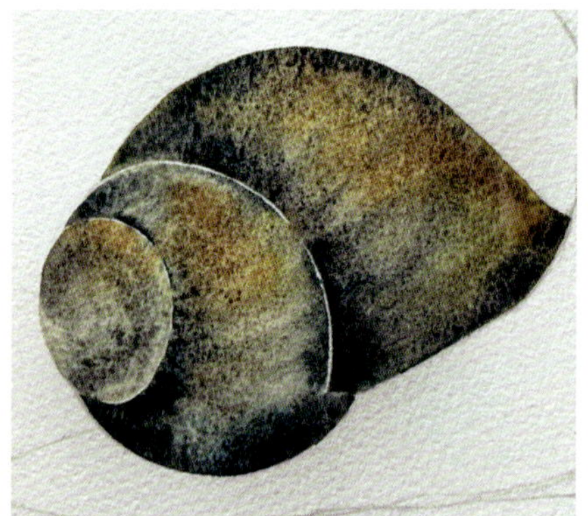

4. Repeat steps 2 and 3 across the entire shell, leaving a discreet line (showing the paper) between each part. It's okay if they touch a little; this can create interesting color blends.

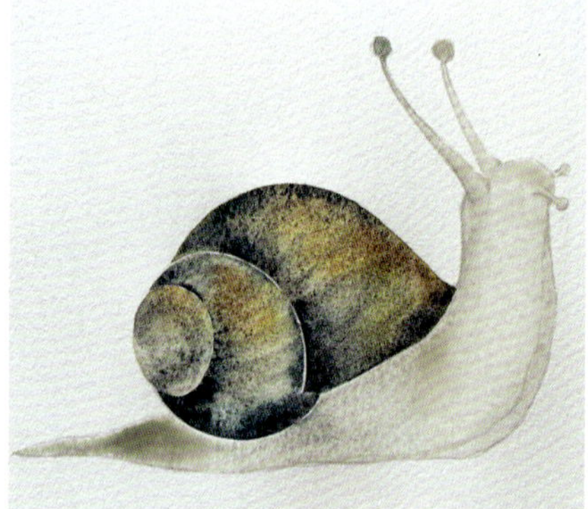

5. Using Mixture 4, paint the body of the snail. Take care not to touch the shell.

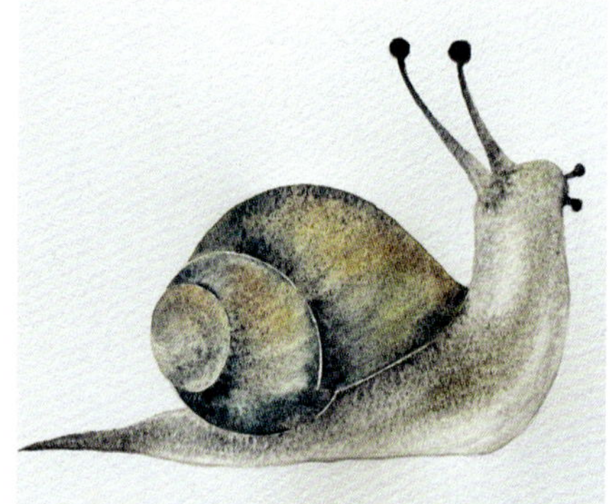

6. In the still-wet watercolor and with Mixture 5, add a few darker touches to emphasize the antennae and the end of the snail. Also add shadows to the part of the body under its shell. Let it dry.

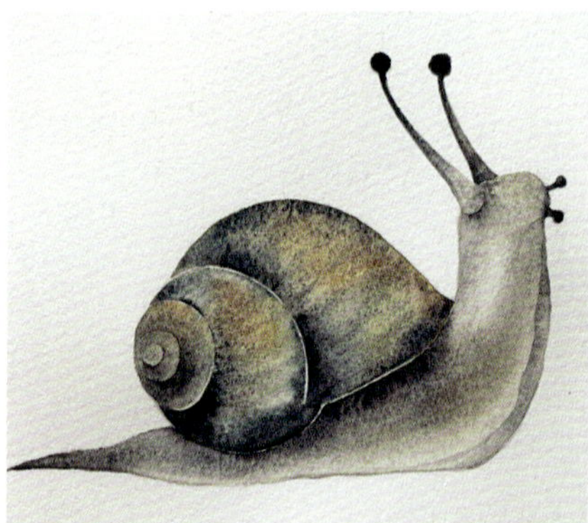

7. Accentuate the darker areas by applying Mixture 3 again, which you can combine with Mixture 5. Use a soft brush to apply the pigments, then using a clean brush, gently blend the color until it disappears. Let it dry.

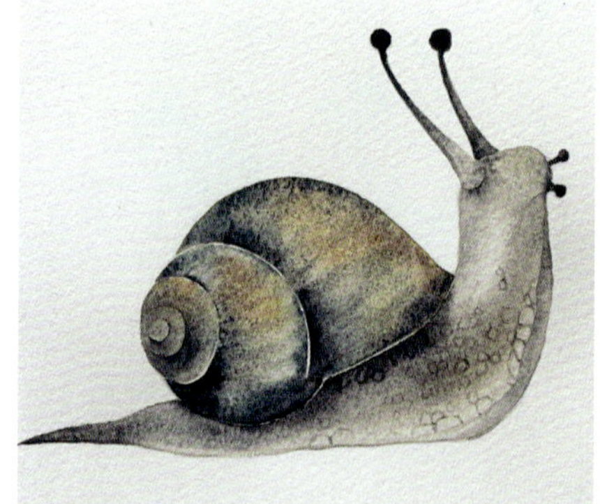

8. Using a small brush and Mixture 6, give a grainy texture to certain parts of the snail's body.

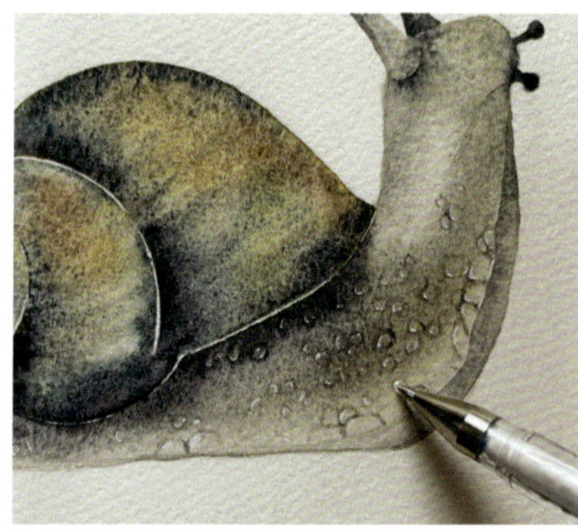

9. Finally, add some light touches with a white gel ink pen.

Take Time to Experiment

We'll discuss how to create scenes later in the book. However, don't let that stop you from adding to your practice watercolor paintings! For example, when I made the snail in my sketchbook, I then added a little strip of grass and mushrooms next to it.

This practice lets you experiment with colors and contrasts without feeling pressure to make it "perfect." For instance, I picked up on some of blue-greens and browns that were created in the snail and really emphasized them in the foliage. The bold grass contrasts nicely with the snail and the mushroom caps, creating balance to this long image. You never know how it will turn out until you try it.

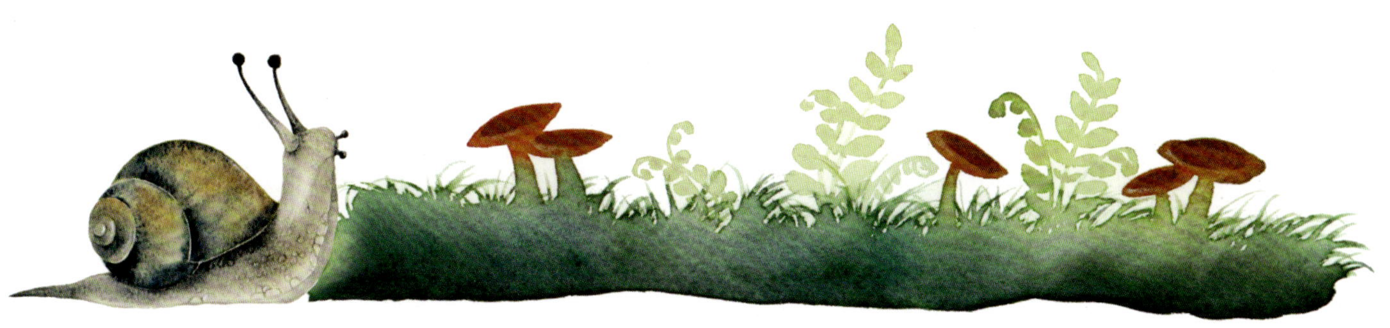

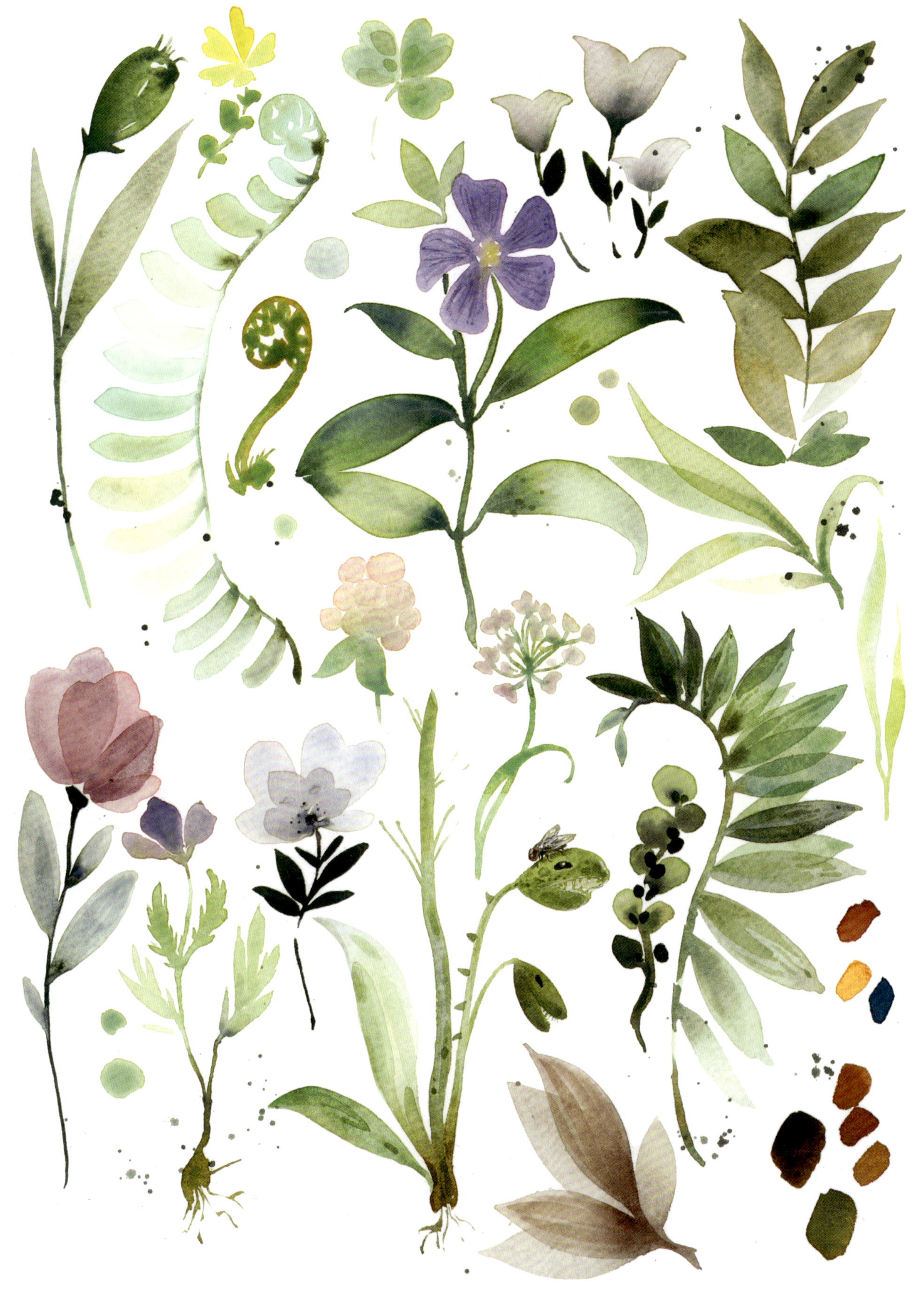

Staging Forest Flowers

Flowers are among my favorite subjects because they are pleasant to paint in watercolor and easy to include in forest scenes, like this bindweed that blends perfectly with the transparent vegetation.

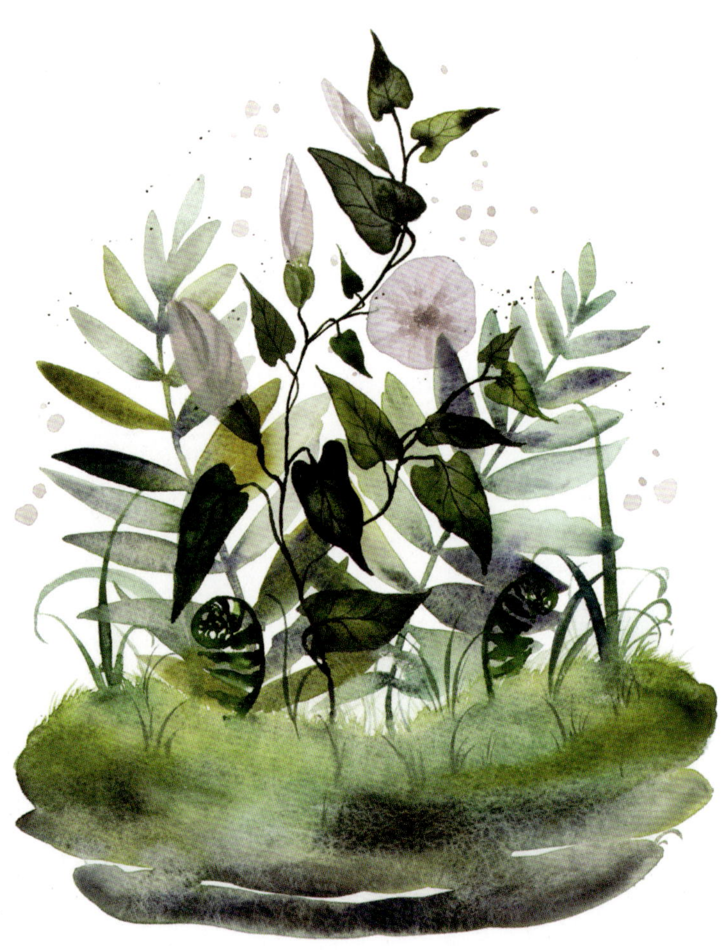

Taking Advantage of Simple Shapes

Wildflowers are often small, discreet, and elegant. They have adapted to forest conditions: low light, high humidity, and often dense vegetation that leaves little room for growth. Essential to the forest's ecosystem and biodiversity, woodland flowers provide food for a large number of pollinating insects and animals thanks to the nectar and seeds they produce.

As you can see, wildflowers are simpler than others that grow in gardens. This is an advantage because you don't need to draw them before painting, which will allow you to maintain your artistic spontaneity. To do this, practice by playing with the flexibility of your brush.

When painting these types of flowers, I mainly focus on the colors, the shape of the petals and leaves, and the features that allow them to be identified.

Painting White Flowers

White flowers are particularly tricky to paint in watercolor because it requires anticipating the placement of white space, especially when the background is dark. In this case, making a sketch will be useful to avoid making mistakes when applying the pigments, as in the step-by-step "Snowdrop Undergrowth" on page 97.

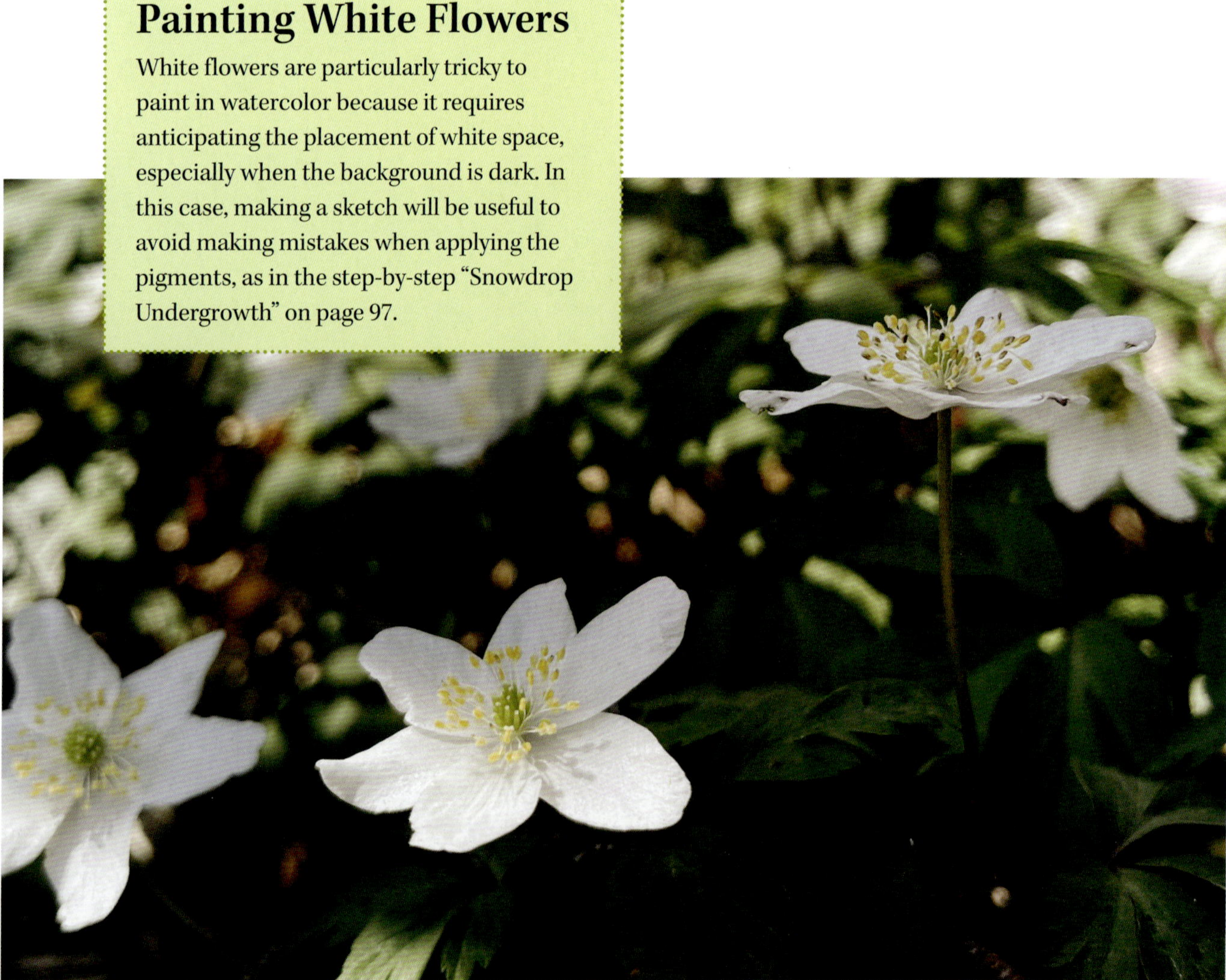

Taking Liberties

When I paint a forest environment, I like to feature different species of very real plants onto the paper. However, in certain forest scenes, it is sometimes difficult to be absolutely faithful to the reference. Indeed, depending on the color I want to use or the space available, I am not always able to respect the characteristics that identity of the plant. This is why I sometimes allow myself to paint according to my imagination, whether it be mushrooms, trees, or flowers. I try not to get stuck on a detail and instead focus on the overall form of my illustration.

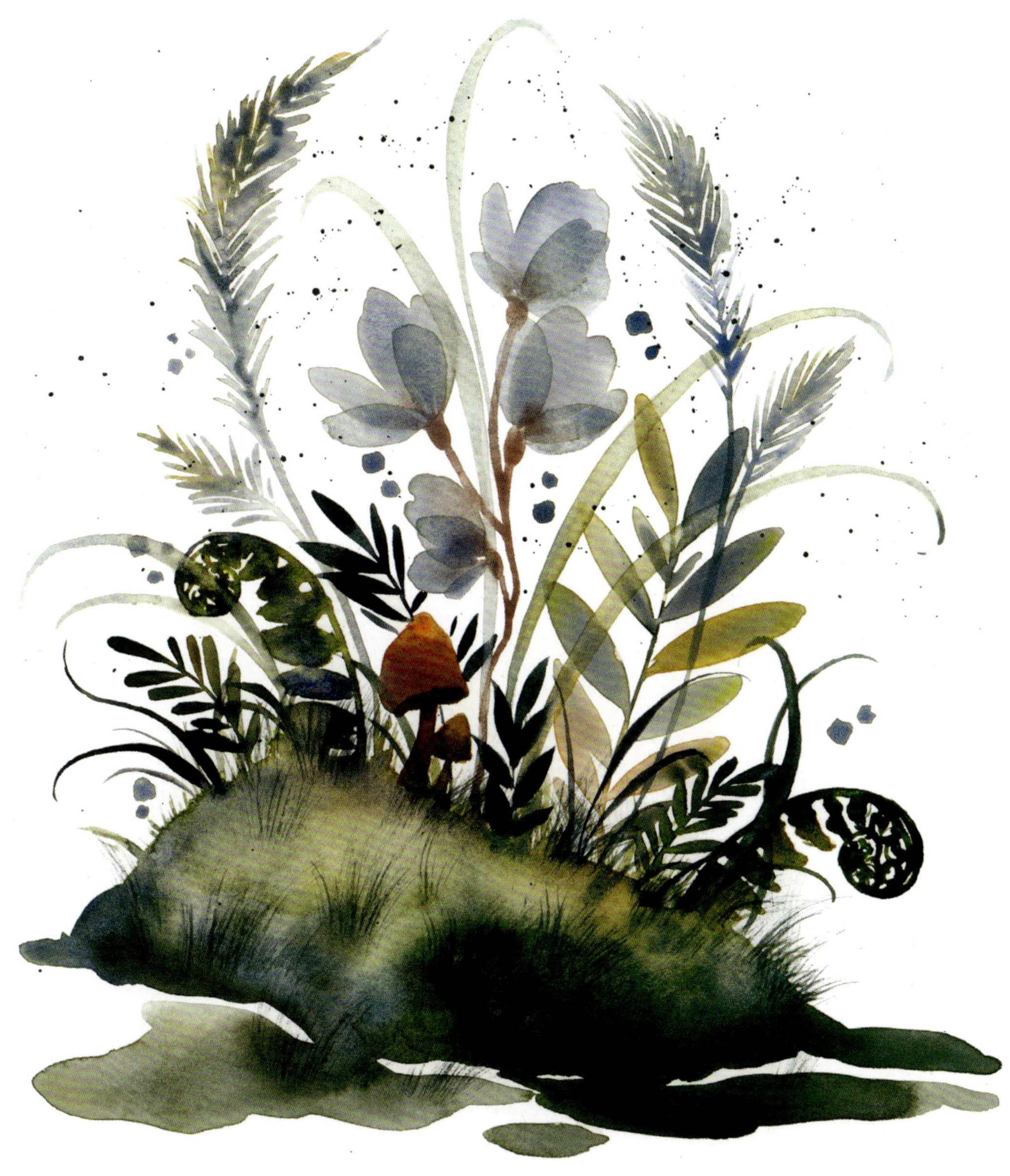

Practice

FORGET-ME-NOT FLOWERBED

I particularly like the simplicity of forget-me-nots. They often appear in numerous clusters of small blue flowers, making them easy to include in a composition. Their color instantly brightens a painting.

1 • **Mixture 1** - Indian yellow + white gouache

2 • **Mixture 2** - Ultramarine blue

3 • **Mixture 3** - Ultramarine blue + sap green + Payne's gray

4 • **Mixture 4** - Indian yellow + sap green

5 • **Mixture 5** - Quinacridone gold + sap green

6 • **Mixture 6** - Mars black + tundra blue (diluted)

7 • **Mixture 7** - Ultramarine blue + phthalo green (diluted)

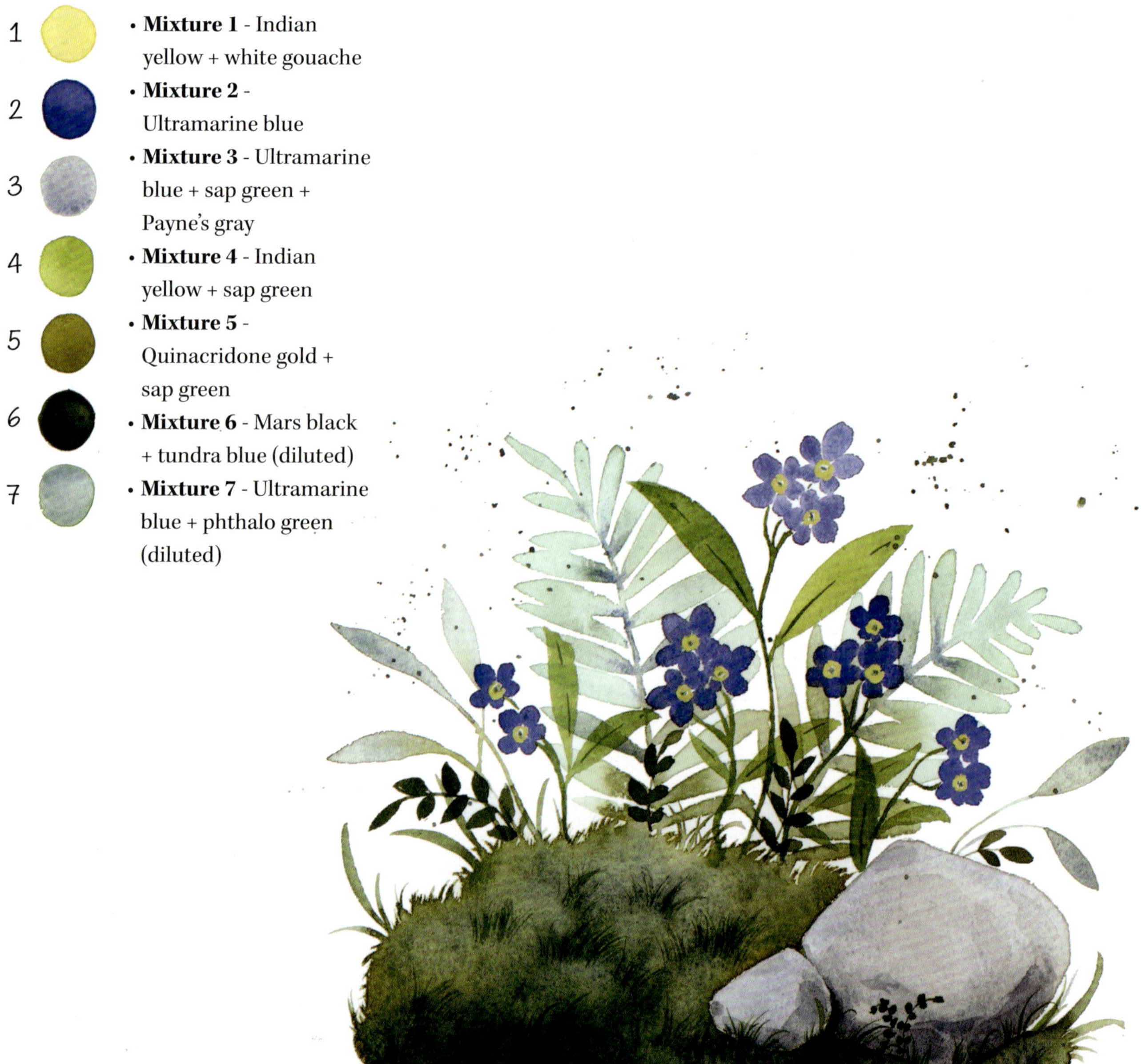

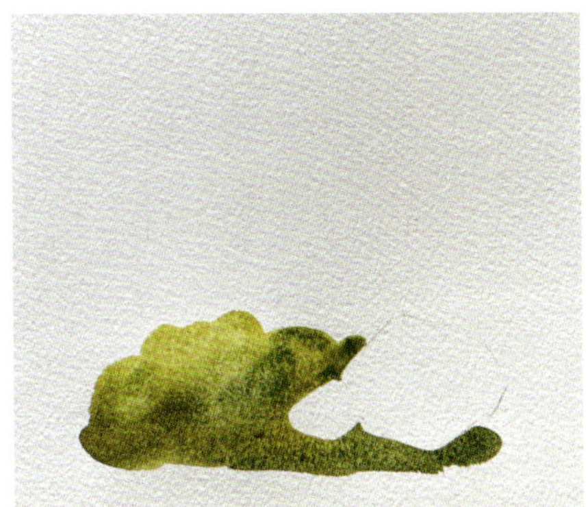

1. Using a pencil, draw two small rock shapes, which should remain blank for now. Then, using a round brush and Mixtures 4 and 5, add the grass around them.

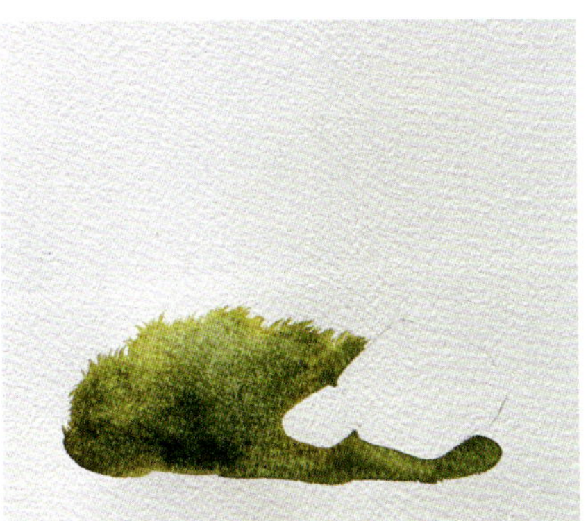

2. In the still-wet watercolor, add blades of grass using a tapered or very fine brush, stretching the pigments already placed on the paper.

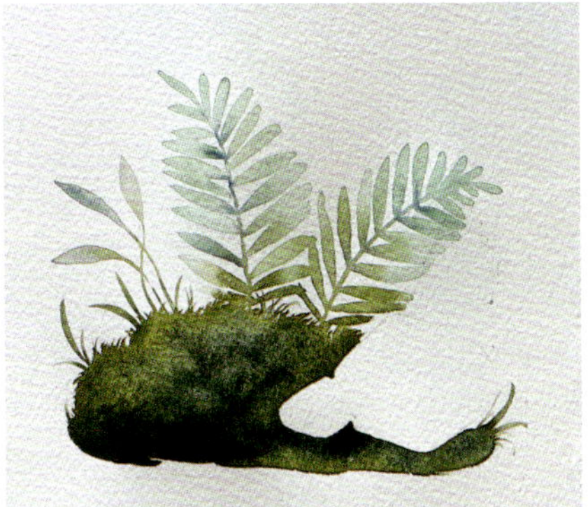

3. In the still-wet watercolor and with Mixture 6, place darker pigments in the grass to create contrast. Using a fine, round brush and Mixtures 4 and 7, create ferns and small, light-colored plants on top of the grass. Let it dry.

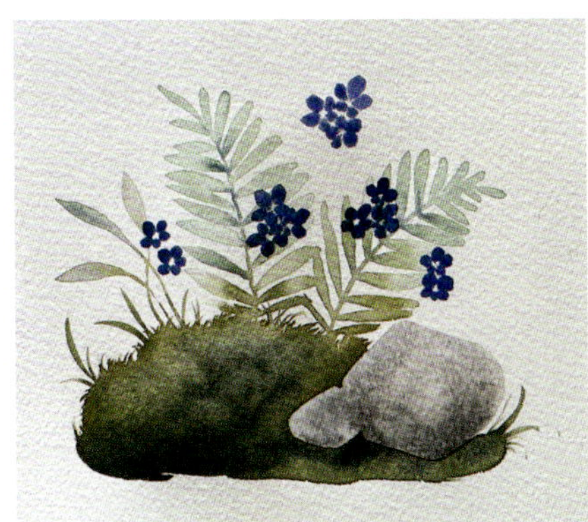

4. With Mixture 2, place small bunches of forget-me-nots in different places, over the vegetation already in place. With Mixture 3, fill the rocks. Wait for the watercolor to dry completely.

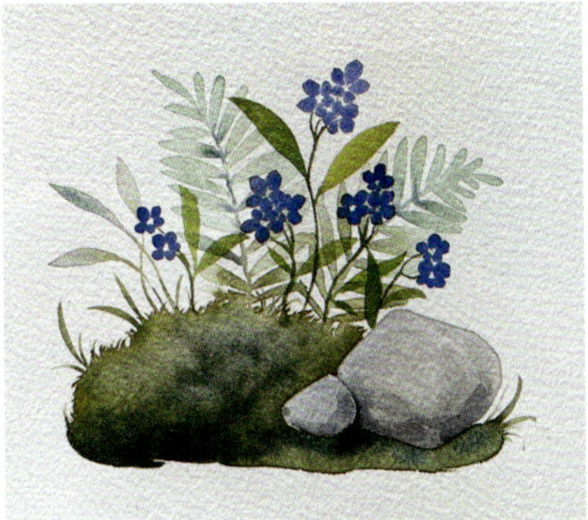

5. Using a fine brush and Mixtures 4 and 5, draw the stems of the flowers as well as their leaves. Add texture to the rocks by applying another layer of Mixture 3. Let it dry.

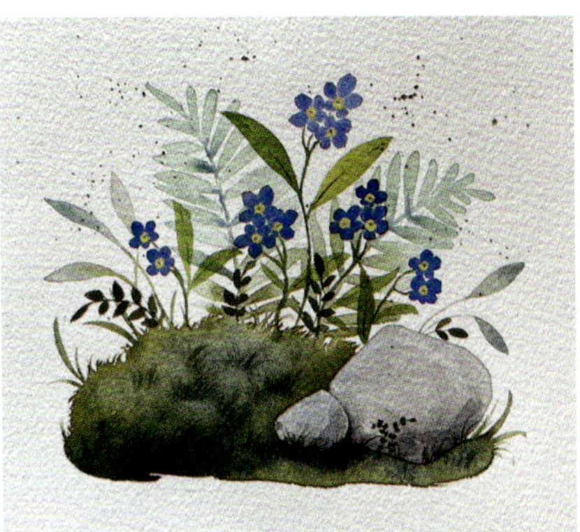

6. With Mixture 6, accentuate the impression of depth by adding plants. With Mixture 1, complete the centers of the forget-me-nots. You can add a few splashes of paint.

LESSER CELANDINE ON ROCKS

Here, I found it interesting to combine the hardness of the rock and the luminous yellow of the lesser celandine, two elements that evoke different reactions in the viewer. Together, they balance each other and create a harmonious scene.

1. • **Mixture 1** - Tundra blue + yellow ochre + Mars black
2. • **Mixture 2** - Sap green + ultramarine blue + lamp black
3. • **Mixture 3** - Sap green
   • **Mixture 4** - Mars black + tundra blue
4. • **Mixture 5** - Indian yellow + quinacridone gold
5.

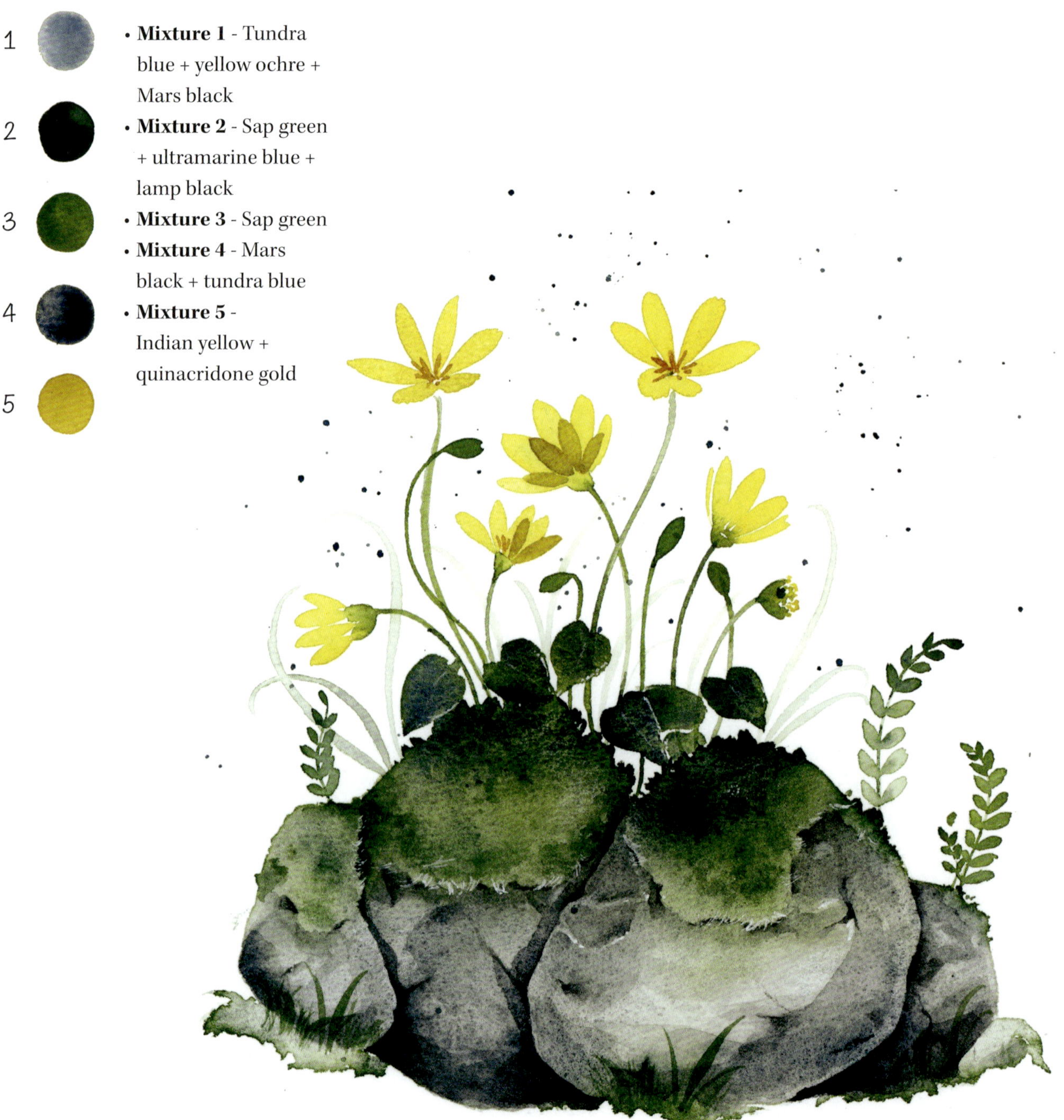

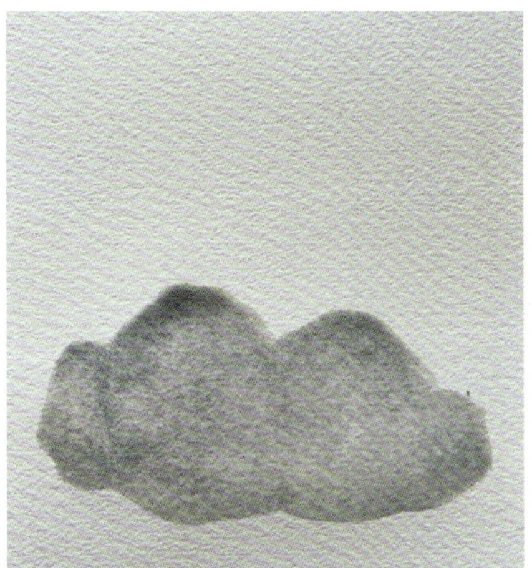

1. Using a soft brush and Mixture 1, paint the rocks.

2. Add moss to the rocks and ground using the same brush and Mixtures 2 and 3.

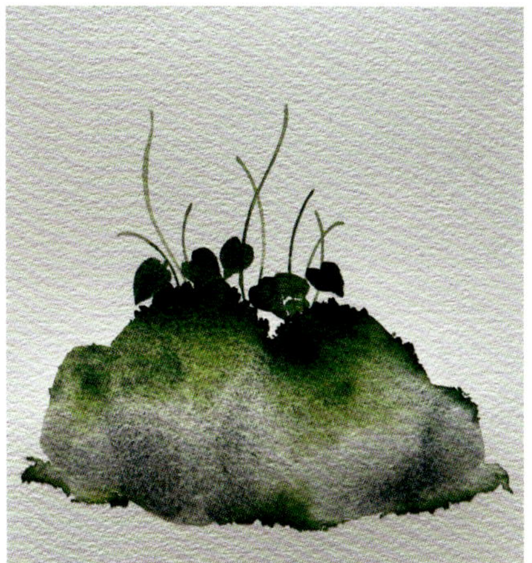

3. Using the still-wet watercolor and Mixtures 2 and 3, create the lesser celandine stems with leaves at their base. Shade the rocks using Mixture 4 and then let them dry.

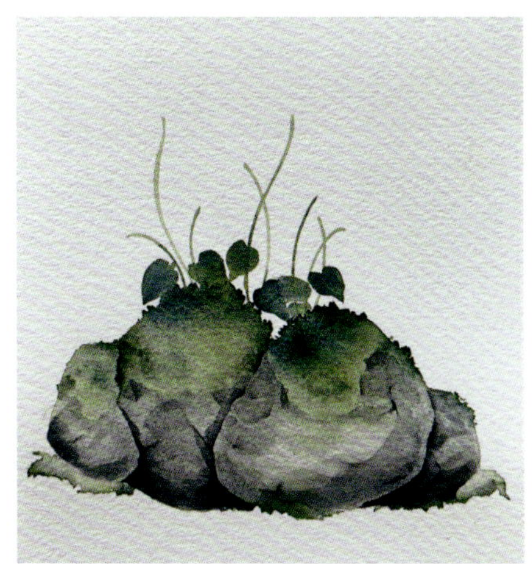

4. Create depth by accentuating the cracks and separation between the rocks using a fine, precise brush and Mixture 4. Give them a mineral appearance by adding more or less intense pigments here and there. Do the same for the moss.

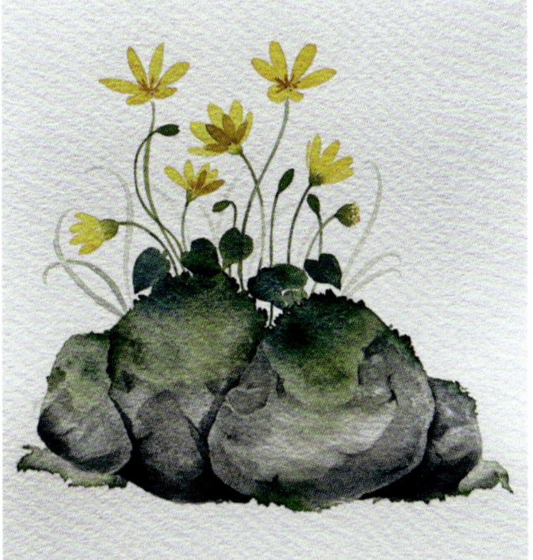

5. Add the lesser celandine flowers to the tops of the stems using Mixture 5. Layer the petals with Mixture 1. Add a few blades of grass and small ferns in different places throughout the watercolor using Mixtures 2 and 3. Let it dry.

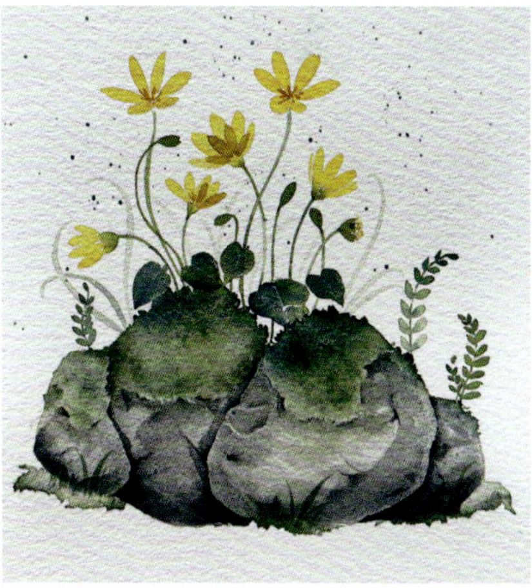

6. Use a white gel pen to highlight some of the leaves or the edges of the moss.

FLOWERING STUMP

In this forest scene, I worked on the realism of the moss and wood because I find it very fun to create. On the other hand, to avoid overloading my watercolor, I simplified certain elements like the flowers and leaves.

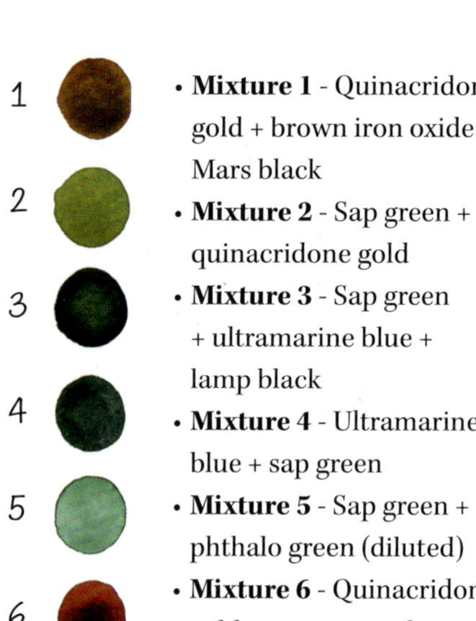

1. • **Mixture 1** - Quinacridone gold + brown iron oxide + Mars black
2. • **Mixture 2** - Sap green + quinacridone gold
3. • **Mixture 3** - Sap green + ultramarine blue + lamp black
4. • **Mixture 4** - Ultramarine blue + sap green
5. • **Mixture 5** - Sap green + phthalo green (diluted)
6. • **Mixture 6** - Quinacridone gold + permanent brown + alizarin crimson
7. • **Mixture 7** - Ultramarine blue + permanent rose
8. • **Mixture 8** - Mars black

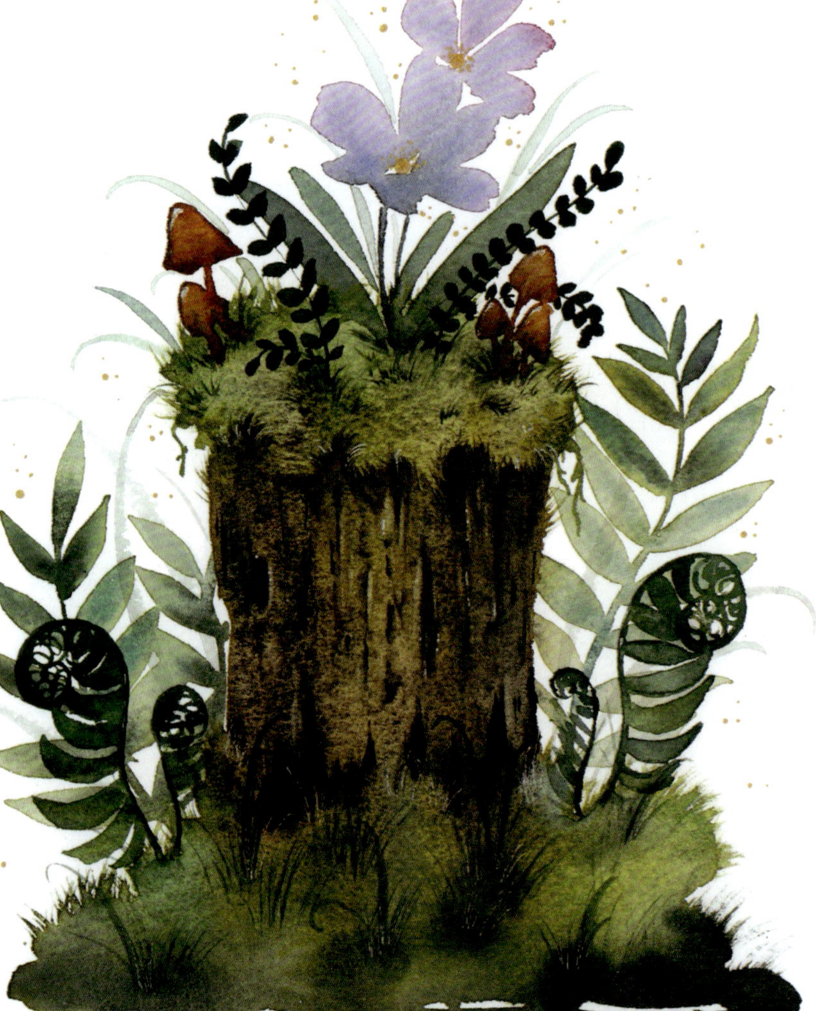

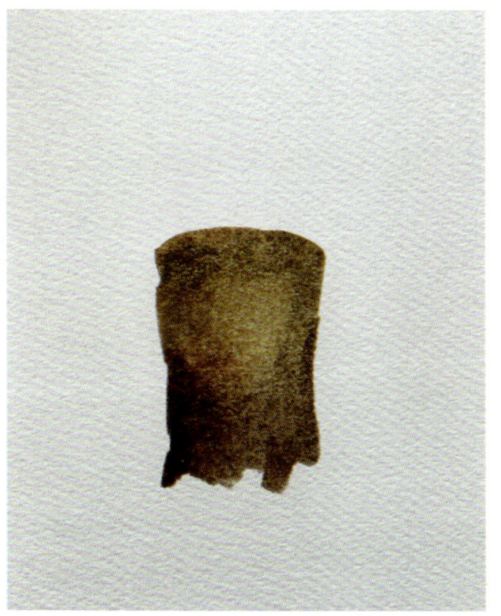

1. Using a soft brush and Mixture 1, paint the tree stump.

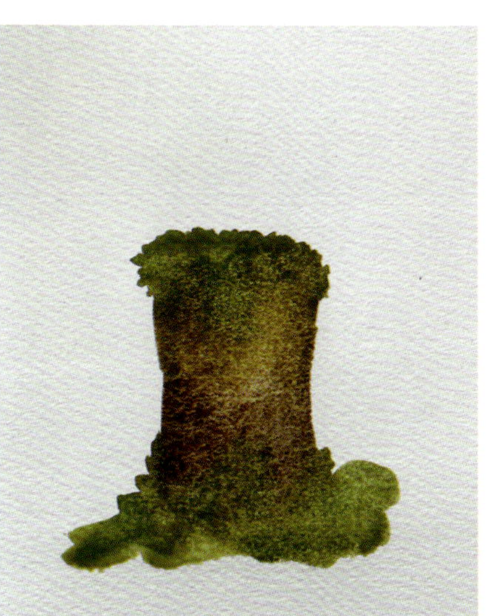

2. Using the same brush and Mixture 2, add moss above and below the stump.

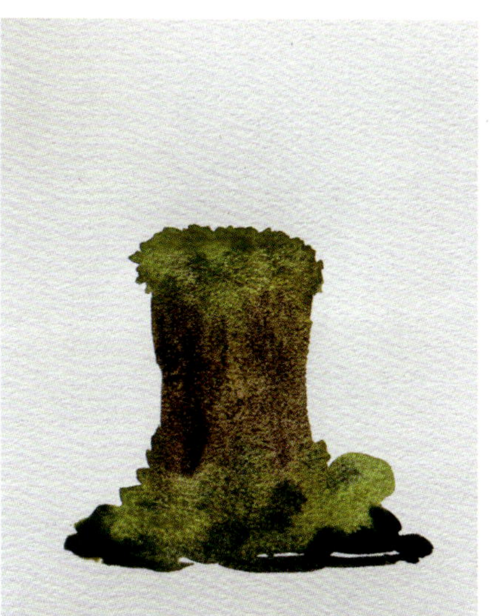

3. Place Mixture 3 on the moss close to the ground to give it contrast. With Mixture 1, shape the stump further by painting a few grooves.

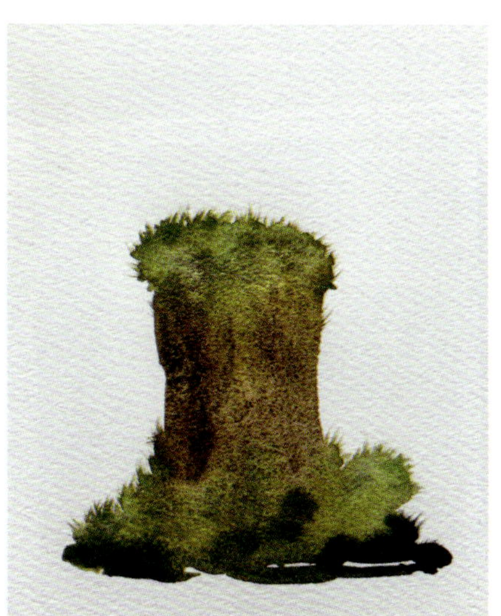

4. In the still-wet watercolor, add blades of grass to the moss by stretching the pigments already placed on the paper using a very fine or tapered brush.

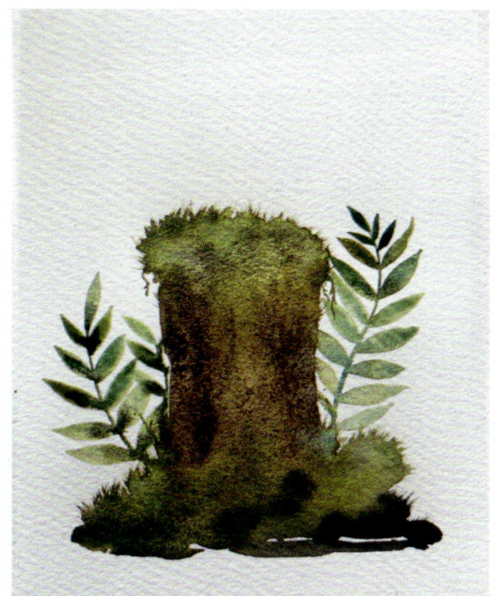

5. Using a fine brush, add some foliage to the right and left of the stump, alternating between Mixtures 2, 3, 4, and 5 to add motion. Let it dry.

Note

Step 5 can be done while the watercolor is still wet, but if you notice the stump starting to dry, then wait until it is completely dry to avoid any possible lines.

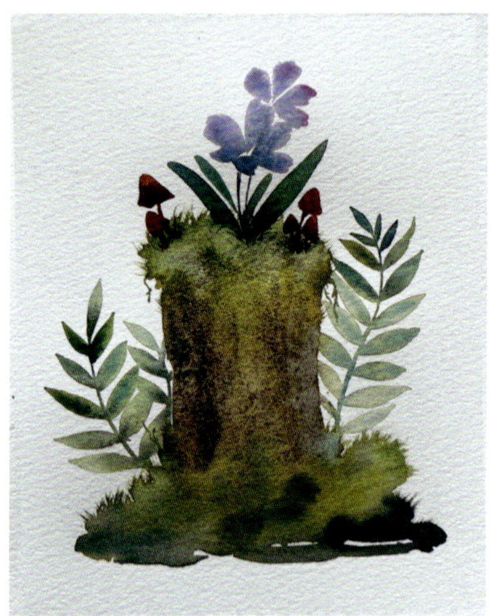 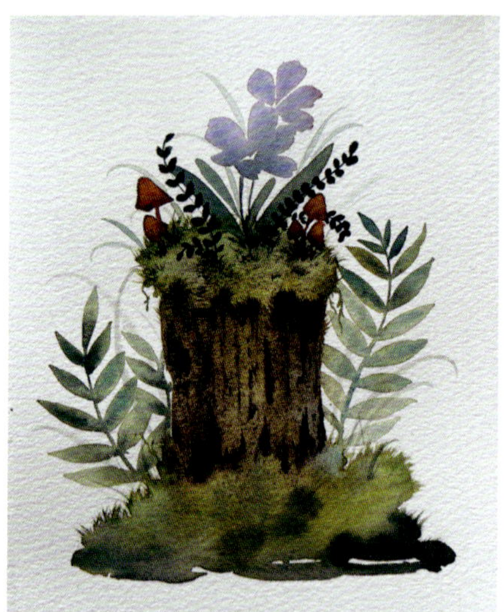 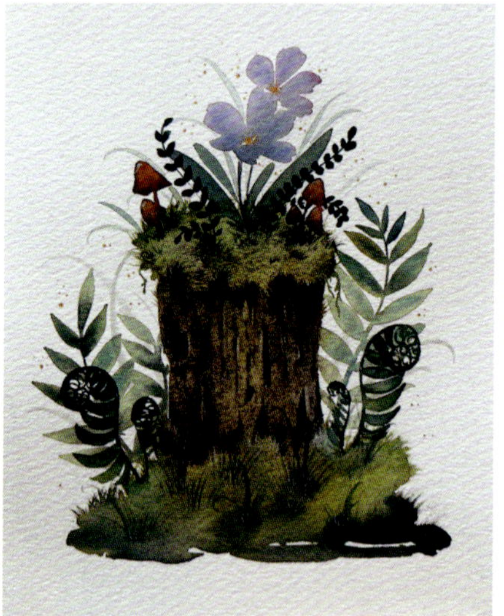

6. Add the mushrooms with Mixture 6, the purple flowers with Mixture 7, and the leaves with Mixture 3. Wait for the watercolor to dry.

7. Using a fine brush and very diluted Mixture 5, draw long blades of grass at the base of the ferns. You can do the same around the flowers and mushrooms. Also add small, very dark leaves to the top of the stump with Mixture 3.

8. Using Mixture 3, place young ferns in front of the foliage, still visible through the transparency. Also add grass to the ground with a fine brush. With a gold gel ink pen, detail the center of the flowers and add dots around your creation.

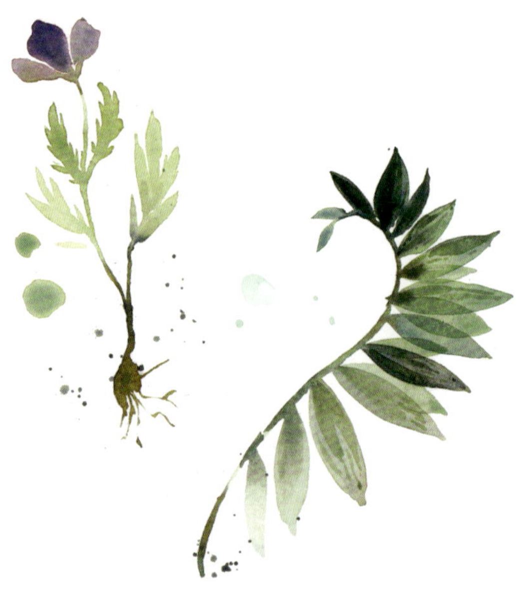

SNOWDROP UNDERGROWTH

To paint these snowdrops, I chose to use masking fluid, which is very useful for freely creating the landscape background while preserving the white of the flowers.

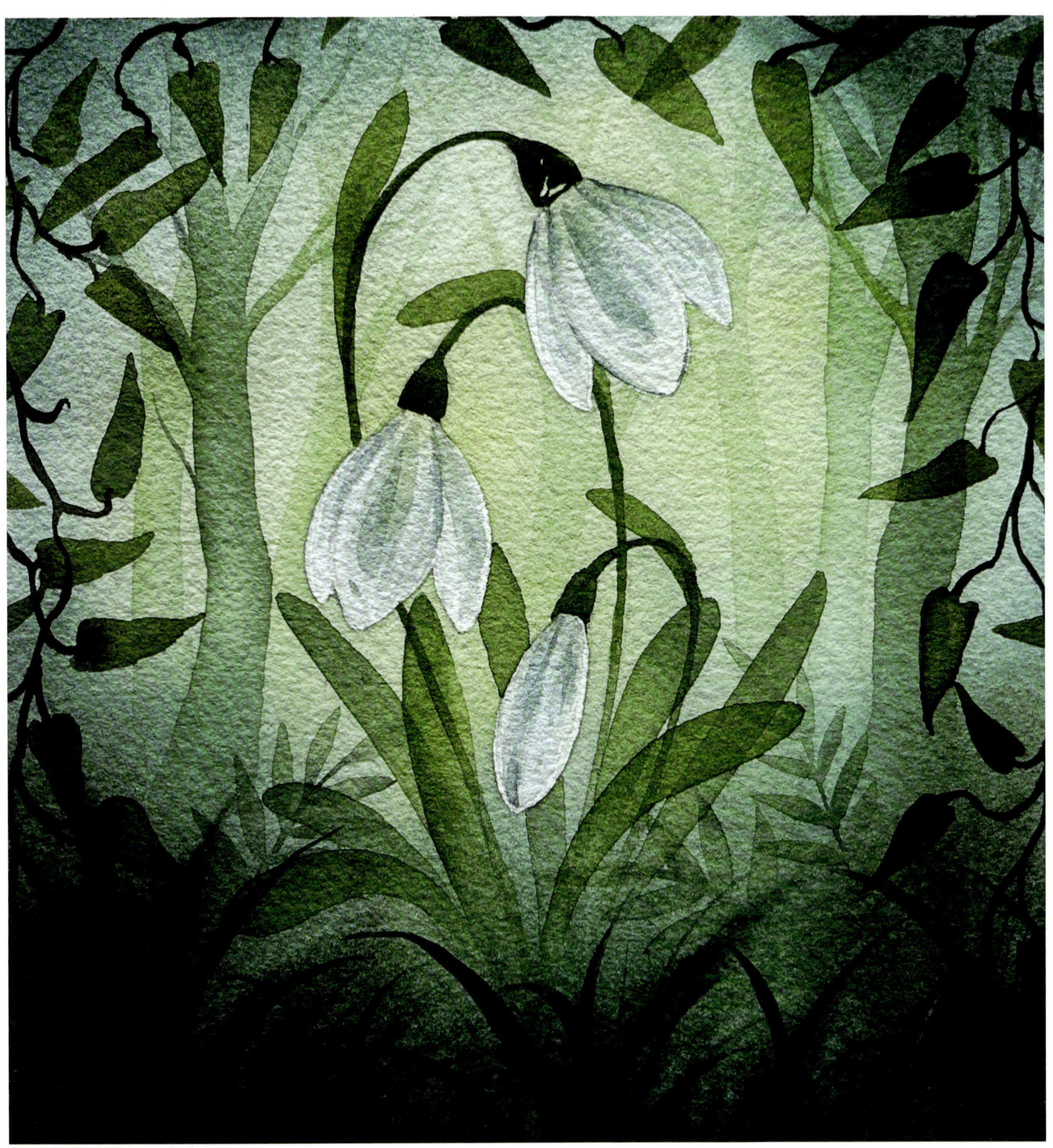

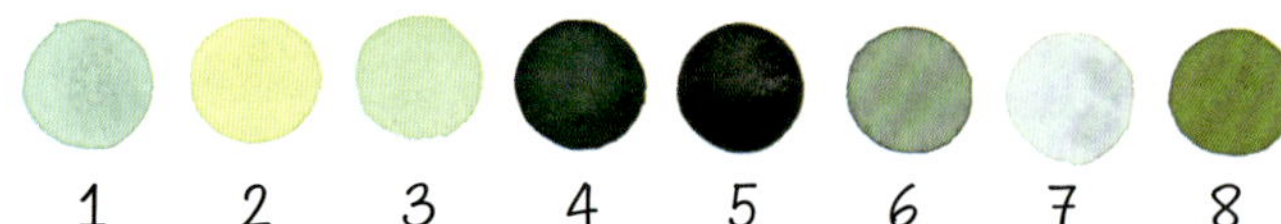

- **Mixture 1** - Phthalo green (diluted)
- **Mixture 2** - Indian yellow (diluted)
- **Mixture 3** - Phthalo green + Indian yellow (diluted)

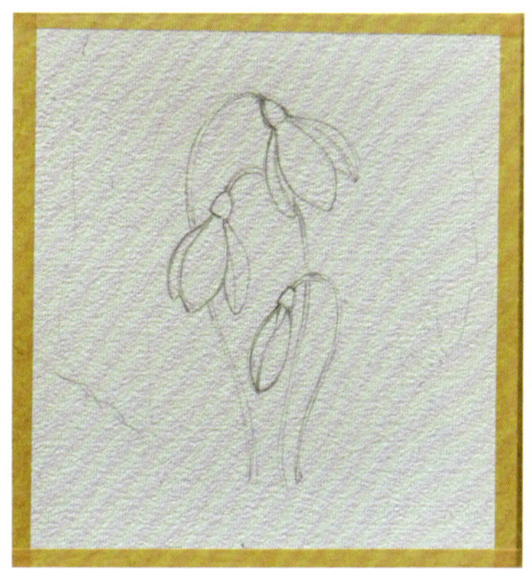

1. Mark out the area to be painted using painter's tape, then draw your snowdrops using a pencil.

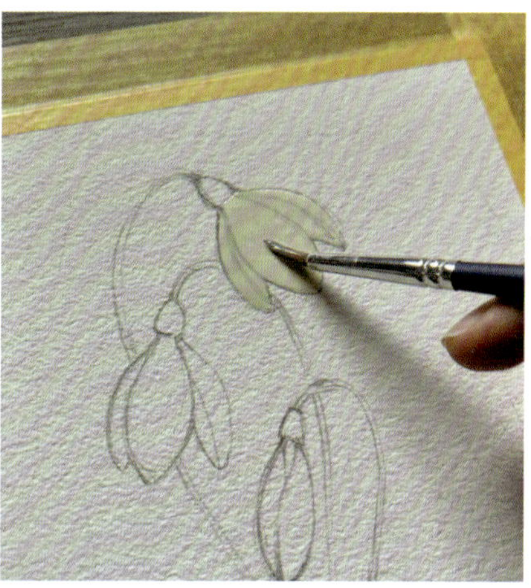

2. Using a slightly damp brush, apply masking fluid to the snowdrop petals, then wait for it to dry completely.

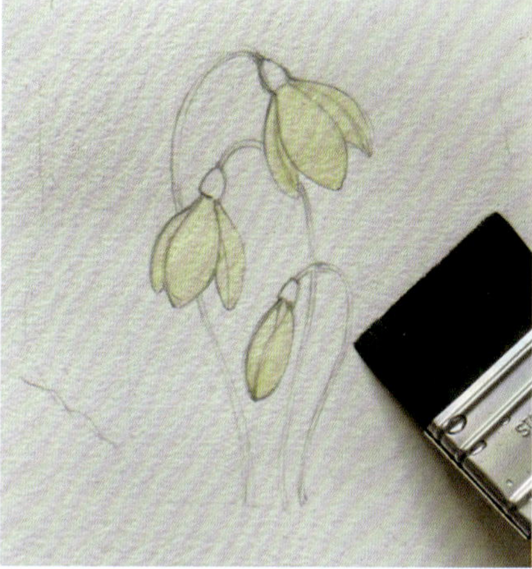

3. Using a large flat brush loaded with water, dampen the entire inside of your frame.

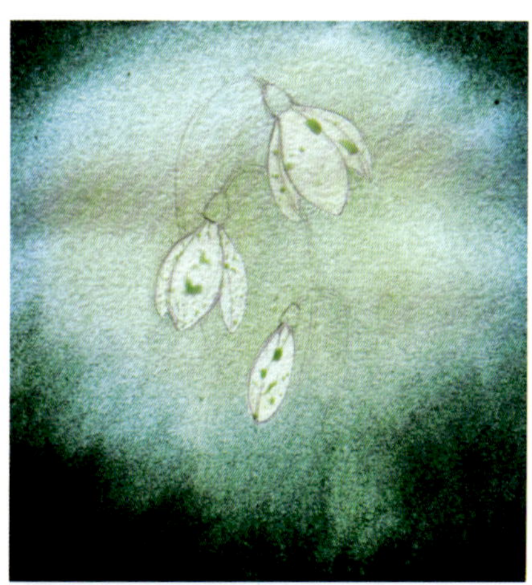

4. Place Mixtures 1, 2, and 3 in the center, then 4 and 5 on the edges, emphasizing Mixture 5 more on the bottom of the watercolor.

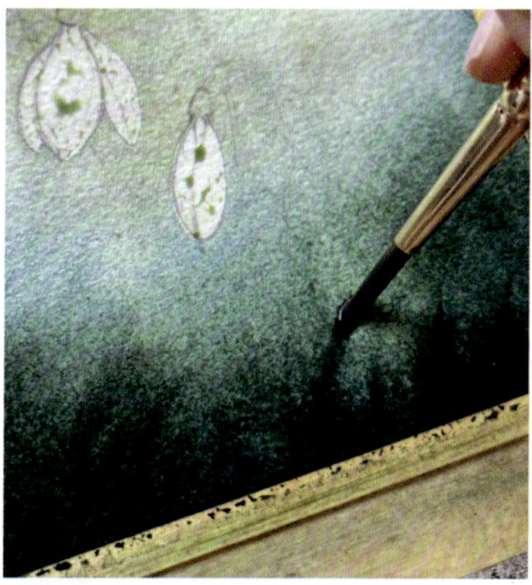

5. In the still-wet watercolor and with a fine, precise brush, draw the first blades of grass using Mixture 5, highly concentrated in pigments. Let it dry.

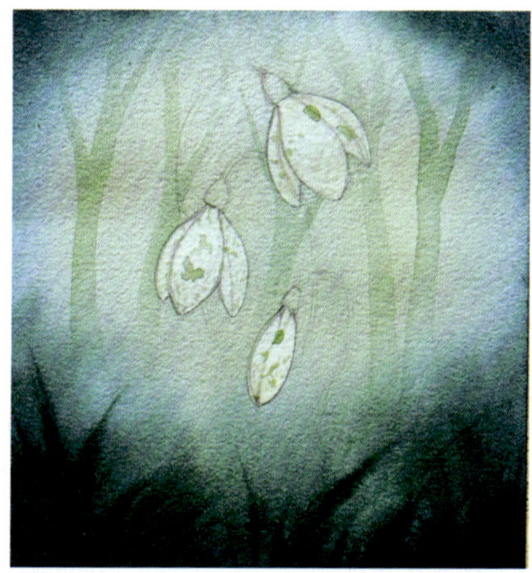

6. Using a precise brush and Mixture 3, draw very light tree shapes. Using a tissue, dab the bottom of the trunk to make it disappear and give the impression of mist. Let it dry.

- **Mixture 4** - Indian yellow + Prussian blue
- **Mixture 5** - Indian yellow + Prussian blue + Payne's gray
- **Mixture 6** - Indian yellow + Prussian blue + Payne's gray (diluted)
- **Mixture 7** - Ultramarine blue + Indian yellow + Payne's gray (diluted)
- **Mixture 8** - Indian yellow + sap green

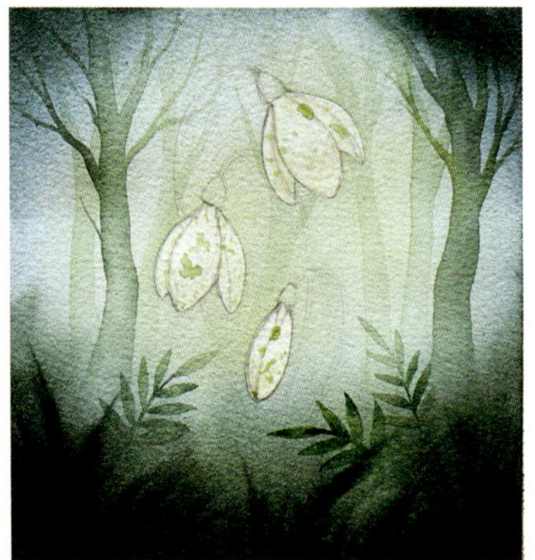

7. Using Mixture 6, draw darker trees in the middle ground. With a clean, damp brush, push the pigments from the trunk upward to soften the pigments at the base of the tree. Use a tissue if necessary. Wait for the watercolor to dry.

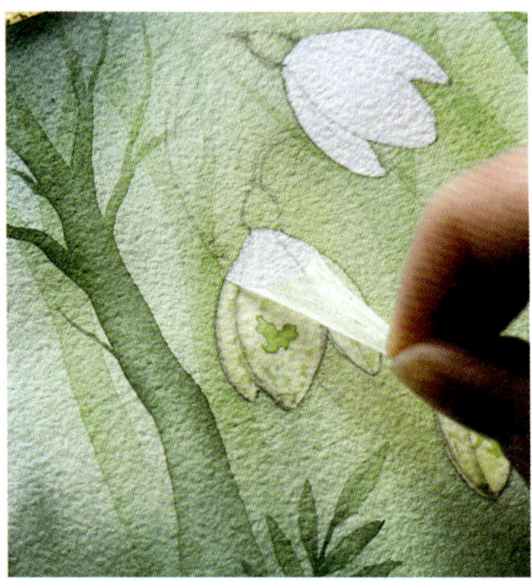

8. Remove the masking fluid by gently rubbing with your finger.

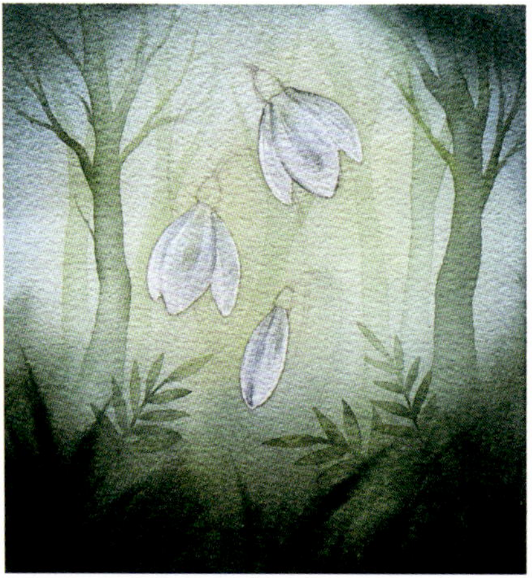

9. Using Mixture 7, paint light shadows on the petals.

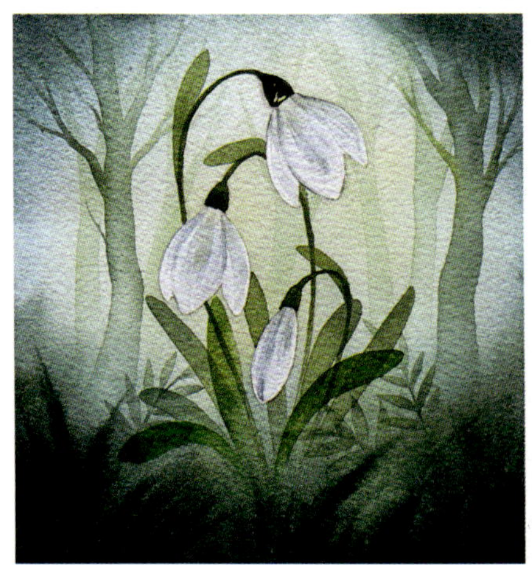

10. Using a precise brush and Mixture 8, paint the stems and leaves of the flowers. As with the trees, soften with a tissue or a clean, damp brush. Let dry and apply new leaves that are semi-transparent.

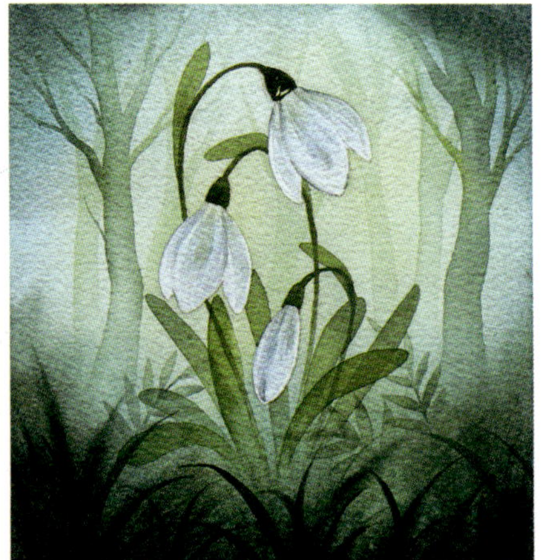

11. Using a precise brush and Mixture 5, add a few blades of grass.

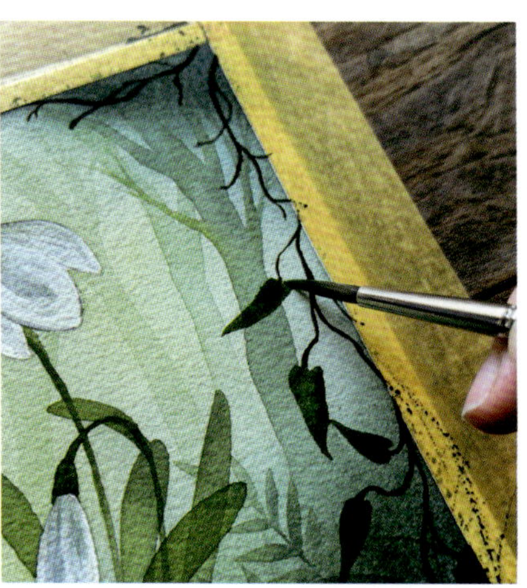

12. Draw an ivy frame using a precise brush and Mixtures 5 and 8. Start by placing the stem, then paint the leaves. Once the watercolor is dry, remove the painter's tape.

VIOLET *KOKEDAMA*

A *kokedama*, which means "moss ball," is a Japanese technique of artistically growing and displaying plants. This flowerpot concept is all the more natural as it recalls the freshness of a mossy undergrowth. This form is ideal for starting to design small forest scenes in a variety of shapes and colors.

1 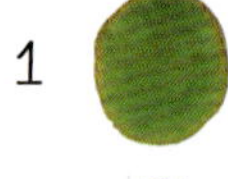 • **Mixture 1** - Cobalt green + quinacridone gold

2 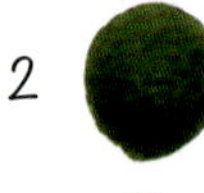 • **Mixture 2** - Sap green

3 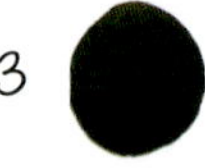 • **Mixture 3** - Sap green + lamp black

4 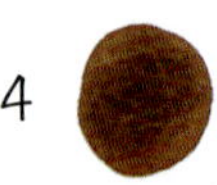 • **Mixture 4** - Brown iron oxide

5 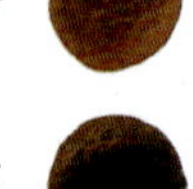 • **Mixture 5** - Brown iron oxide + Mars black

6 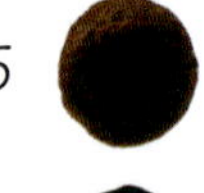 • **Mixture 6** - Sap green + ultramarine blue

7  • **Mixture 7** - Ultramarine blue + permanent rose

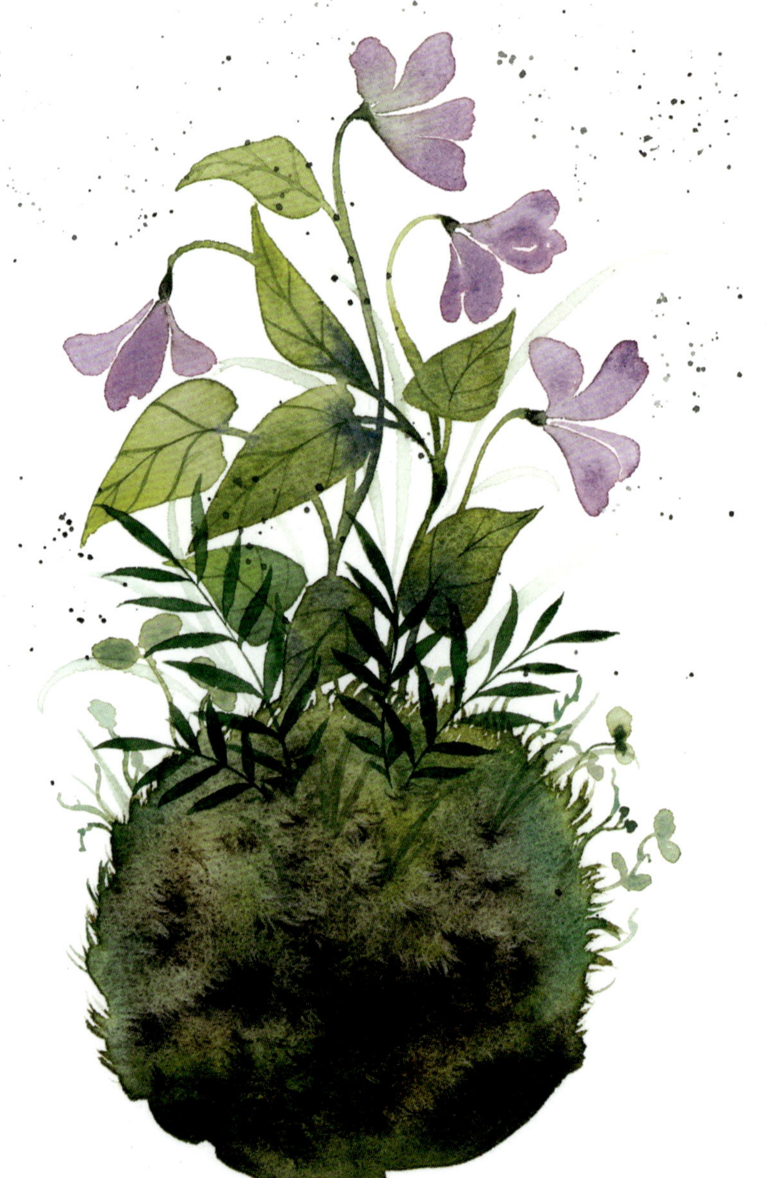

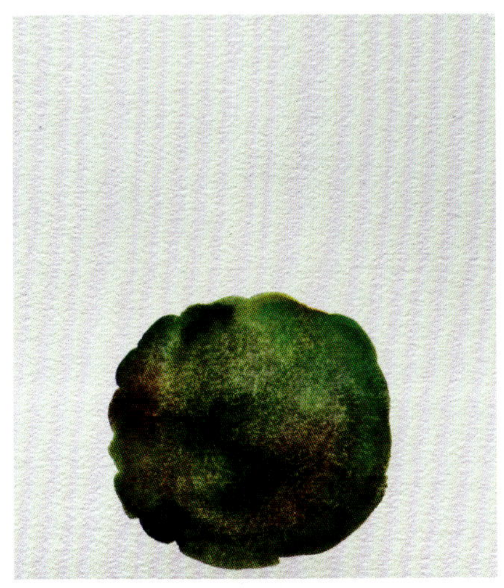

1. Paint an irregular, round shape to create a base for the moss. Use a soft, round brush and alternate between Mixtures 1, 2, 3, and 4. The lower part should be darker.

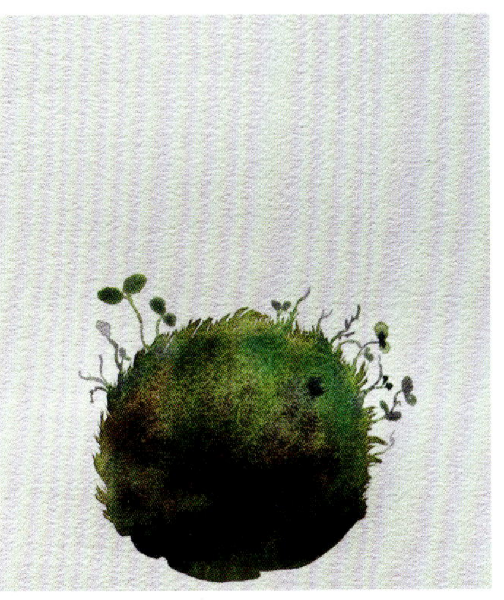

2. In the still-wet watercolor and using Mixture 5, accentuate the color of the earth to bring out the green of the moss. On top of the moss, add blades of grass with a tapered brush and small vegetation with a small brush. If you think marks might be left, let it dry.

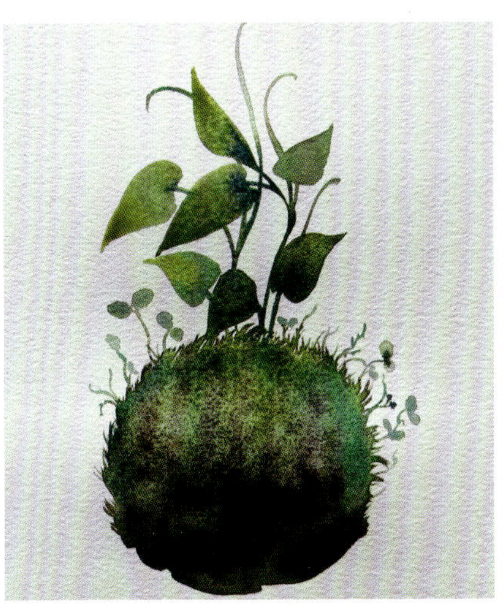

3. Using a fine brush and Mixtures 1 and 2, create the stems and leaves of the violets. Using Mixture 6, vary the shades of green by adding more blue pigments to the stems. Let it dry.

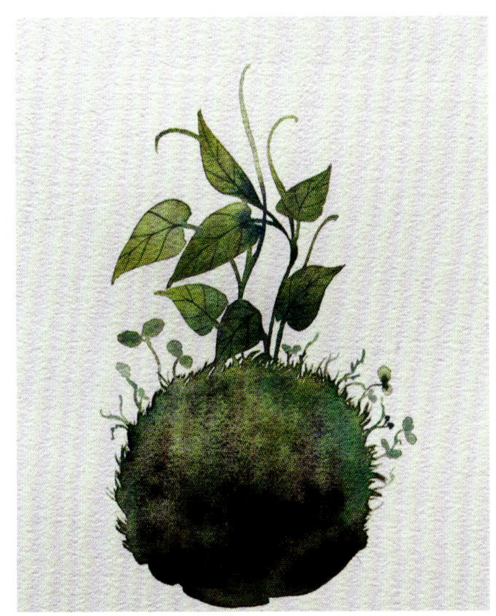

4. Using a fine brush and Mixture 3, add veins to the leaves.

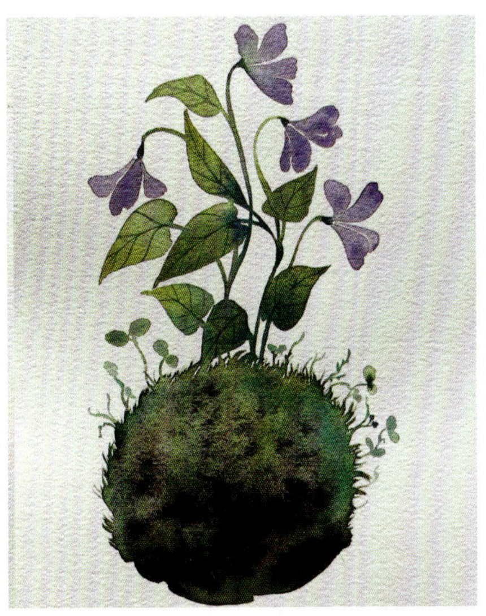

5. Using a small brush and Mixture 7, add the flowers to the ends of the stems. Try varying the angles of the petals and playing with the empty spaces. Add texture to the moss by applying Mixture 5 in places.

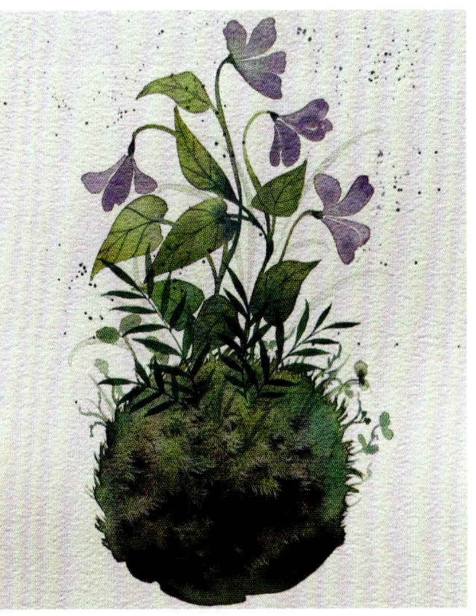

6. Add vegetation with Mixture 3 and semi-transparent long blades of grass with Mixture 2. Add highlights to the moss with a white pencil, and add a few speckles to highlight the artistic character of your creation.

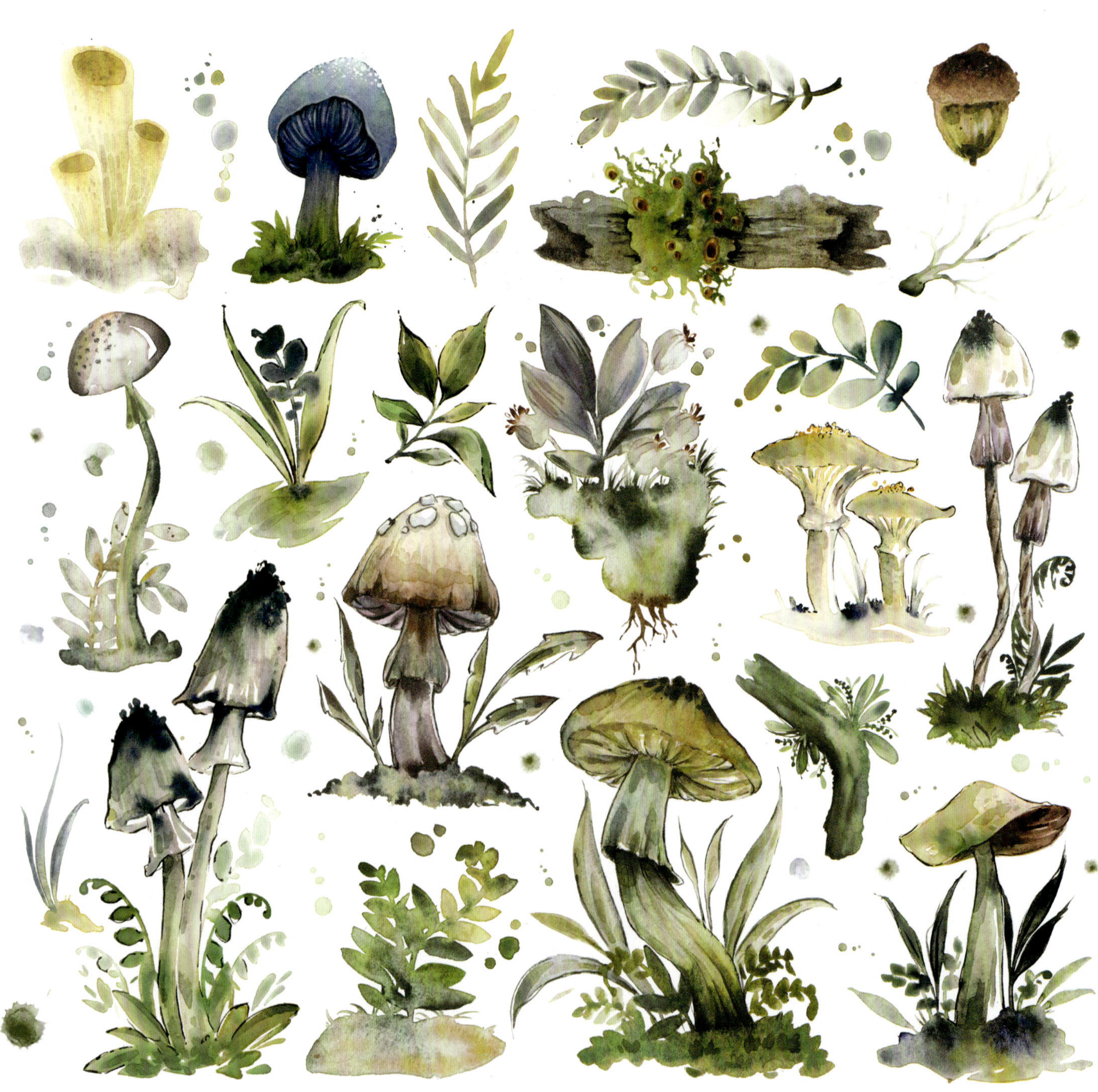

Taming Small Spaces

In the previous chapters, you've learned to observe nature and use the elements to fuel your inspiration. The next step is to delve deeper into different watercolor techniques to create beautiful little forest scenes.

Undergrowth

When I think of undergrowth, I immediately visualize the most isolated and wild part of the forest, a place where the vegetation is dense and where walkers don't venture. I like to imagine these places as if I were a small forest being and all the plants seemed immense to me.

As a child, I often watched the animated movie *FernGully: The Last Rainforest* because I was amazed by the world of this little fairy, who was trying to explain to her human friend that everything that lives in the forest can feel things just as much as he can. Although this cartoon is fictional, it is important not to ignore the fragility of this ecosystem. Everyone must take care of the forest.

In the following step-by-steps, I invite you to work on different ways of approaching nature through the eyes of a small being.

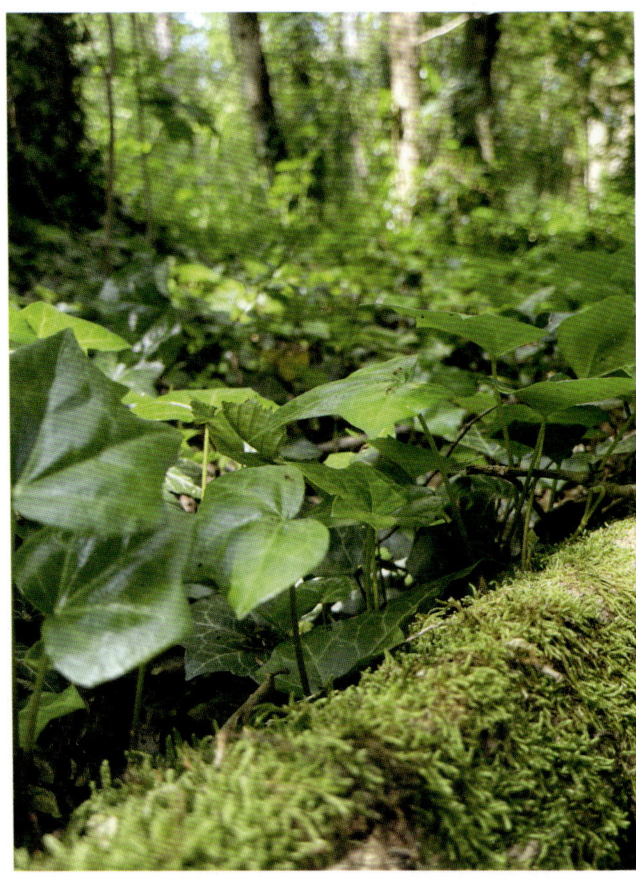

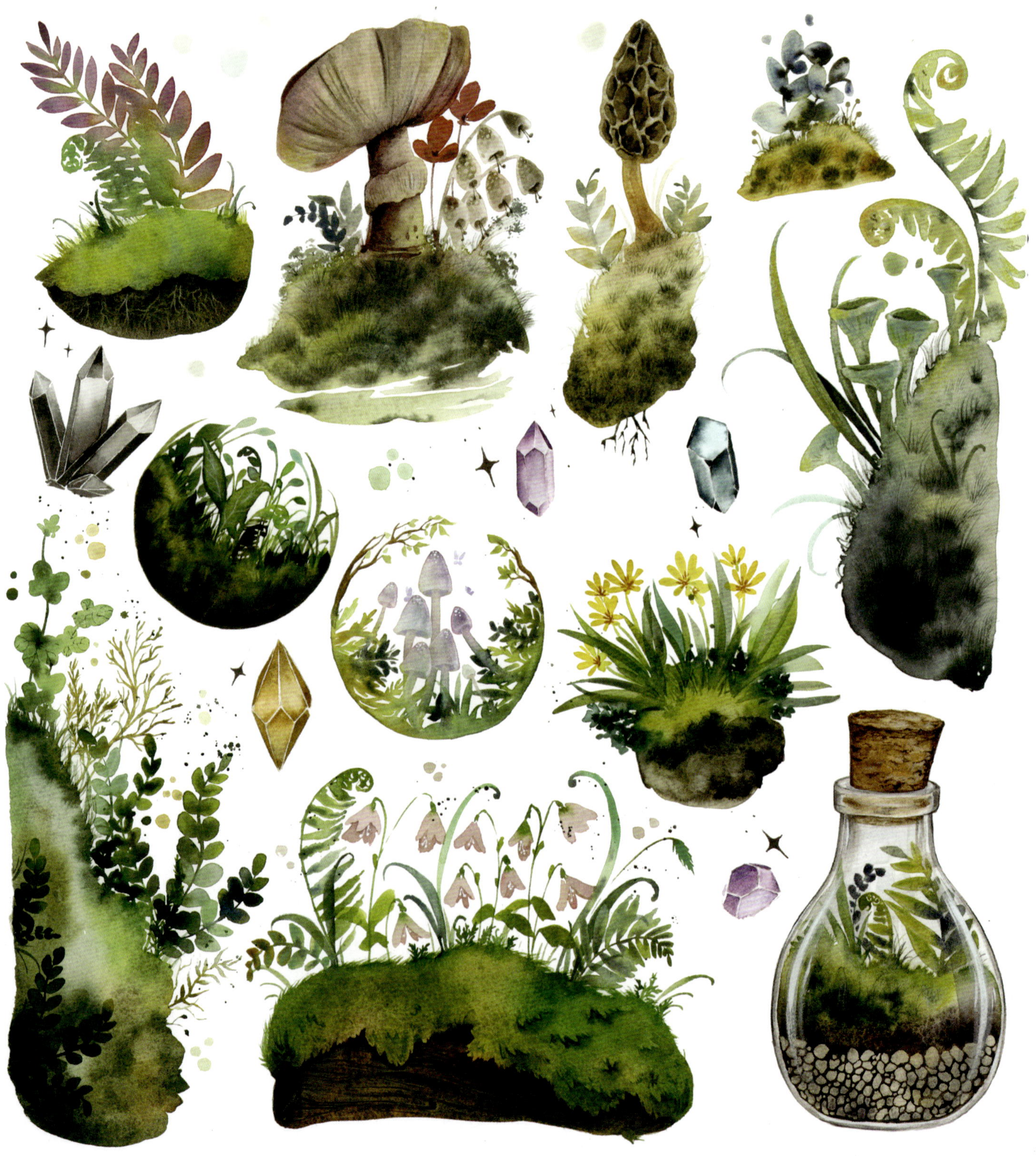

FOREST DWELLERS

But what would the undergrowth be without the little creatures that live there? Essential to their ecosystem, they are fascinating to observe. The forest, in return, provides them with what they need for shelter and food. It has many places to hide, both underground and above ground: moss, dead wood, leaves, soil, etc. Each little creature will find what it needs. You will probably have difficulty spotting these inconspicuous critters, but by being patient and attentive, you will be able to admire the activities of these fragile little creatures that we must protect.

Indulge your inner scientist by treating your notebooks as field studies.

LUSH VEGETATION

To document a rich and varied universe within small scenes, you will often need to work your watercolor in two stages:

- Wet, to adjust the color tones before the watercolor dries.
- Transparent, to give a beautiful depth to the vegetation by superimposing layers.

You will also need to know how to vary the plants in order to create a harmonious composition without weighing it down.

To put these principles into practice, follow the exercise "Small Undergrowth Scenes" on the next page.

SPACE

What I find interesting about creating these little scenes is being able to explore them from different angles and shapes. This allows for a great deal of innovation in the way we approach them. The step-by-steps "Mushroom Sphere" (page 118) and "Forest-Style Terrarium" (page 115) are examples of exercises where you can have fun with the shape.

Painting a terrarium is a bit more complex, as you'll need to think about the shape of your jar, but I don't think you need to be too particular about symmetry; instead, consider the ecosystem inside with enthusiasm.

Practice

SMALL UNDERGROWTH SCENES

I draw inspiration from photographs taken close to the ground and very close to the subject, as if I were seeing the scene through the eyes of a small being. This makes each element even more vivid and exciting to observe. Approach these three landscapes differently by using a variety of plants.

Slippery Jack Mushroom Undergrowth

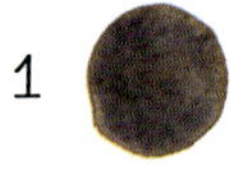 1

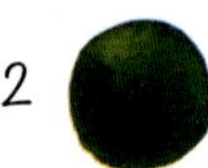 2

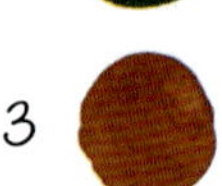 3

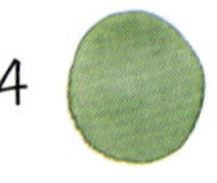 4

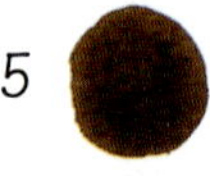 5

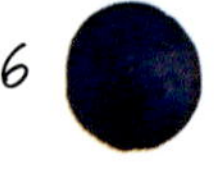 6

 7

- **Mixture 1** - Tundra blue + brown iron oxide
- **Mixture 2** - Sap green + ultramarine blue
- **Mixture 3** - Burgundy red ochre + quinacridone gold + permanent brown
- **Mixture 4** - Phthalo green + sap green (diluted)
- **Mixture 5** - Brown iron oxide
- **Mixture 6** - Ultramarine blue + permanent rose
- **Mixture 7** - Sap green + ultramarine blue + Payne's gray

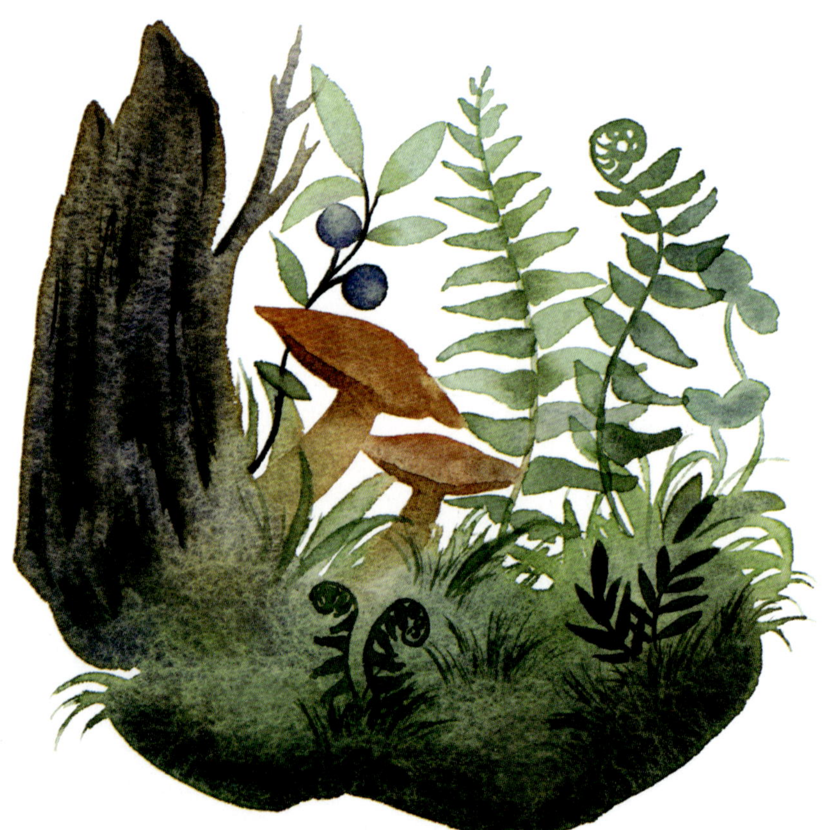

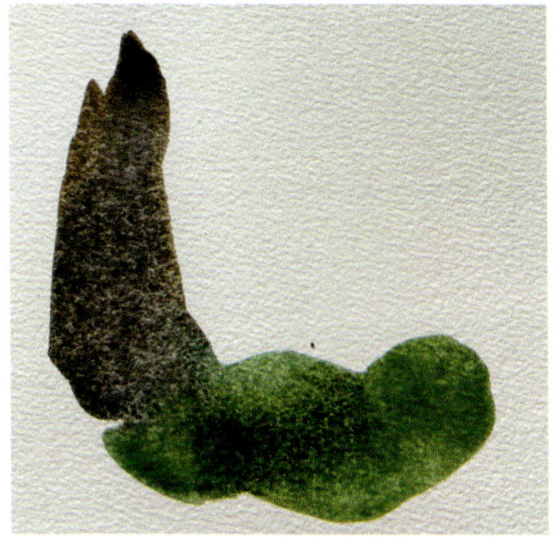

1. Using a soft, wide brush, apply Mixture 1 to form the tree stump. Create the mossy area using Mixture 2. Take care to vary the concentration of pigments and water to create depth.

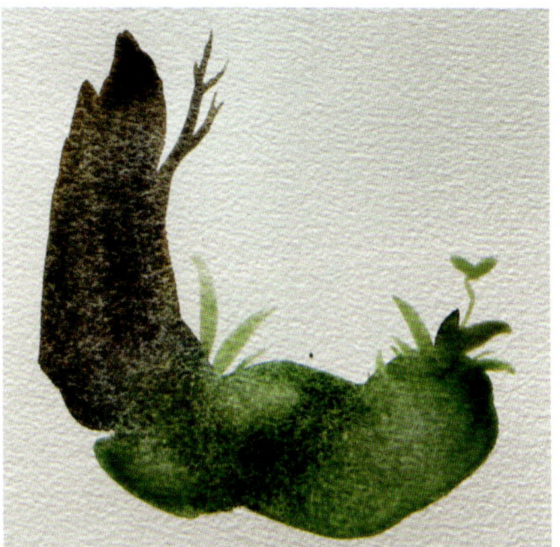

2. Using a thinner, pointed brush, stretch the pigments already placed to represent vegetation on the surface of the moss and a branch on the trunk.

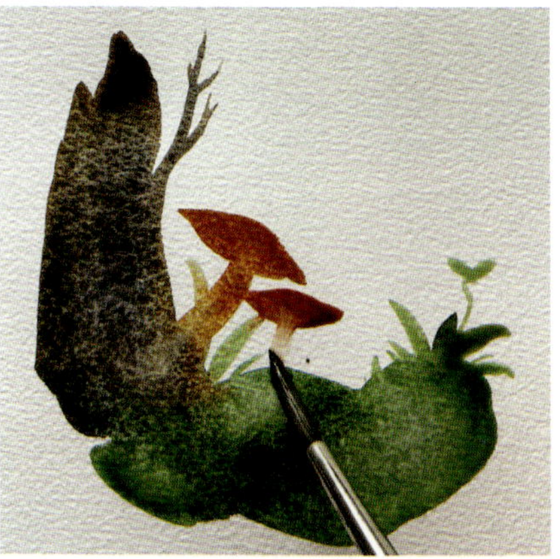

3. In the still-wet watercolor, paint two mushrooms with Mixture 3. Stretch the pigments down to the moss so that they merge together.

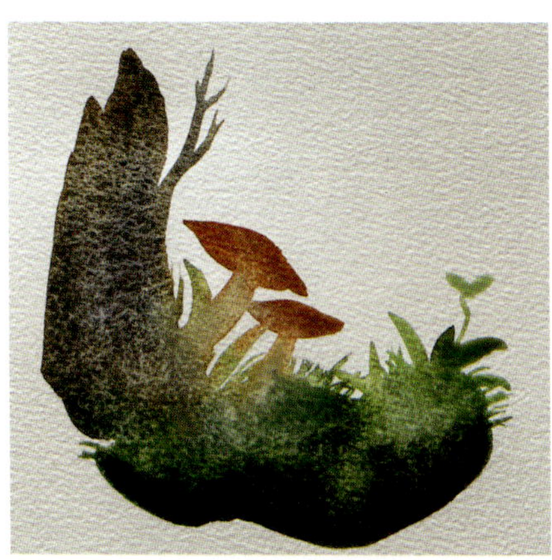

4. While the watercolor is still wet, use a very fine or tapered brush to add denser blades of grass. When you are satisfied with the result, let it dry.

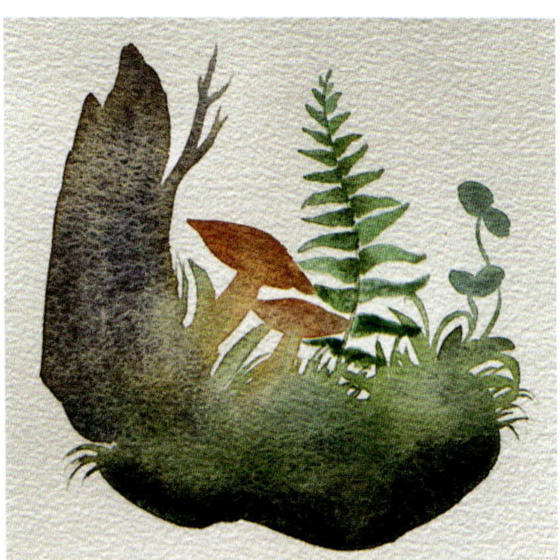

5. Using the same brush and Mixture 4, create the first fern. Wait for the watercolor to dry.

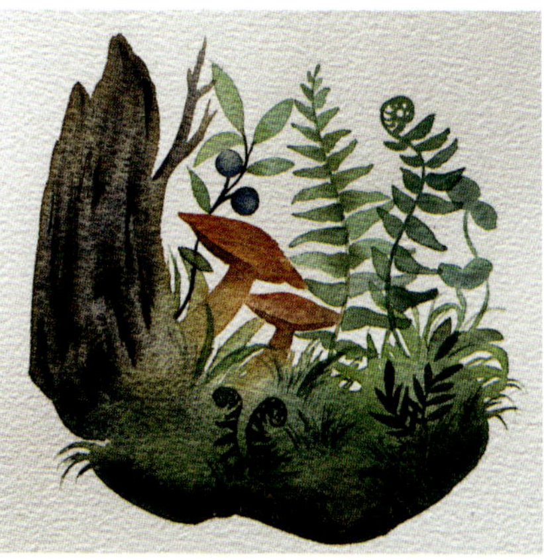

6. Gradually add new vegetation. Paint stems and berries around the mushrooms with Mixtures 5 and 6, and semi-transparent vegetation with Mixture 7 to give an impression of depth.

Flower and Mushroom Undergrowth

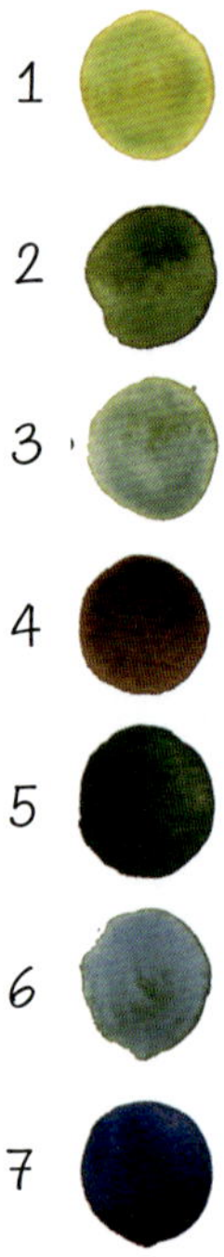

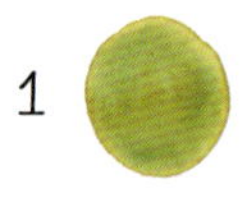

1 • **Mixture 1** - Indian yellow + quinacridone gold + cobalt green (diluted)

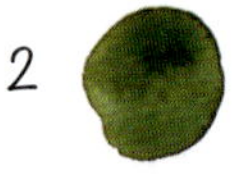

2 • **Mixture 2** - Sap green + cobalt green + lamp black

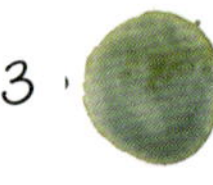

3 • **Mixture 3** - Cobalt green deep + ultramarine blue + quinacridone gold (diluted)

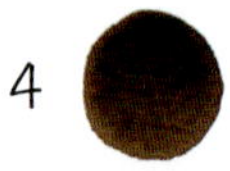

4 • **Mixture 4** - Brown iron oxide + Mars black

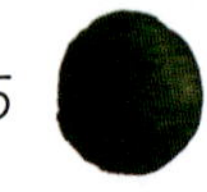

5 • **Mixture 5** - Sap green + cobalt green dark + lamp black

6 • **Mixture 6** - Cobalt green dark + cobalt turquoise light + sap green + ultramarine blue

7 • **Mixture 7** - Tundra blue

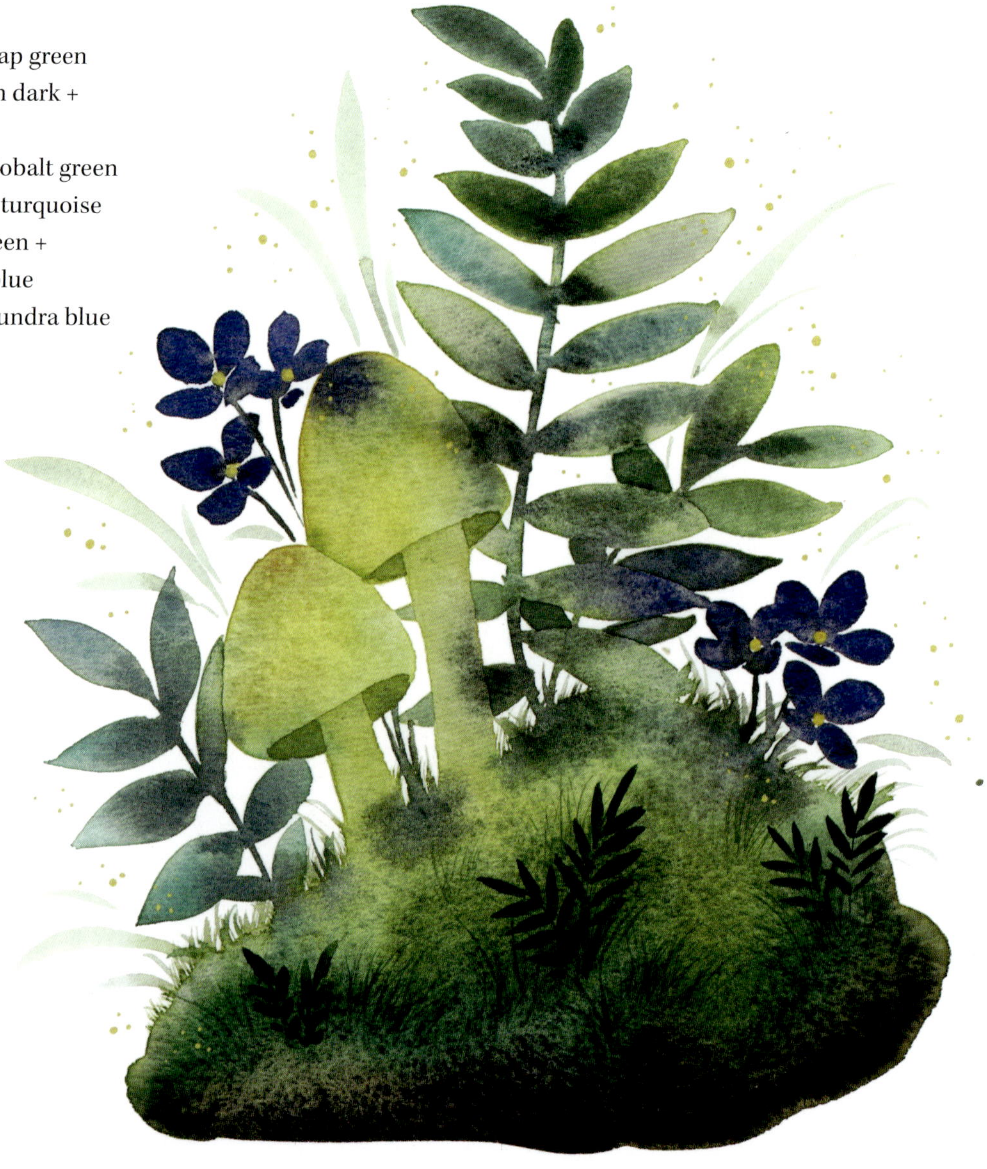

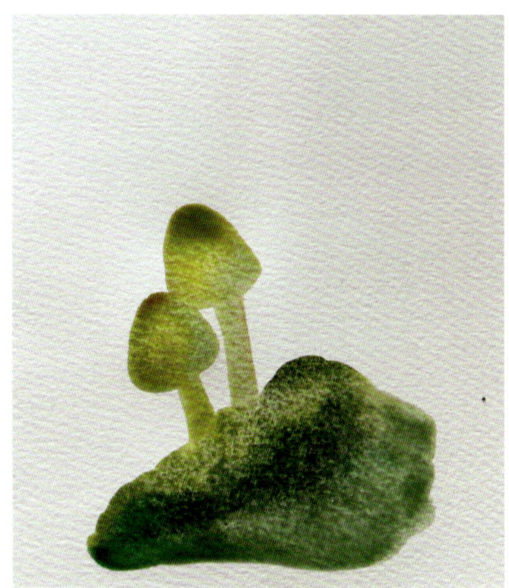

1. Using a soft, round brush, paint two mushrooms with Mixture 1. In the still-wet watercolor, place the moss at the base of the mushrooms using Mixtures 2 and 3.

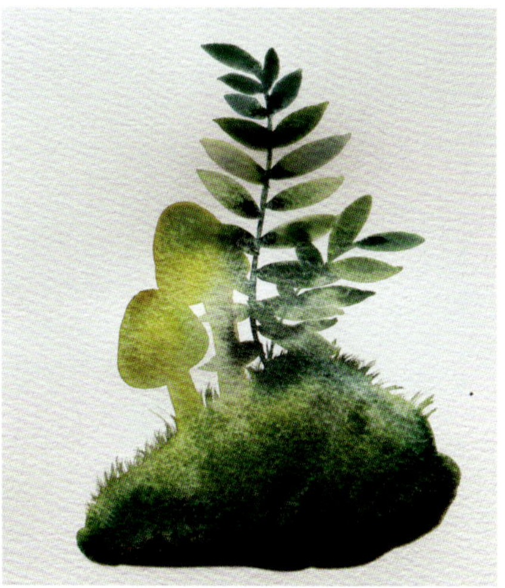

2. Using a tapered or very fine brush, paint small blades of grass. Add two ferns, giving them some nice movement. Have fun using Mixtures 1, 2, and 3. For the stem, use Mixture 5 to create contrasts. On the bottom of the moss, place Mixture 4 for the soil.

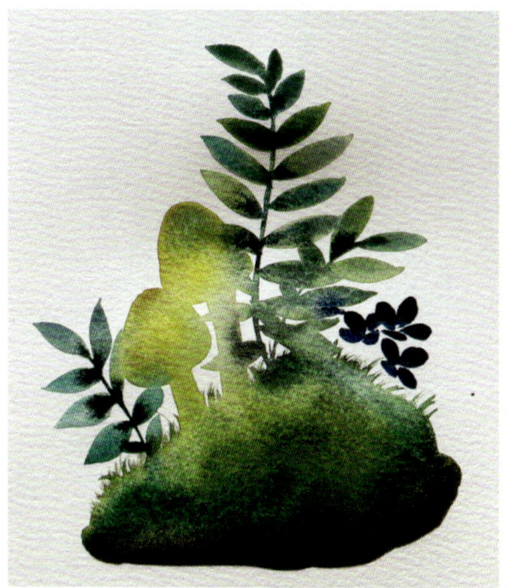

3. Without changing brushes, use Mixture 6 to create new foliage. Continue using Mixture 5 for the stem. Using Mixture 7, paint small clusters of blue flowers in the empty spaces.

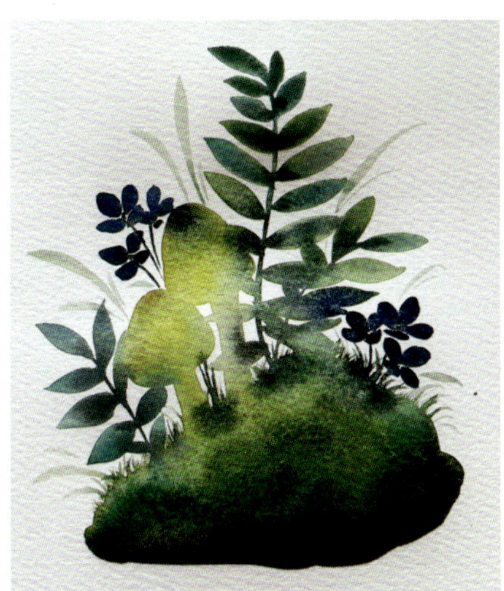

4. Using an even finer brush, place blades of grass in different areas of your painting to add dynamism. Let it dry.

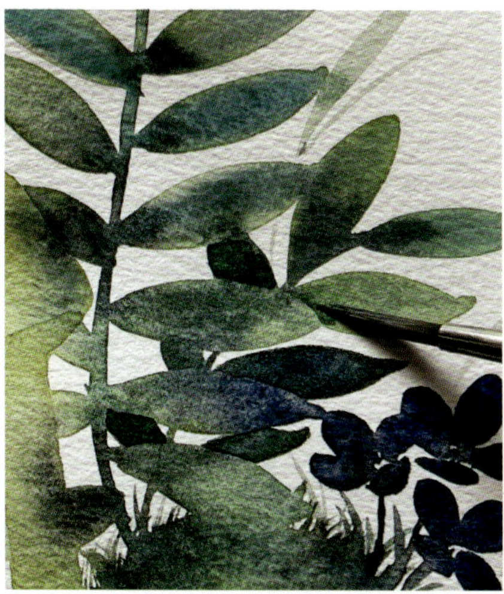

5. Add the final details of your undergrowth using a fine brush. To create volume, separate the leaves that had blended in with others by using a slightly darker mixture than the one you've already used.

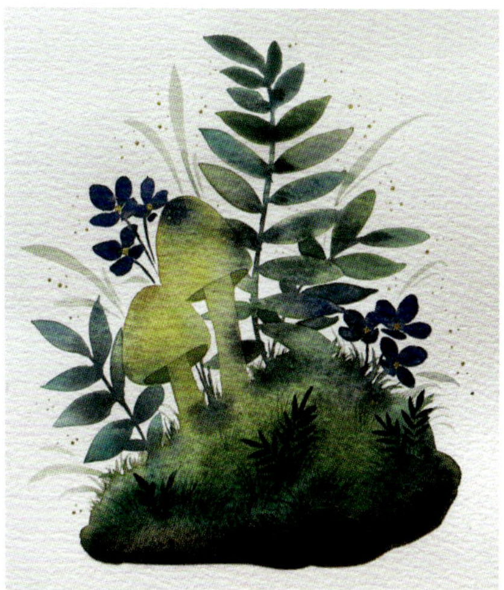

6. Add even more depth by painting small, darker leaves on the moss using Mixture 5. Add a center to the blue flowers using a gold gel pen, also adding small dots all around your piece to give it a whimsical touch.

Scarlet Elf Cup Undergrowth

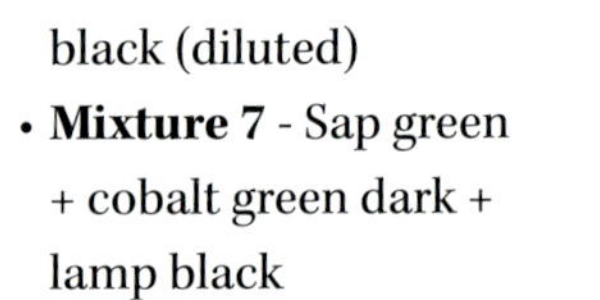

1 • **Mixture 1** - Buff titanium

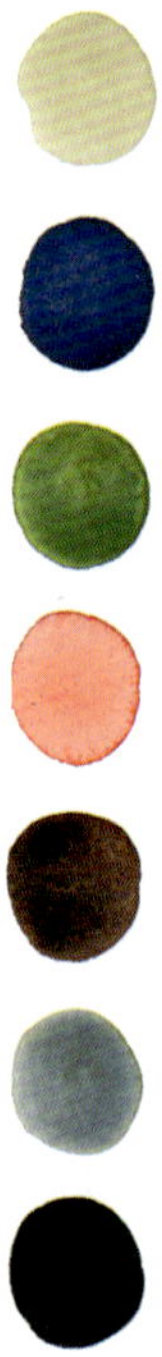

2 • **Mixture 2** - Tundra blue + ultramarine blue + cobalt turquoise light

3 • **Mixture 3** - Sap green + quinacridone gold + cobalt green deep

4 • **Mixture 4** - Permanent rose + pyrrole orange (diluted)

5 • **Mixture 5** - Brown iron oxide + Mars black + tundra blue

6 • **Mixture 6** - Cobalt green dark + tundra blue + Mars black (diluted)

7 • **Mixture 7** - Sap green + cobalt green dark + lamp black

> ### Note
> *I created this undergrowth without a specific plan in mind. I simply wanted to paint with spontaneity and letting my creativity go to work to the maximum with fun shapes.*

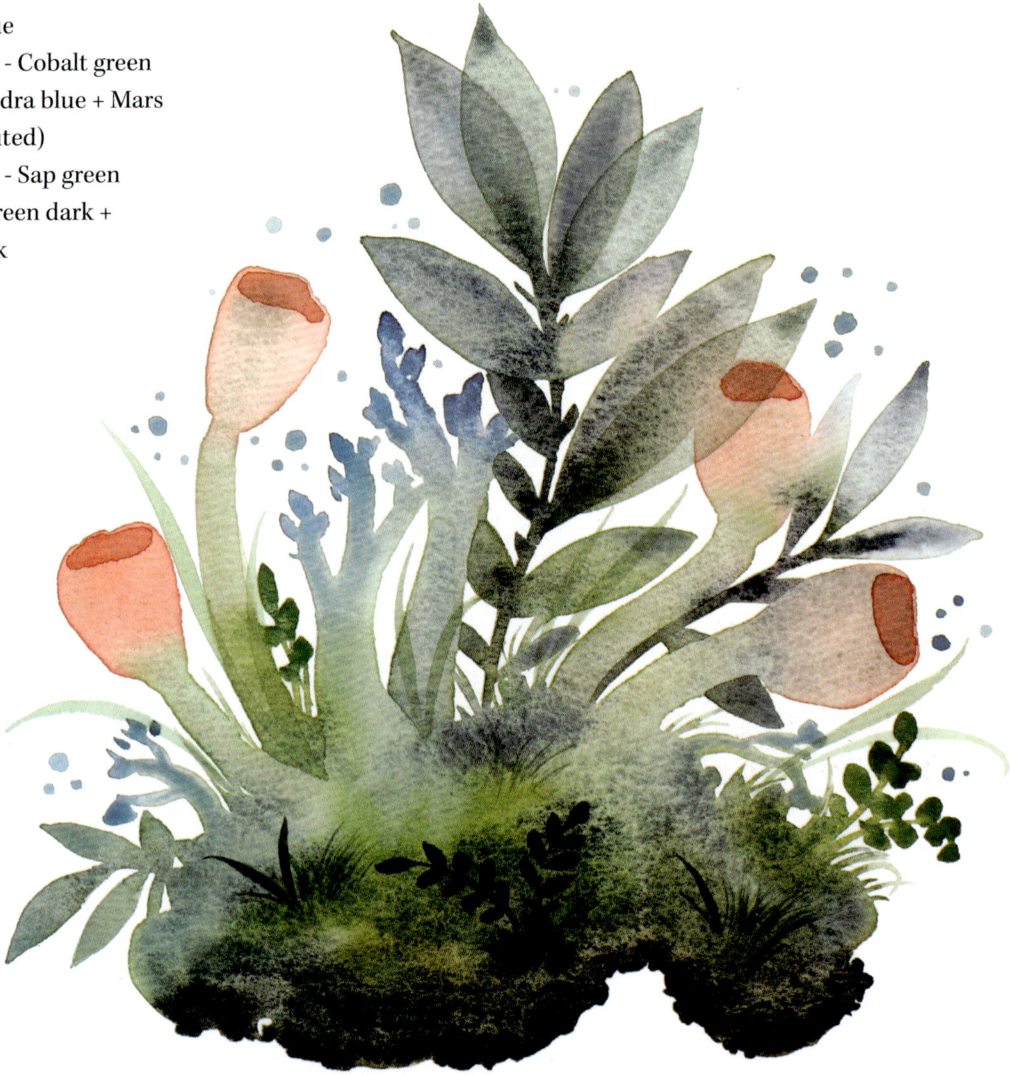

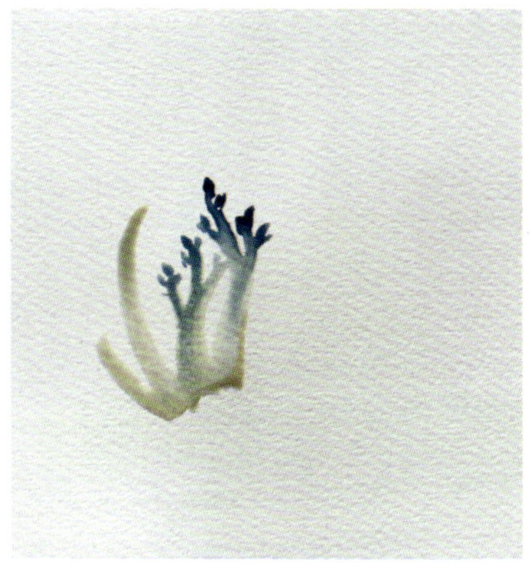

1. Draw the mushroom stems using a fine, round brush and Mixture 1. On the right mushrooms, add small branches with a few oval ends using Mixture 2.

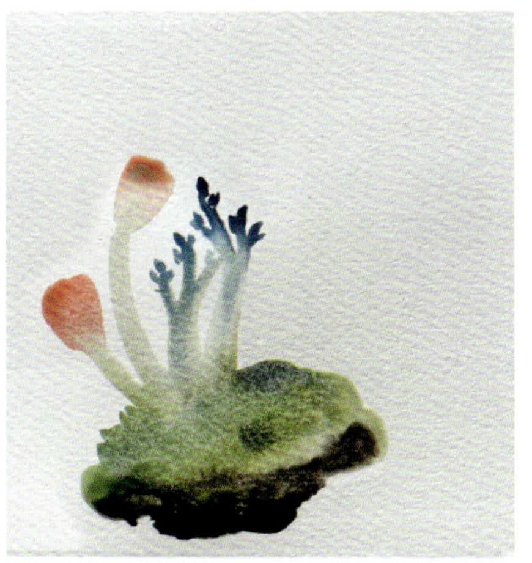

2. On the two left mushrooms, place two bowl-shaped hats with Mixture 4. Underneath, make the moss with Mixture 3 and, at the very bottom, add the soil with Mixture 5.

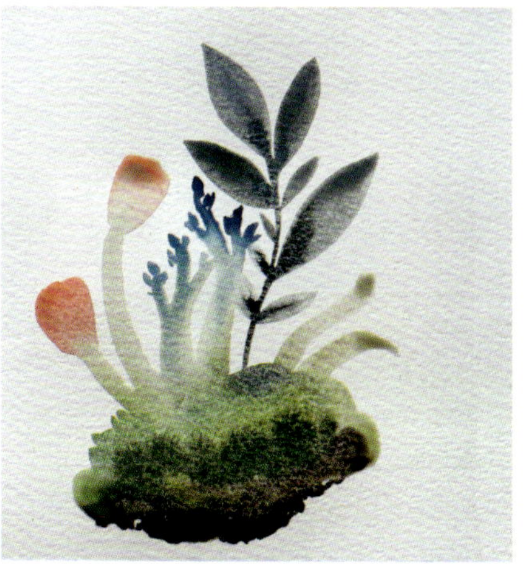

3. On the right side, add two new mushroom stems with Mixture 1, then a blue foliage with Mixture 6. Add a little Mars black to this mixture to darken the stem.

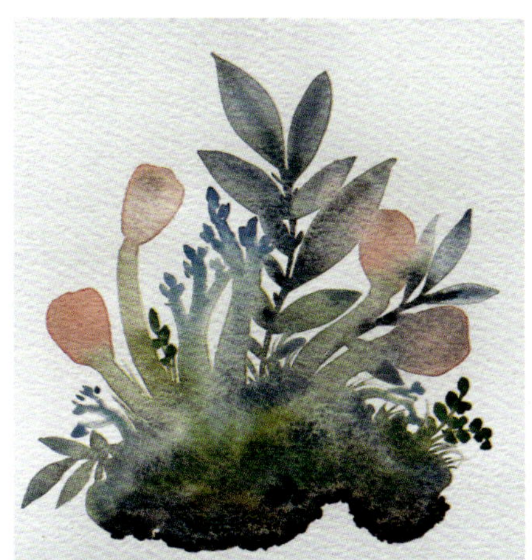

4. On the two new plants, add caps as in step 2. Using your imagination and the previous mixtures, fill the space around the main elements with vegetation. When you are satisfied with the density, let it dry.

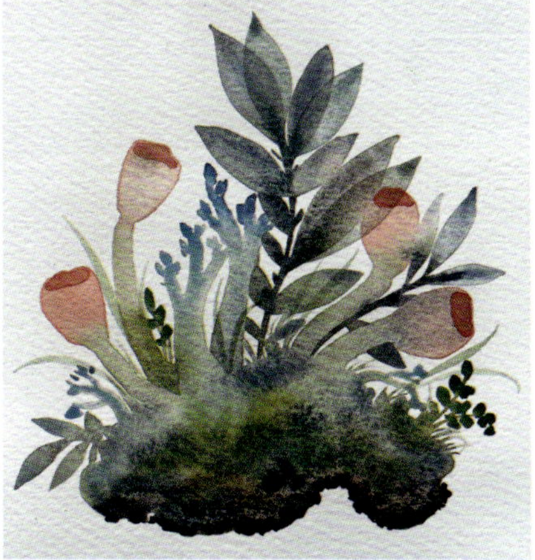

5. Create the illusion of depth on the mushroom caps by placing a small oval shape in their center with a slightly more concentrated Mixture 4. Have fun creating volume by making the mushroom stems pass either in front of or behind the other elements.

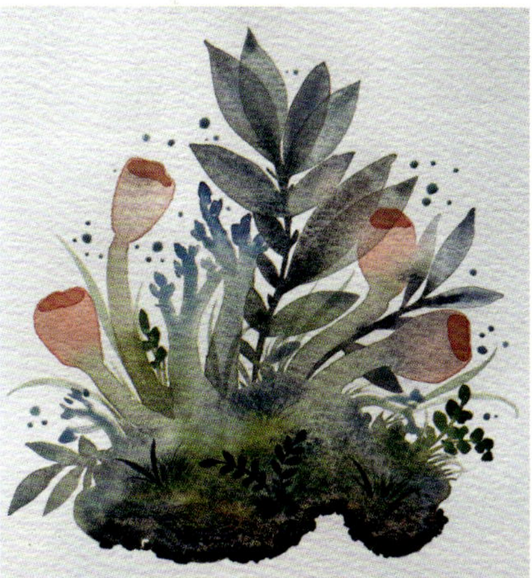

6. On the front of the moss, add dark green plants with Mixture 7 and dots all around your creation with Mixtures 3 and 6.

HEDGEHOG

For this watercolor, the work is done in two stages: first the hedgehog, then the vegetation. I preferred not to sketch on the sheet before painting so as not to intimidate beginners to drawing; however, you can make some sketches with a pencil if that helps you.

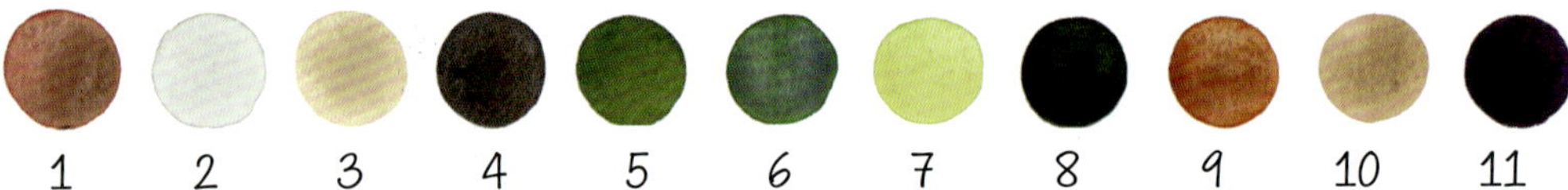

- **Mixture 1** - Brown iron oxide + alizarin crimson + yellow ochre
- **Mixture 2** - White gouache + Payne's gray (diluted)
- **Mixture 3** - Buff titanium
- **Mixture 4** - Payne's gray + brown iron oxide
- **Mixture 5** - Sap green
- **Mixture 6** - Dark ultramarine blue + phthalo green + Indian yellow
- **Mixture 7** - Sap green + Indian yellow (diluted)
- **Mixture 8** - Sap green + Payne's gray
- **Mixture 9** - Burgundy red ochre
- **Mixture 10** - Burgundy red ochre + buff titanium
- **Mixture 11** - Dark ultramarine blue + permanent rose

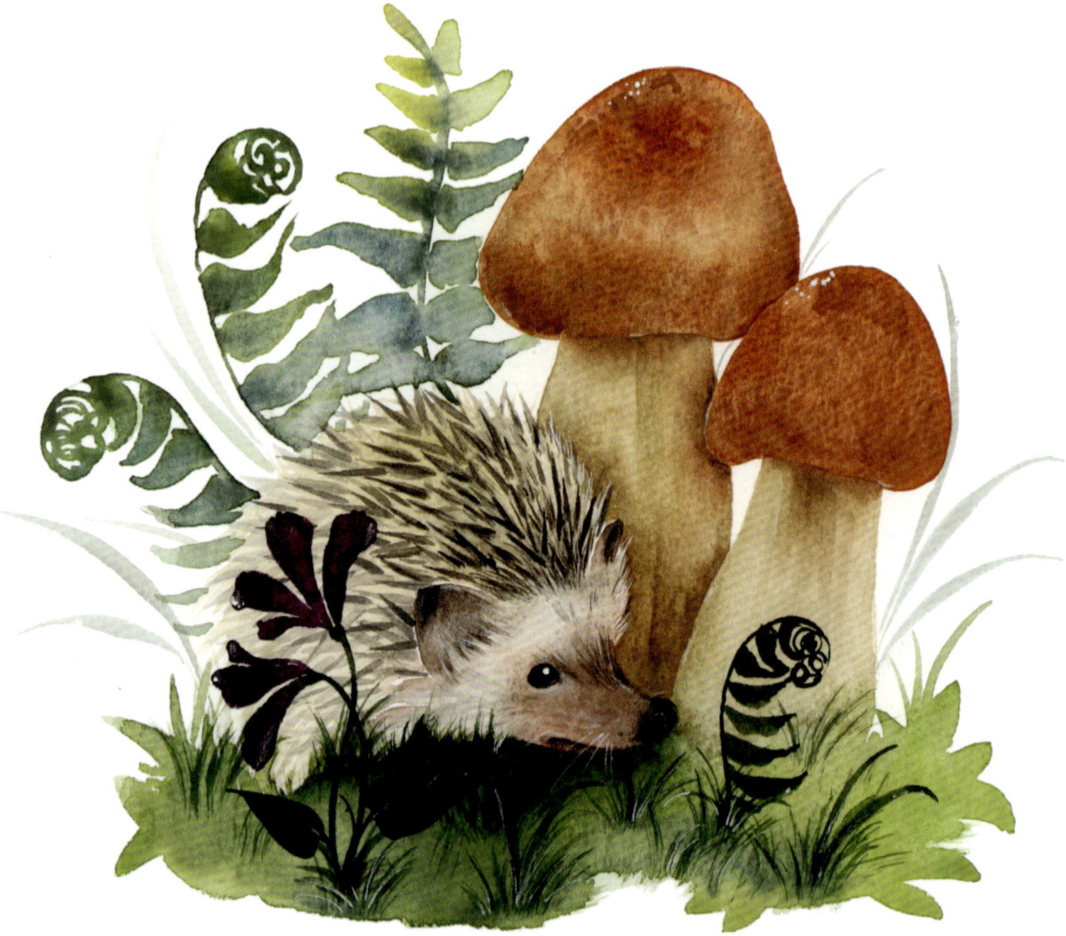

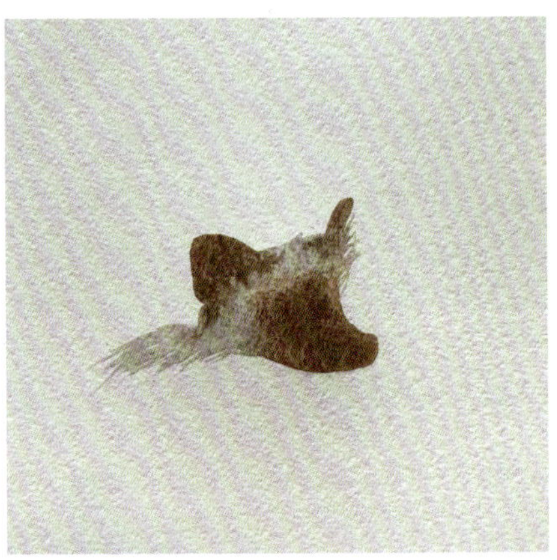

1. Paint the hedgehog's snout using a soft, round brush and Mixture 1. Add the hair above with Mixture 2, then repeat Mixture 1 for the ears.

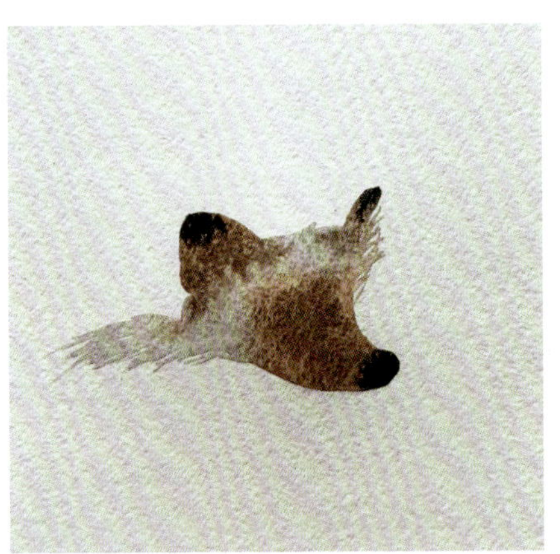

2. In the wet watercolor, add Mixture 4 to the tip of the muzzle and the tips of the ears.

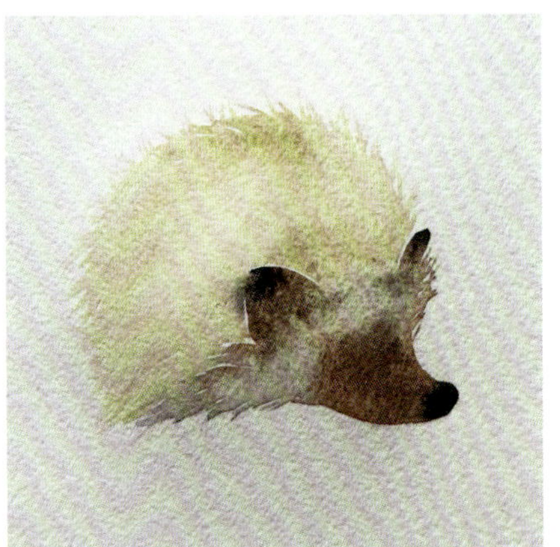

3. In the still-wet watercolor, paint the hedgehog's body using Mixture 3. Be careful not to touch the ears, leaving a thin strip of paper between. Use a fine brush to sketch the first spines. Let it dry.

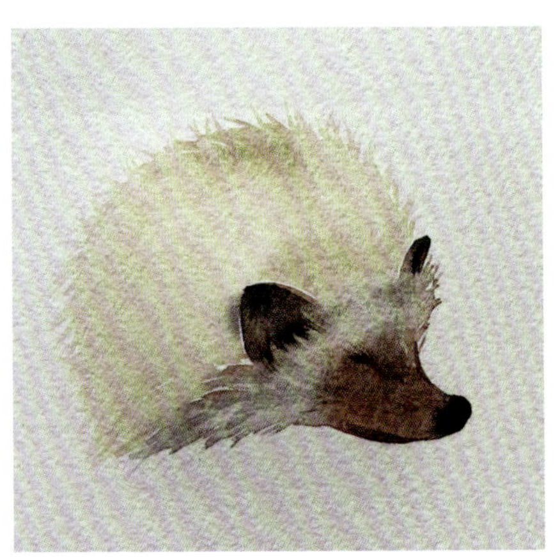

4. Shade the muzzle with Mixture 1 and the hair above with Mixture 2.

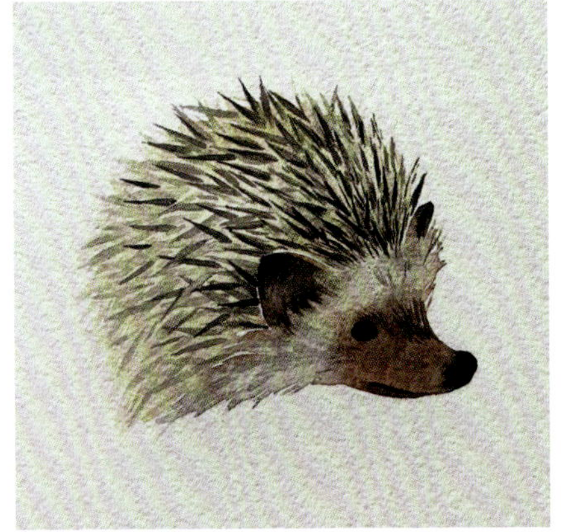

5. Using a liner brush and Mixture 4, add spines. Occasionally dilute the mixture a little by alternating their color, and add movement by varying their orientation. Then draw the hedgehog's eye and lightly outline its mouth. Let it dry.

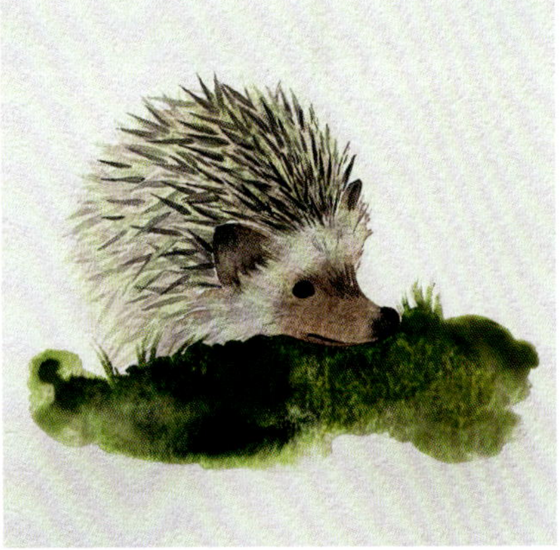

6. Paint the grass using a soft brush and alternating between Mixtures 5, 6, and 7. Work as close to the hedgehog as possible. Make small grass blades with a fine brush.

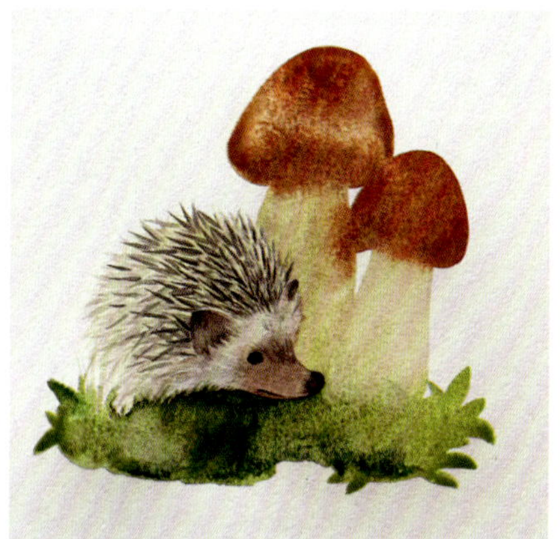

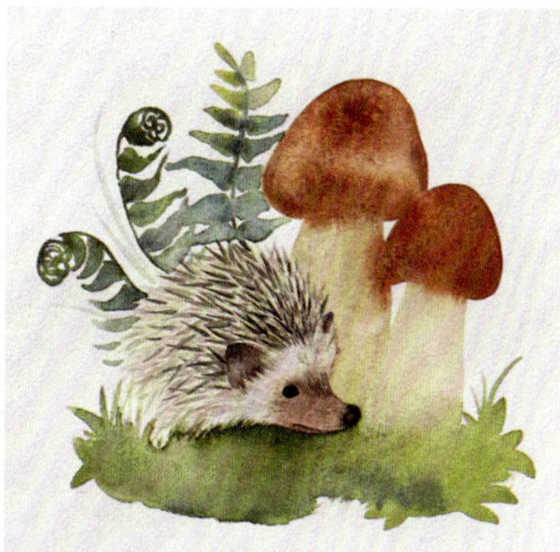

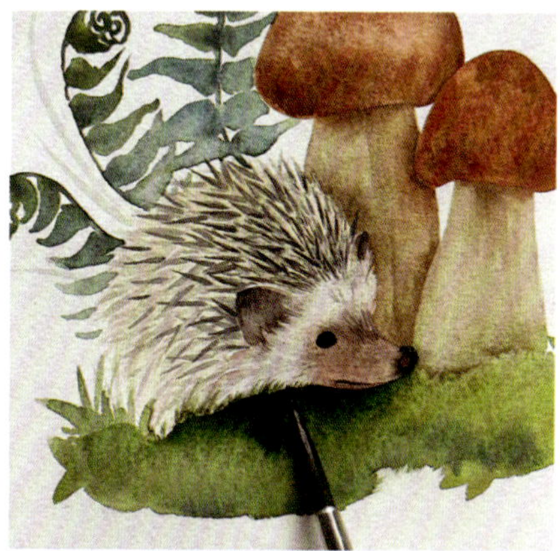

7. Using a soft brush and still-wet watercolor, paint two porcini mushrooms. Use Mixture 9 for the caps and 3 for the stems; they should blend in with the grass. Let it dry.

8. Paint three ferns behind the hedgehog, playing with Mixtures 5, 6, 7, and 8 to vary the contrasts. Wait for the watercolor to dry.

9. Using Mixture 10, apply shadows under the mushroom caps and stems. Using a precise brush and Mixture 8, accentuate the green under the hedgehog.

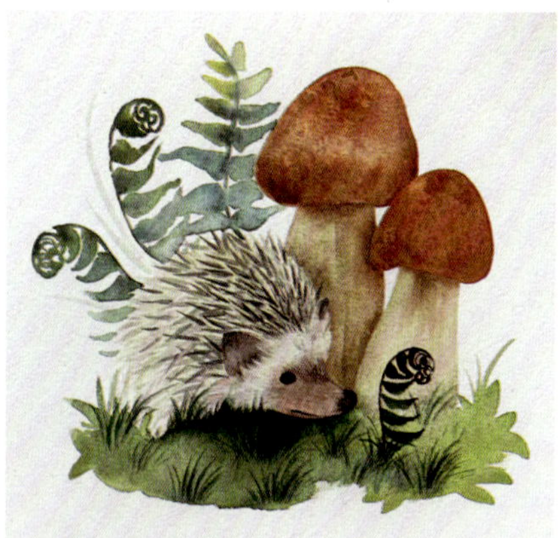

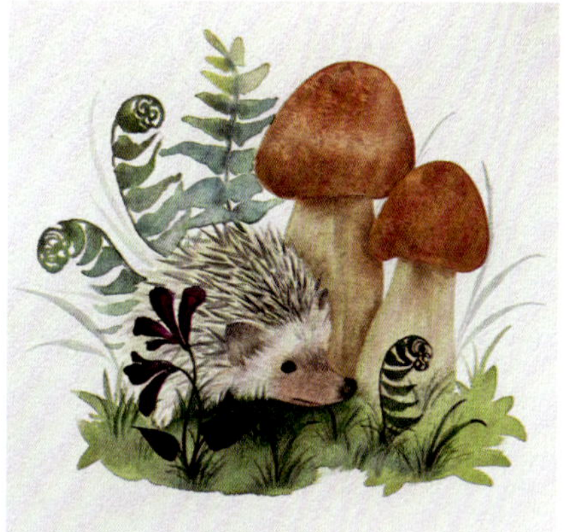

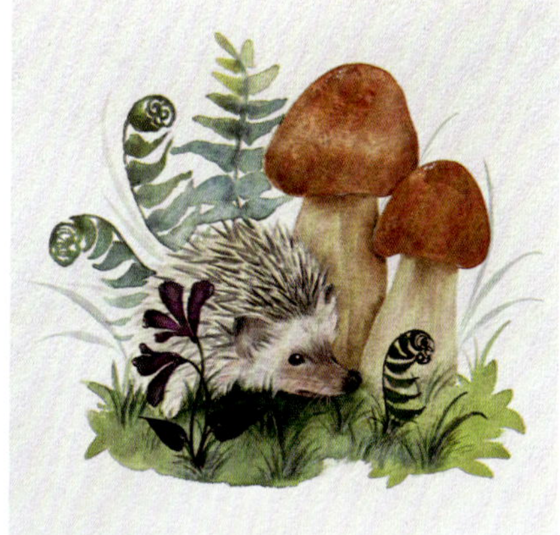

10. Using a fine brush and Mixture 8, sketch some blades of grass on the ground and a fern in front of the mushrooms.

11. Without changing brushes, place two violets in front of the hedgehog using Mixture 11 for the flowers and Mixture 8 for the leaves and stems. Using a fine brush and Mixture 6, add tall grass to the back.

12. Add a shine to the eye and mushrooms, and add whiskers. Use a white colored pencil for a light touch and a white gel ink pen for a more intense touch.

FOREST-STYLE TERRARIUM

Learning how to paint terrariums will give you a new artistic perspective on creating your forest scenes.

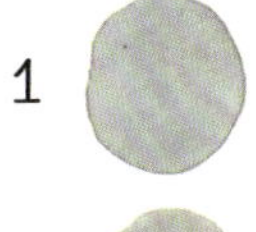 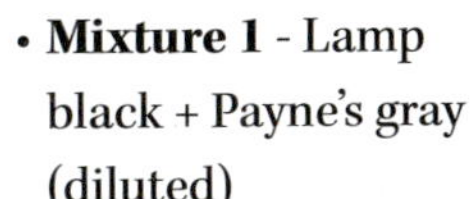

1 • **Mixture 1** - Lamp black + Payne's gray (diluted)

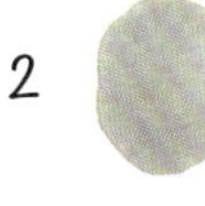

2 • **Mixture 2** - Tundra blue + Mars black + yellow ochre (diluted)

3 • **Mixture 3** - Brown iron oxide + Mars black

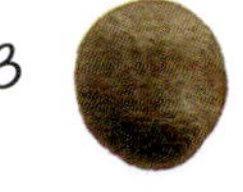

4 • **Mixture 4** - Sap green + ultramarine blue + cobalt green

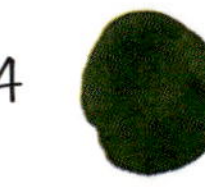

5 • **Mixture 5** - Indian yellow + sap green

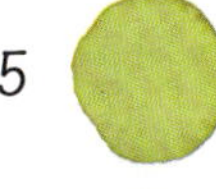

6 • **Mixture 6** - Phthalo green + ultramarine blue

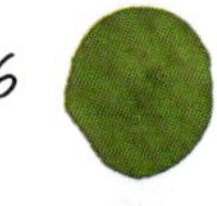

7 • **Mixture 7** - Sap green

• **Mixture 8** - Sap green + lamp black + ultramarine blue (diluted)

8

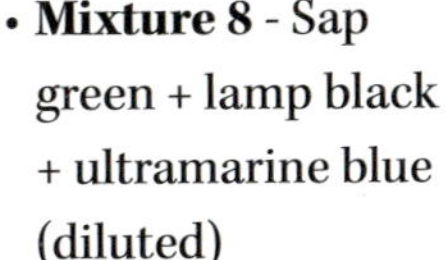

9 • **Mixture 9** - Permanent rose + ultramarine blue

10 • **Mixture 10** - Brown iron oxide + yellow ochre

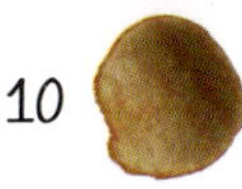

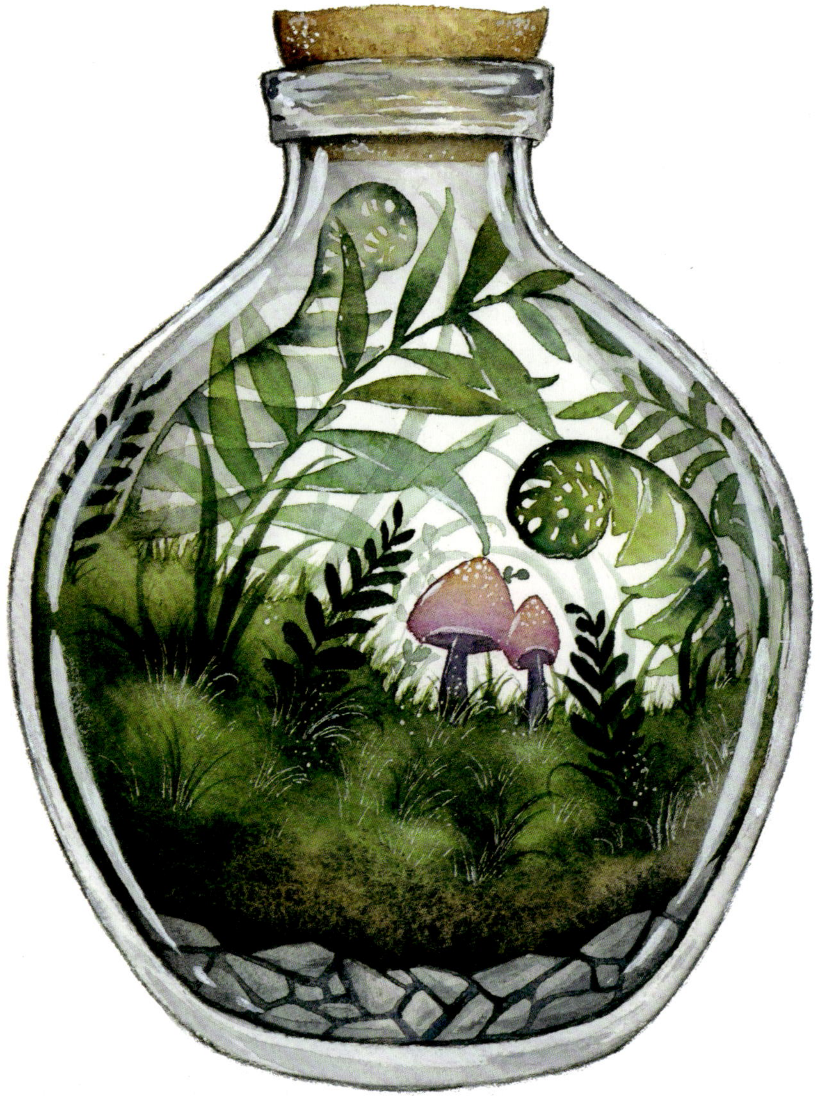

Advice

I prefer to paint the reflections of the jar before the vegetation rather than at the very end because, this way, I do not run the risk of moving the pigments and therefore damaging my watercolor.

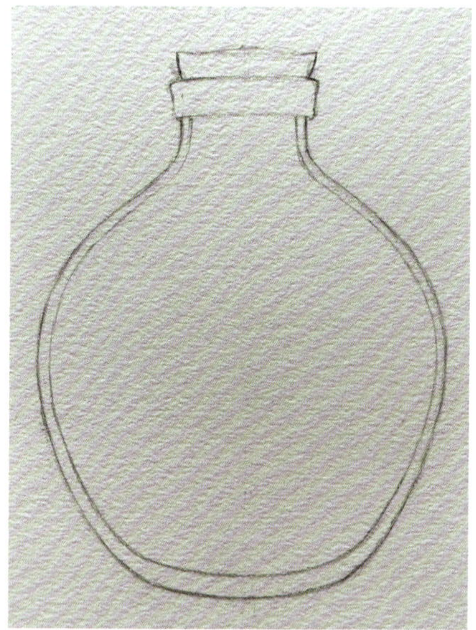

1. Using a pencil, sketch the shape of a jar for the terrarium. Be sure to mark the thickness of the bottle glass with a thin inner line.

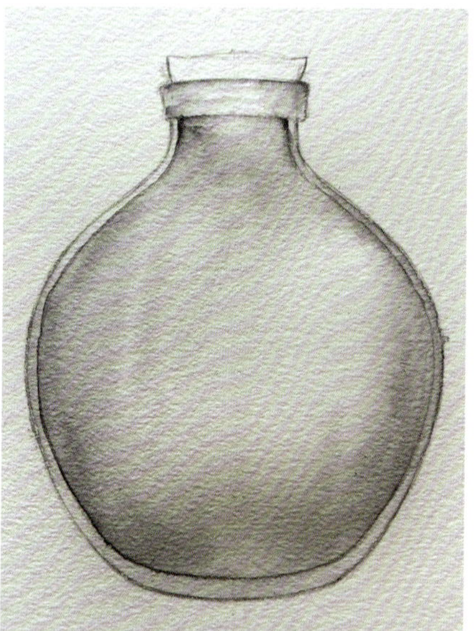

2. Using a brush loaded with water, moisten the inside of the jar without going beyond the inner line. In the wet watercolor, mark the shaded areas with the very diluted Mixture 1. Let it dry.

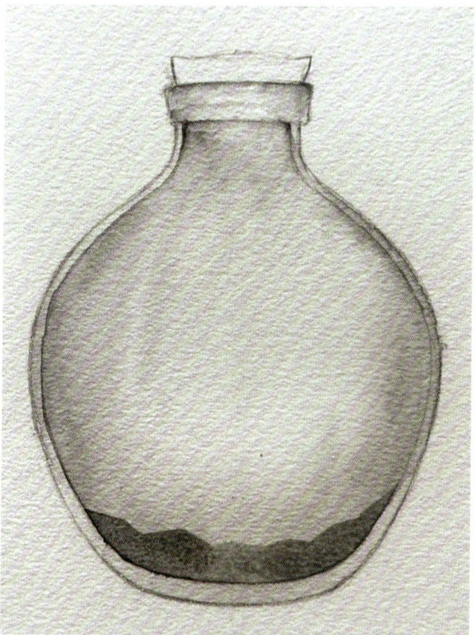

3. Place Mixture 2 on the bottom of the jar, forming small mounds that will later become the rocks at the bottom of the terrarium. Wait for the watercolor to dry.

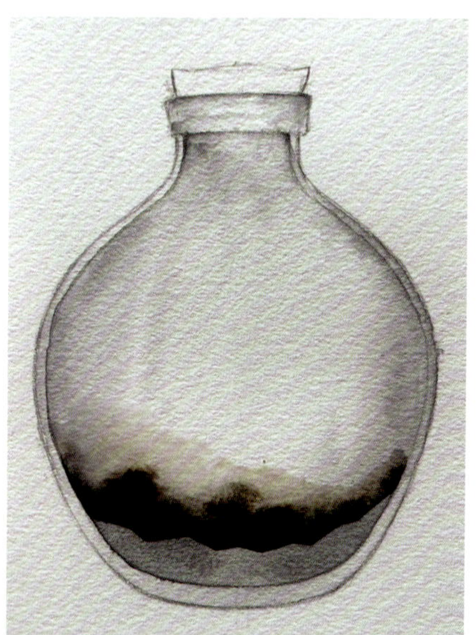

4. On top of the rocks, place Mixture 3 to make the terrarium soil.

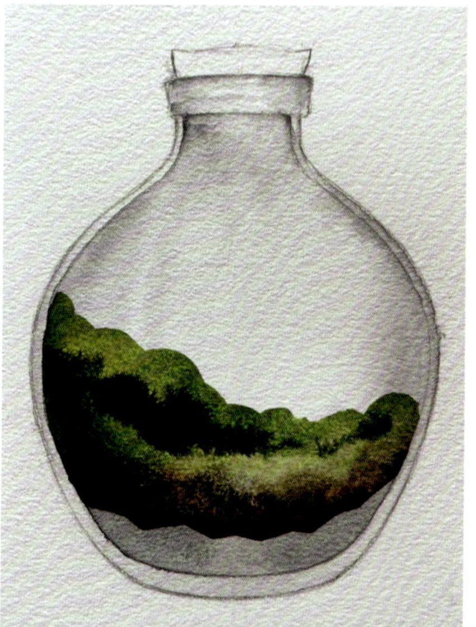

5. Just above the still-wet soil, paint grass in small clouds with your brush. Vary the shades of green and water to add depth and texture, using Mixtures 4, 5, 6, and 7.

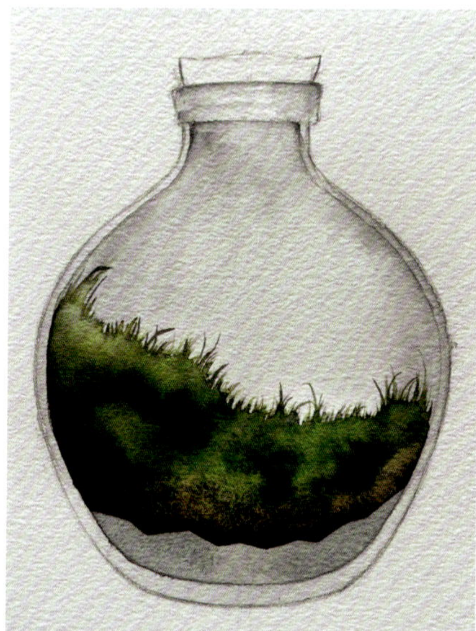

6. Using a tapered or very fine brush and the mixtures from the previous step, add small blades of grass. Wait for the watercolor to dry.

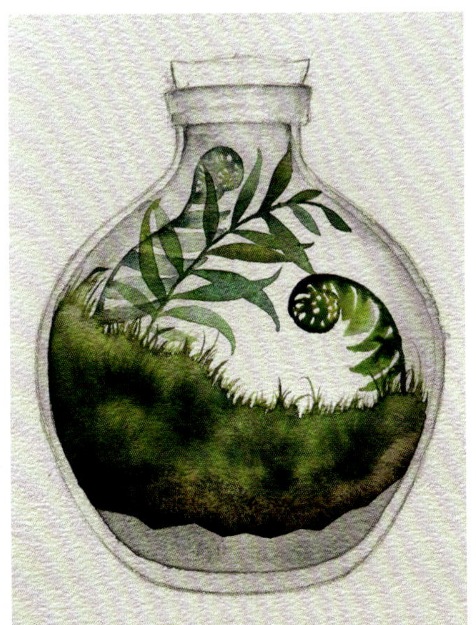

7. Form the vegetation above the grass by painting different styles of ferns with Mixtures 5, 6, and 8. When the first ones are dry, layer new ones on top. Let it dry.

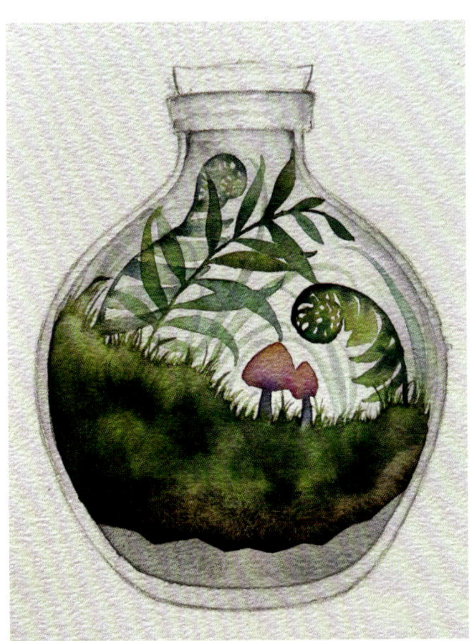

8. To add a little color, draw two small mushrooms with Mixture 9, adding a little extra ultramarine blue to the mushroom stems.

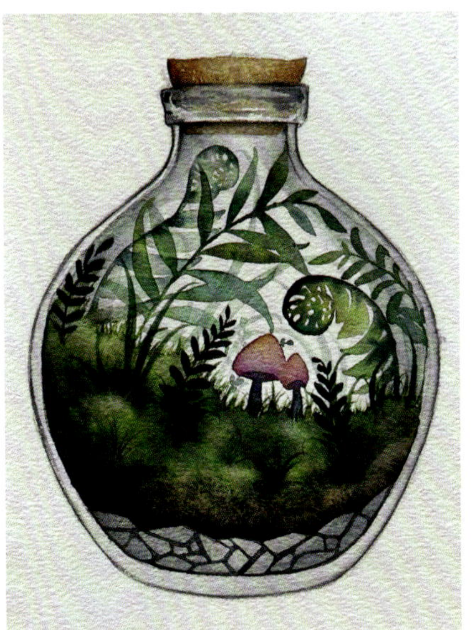

9. With Mixture 7, a little heavier in lamp black, add vegetation to the jar in the foreground. With Mixture 2, a little heavier in Mars black, form the small rocks in the lower part of the terrarium. Add the cork top with Mixture 10, then add more shadows to the glass with Mixture 1 (a little heavier in Payne's gray) to give it a shiny effect.

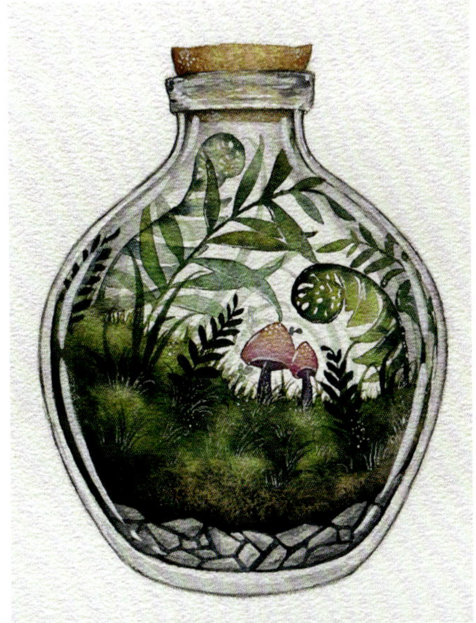

10. Finish with light. Use white gouache to add highlights to the jar and a white gel ink pen for the vegetation and cork.

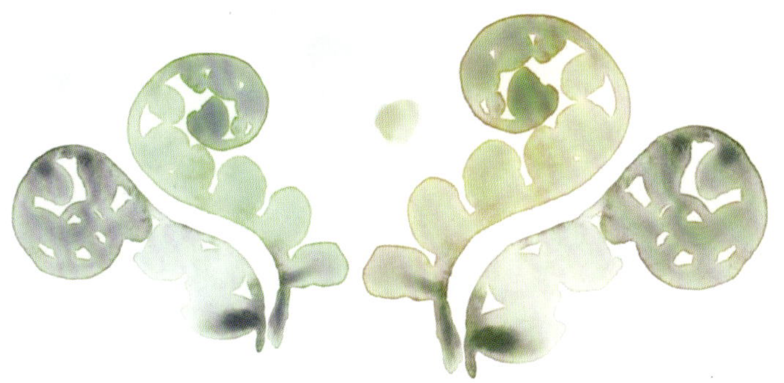

MUSHROOM SPHERE

Another way to think about space is to paint inside a sphere. This allows you to focus your attention—here, on the crystals in the center—and thus give more intensity to the painting and the message you wish to convey.

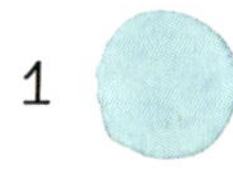 1   • **Mixture 1** - Phthalo green + Prussian blue (diluted)

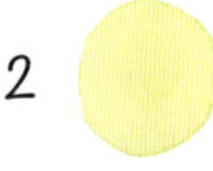 2   • **Mixture 2** - Indian yellow (diluted)

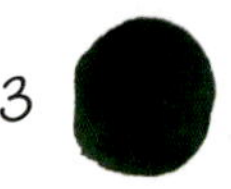 3   • **Mixture 3** - Sap green + Prussian blue + Payne's gray

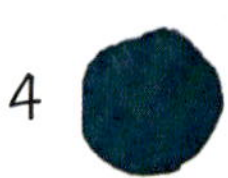 4   • **Mixture 4** - Prussian blue + phthalo green

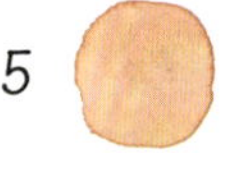 5   • **Mixture 5** - Alizarin crimson + quinacridone gold

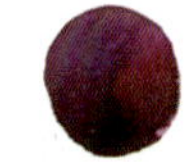 6   • **Mixture 6** - Permanent rose + ultramarine blue

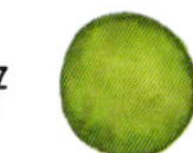 7   • **Mixture 7** - Sap green + Indian yellow

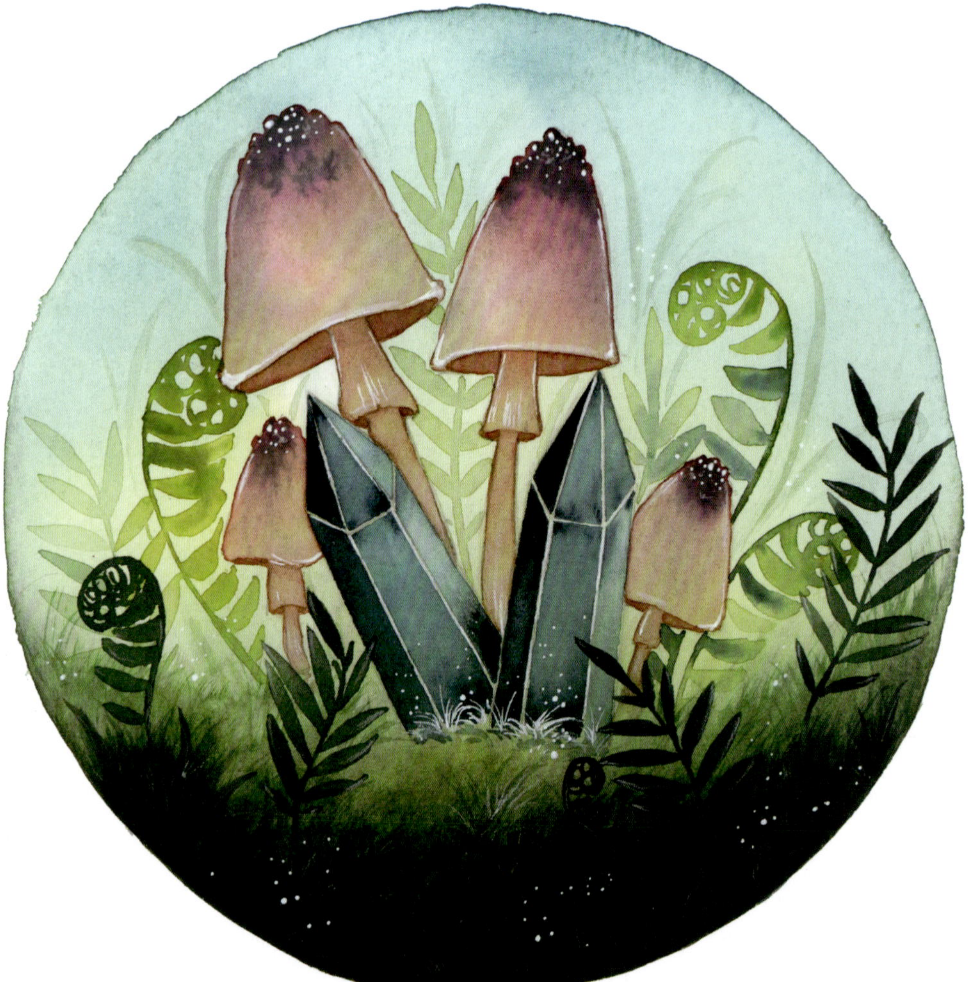

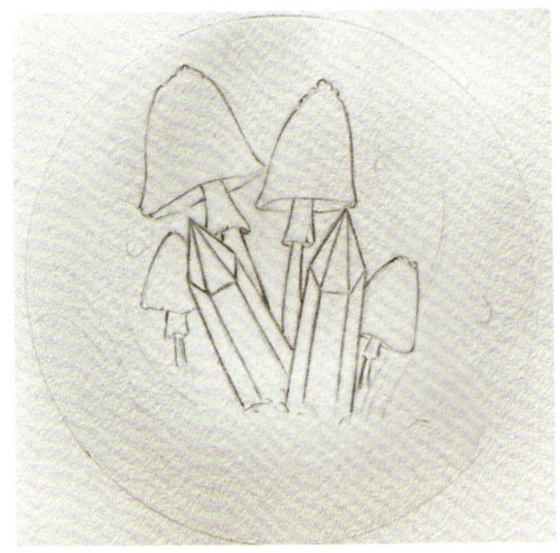

1. Draw a circle using a compass. With a pencil, make a small sketch of four mushrooms behind two precious stones. Once this is done, completely moisten the inside of the circle.

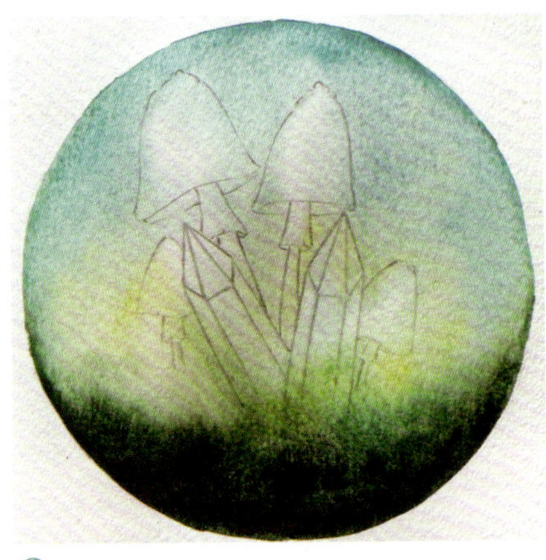

2. Using a round brush, create a color gradient by applying Mixture 1 to the top, 2 to the middle, and 3 to the bottom of the circle.

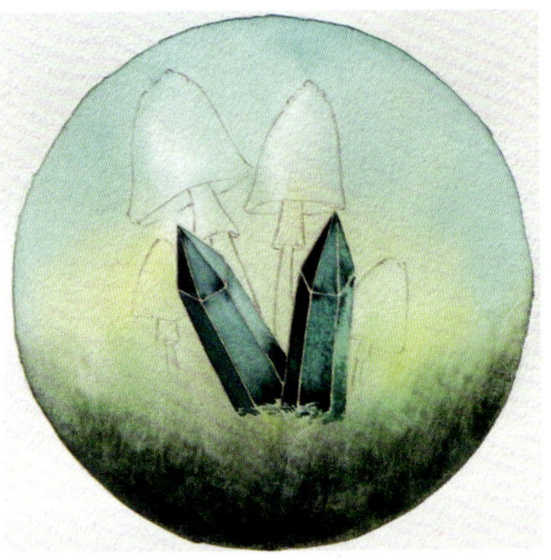

3. Using a small, round brush, apply Mixture 4 to the inside of the gemstones, making sure to lighten them more in the center and on the right sides. Avoid letting the crystals' faces touch each other by creating a thin band of light on each edge. Let dry.

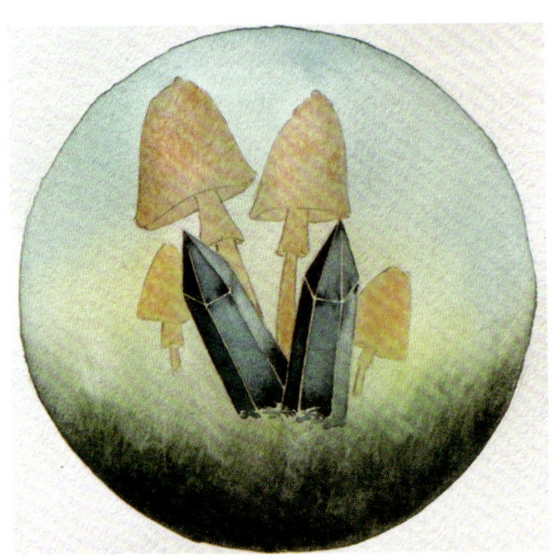

4. Using a soft brush and Mixture 5, fill the four mushrooms.

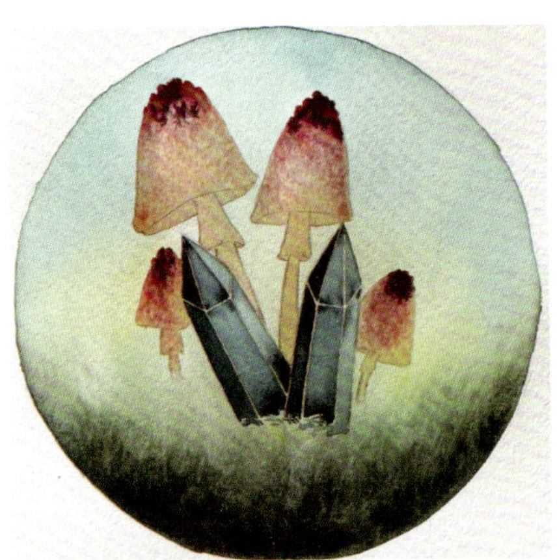

5. In the still-wet watercolor, place a touch of Mixture 6 on the mushroom caps. Let it dry.

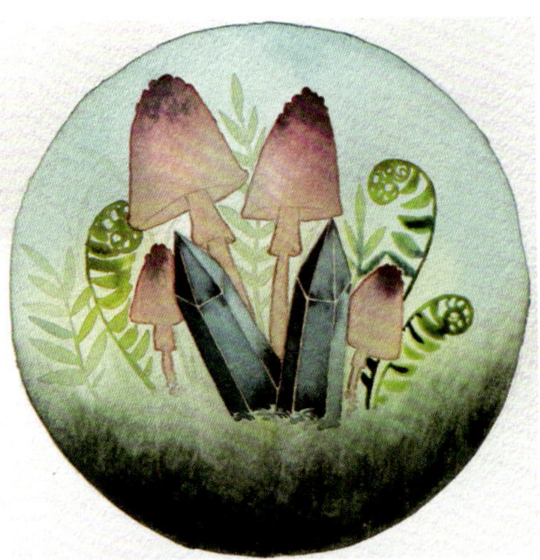

6. Using a thin, round brush, add vegetation around the mushrooms. Use different types of greens, including those from Mixtures 3 and 7.

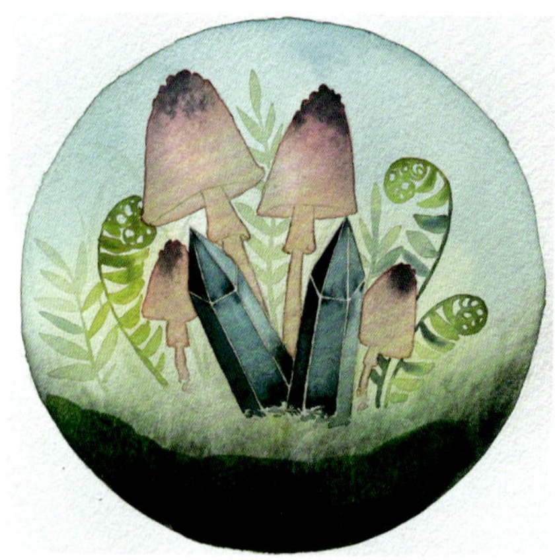

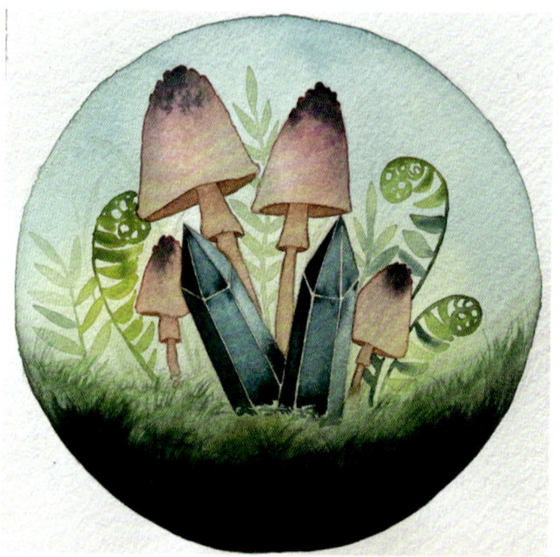

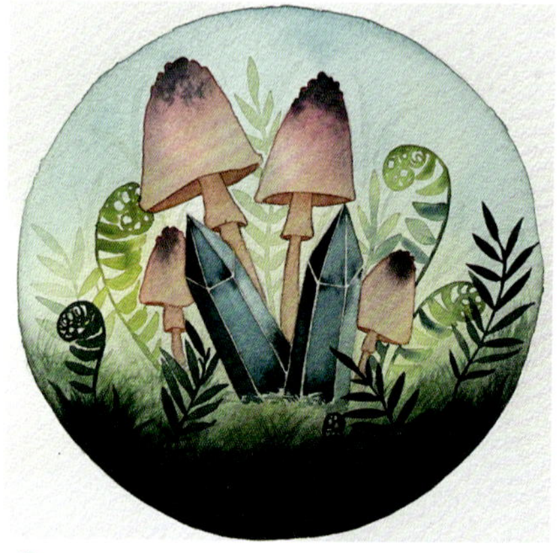

7. Using a soft brush, add Mixture 3 to the bottom of the sphere, on the moss at the base of the mushrooms.

8. Using a very fine or tapered brush, stretch the pigments you have just applied to create grass blades. Use Mixture 3 for the foreground and Mixture 7 for the background. This will allow you to accentuate the depth of the ground. With Mixture 5, paint the shadow under the mushroom caps.

9. Using a precise brush and Mixture 3, paint small ferns in the foreground to create depth.

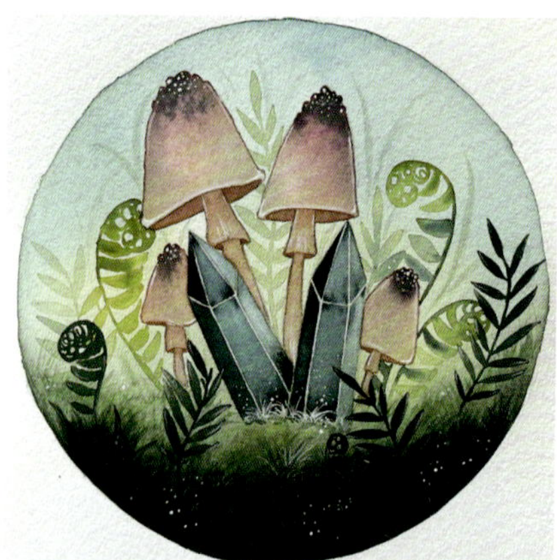

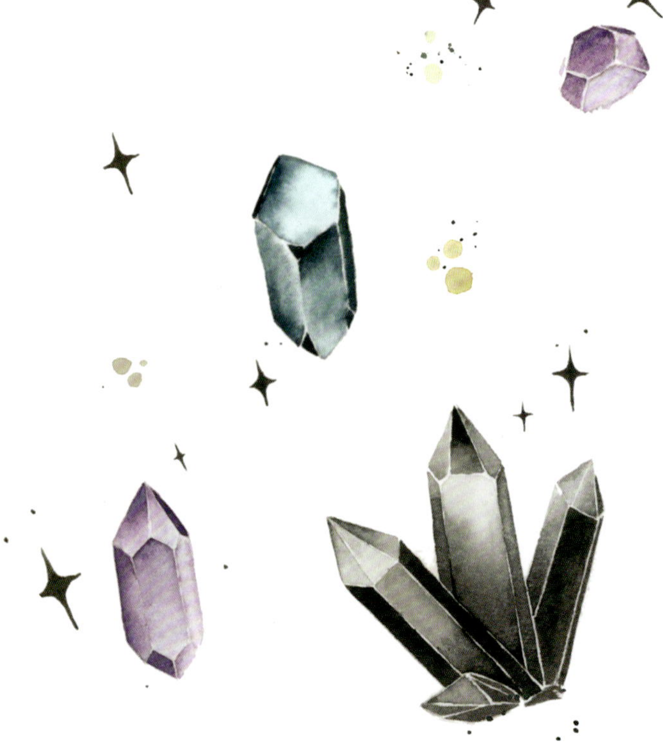

10. Using a white gel pen, add small touches of light to different areas of the watercolor; for example, at the base of the crystals or on the caps of the mushrooms.

WOOD FRAME OF FERNS

In this step-by-step guide, I show you how to create a transparent and beautifully framed fern undergrowth using the different shades of green. If necessary, adapt this exercise with the fern species presented on pages 69–72.

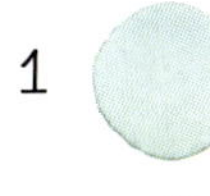

1 • **Mixture 1** - Phthalo green + ultramarine blue (diluted)

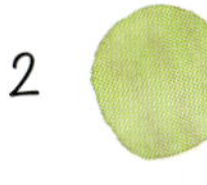

2 • **Mixture 2** - Sap green (diluted)

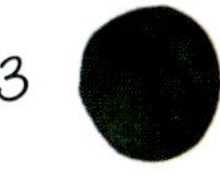

3 • **Mixture 3** - Sap green + Prussian blue + lamp black

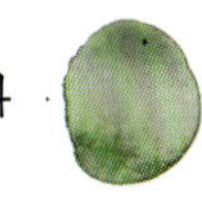

4 • **Mixture 4** - Sap green + Prussian blue (diluted)

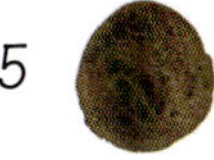

5 • **Mixture 5** - Brown iron oxide + Mars black

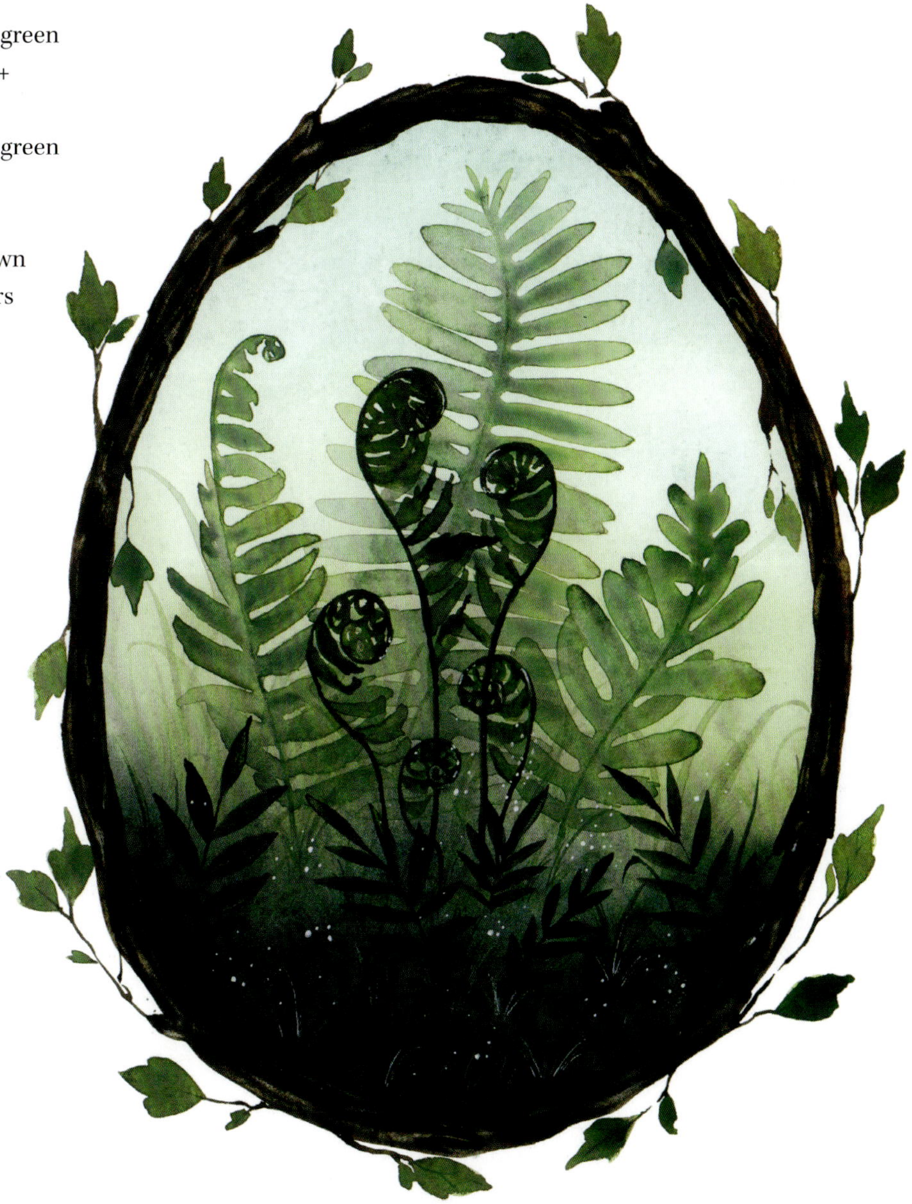

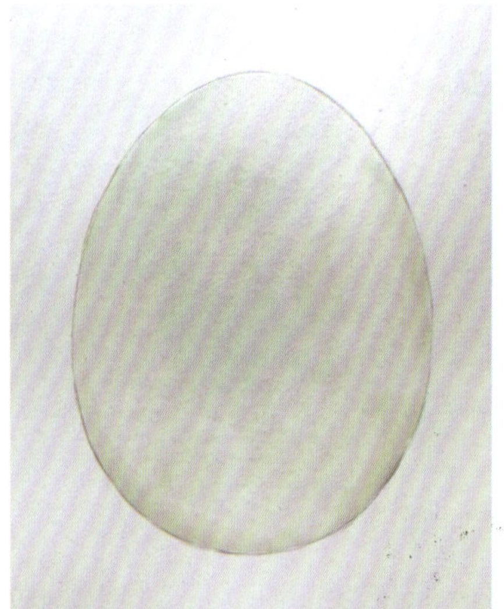

1. Draw an oval shape with a pencil. Fill the entire shape with a very diluted combination of water and Mixture 4.

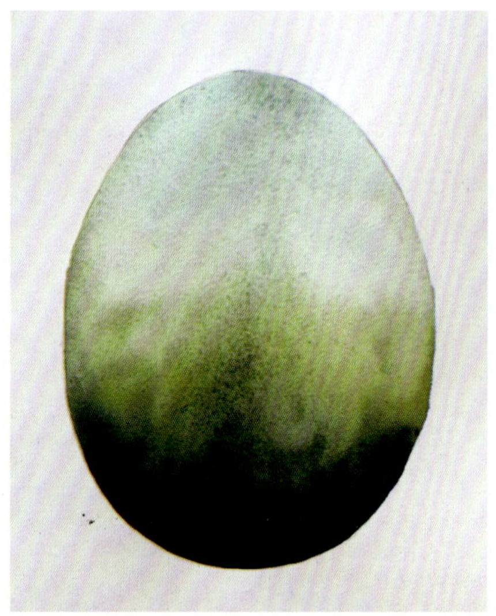

2. In the still-wet watercolor, create a color gradient: Mixture 1 on top, Mixture 2 in the middle, and Mixture 3 at the bottom. Wait for the watercolor to dry.

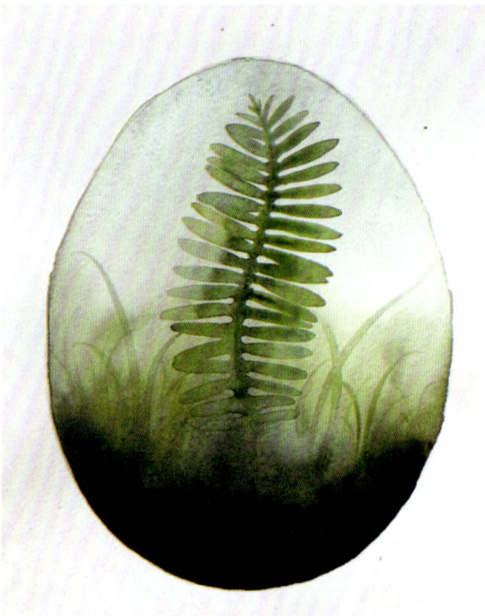

3. Make a first fern, fairly light and centered inside your oval. Preferably use Mixtures 2 and 4, but all kinds of warm and cool greens will work. Let it dry. Add grass blades with these same mixtures.

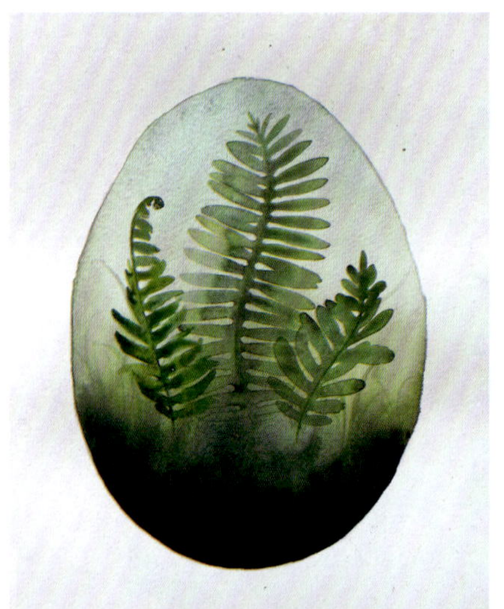

4. Add two new ferns on the sides of the first, taking care to add movement. You can use Mixtures 2 and 4 again, but do not dilute your mixes as much to add depth. Wait for the watercolor to dry.

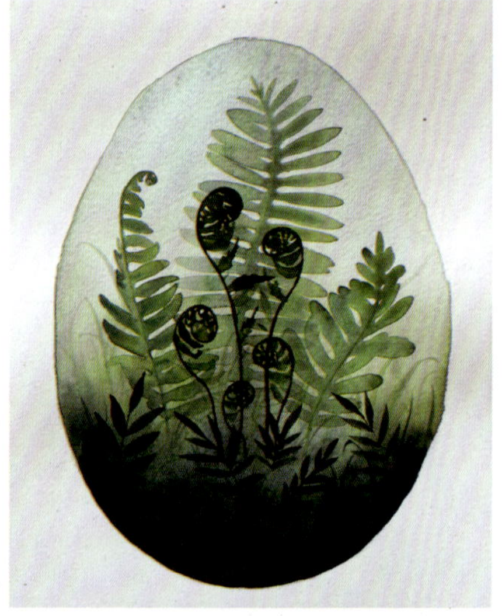

5. With Mixtures 2 and 3, add grasses, young ferns, and other plants of various shapes to your foreground.

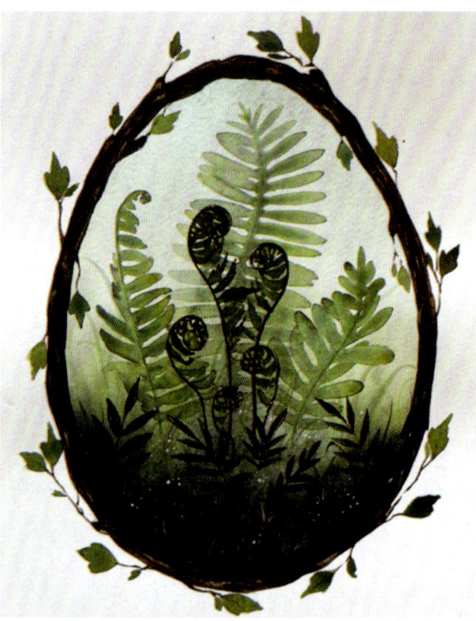

6. Using Mixture 5, create the wooden frame. The outline should be slightly irregular to imitate wood. Make small leafy branches. Add lighting effects with a white gel ink pen.

INSECT BRANCH

When I want to include insects in specific places in the composition or when there are a lot of them, I first sketch their shape to better prepare myself and adapt the scale of the different elements.

1 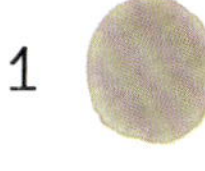 • **Mixture 1** - Brown iron oxide + tundra blue (diluted)

2 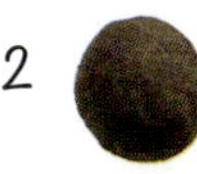 • **Mixture 2** - Brown iron oxide + tundra blue

3 • **Mixture 3** - Sap green + ultramarine blue

4 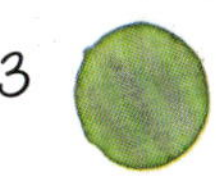 • **Mixture 4** - Sap green + Prussian blue + Payne's gray

5  • **Mixture 5** - Burgundy red ochre + pyrrole orange + permanent rose (diluted)

6 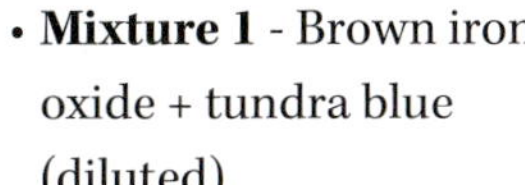 • **Mixture 6** - Ultramarine blue + cobalt green (diluted)

7  • **Mixture 7** - Pyrrole orange + permanent rose + yellow ochre (diluted)

8 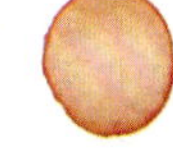 • **Mixture 8** - Indian yellow + cobalt green + phthalo green

9 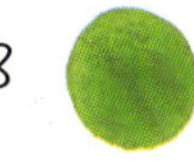 • **Mixture 9** - Indian yellow

10 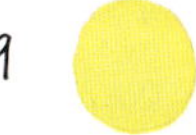 • **Mixture 10** - Prussian blue + phthalo green + Payne's gray

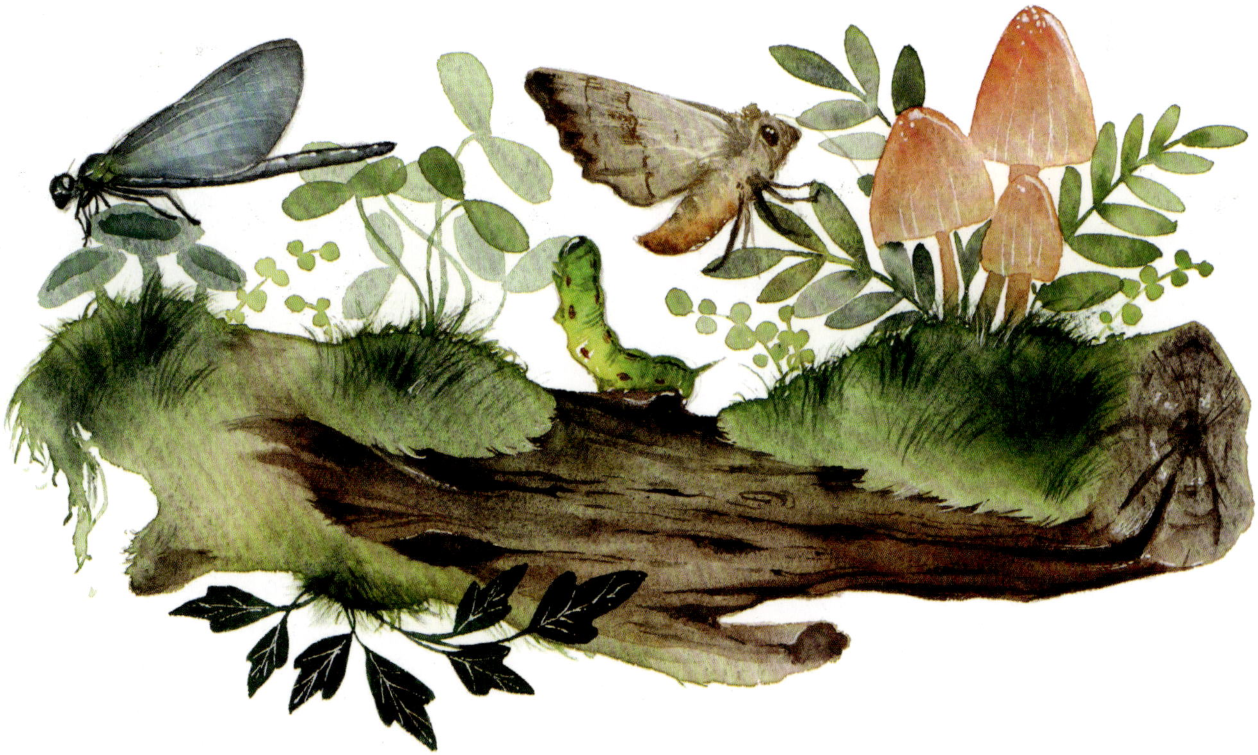

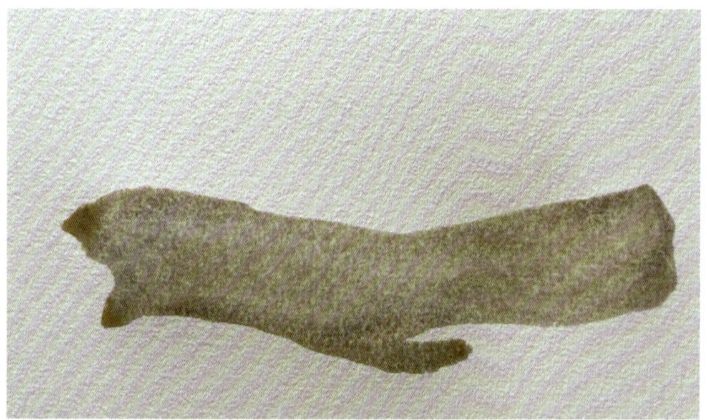

1. Using a soft brush and Mixture 1, paint the shape of the tree trunk.

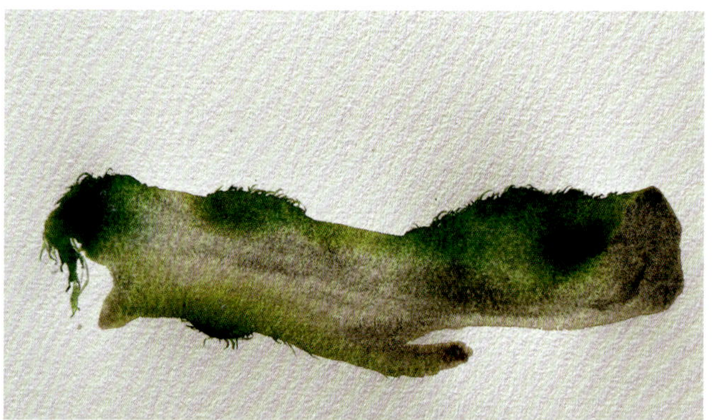

2. While the watercolor is still wet, use Mixtures 3 and 4 to create the moss. With Mixture 2, start tracing the grooves on the wood and let it dry.

3. Using a small brush and Mixture 2, deepen the grooves in the wood, varying their width to add realism, then add the shadow between the moss and the wood. Let it dry.

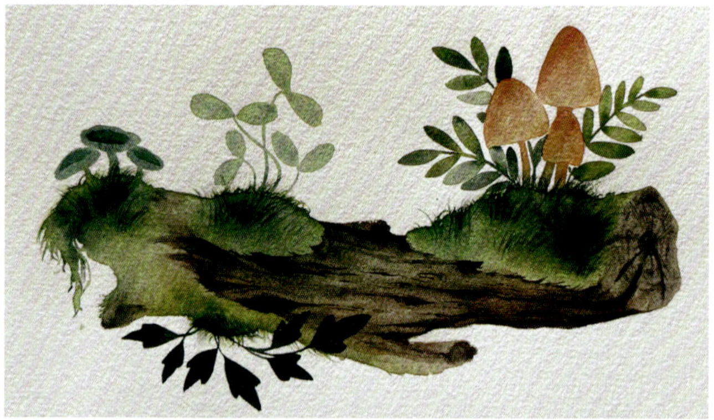

4. Using a soft, small brush, add vegetation above and below the trunk. Use Mixtures 5 and 7 for the mushrooms, 3 for the leaves, 6 for the lichen, 3 and 4 for the foliage around the mushrooms, and 4 for the ivy under the branch. Using a fine or tapered brush, draw small blades of grass with Mixture 4. Let it dry.

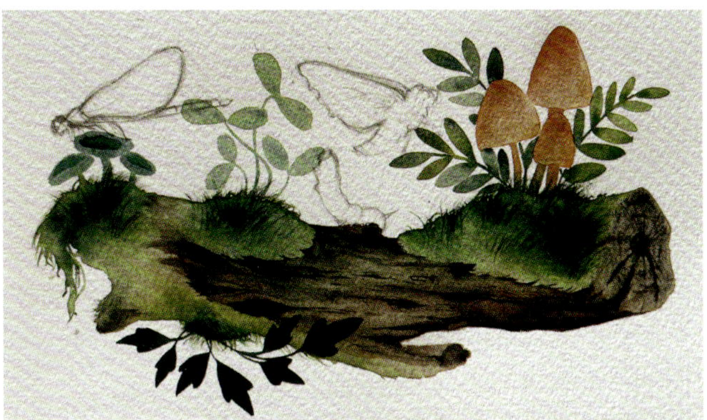

5. Sketch the insects to make them easier to position. Choose the ones you like best. For me, it's a caterpillar, a moth, and a dragonfly.

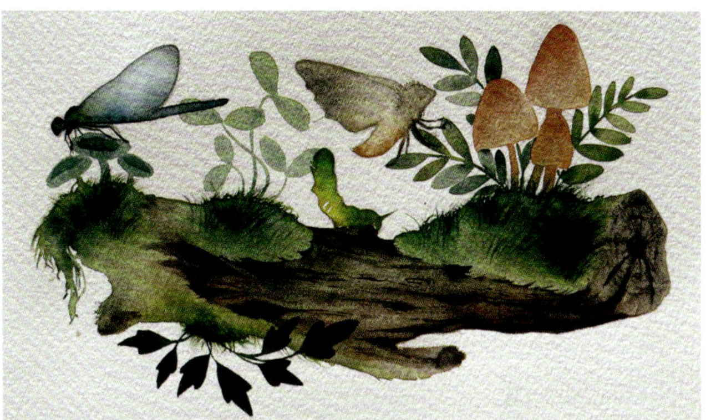

6. Apply the first colors to your insects. Here, I chose Mixture 10 for the dragonfly, Mixtures 1 and 5 for the butterfly, and Mixtures 8 and 9 for the caterpillar. Let them dry.

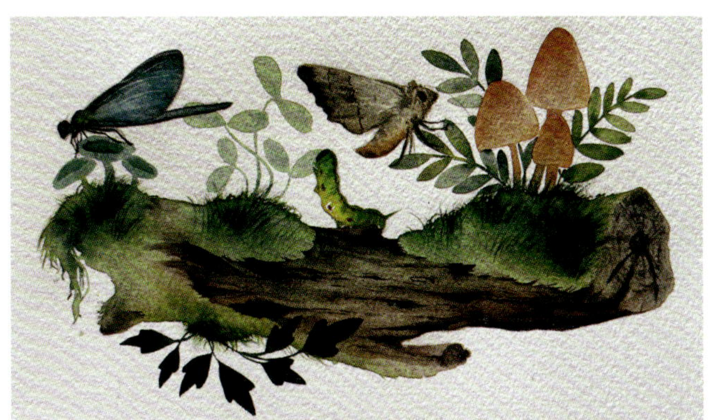

7. Intensify the colors by applying a new, slightly darker layer to give them volume.

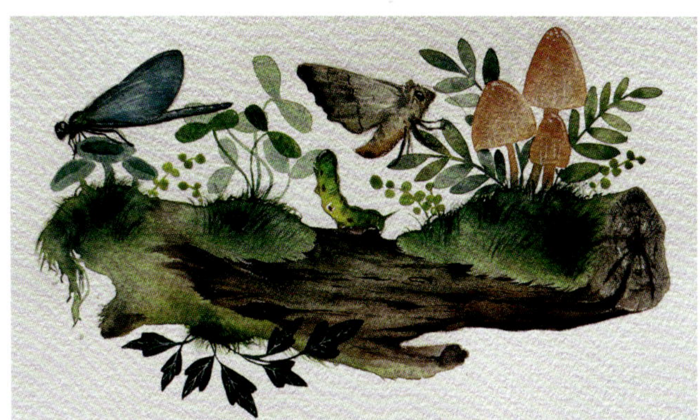

8. Add some small vegetation to fill in the white spaces. With a white gel ink pen, add touches of light to the insects, plants, and log.

FOREST SCENE: WILD STRAWBERRIES AND BUMBLEBEE

Wildflowers attract many pollinating insects, and I found it interesting to create a watercolor depicting this little bumblebee in action. This step-by-step guide will allow you to explore the softness of a bed of wild strawberries, while working on the transparency of the vegetation.

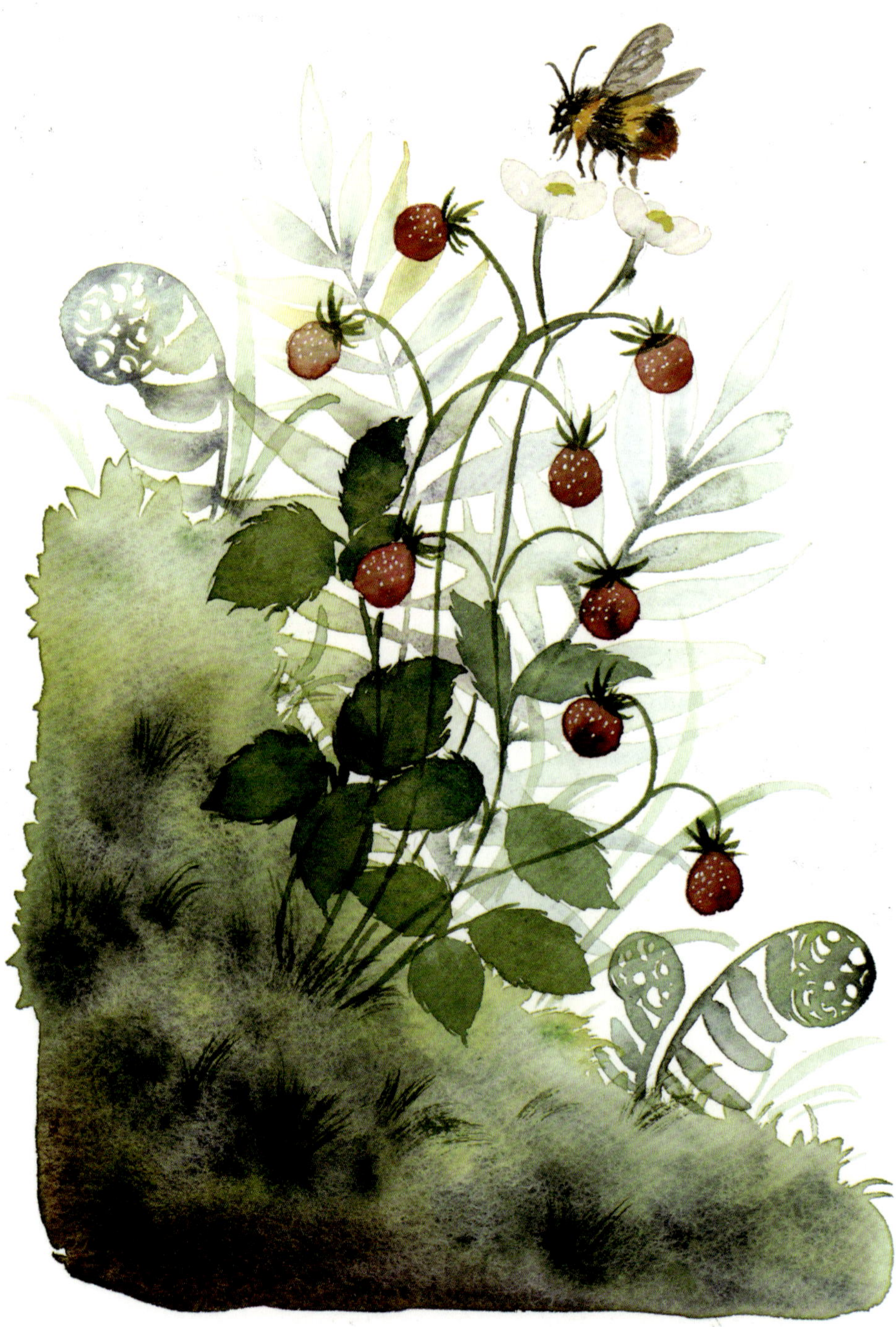

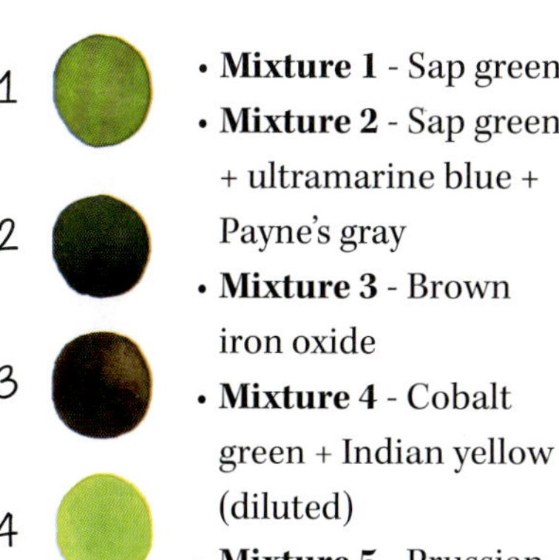

1

2

3

4

5

- **Mixture 1** - Sap green
- **Mixture 2** - Sap green + ultramarine blue + Payne's gray
- **Mixture 3** - Brown iron oxide
- **Mixture 4** - Cobalt green + Indian yellow (diluted)
- **Mixture 5** - Prussian blue + sap green + buff titanium (diluted)

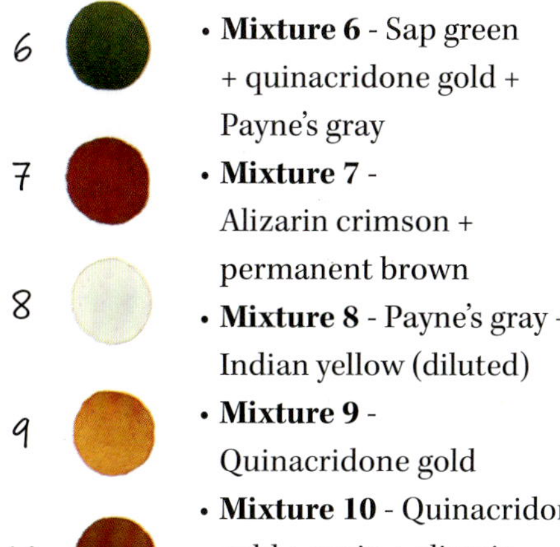

6

7

8

9

10

- **Mixture 6** - Sap green + quinacridone gold + Payne's gray
- **Mixture 7** - Alizarin crimson + permanent brown
- **Mixture 8** - Payne's gray + Indian yellow (diluted)
- **Mixture 9** - Quinacridone gold
- **Mixture 10** - Quinacridone gold + sepia + alizarin crimson

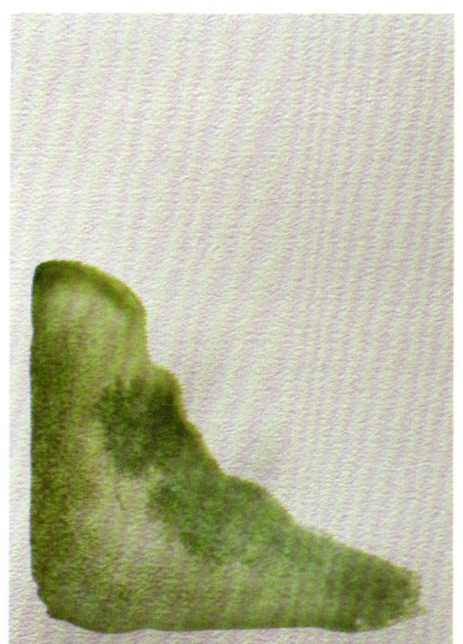

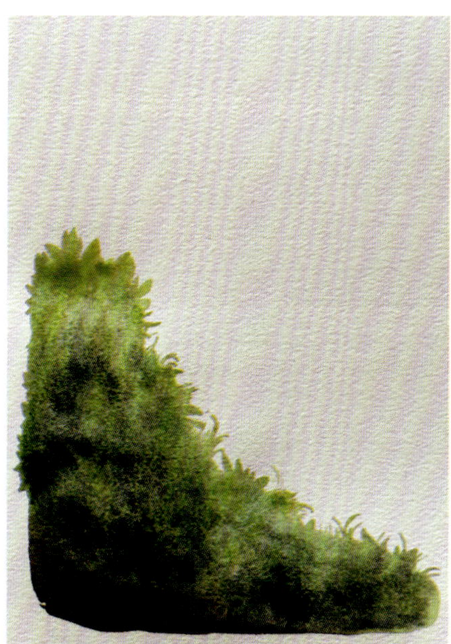

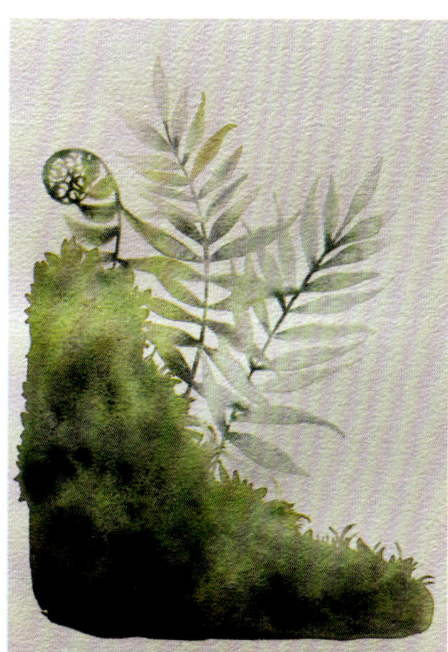

1. Paint the base of the moss in the bottom-left corner of your sheet using a thick, soft, round brush and Mixture 1.

2. Using a more precise brush and Mixture 4, place plant shapes on top of the moss. Add different concentrations of Mixture 2 to give it texture and irregularity. At the very bottom, represent the earth with Mixture 3. If you are worried about lines, wait until the watercolor dries completely.

3. In the still-wet watercolor, using a fine brush and Mixture 5, paint three ferns, one of which is still budding. With Mixture 6, apply a few touches of pigment to the stems of the ferns to bring out the colors. You can also add Mixture 4 to a few leaves to create warm contrasts. Let it dry.

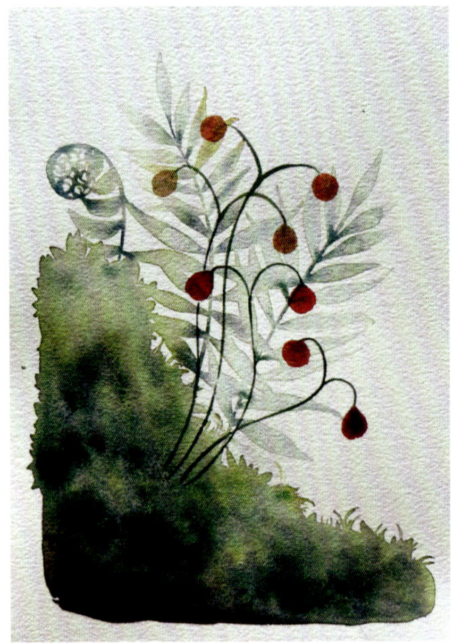

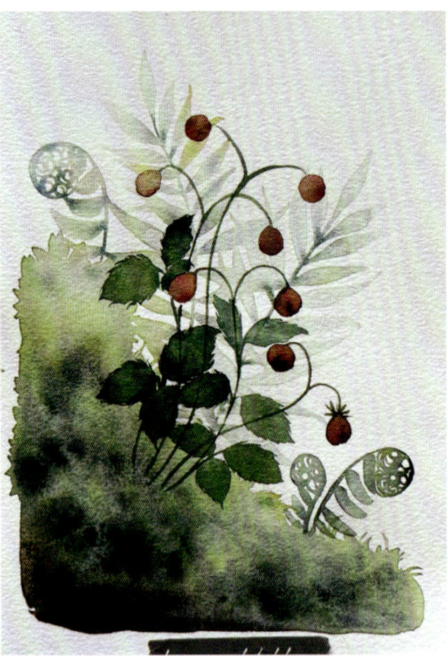

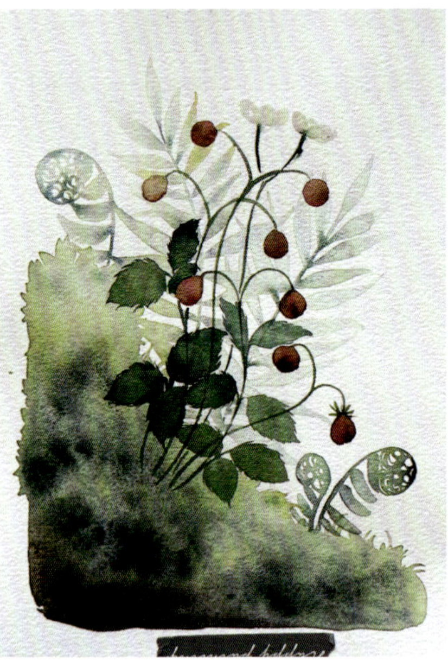

4. Using a fine brush and Mixture 6, draw the stems of the wild strawberries in the middle of the moss. Use Mixture 7 to paint the fruit. Let it dry.

5. Using the same brush and Mixture 6, add the wild strawberry leaves. Make them serrated using the tip of the brush.

6. Using Mixture 8, form strawberry flowers in an empty space so that their whiteness stands out better, then add small stems to connect them to the others.

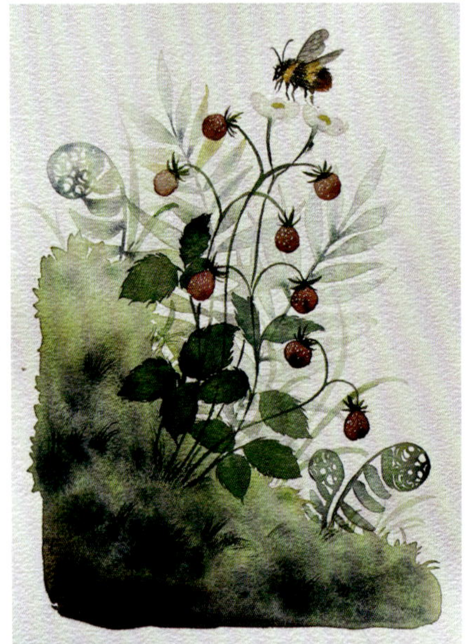

7. Paint the centers of the flowers with a fine, precise brush and a slightly diluted Mixture 9. Using Mixtures 9 and 10, add the bumblebee ready to forage.

Advice

If you feel an imbalance between the elements in your illustration, don't hesitate to add additional vegetation. For my part, I preferred to paint two ferns in the bottom-right corner to fill an empty space. Use your different shades of green and the same brush as the fern on the left.

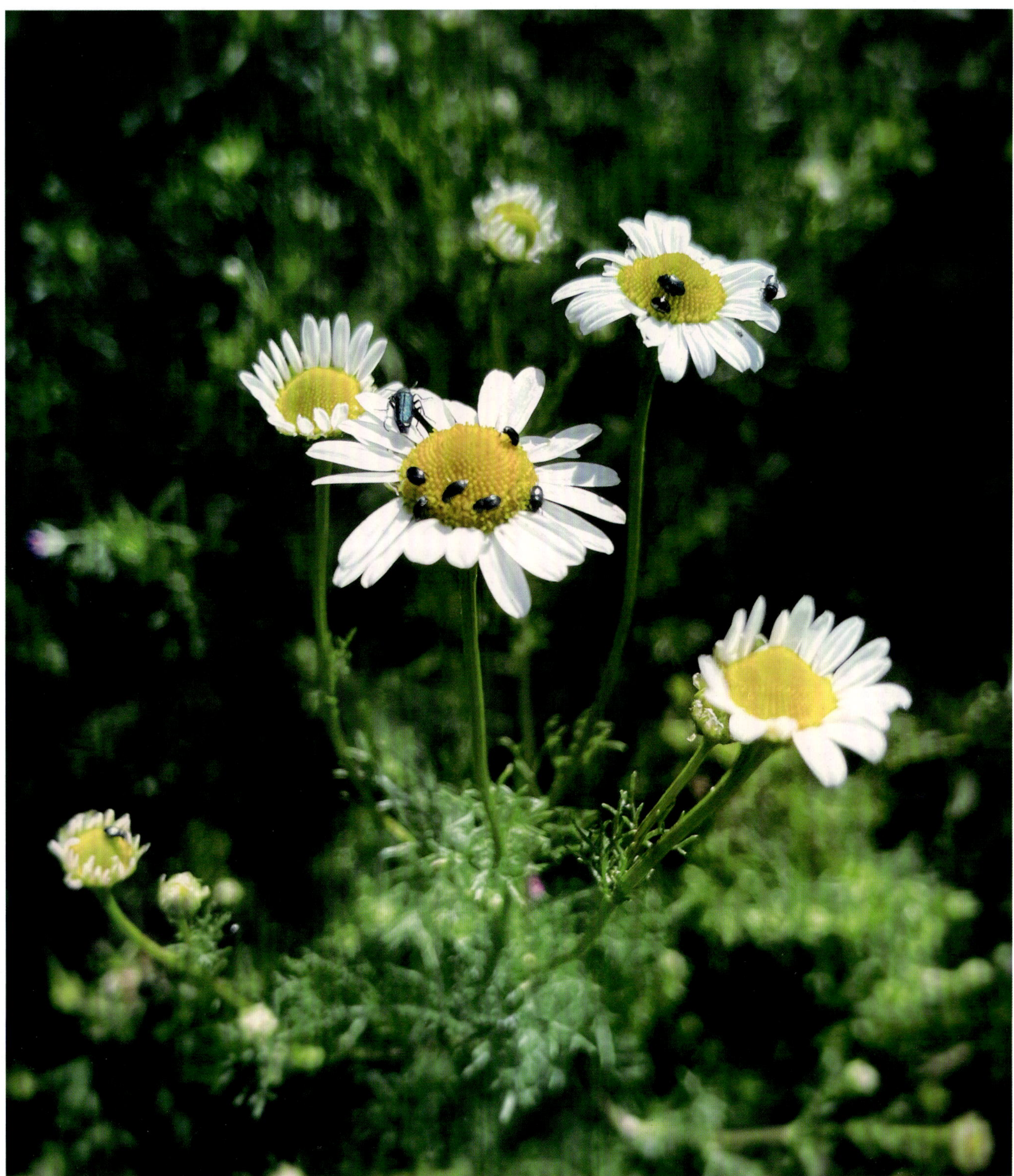

Photos help when picking colors. Even though the petals are white, the shadows on them are blue and green. You can make those shades much easier than white!

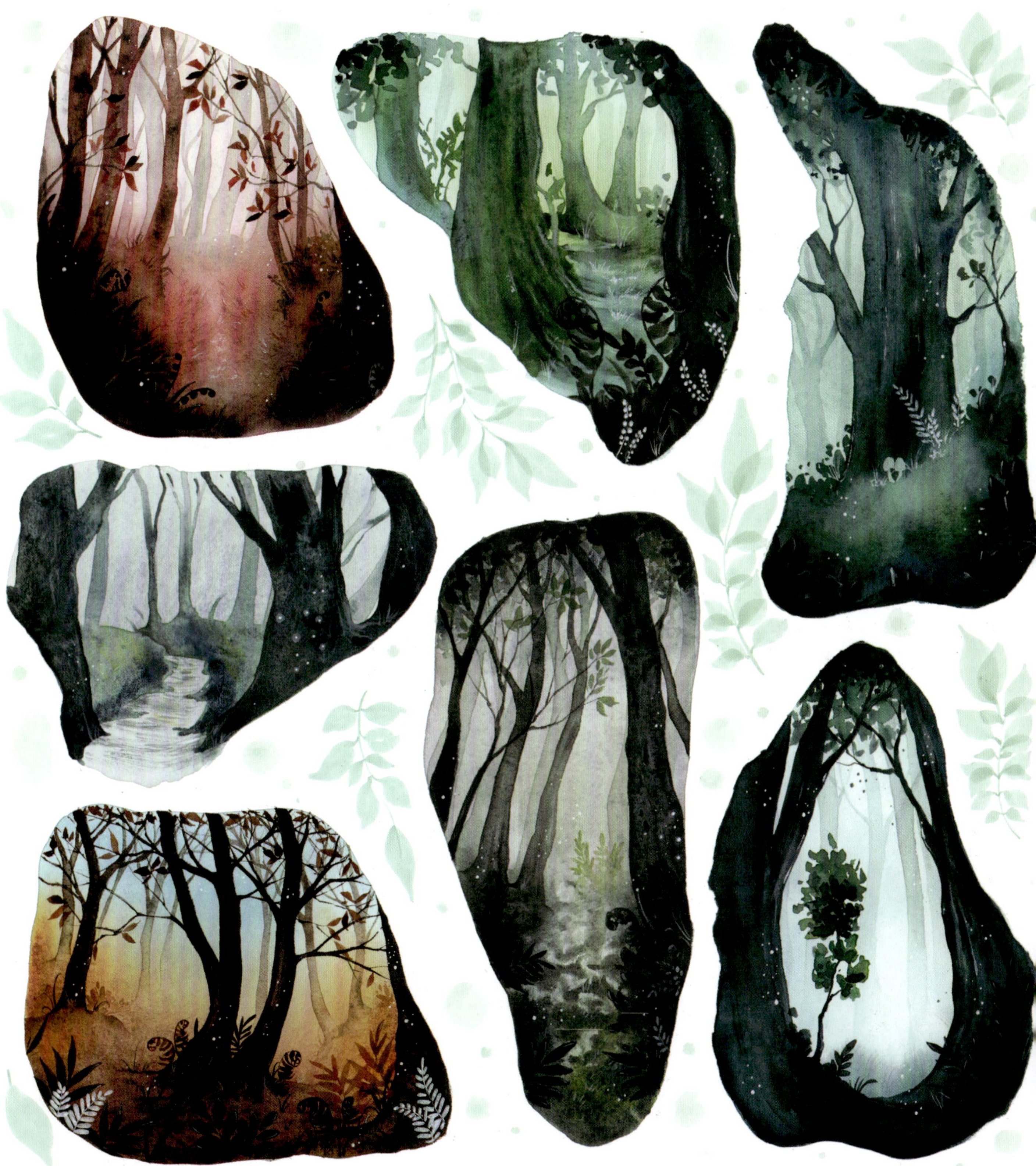

Painting Forest Landscapes

In this final chapter, expand your horizons to see the forest from a broader perspective. Unlike the small undergrowth scenes mentioned earlier, focus more on the forest's overall atmosphere here while simplifying the details of the vegetation.

Perspective

Until now, I've often advised you to emphasize details; for example, by depicting the grooves in the wood or the veins in the leaves. Here, the elements will often be too small and numerous to do so. This is partly due to the illusion of depth.

To create perspective, you will need to play with:

- **Colors**, because the further away an element is, the paler its shades. Conversely, the closer it is, the more contrasting and vibrant the colors are.

- **Shapes**, because the closer the elements of your landscape are to the foreground, the larger and more detailed they appear—and they are located in the lower part of the paper, as seen with the trees in the following step-by-steps.

- **Layers**, because you will need to superimpose several elements on top of each other to create the illusion of depth. The more planes there are, the greater number of elements.

- **Horizon lines**, because this line demarcates the place between the earth and the sky. It will be very useful to establish the perspective between your different elements.

- **Vanishing points**, because if you want to add an element that is present on different planes, you will have to think about modifying its size on each one. For example, a path that disappears into the distance will become smaller and smaller as it moves away.

> ## *Tip*
> *To avoid redundancy, try varying the shape of the trees and branches by practicing with the first exercise in this chapter (starting on page 133).*

Forest Atmosphere

No matter the day, season, or weather, the forest offers us an incredible array of colors and atmospheres. In spring, bright, intense greens dominate the woods; in autumn, the leaves turn red, orange, and brown, giving nature a warm and soothing atmosphere. In the morning, the sunrise floods the undergrowth with a soft, reassuring light; the evening gives way to shadow and darkness. The forest arouses many emotions in us, because its aura—sometimes magical, sometimes unsettling—is the site of countless fascinating stories.

A place widely exploited in cinema and art in general, the forest is associated with many spiritual meanings and messages. Directors and artists use this natural setting to develop plays of light and shadow, color contrasts, and artistic blur.

Desaturated and cool colors often inspire a feeling of worry or unease, while warm and bright colors reassure us. Other elements can also add a special aura to the forest, such as the various shapes that inhabit it.

For example, the drier and more twisted the trees, the greater the sense of unease.

In my opinion, watercolor is one of the best mediums for exploring and replicating the many facets of the forest. Its transparency is an incredible asset that will allow you to use several artistic effects.

Wash Technique

In this chapter, we will often use it to create the backgrounds of landscapes. The wash technique consists of applying a first layer of diluted color to cover a large surface. It serves as the base of the painting before applying the colors that contribute to the atmosphere of the landscape.

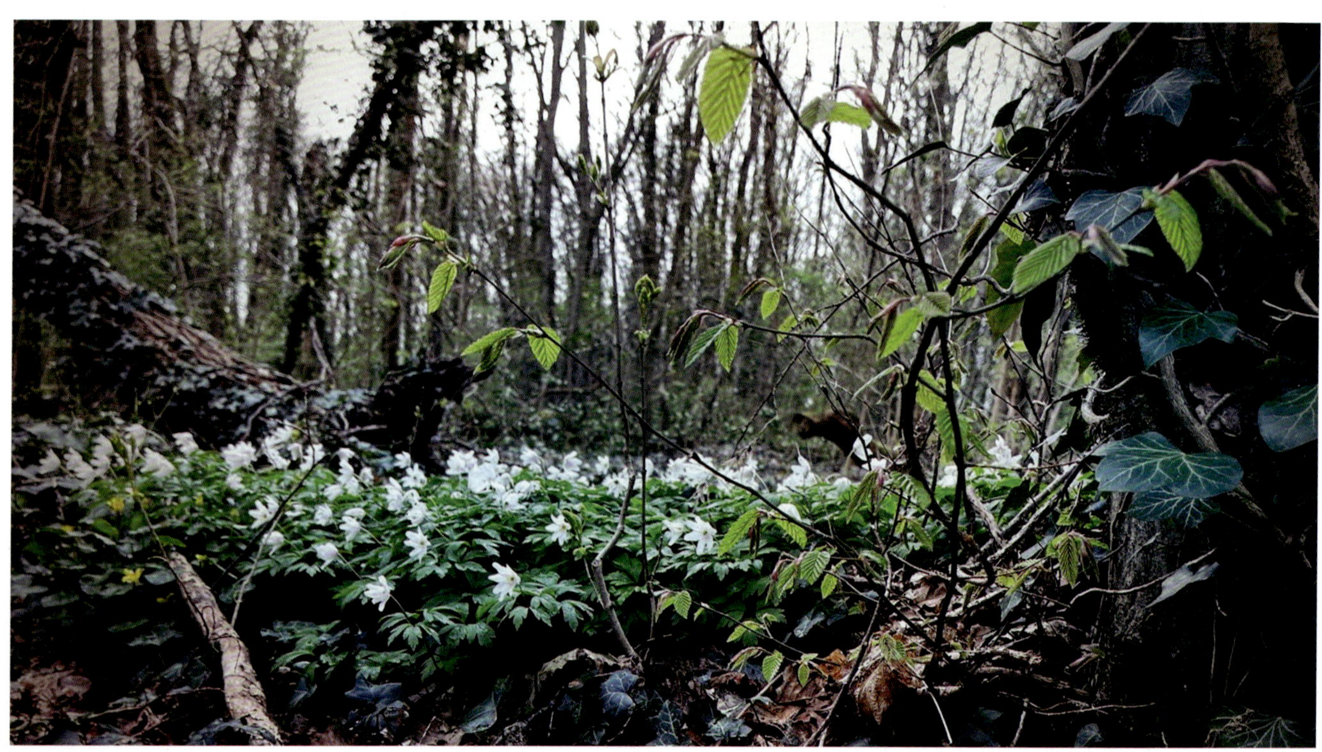

Practice

TREES

Before you start creating landscapes, I suggest you practice drawing your first trees. Understanding how a tree is made will help you better choose what you want to depict in your forest scenes.

Autumn Tree

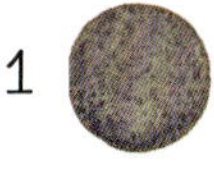 1 • **Mixture 1** - Tundra blue + brown iron oxide

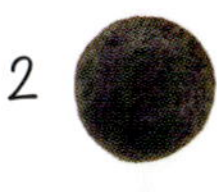 2 • **Mixture 2** - Tundra blue + brown iron oxide + Mars black

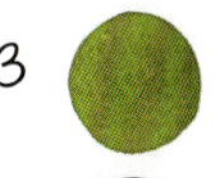 3 • **Mixture 3** - Sap green + Indian yellow

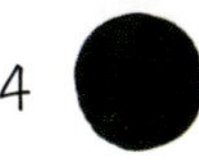 4 • **Mixture 4** - Sap green + ultramarine blue + Payne's gray

> *Note*
>
> *I generally don't depict entire trees. I use them more as a framing choice, which typically doesn't allow me to detail the tree species. This doesn't bother me, as I prefer to emphasize the atmosphere.*

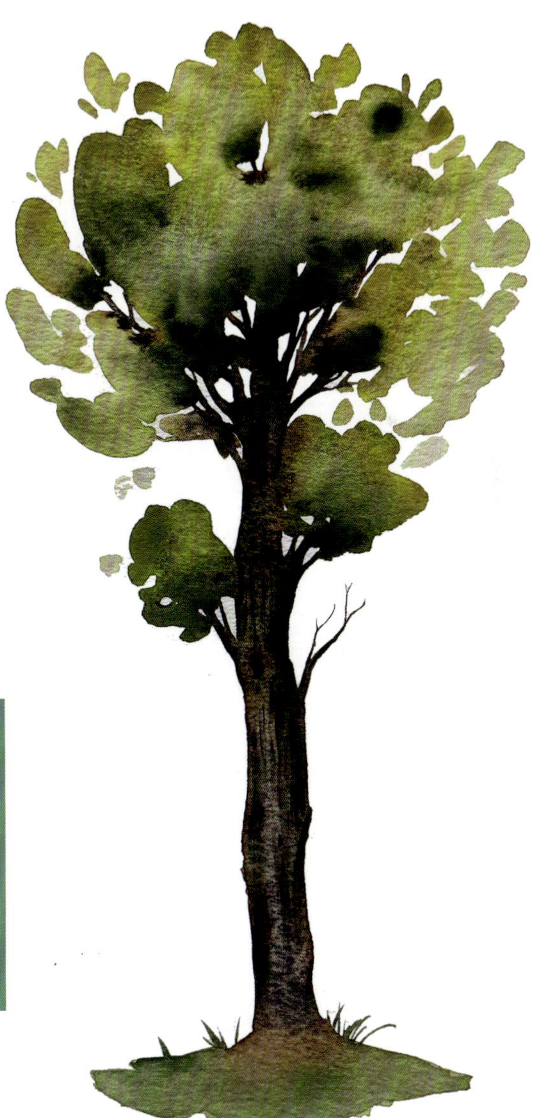

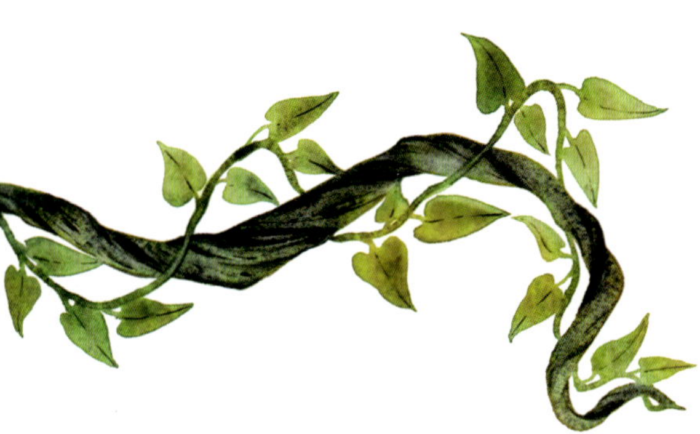

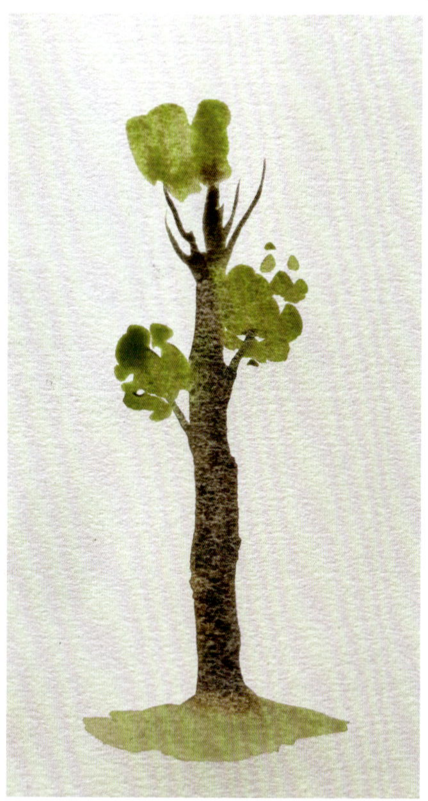

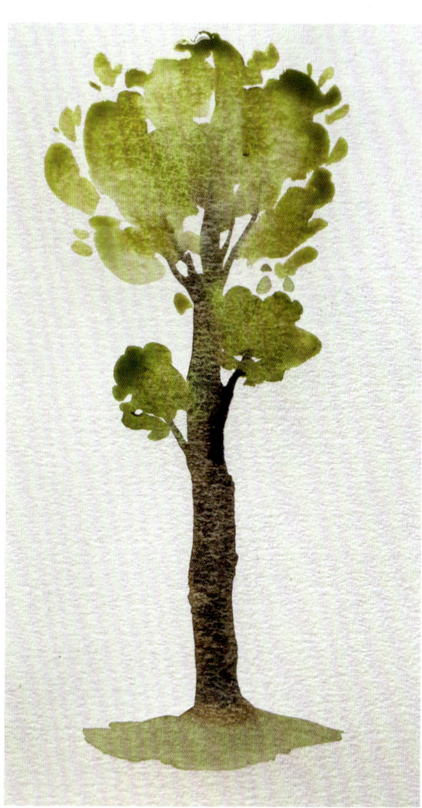

1. Using a soft brush, paint the trunk with Mixture 1 and the grass at its base with Mixture 3.

2. Using a small brush and Mixture 1, shape the upper part of the trunk including small branches. Then add a few leaves with Mixture 3.

3. Using a soft brush and Mixture 3, create small cloud-shaped areas to represent the foliage.

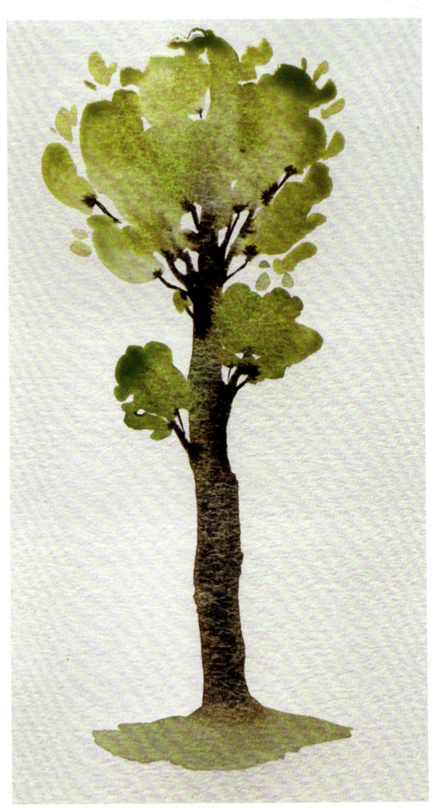

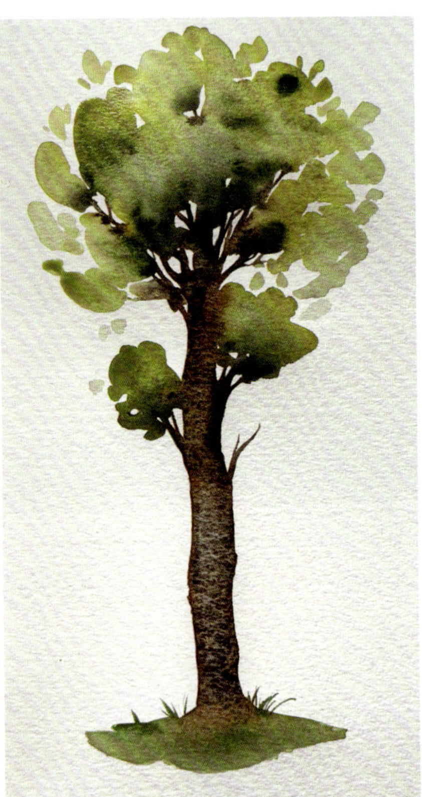

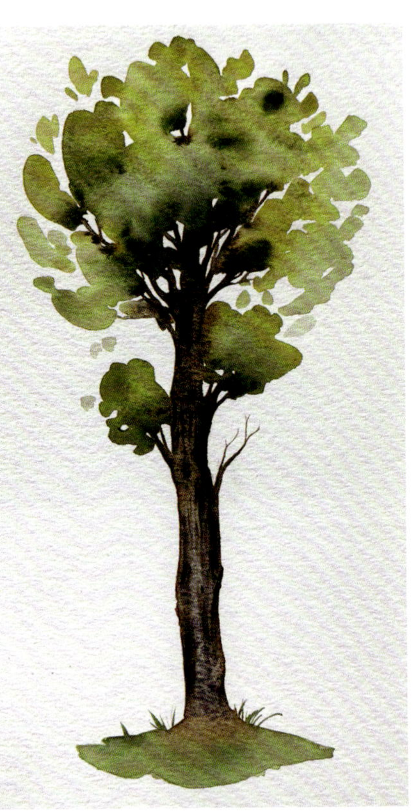

4. In the still-wet watercolor, using a precise brush and Mixture 2, draw darker branches under the foliage.

5. Create the shadow under the leaves and a few blades of grass at the base of the tree by adding Mixture 4 to the still-wet watercolor. You can also add more color to your tree if necessary. Wait for the watercolor to dry.

6. Using a very fine brush and Mixture 2, draw fine grooves on the trunk and darken the shadows.

Spring Tree

1 • **Mixture 1** - Permanent brown + brown iron oxide + Mars black

2 • **Mixture 2** - Sap green + Indian yellow

3 • **Mixture 3** - Indian yellow + Prussian blue

4 • **Mixture 4** - Indian yellow + Prussian blue + Payne's gray

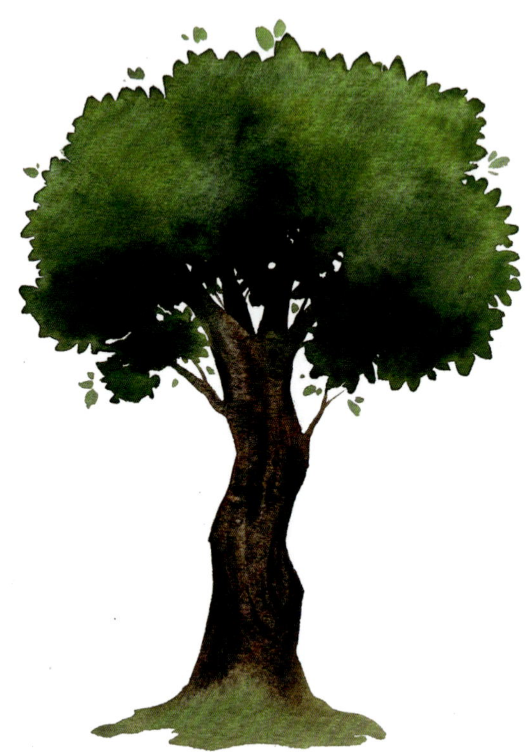

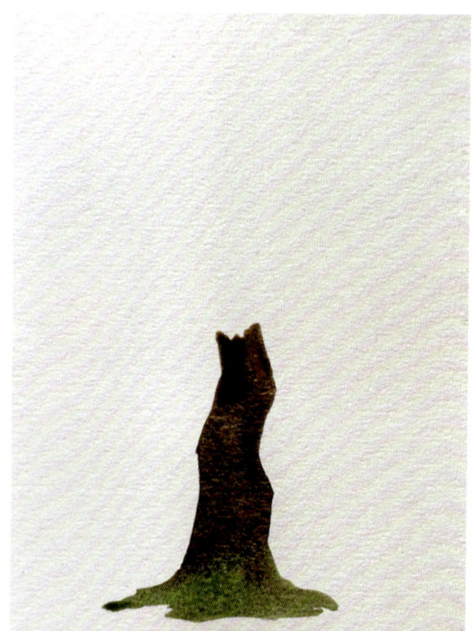

1. Using a soft brush and Mixture 1, paint the bottom of the tree trunk. In the wet watercolor, add the grass at the base of the trunk using Mixture 2.

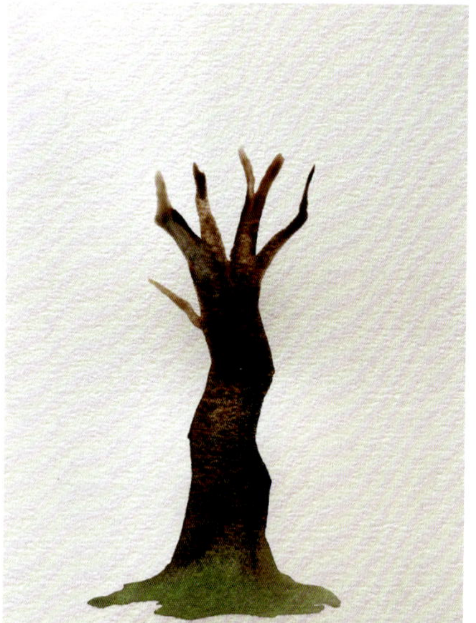

2. Using the same brush and Mixture 1, continue painting the trunk with branches.

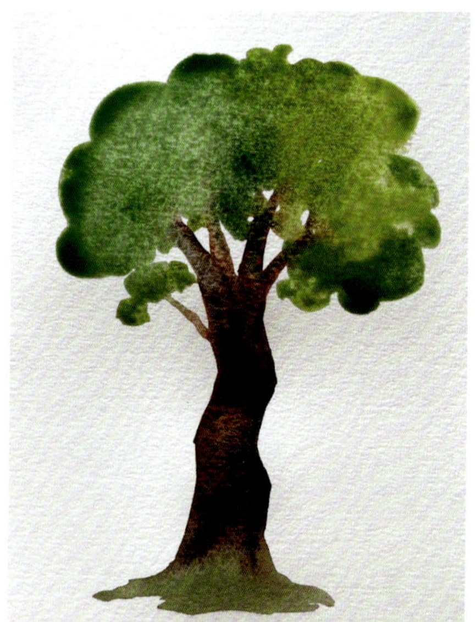

3. In the wet watercolor and alternating Mixtures 2 and 3, create the foliage of the tree.

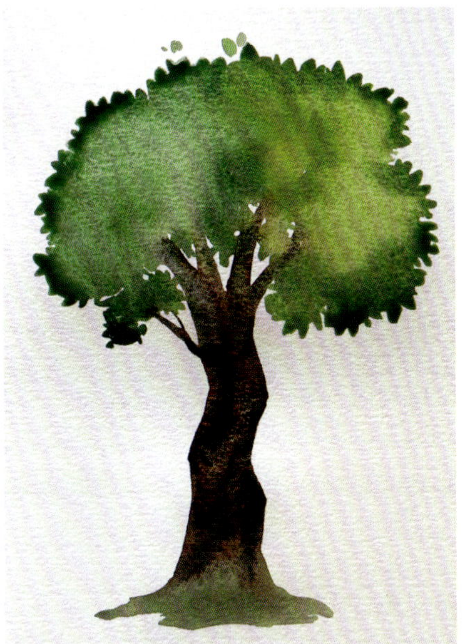

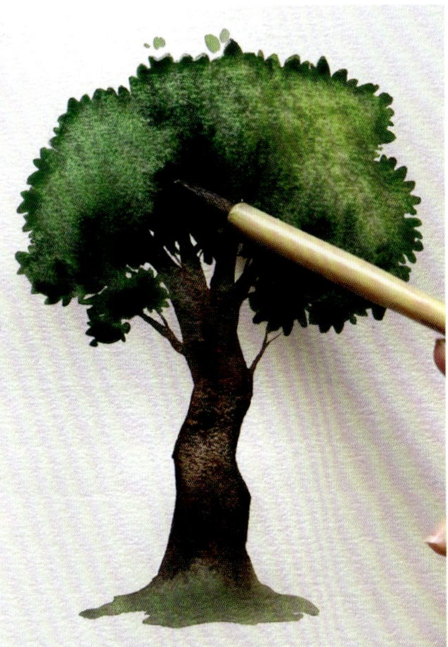

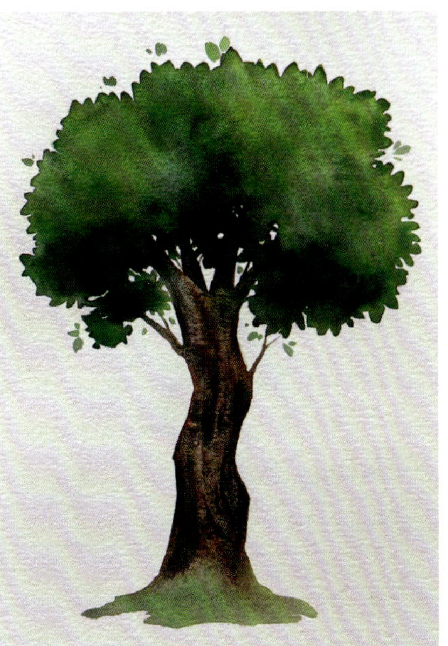

4. In the still-wet watercolor, using the tip of your brush and Mixtures 2 and 3, make the edge of the foliage serrated.

5. Use Mixture 4 to add depth and volume to the foliage. Wait for the watercolor to dry.

6. Using a fine brush and Mixture 1, draw the grooves on the trunk. Darken some of the branches to indicate different layers. The darkest branches represent the furthest ones.

Tip

Once the watercolor is dry, you can further work on the depth of the foliage by bringing out leaf shapes here and there in the shaded part of the tree.

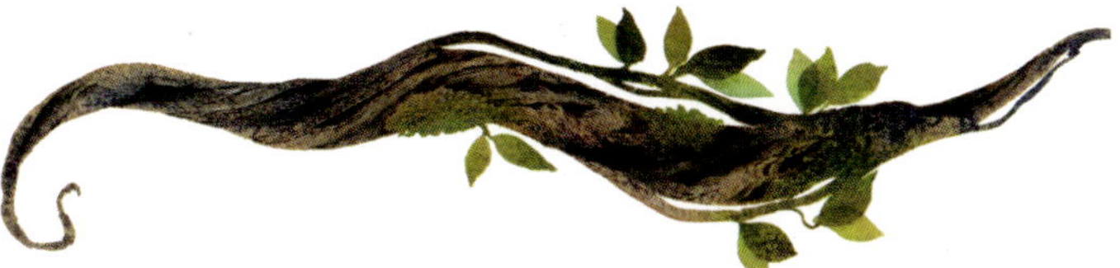

Winter Tree

- **Mixture 1** - Brown iron oxide + tundra blue
- **Mixture 2** - Brown iron oxide + blue tundra + Mars black

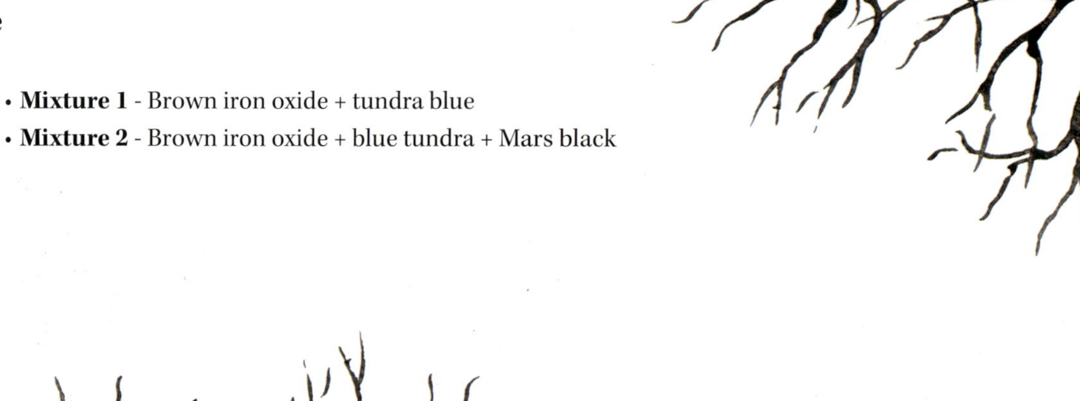

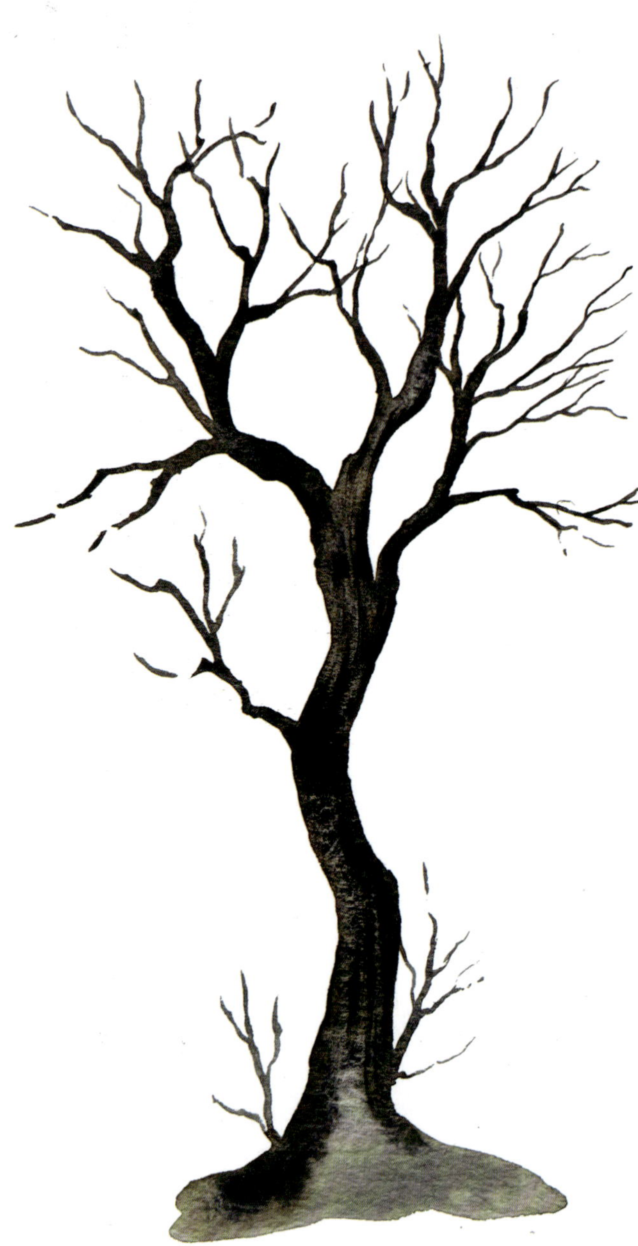

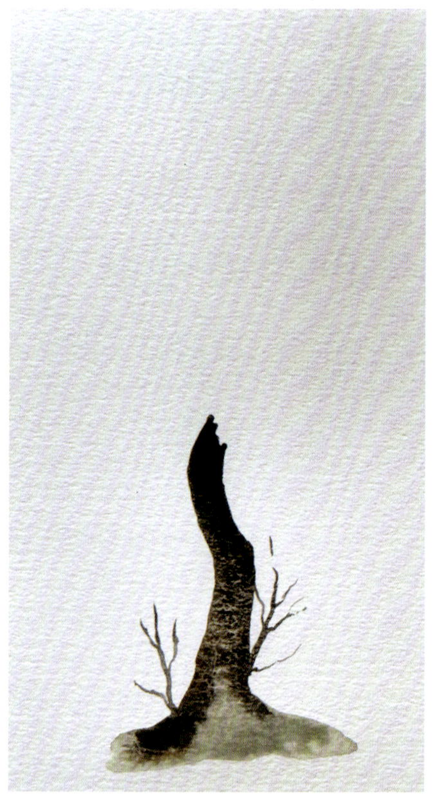

1. Start by painting the ground and the trunk with Mixture 1. Use more water with the mixture to indicate the ground.

    Painting the Secrets of the Forest with Watercolors

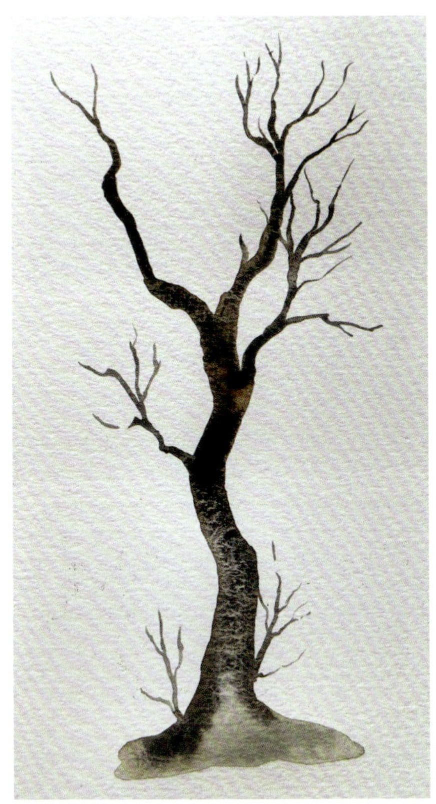

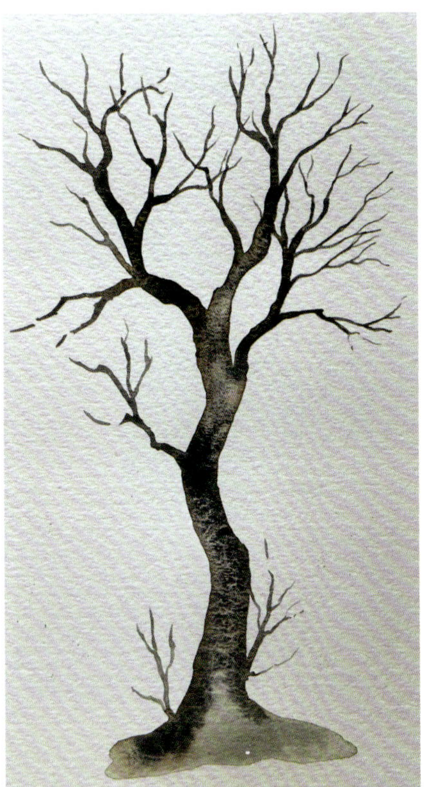

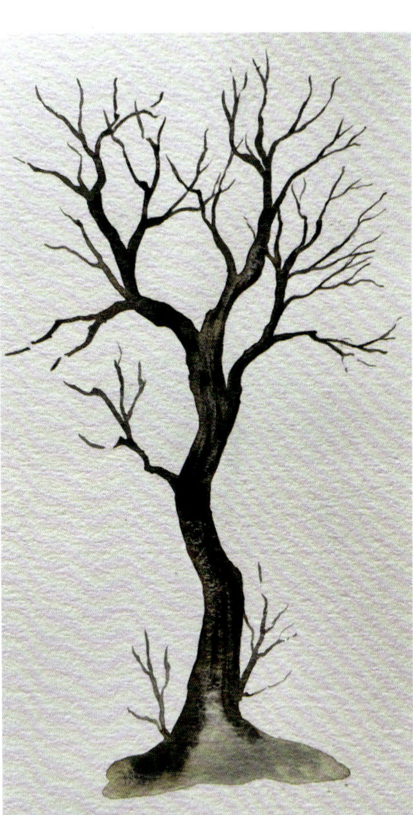

2. Using a precise brush, gradually move up the trunk to divide it into branches.

3. Divide the branches again into several smaller, increasingly thinner branches, while giving the tree a uniform structure. Be sure to alternate the amount of pigment or use the pigment-removal technique (see pages 23–24) to bring areas of light onto the trunk. Let it dry.

4. Using a fine brush and Mixture 2, add grooves and shadows to the tree trunk.

THE FOREST THROUGH THE SEASONS

A great way to explore the different moods of the forest is to paint the seasons. Practice working with washes by applying your colors to the background that will serve as the base for your composition's atmosphere.

Spring

1 • **Mixture 1** - Ultramarine blue + phthalo green (diluted)

2 • **Mixture 2** - Sap green

3 • **Mixture 3** - Sap green + Indian yellow

4 • **Mixture 4** - Ultramarine blue + Indian yellow

5 • **Mixture 5** - Sap green + ultramarine blue + Payne's gray

6 • **Mixture 6** - Permanent rose + ultramarine blue (diluted)

7 • **Mixture 7** - Permanent rose + ultramarine blue

8 • **Mixture 8** - Ultramarine blue

9 • **Mixture 9** - Sepia (diluted)

10 • **Mixture 10** - Sepia + Mars black

> ## Note
> *Let the watercolor dry thoroughly between each new layer of trees.*

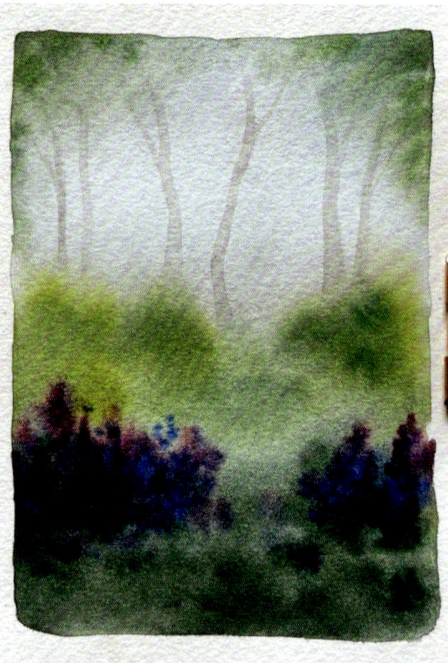

1. Dampen a rectangle with a water-filled paintbrush. Apply Mixture 1 to the top half of the rectangle and Mixtures 2 and 4 to the bottom half, using Mixture 2 to slightly overlap Mixture 1. With a more precise brush, apply Mixture 4 to the top corners. Use Mixtures 6, 7, and 8 to place the flowers in the landscape. Strengthen the soil with small touches of Mixture 5. Let it dry.

2. Paint several trees to add depth to the landscape with Mixture 9. The further apart the trees are, the lighter they will be, so this layer will be the lightest. Blend in the lower parts of the trunks with a clean, damp brush to blend the color.

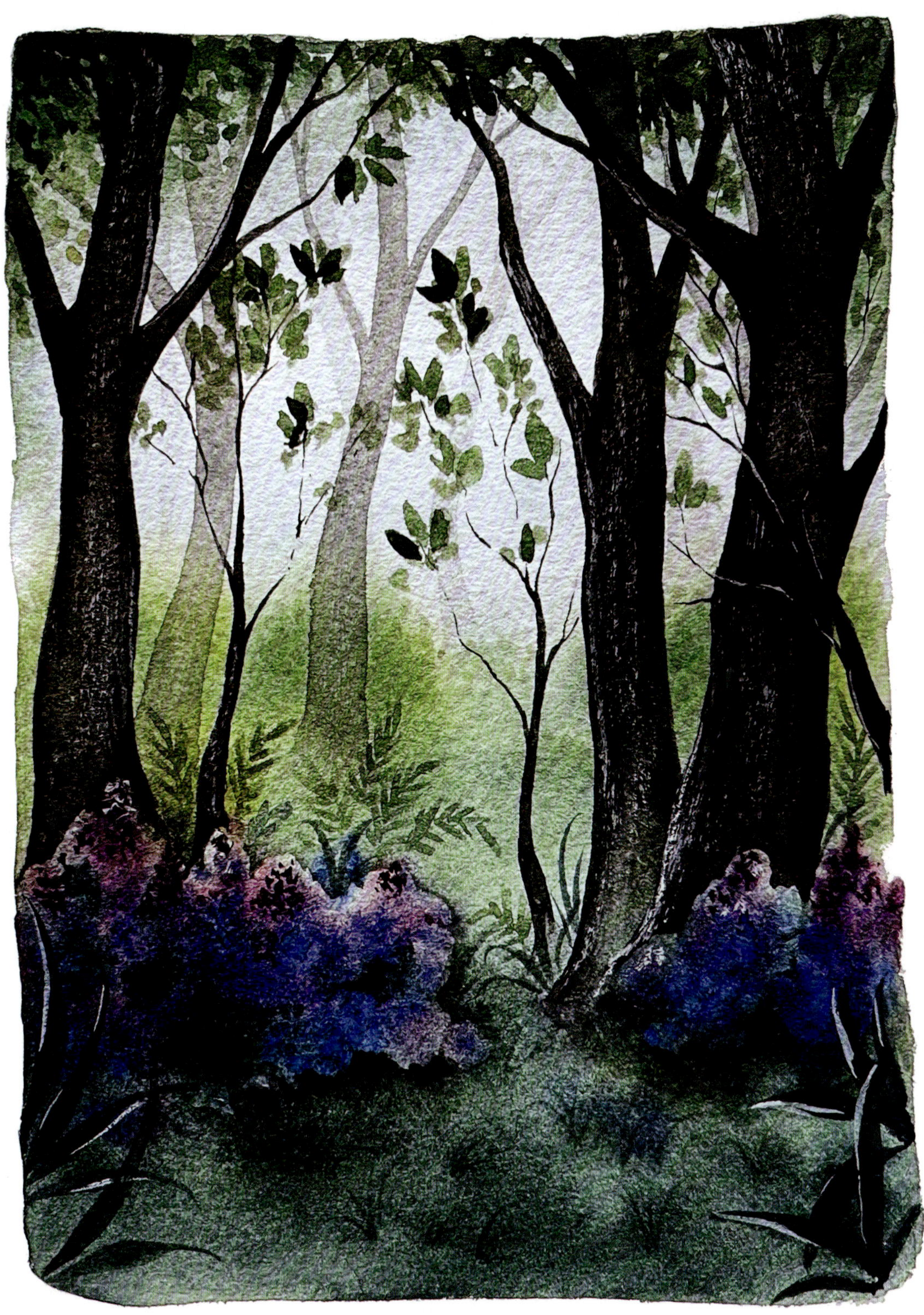

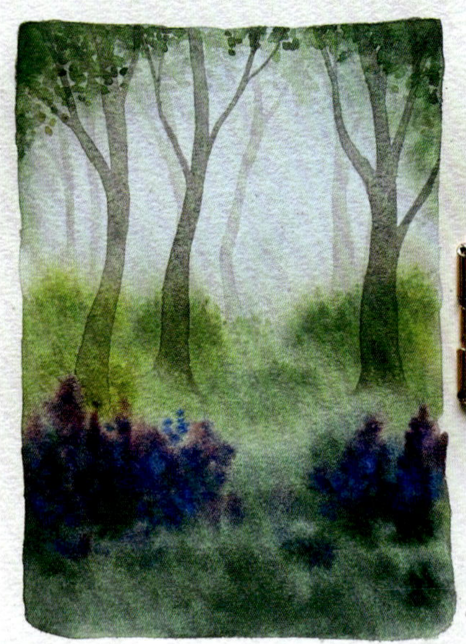

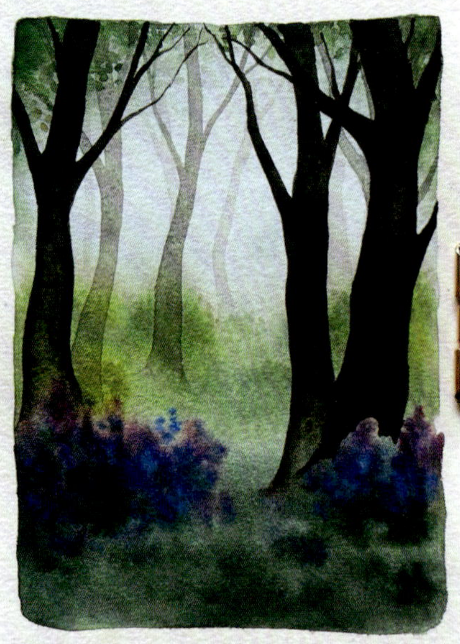

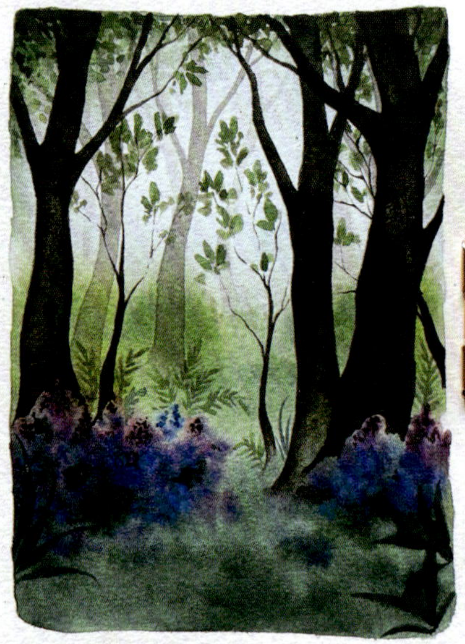

3. Paint a new layer of trees, gradually intensifying Mixture 9 but not reaching the intensity of Mixture 10. Create foliage using Mixture 4.

4. Paint a new layer of trees using Mixture 10. Hide the bases of the trunks in the foreground behind the flowers, taking care to preserve their shape. Let it dry.

5. Add more detail to the flowers using darker pigments. Also add vegetation to the ground and leaves to the few branches that appear in the painting. Let it dry.

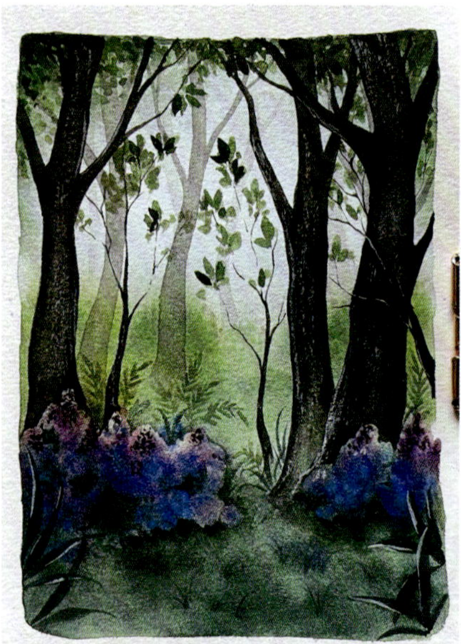

6. Highlight a few areas using a white gel ink pen. I used on some of the darkest trees and leaves to indicate how they overlap.

Advice

You may not realize it here, but the four landscapes in this exercise each measure about 5½" x 3½" (14 x 8.9cm). That's quite small, but perfect for practicing. Therefore, I advise you to start with small thumbnails like these in order to gain confidence before moving onto larger formats.

Summer

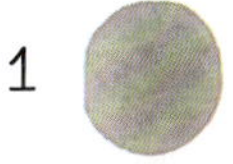

1

- **Mixture 1** - Shadow violet (diluted)

2

- **Mixture 2** - Sap green (diluted)

3

- **Mixture 3** - Sap green + sepia (diluted)

4

- **Mixture 4** - Sap green + ultramarine blue + Payne's gray

5

- **Mixture 5** - Payne's gray + sepia (diluted)

6

- **Mixture 6** - Payne's gray + sepia

7

- **Mixture 7** - Mars black (diluted)

8

- **Mixture 8** - Quinacridone gold + Indian yellow + sap green

1. Fill a small rectangle with Mixture 1, taking care to dilute it well with water. Then, using a soft brush, apply Mixtures 2 and 3 to the bottom of the frame. This will establish the forest floor.

2. Make streaks in the still-wet watercolor and with a more concentrated Mixture 1, starting diagonally from the upper-left corner of the frame. This effect will give the impression that rays of sunlight are piercing the foliage. Place touches of Mixture 4 on the ground to create volume.

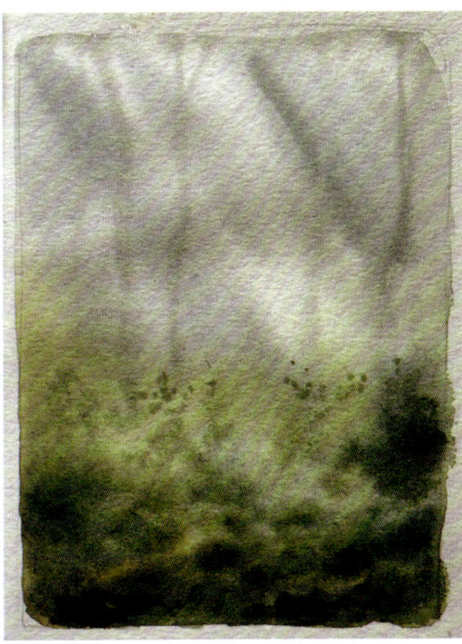

3. In the still-wet watercolor, add trees at the very back of the painting with Mixture 5. Continue working the ground textures by adding and removing some green pigments. Let it dry.

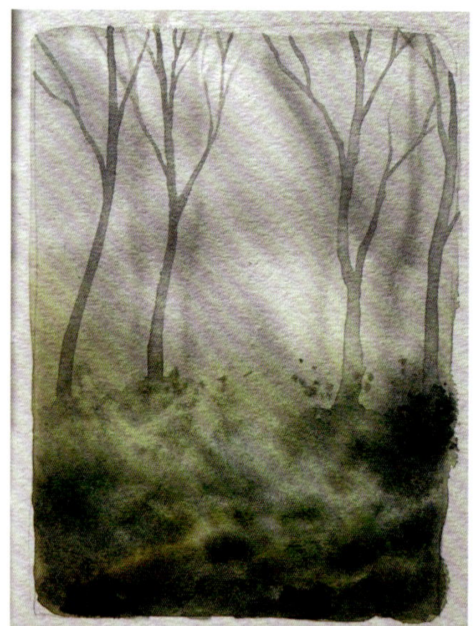 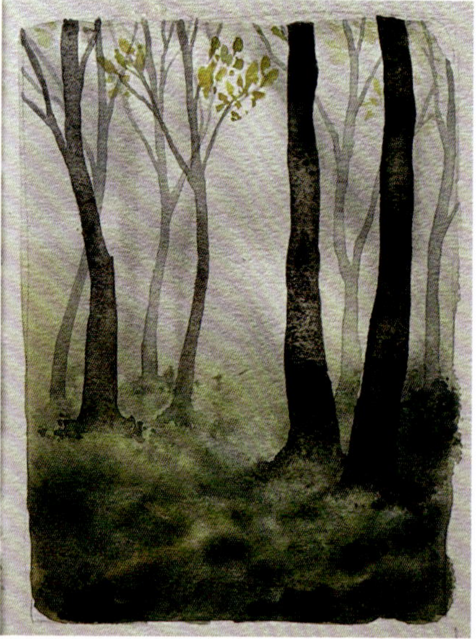 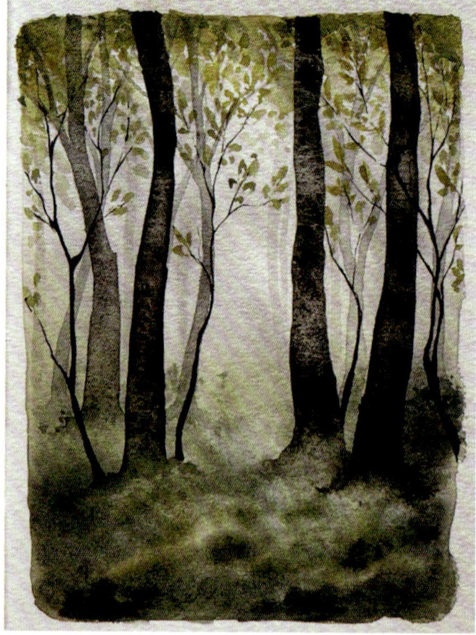

4. Add several layers of trees, gradually increasing the pigments of Mixtures 6 and 7 as the layers get closer. The further away the trees are, the lighter they are.

5. Dress the tops of the trees with foliage using Mixtures 2, 3, and 8. Dab the trunks with a damp brush to blend the color.

6. Finish with small, very dark branches to further detail the vegetation.

Note

Let the watercolor dry thoroughly between each new layer of trees.

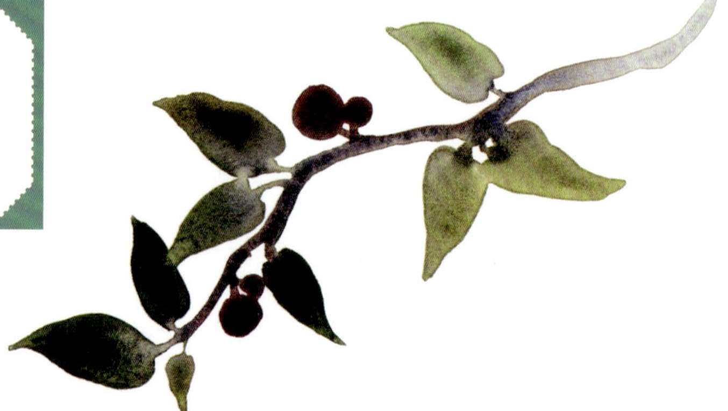

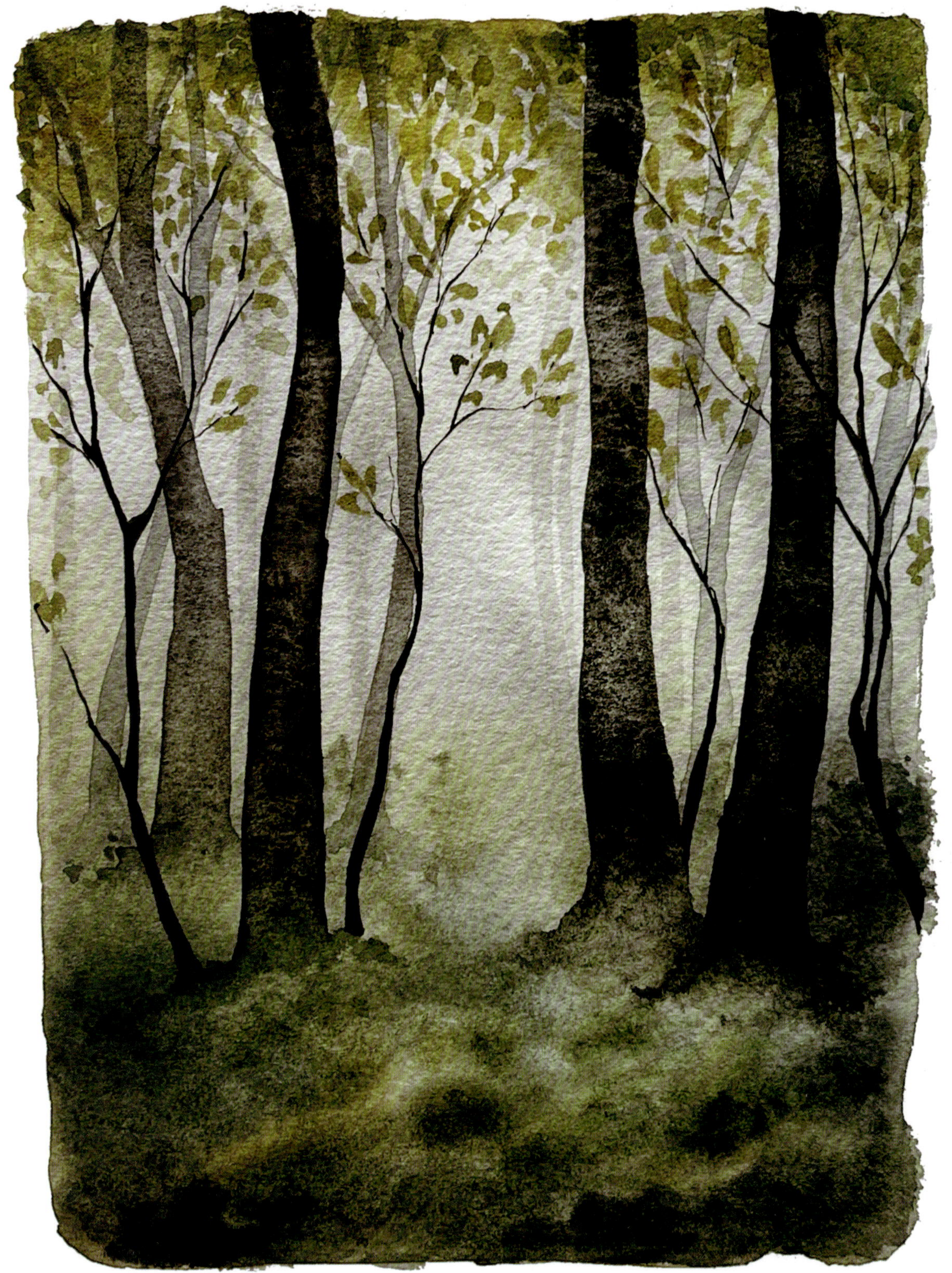

Autumn

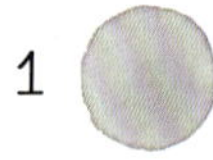

- **Mixture 1** - Payne's gray + umber violet (diluted)

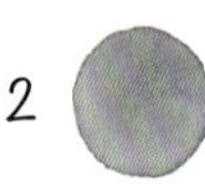

- **Mixture 2** - Payne's gray + Prussian blue (diluted)

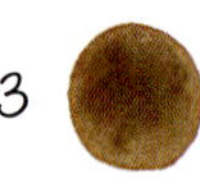

- **Mixture 3** - Burgundy red ochre + yellow ochre + brown iron oxide

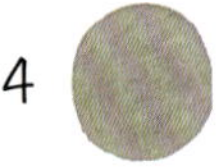

- **Mixture 4** - Sepia + Payne's gray (diluted)

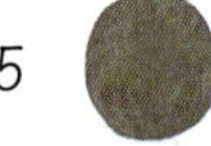

- **Mixture 5** - Sepia + Payne's gray

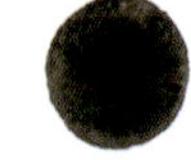

- **Mixture 6** - Sepia + Mars black

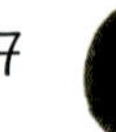

- **Mixture 7** - Mars black

> ### Note
> *Let the watercolor dry thoroughly between each new layer of trees.*

1. Fill a rectangle with Mixture 1, then paint the forest floor with Mixture 3.

2. Framing the top half of the rectangle, add Mixture 2 to create a misty halo. Using the pigment-removal technique (see pages 23–24), create texture on the ground to represent the orange moss. Wait for the watercolor to dry.

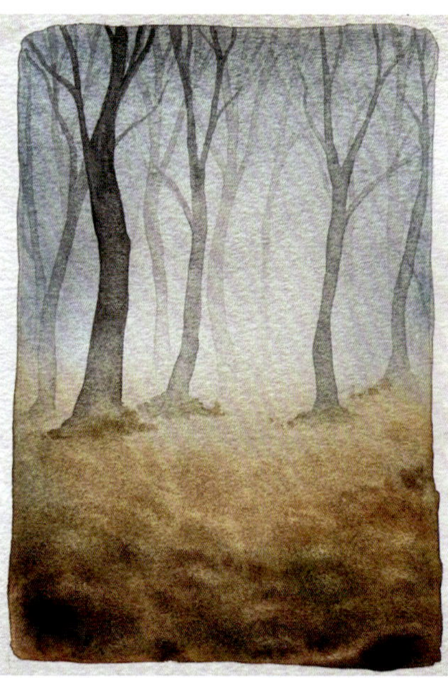

3. Using a precise brush, create several layers of trees using Mixtures 4, 5, 6, and 7 in stages. The closer the trees are to the foreground, the more intense and concentrated the pigments will be.

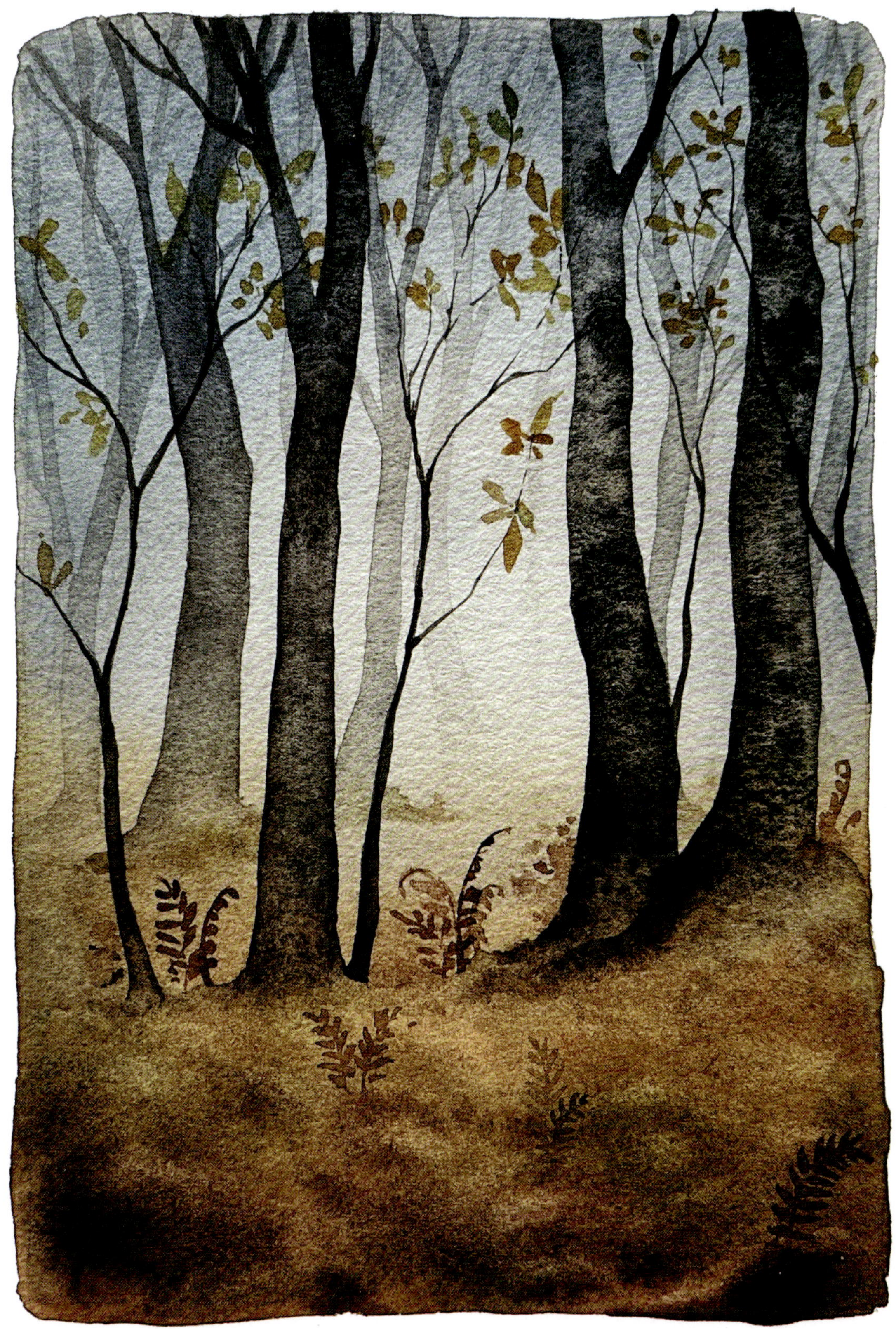

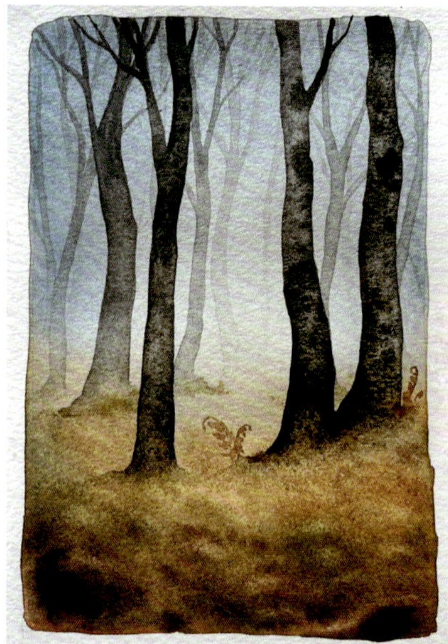 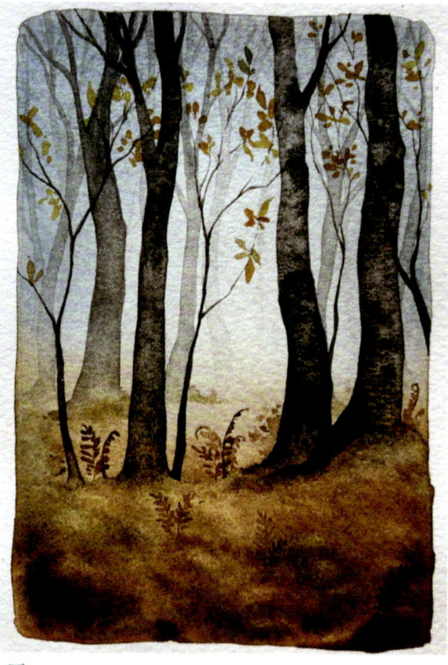

4. Using a small paintbrush and Mixtures 3 and 6, add ferns to the base of the trees and let them dry.

5. Using Mixture 3, add leaves to the branches. Add some unruly branches to the front layer of trees using Mixture 7.

Note

Mars black in Mixture 7 is a naturally grainy pigment that will perfectly mimic the texture of bark.

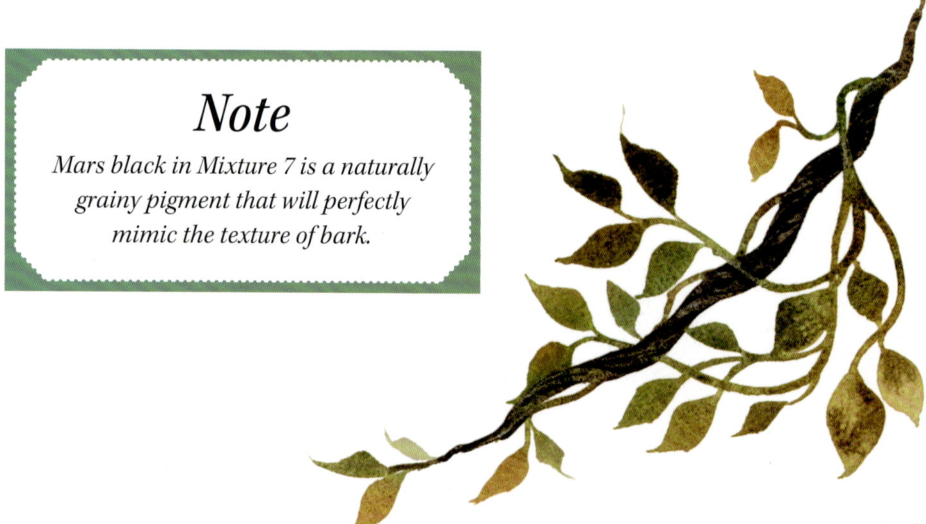

Winter

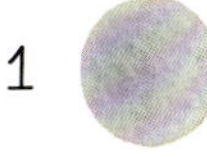 1
- **Mixture 1** - Shadow violet + ultramarine blue (diluted)

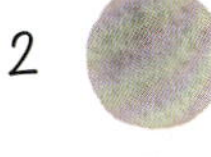 2
- **Mixture 2** - Shadow violet (diluted)

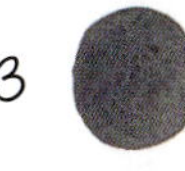 3
- **Mixture 3** - Shadow violet + ultramarine blue + Payne's gray

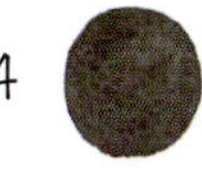 4
- **Mixture 4** - Payne's gray + sepia (diluted)

 5
- **Mixture 5** - Payne's gray + sepia

 6
- **Mixture 6** - Ultramarine blue (diluted)

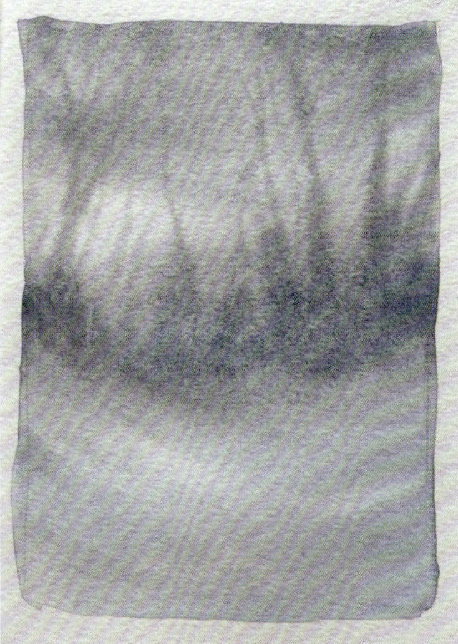

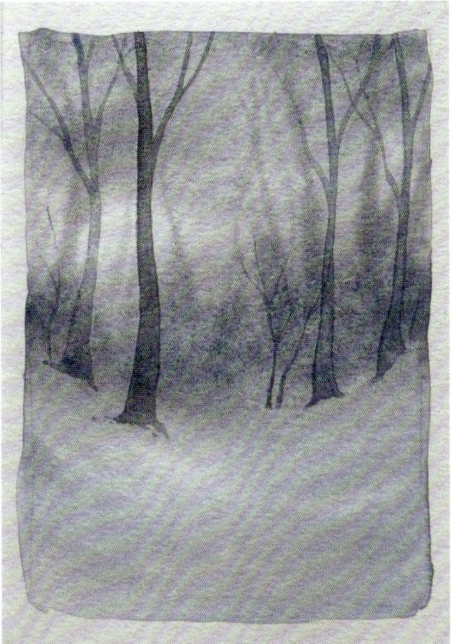

1. With a wide, soft brush, fill a rectangle using Mixture 1 (see sidebar on page 132). In the wet watercolor, create a background with Mixtures 2 and 3 by drawing vertical lines at different angles in the upper half to look like trees in the distance. In the lower half, add streaks that dip toward the center to suggest a snowy slope. Let it dry.

2. As in previous seasons, create several overlapping layers of trees to give the landscape a sense of depth. The closer they are, the more intense the watercolor will be and the more concentrated the pigments.

Note

Let the watercolor dry thoroughly between each new layer of trees.

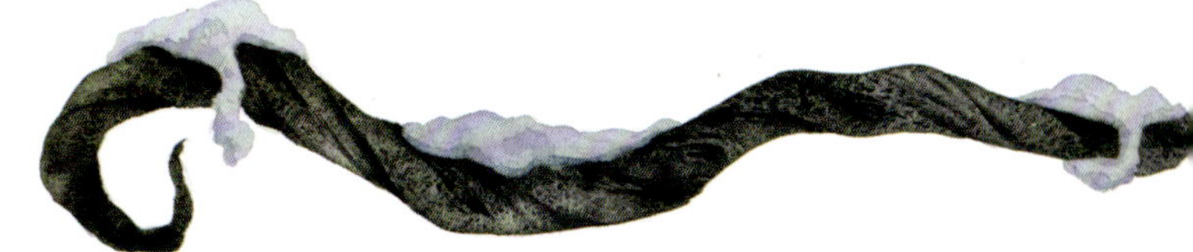

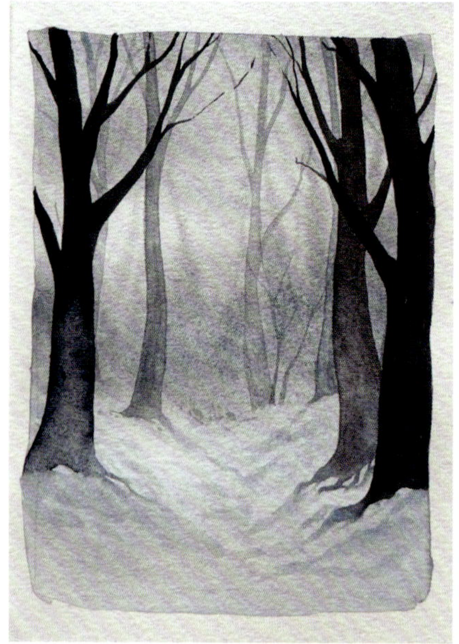 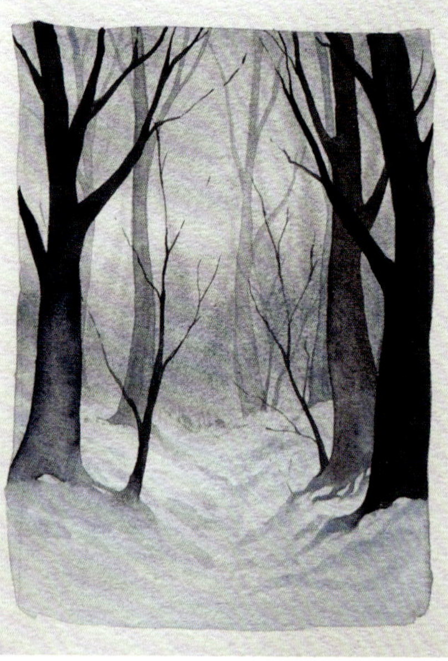 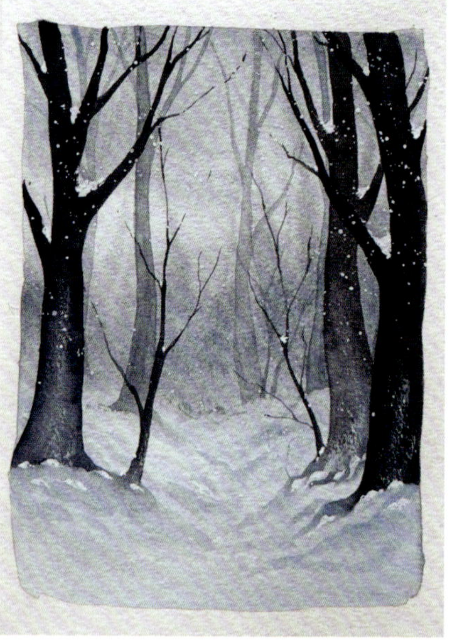

3. At the bottom of each tree base, add small banks of snow falling toward the middle of the paper using Mixture 6.

4. Using Mixture 5, add two young trees in the center and foreground.

5. Using white gouache or a white gel ink pen, add snowflakes and touches of snow in the hollows of the branches to enhance the winter atmosphere.

Advice

Be sure to check out page 21 to learn how to control pigments in water.

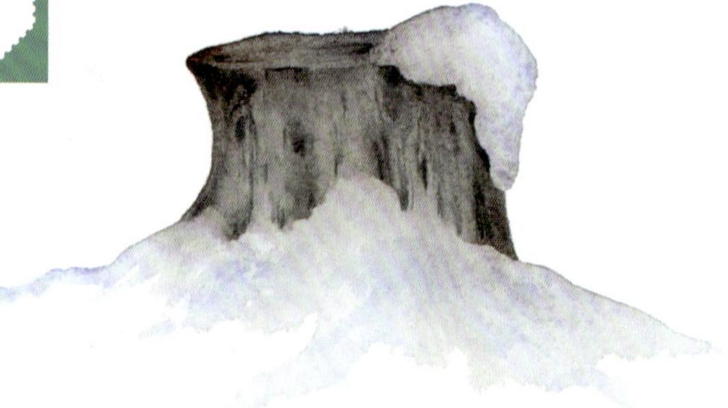

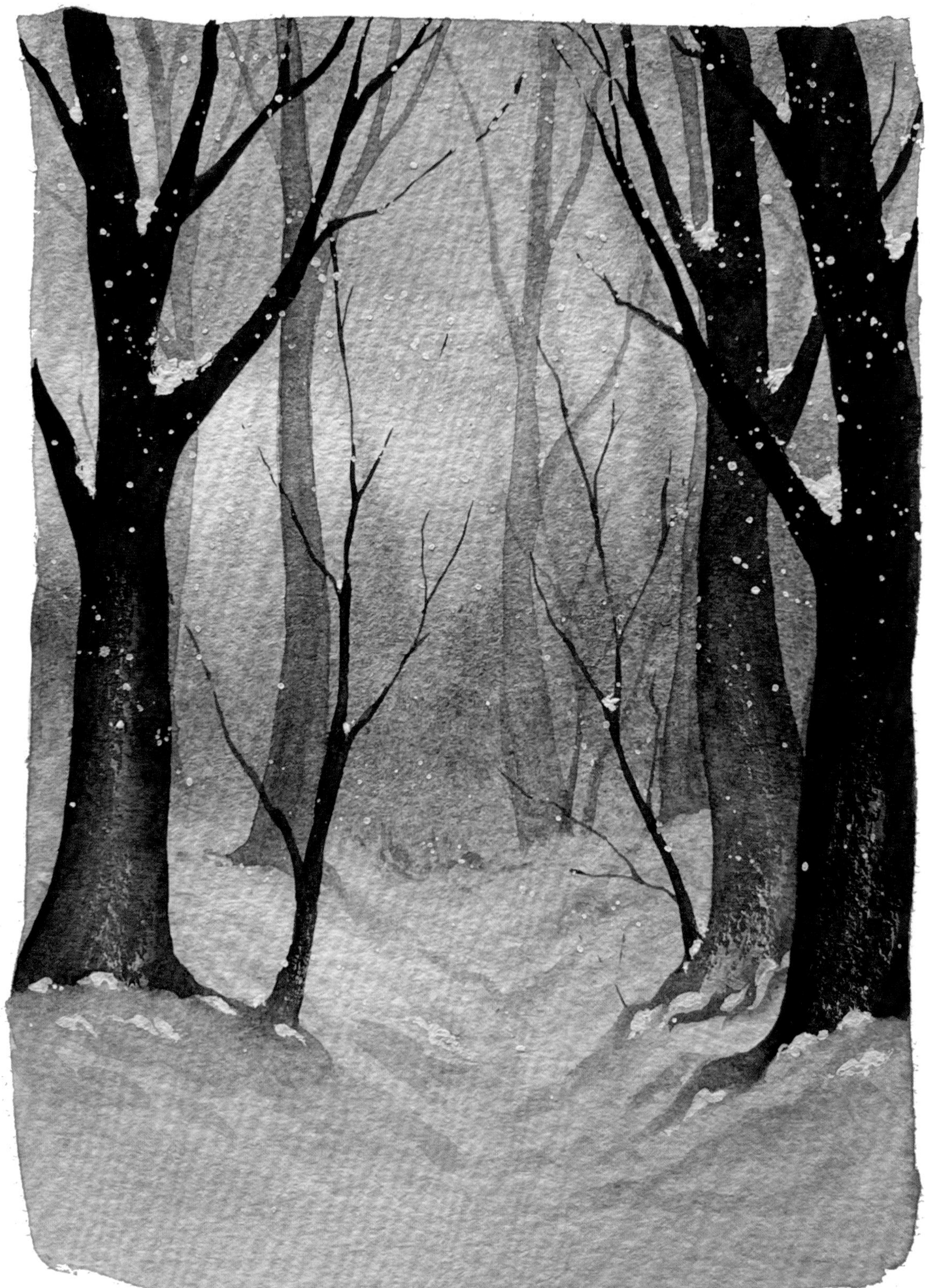

A DARK FOREST

Painting in monochrome is a great way to understand the importance of color values to create depth in a landscape. To learn how to lighten a color, see "Playing with Value" on page 25.

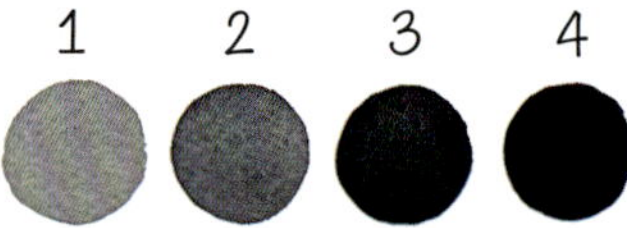

- **Mixtures 1–4** - Make a single mixture in four levels of clarity: lamp black + shadow violet + Payne's gray.

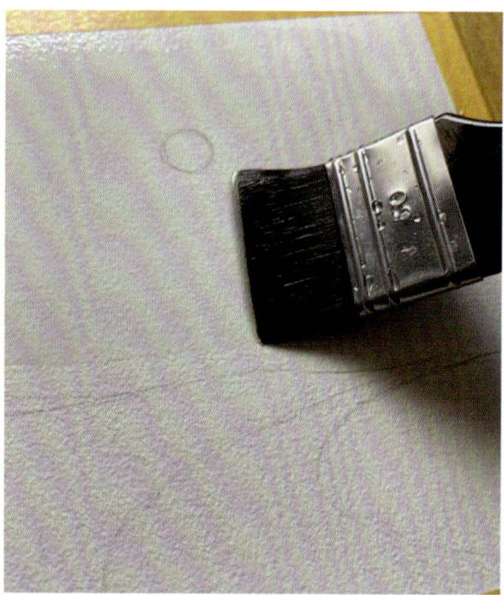

1. Place your painter's tape. With a pencil, draw some markers that will guide you for the first layer of watercolor: the path, horizon line, and moon.

2. Moisten the entire surface using a large, flat brush loaded with water.

3. Using a thick, soft brush, apply Mixture 1, sweeping it across the paper to create misty streaks in the sky.

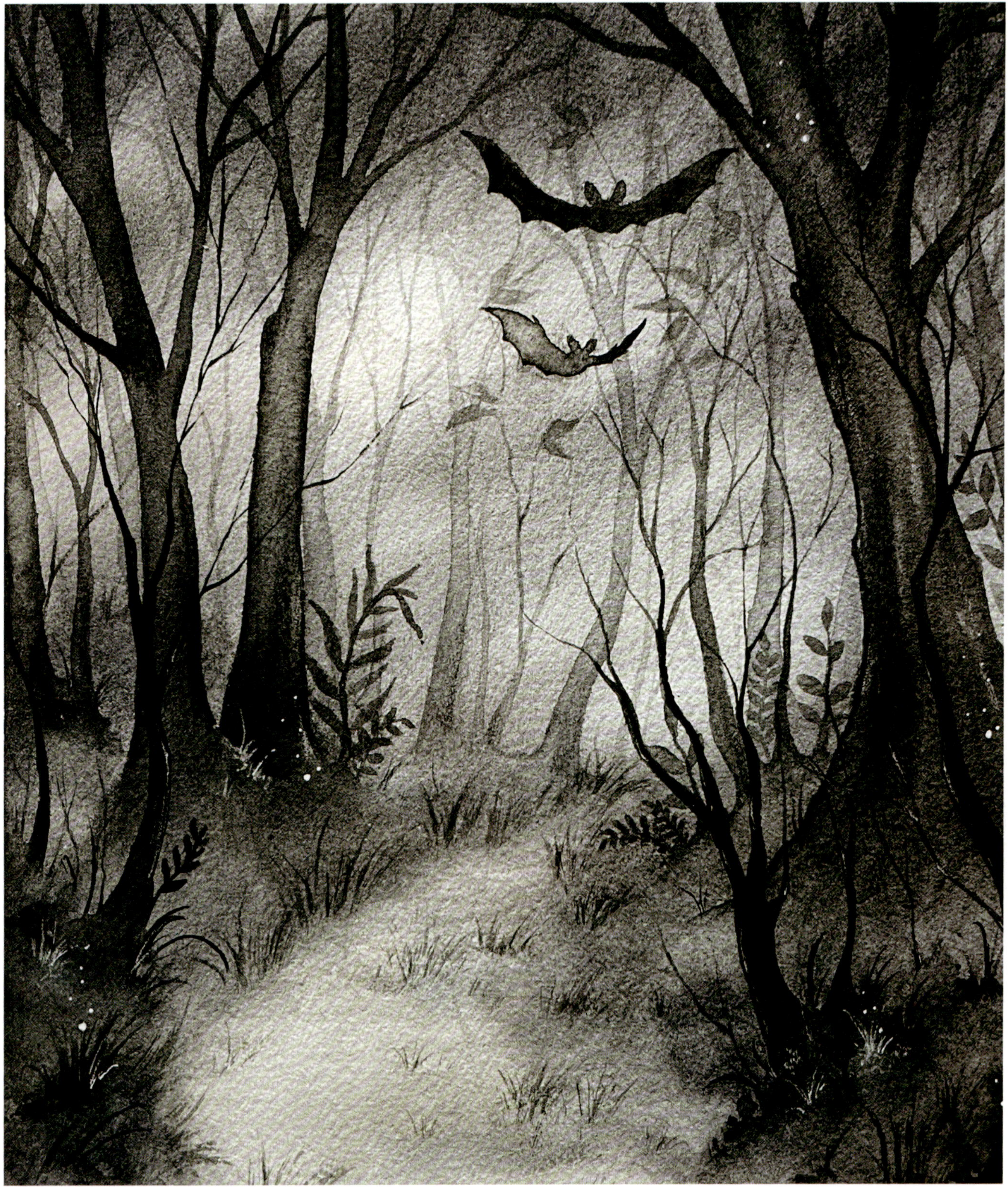

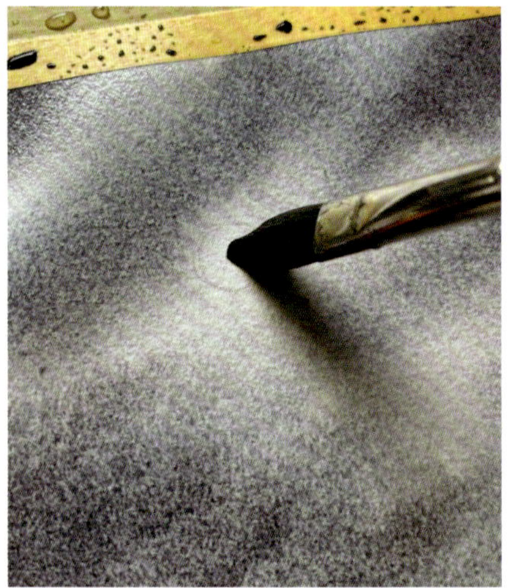

4. Add a little clear water to the moon to repel the pigments and create a halo of light.

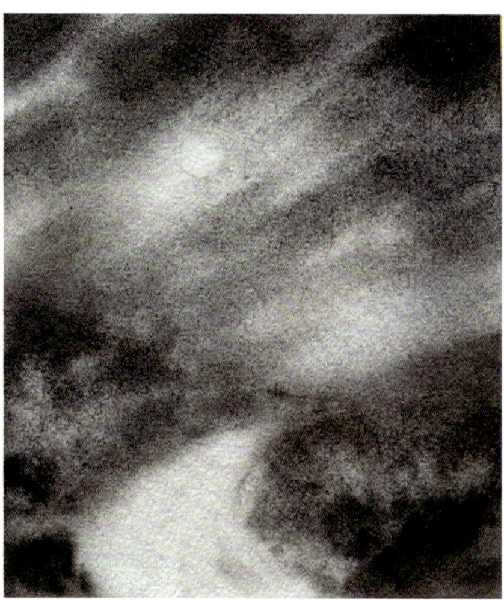

5. Using Mixtures 2 and 3, place the watercolor on the ground, avoiding the path. With a little clear water in your brush, create small "blotchy" effects on the dark part of the ground. Let it dry.

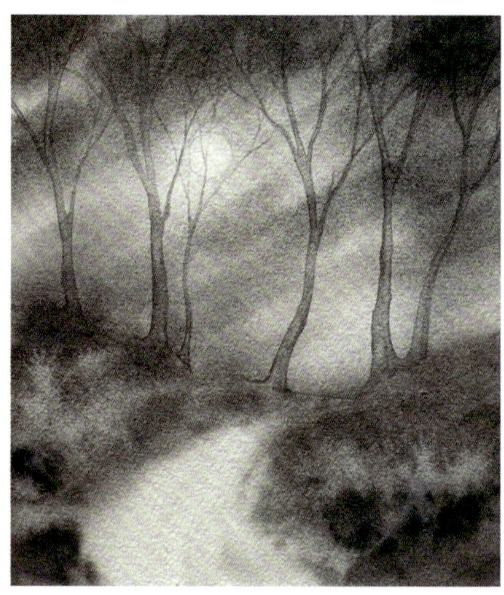

6. Using a precise brush and the diluted mixture, paint the first layer of trees in the distance. Wait for the watercolor to dry.

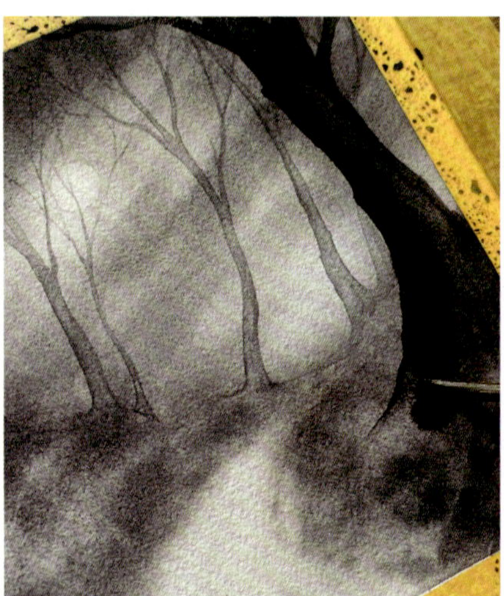

7. Without changing brushes, paint more trees, wider and lower on the sheet. Accentuate the intensity of the blending pigments to cover the trees in the background. With a clean brush, blend the tree bases into the ground.

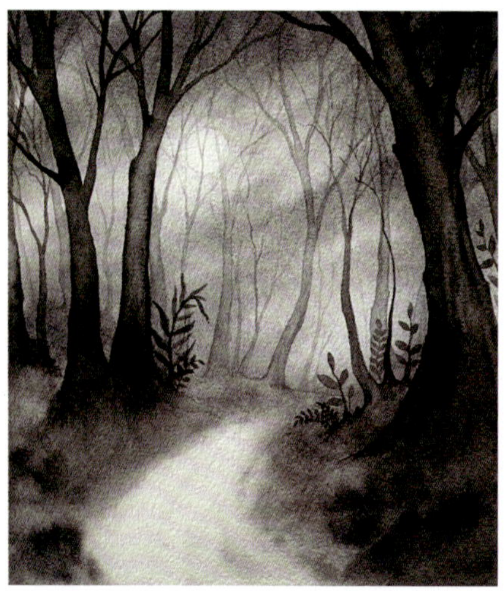

8. If you notice any gaps that are too empty, fill them with new trees. Gradually add vegetation using a fine brush and the same mixture.

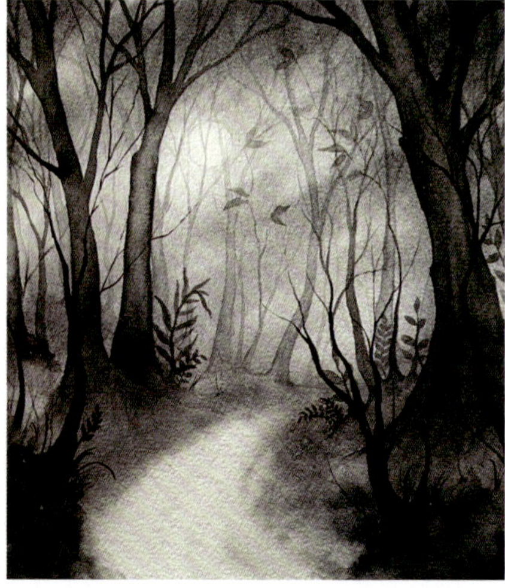

9. Using a fine brush and Mixture 4, draw branches in the foreground. Take care to accentuate the pigments at their base to bring out the foreground and accentuate the depth. Add a few leaves here and there, mixing the pigment with clear water. Let it dry.

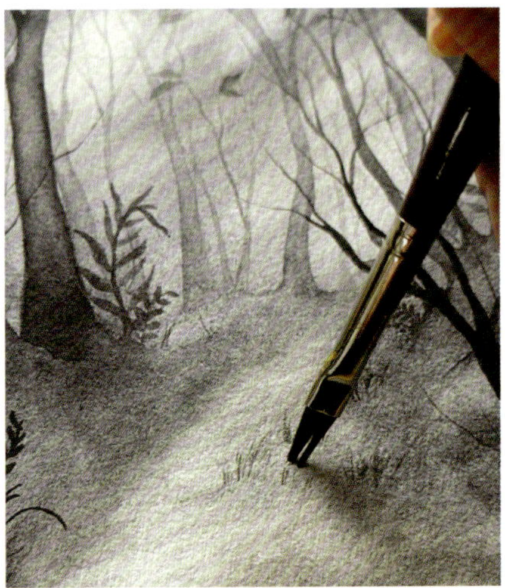

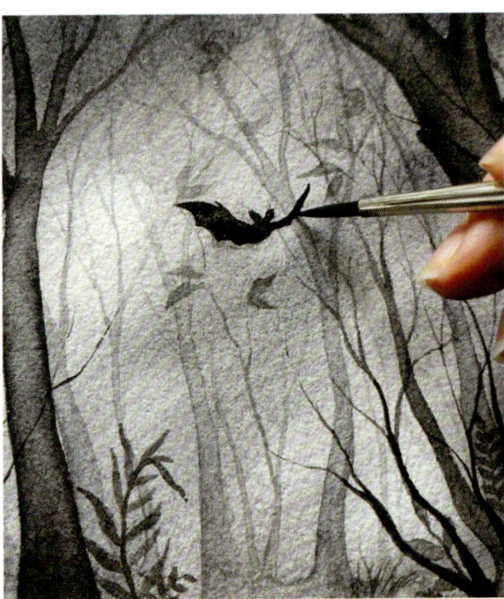

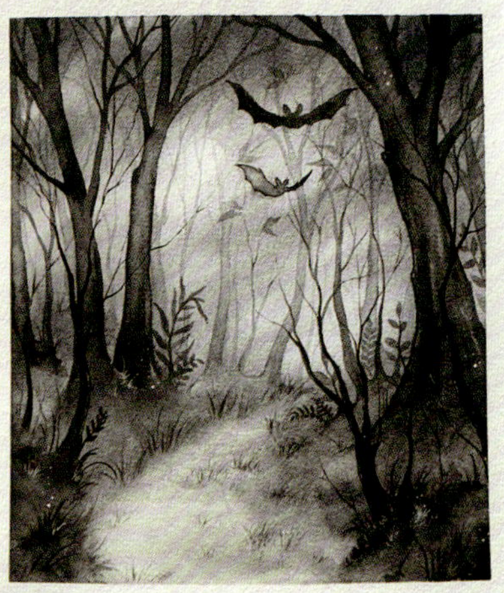

10. With Mixture 1 and a tapered brush, create small shadows on the path and add a few blades of grass.

11. Using a fine brush and Mixture 4, add bats to make the atmosphere of this landscape even darker.

12. Using a white colored pencil, add touches of light where the moonbeams would hit the ground and vegetation. Once finished, carefully remove the painter's tape.

Advice

To achieve a very thin line for the branches, lightly dry your brush on your cloth to obtain a finer tip. Trace the tip of the branch with pure pigments for a very dark effect, or stretch the still-wet pigments as far as possible until they disappear.

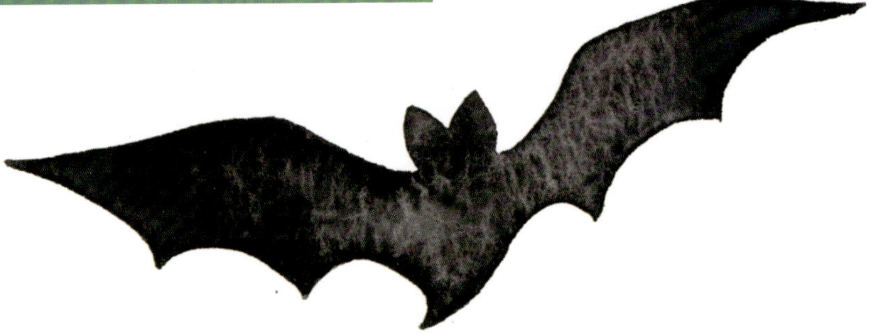

A MYSTERIOUS FOREST

Creating magical worlds is something I enjoy very much because I like to associate the forest with a world filled with mystery. I wanted to conclude this final step-by-step with a forest landscape style that I particularly enjoy. Learn how to play with warm and cool colors here.

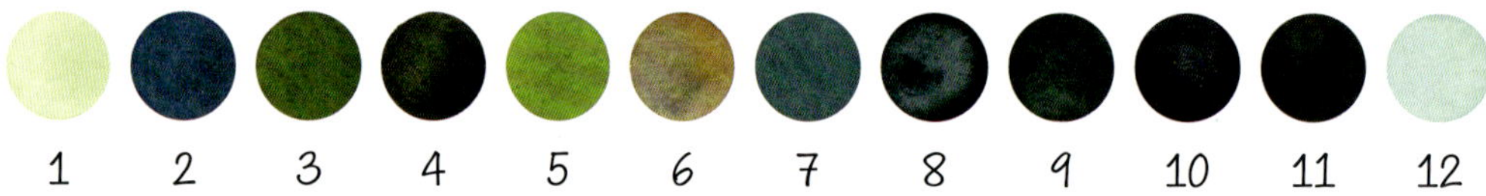

- **Mixture 1** - Phthalo green + Indian yellow (diluted)
- **Mixture 2** - Prussian blue + phthalo green
- **Mixture 3** - Sap green + phthalo green
- **Mixture 4** - Payne's gray + phthalo green
- **Mixture 5** - Indian yellow + phthalo green
- **Mixture 6** - Shadow violet + yellow ochre
- **Mixture 7** - Phthalo green + Prussian blue + sap green
- **Mixture 8** - Phthalo green + Prussian blue + sap green + Payne's gray
- **Mixture 9** - Sap green + ultramarine blue + Payne's gray
- **Mixture 10** - Sap green + ultramarine blue + lamp black
- **Mixture 11** - Sap green + phthalo green + lamp black
- **Mixture 12** - White gouache + phthalo green (diluted)

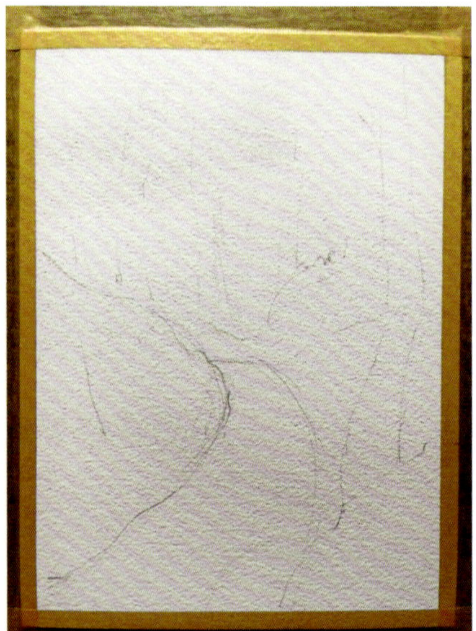

1. Place your painter's tape. With a pencil, draw the main features of your landscape: path, vegetation, trees, etc. This will guide you for the first layer of watercolor.

2. Using a flat brush loaded with water, wet the entire surface of the paper.

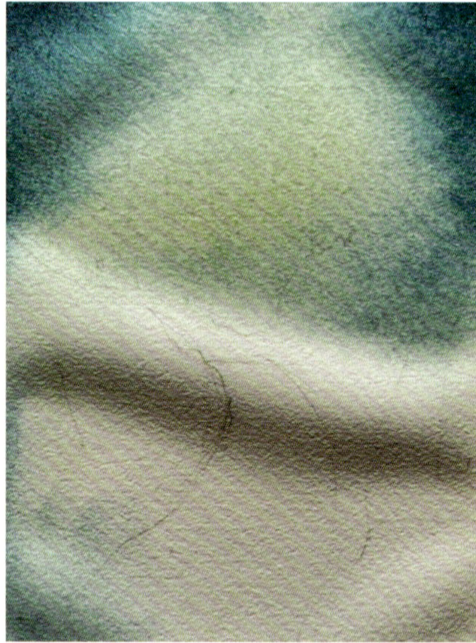

3. Using a thick, soft brush, apply Mixture 1 to the center of your paper and Mixture 2 to the upper corners, accentuating the light in the center.

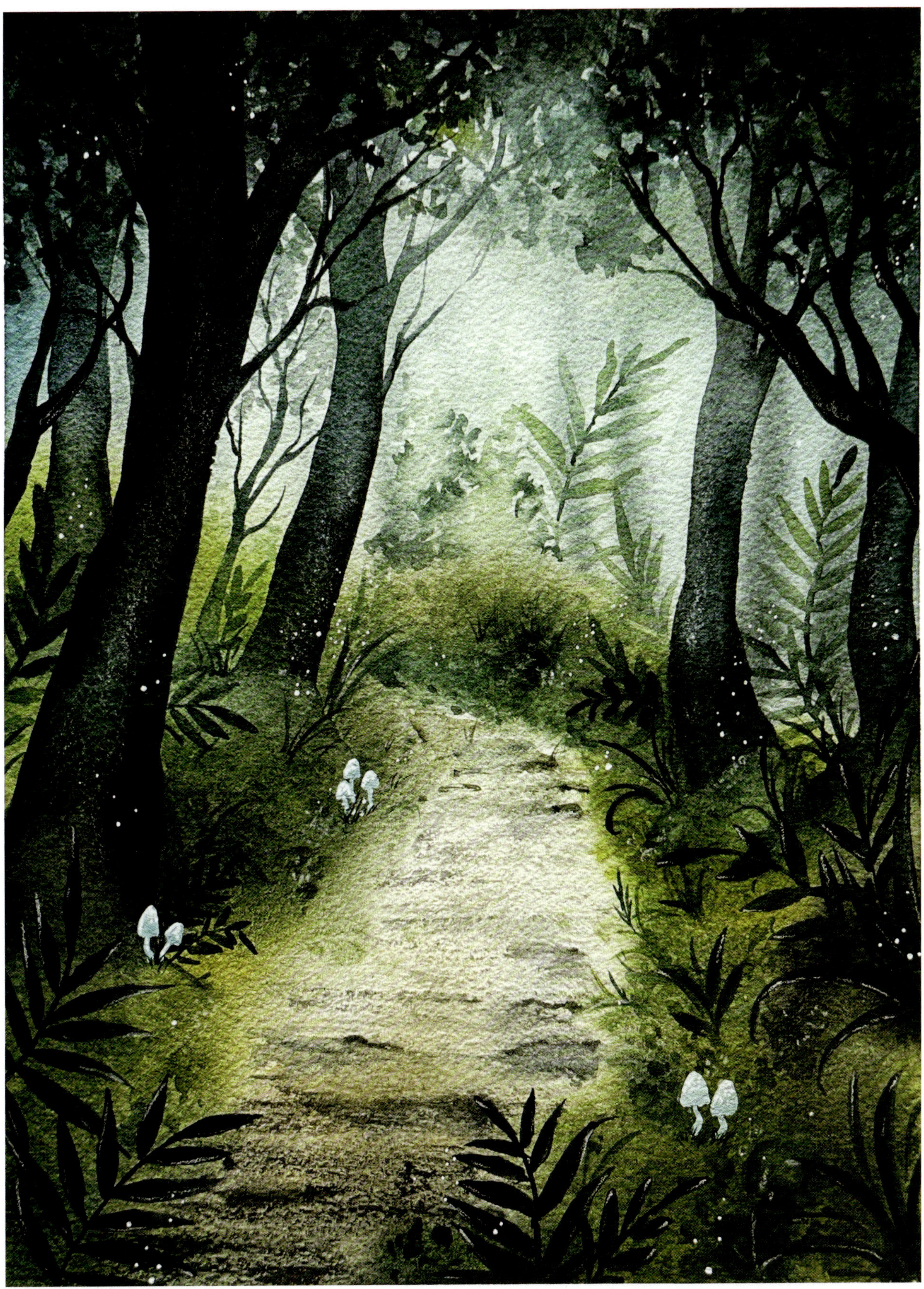

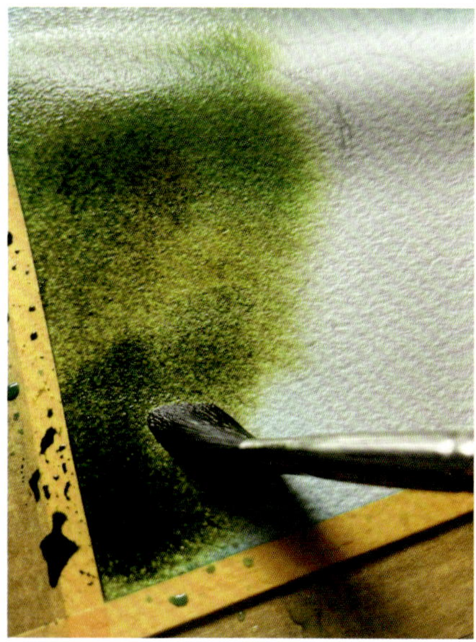

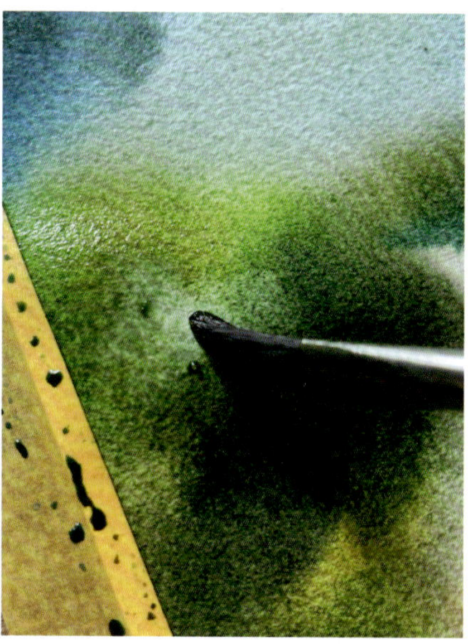

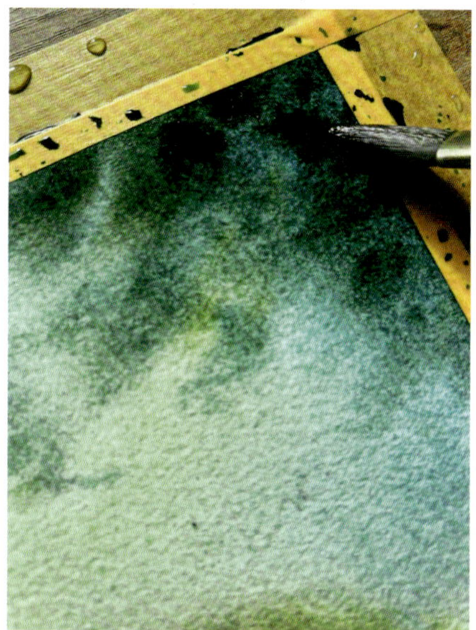

4. In the still-wet watercolor and without changing brushes, paint the vegetation on the ground, taking care to leave a light area for the path. Have fun varying the shades of Mixtures 3, 4, and 5.

5. Push the pigments back from time to time with water to create texture.

6. In the still-wet watercolor, place Mixtures 3, 7, and 8 in the upper corners of the sheet, using the tip of a more precise brush to sketch the vegetation of the trees in the distance.

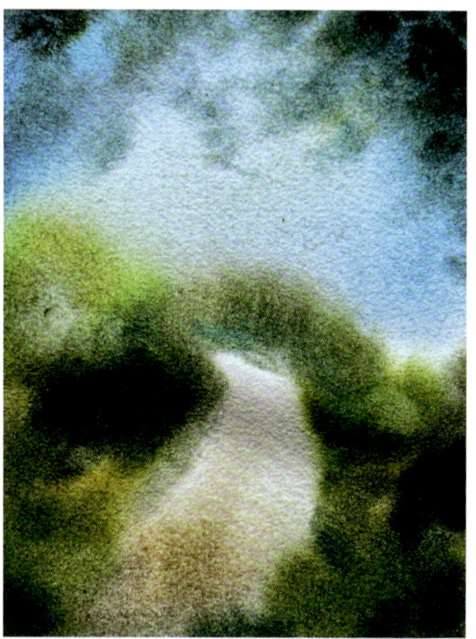

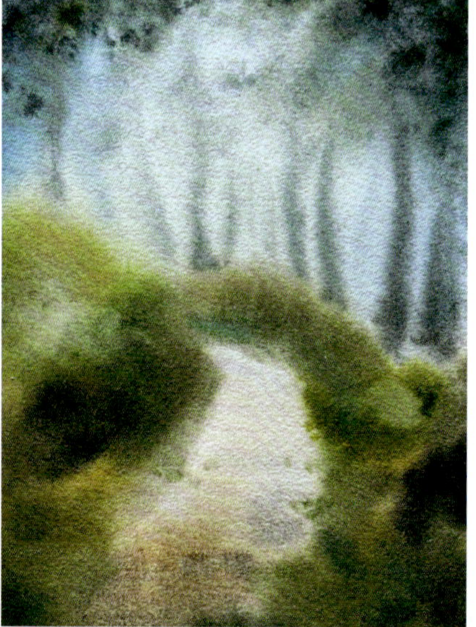

7. Using the same brush, apply Mixture 6 to give the path its color.

8. In the still-wet watercolor, draw tree trunks in the background using Mixture 7. Continue to darken the tree vegetation with Mixture 8. Wait for your watercolor to dry completely.

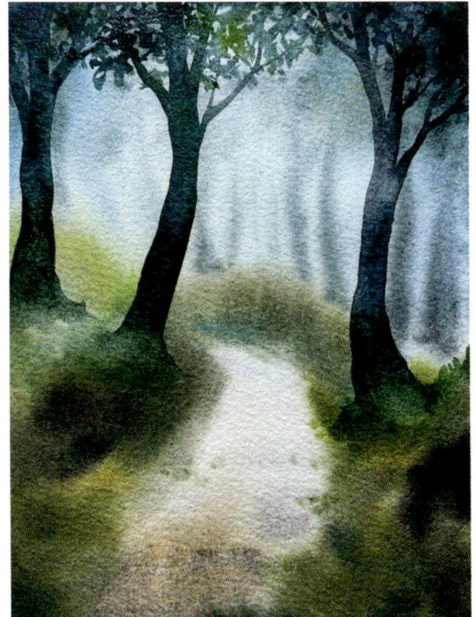

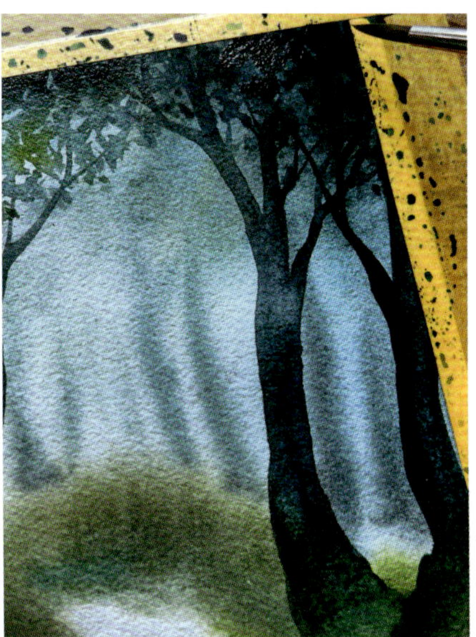

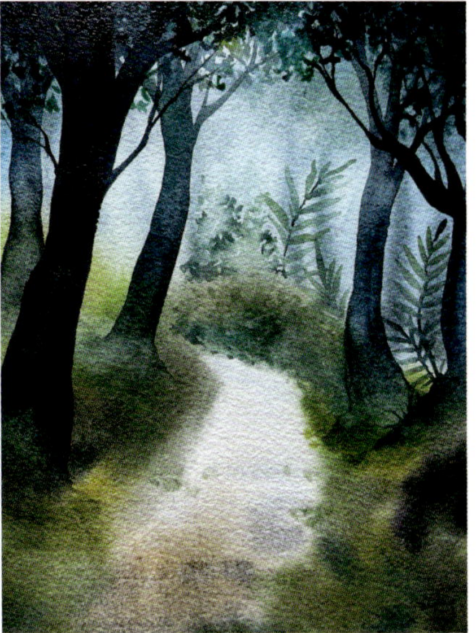

9. Paint the first foreground trees, which disappear out of the frame. Tap with the tip of the brush to further detail the foliage of some trees. Use Mixture 8 for the trees and, occasionally, Mixture 3 to bring a little light into the foliage. Let dry.

10. Add another layer of trees on top of the ones from the previous step with Mixtures 9, 10, and 11, becoming darker and more concentrated as they get closer to the foreground.

11. Paint the ground vegetation with Mixtures 3, 4, 5, and 7, as trees are added. To add texture to your different plants, gently touch the watercolor pigments with your fingertip.

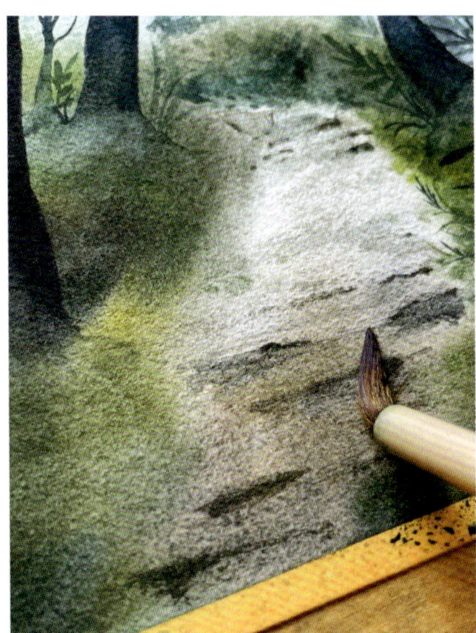

12. With a soft, almost dry brush, add texture to the path by using Mixture 6. Rub the surface of the paper to create a cracked effect on the ground.

Tip

To create all sorts of texture effects, I sometimes play around with tools I find around me. Here, I'm using the tip of my finger, but it can be a small piece of paper or plastic, or even a toothbrush. Don't hesitate to repurpose different materials from everyday life.

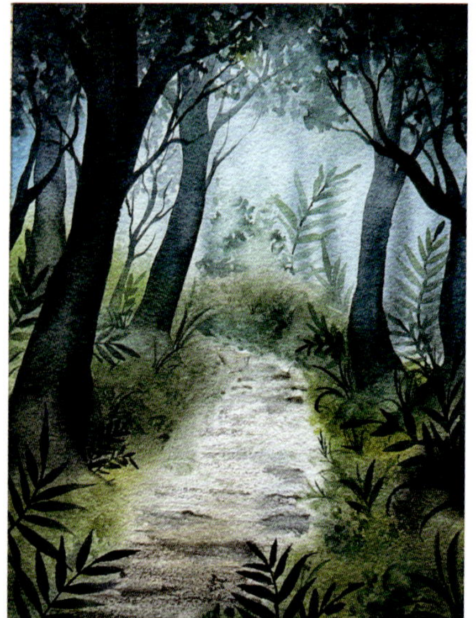 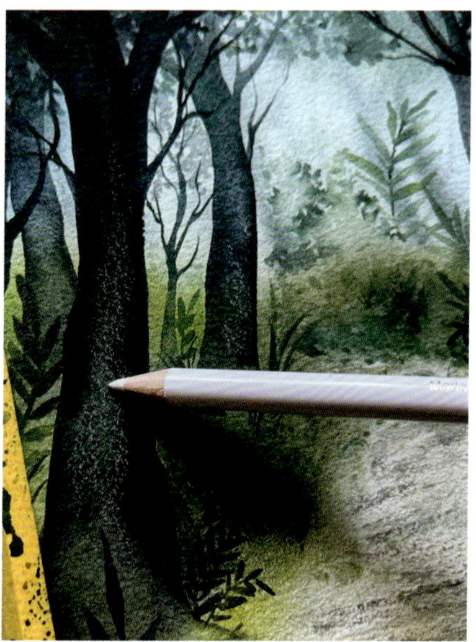 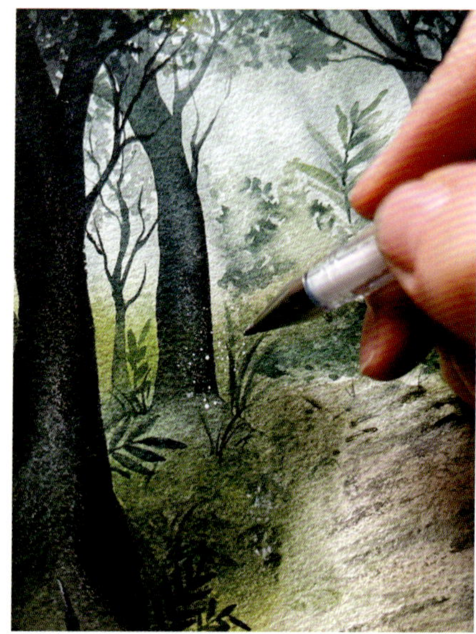

13. With a precise brush and Mixture 11, add some plants to the foreground.

14. Add touches of light to your painting with a white colored pencil. Use the flat end of the pencil for the bark and the tip for the vegetation.

15. Continue with a white gel ink pen. This will be useful for drawing dots in different areas of the landscape.

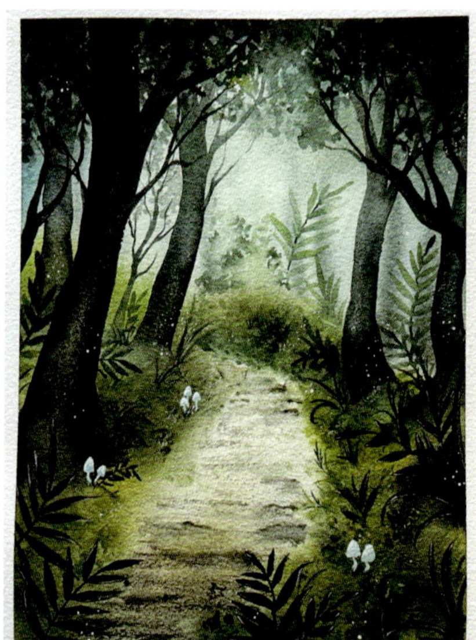

16. Using Mixture 12, add small white mushrooms to enhance the magical atmosphere of your forest. Carefully remove the painter's tape.

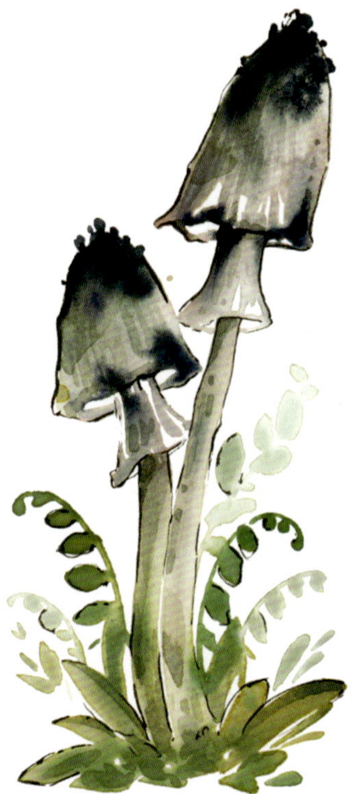

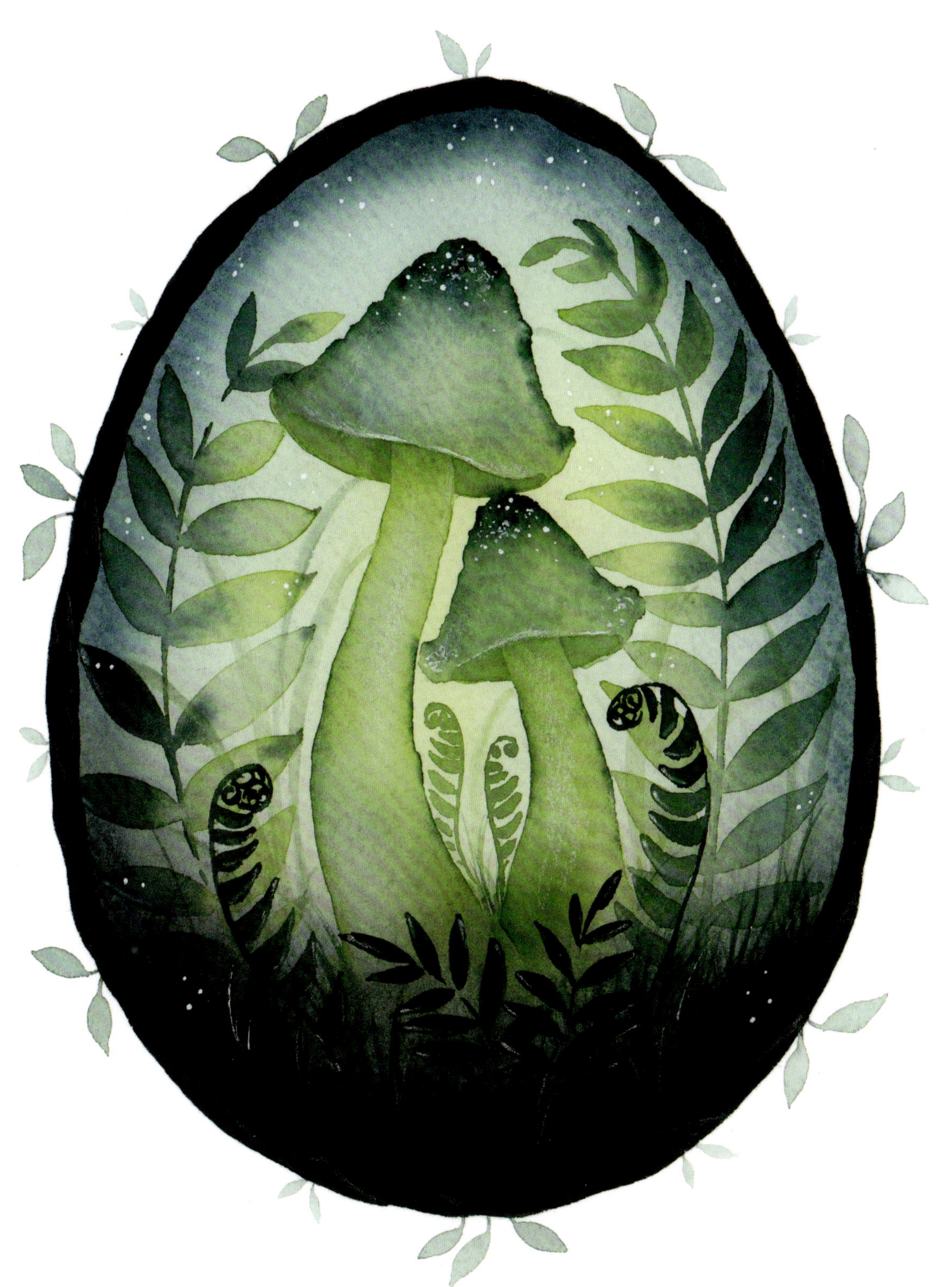

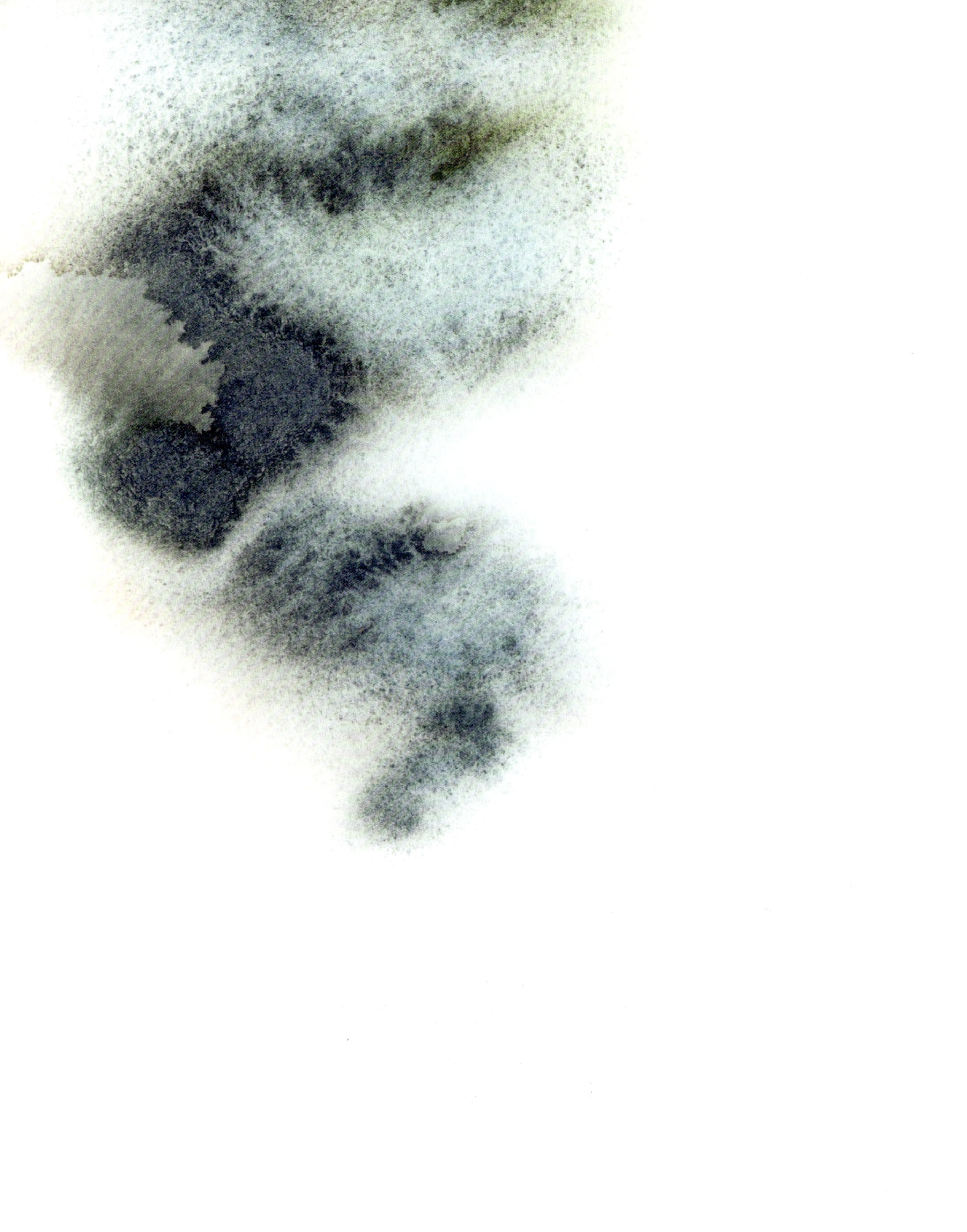

Thanks

First of all, I would like to thank the entire Éditions Eyrolles team for once again supporting one of my publishing projects with dedication and professionalism. I wish to express my deep gratitude to Nathalie, Hélène, and Armelle for giving me the opportunity to freely explore my creativity in writing this book.

Thank you to my husband and my adorable daughters, my greatest supporters, who allow me to give the best of myself to the projects so dear to my heart.

Thank you to my parents, who influenced my love of nature and giving it the respect it deserves. The moments I shared with them remain etched in my memory and have helped shape me into the person I am today.

Thanks to Dalbe, my dear collaborators with whom I have worked for several years and who have accompanied me since the beginning of my artistic adventure.

Finally, I wanted to thank this incredible community of artists with whom I share my passion on Instagram. Their kindness makes this creative experience beautiful, gentle, and inspiring.

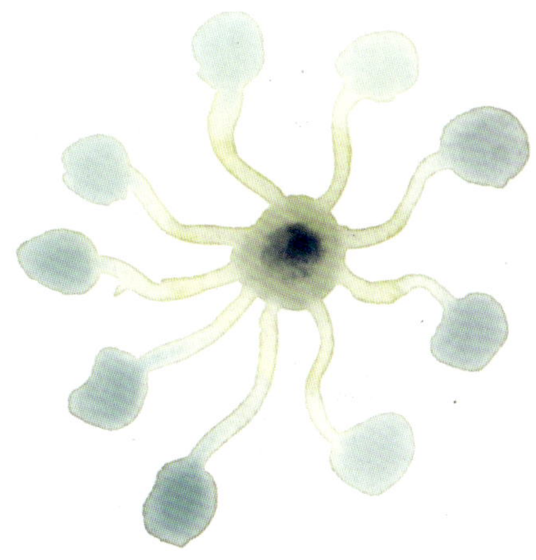

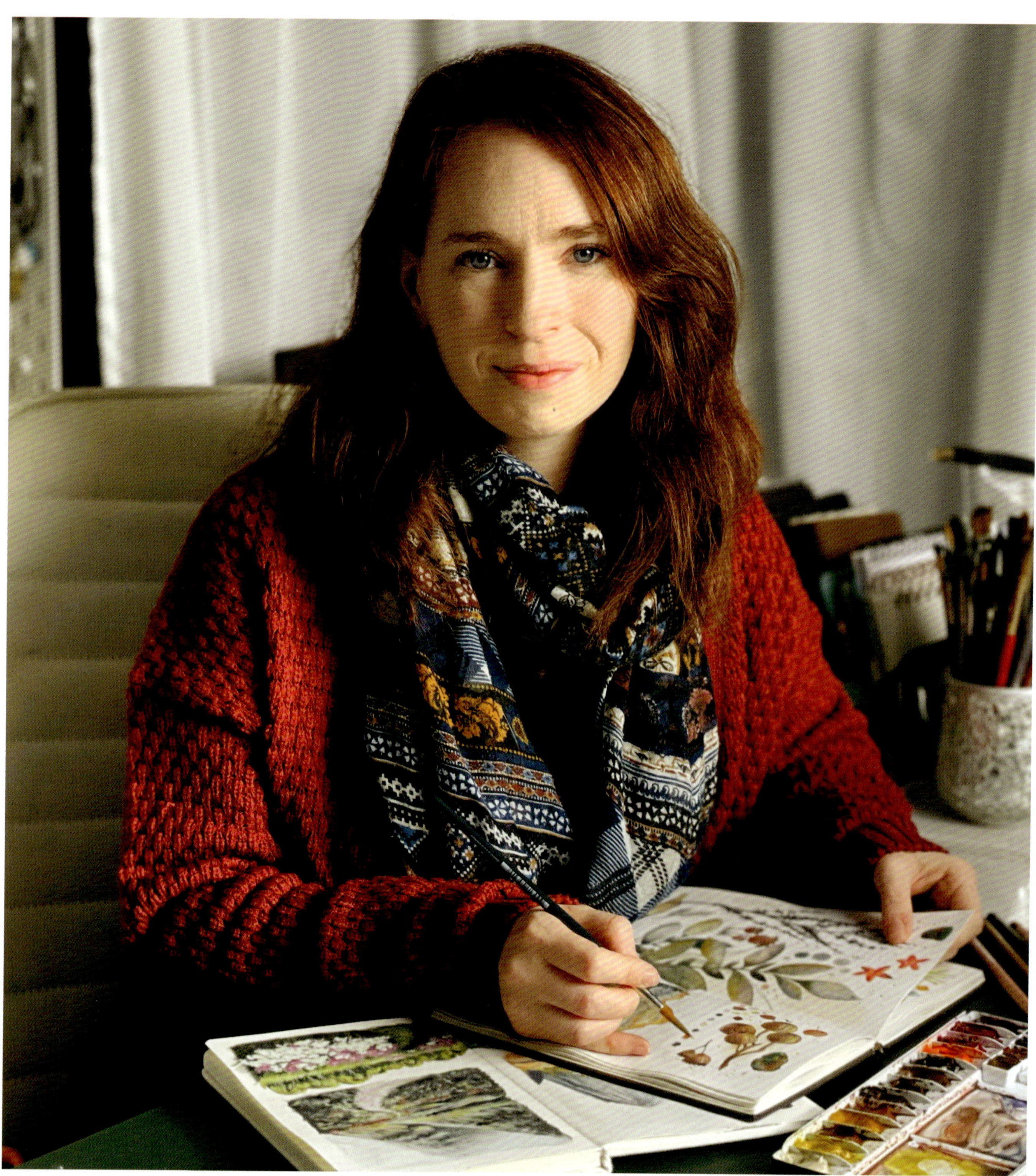

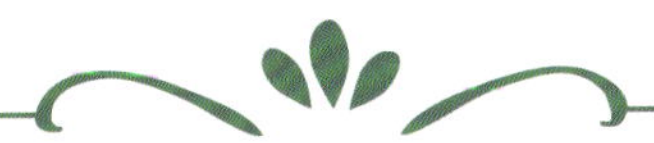

About the Author

My artistic journey began in 2016, during my parental leave, with a simple desire to share my drawings with my loved ones. Four years later, in 2020, this adventure has transformed into a full-time profession.

After writing my first book, I Dare Watercolor, in 2021, I continued to explore and flourish in my artistic practice. In reality, I've never stopped creating, as spontaneity and passion are essential drivers for me.

Nature has always been at the heart of my art, a fascination that dates back to my childhood spent observing it and marveling at its mysteries. This is how I naturally immersed myself in the world of the forest, an environment I know intimately thanks to my childhood memories spent at the edge of the woods.

Watercolor is my preferred medium and offers an infinite palette of artistic possibilities thanks to the play of transparency. With a few colors, I can bring a multitude of different worlds to life. As I write these lines in October 2023, I realize that I have been painting in watercolor for almost seven years. It is rare that I go a day without touching my colors, even just a little. Painting and creating are an integral part of my life, as natural as the need to eat and drink. My goal is to continue sharing my passion for nature and art, and I am delighted to share it once again in this new book.

Find me online:
Website: https://jennyillustrations.com
Instagram: @Jenny_illustrations
YouTube: @Jenny Illustrations

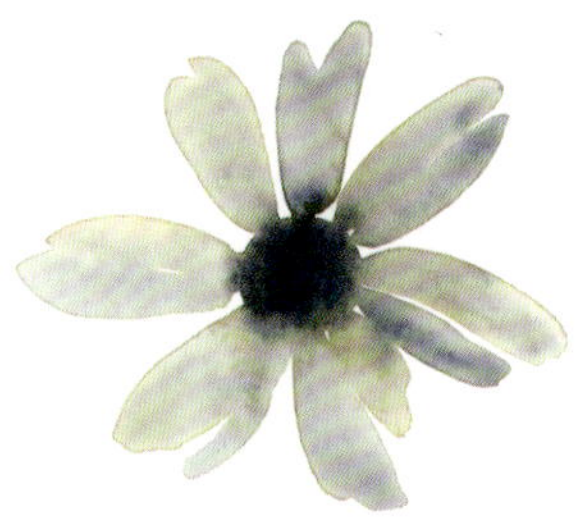

Index